UNREASONABLE FAITH

How William Lane Craig Overstates the Case for Christianity

James Fodor

HYPATIA PRESS

Copyright © 2018 James Fodor

All rights reserved. No part of this publication may be reproduced, stored in or introduced into a retrieval system or transmitted in any form or by any means, electronic, mechanical, photocopying, recording or otherwise without prior written permission from the publisher.

Published by Hypatia Press in the United States

ISBN: 978-1-83919-264-7

Cover design by Claire Wood

www.hypatiapress.org

About the Author

James Fodor has a graduate degree in physics from the University of Melbourne, and is a research assistant in structural biology at Monash University. With a keen interest in philosophy, he writes for the Rationalist magazine on various subjects in religion and epistemology. As former president of the University of Melbourne Secular Society, he has engaged in numerous discussions and public debates concerning religion, with a focus on secular morality and the evidence for the resurrection of Jesus. He also has an interest in effective altruism and computational neuroscience.

Synopsis

William Lane Craig is arguably the world's leading Christian apologist, having engaged in dozens of public debates concerning the existence of God and the resurrection of Jesus, and with a large online following through his Reasonable Faith ministry. Although many philosophers, scientists, and historians have responded to various aspects of Craig's work, a single integrated in-depth response to Craig's apologetic as a whole has hitherto been lacking. This book aims to fill this gap by providing the first book-length critical response to all of Craig's main apologetic arguments, building upon previous responses to develop several new and innovative lines of critique. Craig's much-discussed kalam cosmological argument is considered from both a philosophical and scientific standpoint, integrating previously disparate criticisms developed by scholars such as L. Nathan Oaklander, Quentin Smith, Graham Oppy, and Sean Carroll. It is contended that Craig's argument suffers from a hitherto unappreciated flaw, namely that the very same reasons Craig uses to establish the tensed theory of time (necessary for the kalam to succeed), actually serve to undermine his arguments that the universe began to exist. A similarly novel approach is taken with respect to the fine-tuning argument, where Craig's key assumption that fine-tuning of the universe for life is a well-established scientific fact is shown to be based on an equivocation concerning what type of life is being referred to. The discussion of Craig's moral argument is considerably more comprehensive than any previously published critiques, and focuses on Craig's failure to specify any properties that render God a superior foundation for objective moral values than any of the many non-theistic alternatives developed by philosophers. With regard to Craig's argument for resurrection of Jesus, a new theory is developed to account for the key historical facts without needing to appeal to divine intervention. Drawing upon work by thinkers such as Gerd Lüdemann and Richard Carrier, as well as extensive research from sociology, psychology, and comparative religion, it is shown how a combination of hallucinations, memory biases, and social reinforcement could have operated to lead Jesus' followers to report seeing the risen Jesus. Written in a clear and accessible style, this book provides a robust and comprehensive response to Craig's arguments for Christianity, and will be of interest to believers and non-believers alike.

Contents

Chapter One   1

Introduction

   The Purpose of This Book   1

   A Brief Biography of Craig   2

   The Purpose of Craig's Arguments   4

   The Structure of This Book   7

   A Note to the Reader   10

Chapter Two   12

The Kalam Cosmological Argument

   Overview of The Argument   12

   Premise One: Time is Tensed   14

     The Inelimibility of Tense from Language Implies the Reality of Tense   18

       Tensed and Tenseless Sentences   18

       The Token Indexical Tenseless Theory of Language   19

       The Problem of Untokened Sentences   25

       Tensed Statements as Enablers of Timely Action   27

       Should Tensed Language be Taken as Veridical?   29

     Our Direct Experience of Time Shows That it is Tensed   32

       Our Direct Experience of Presentness   32

       Our Differential Attitudes Towards Past and Future   34

       Our Experience of the Reality of Temporal Becoming   37

       Relativity Does Not Undermine Tensed Theories of Time   41

Special Relativity and the Tensed Theory of Time	41
The General Theory of Relativity	44
Further Responses to General Relativity	49
The Tenseless Theory of Time Leads to Absurd Conclusions	54
The Alleged Absurdities of Perdurantism	54
The Removal of Temporal Relations from Tenseless Time	59
Presentism and the Difference Between Past and Future	62
The Problem of the Extent of the Present	65
Summary	68
PREMISE TWO: THE UNIVERSE BEGAN TO EXIST	69
An Actual Infinite is Impossible	70
Cantor's Arithmetic	70
The Problem of Hilbert's Hotel	71
Subtraction of Infinite Quantities	76
Spatial and Temporal Intervals	78
Is an Infinite Regress of Events an Actual Infinite?	81
The Impossibility of Forming an Infinite by Successive Addition	88
Counting to Infinity	88
Zenoian Considerations	91
Coordinated Events	93
The Tristram Shandy Paradox	94
Finishing an Infinitely Long Count	97
Is the Temporal Series of Events Formed by Successive Addition?	99

There is Powerful Empirical Evidence for a Beginning of the Universe	101
The Big Bang Theory	101
The Borde-Vilenkin-Guth Theorem	103
Closed timelike curves	110
Quantum Cosmology	111
The Second Law of Thermodynamics	114
Summary	117
PREMISE THREE: EVERYTHING THAT BEGINS TO EXIST HAS A CAUSE	118
That Nothing Comes from Nothing is a Basic Metaphysical Principle	119
On Popping Out of Nothing	119
'Beginning to Exist' and the Tensed Theory of Time	121
The Reliability of Metaphysical Intuitions	123
If Universes Could Come from Nothing Then So Could Anything	125
We Have Strong Evidence in Favour of This Principle	128
PREMISE FOUR: IF THE UNIVERSE HAD A CAUSE, THAT CAUSE MUST BE PERSONAL	129
There Are No Other Plausible Candidates	130
A Material Cause of the Universe	130
Possible Non-Material, Non-Personal Causes	133
Free Agency is the Only Way for Change to Come from Changelessness	137
The Alleged Need for Agent Causation	137
The Plausibility of Substance Dualism	141

Summary of the Argument	148
Chapter Three	**152**
The Fine-Tuning Argument	
Overview of the Argument	152
Premise One: The Universe is Fine-Tuned for Intelligent Life	153
The Evidence for Fine-Tuning	154
The Possibility of Other Forms of Life	156
Examining Martin Rees' Six Numbers	161
The Dimensionality Problem	170
The Representativeness Problem	175
Premise Two: The Explanation of Fine-Tuning is Either Chance, Necessity, or Design	180
Premise Three: Chance and Physical Necessity are not Plausible Explanations	181
Chance as an Explanation	181
Physical Necessity as an Explanation	185
Summary of the Argument	186
Chapter Four	**188**
The Moral Argument	
Overview of the Argument	188
Premise One: Moral Facts Require Grounding	190
Premise Two: Objective Moral Facts Exist	192
Cognitivism and Non-Cognitivism	193
Relativism and Universalism	196
Craig's Mutually-Conflicting Arguments	197

Possible Defeaters of Our Moral Experience	198
PREMISE THREE: GOD PROVIDES A FOUNDATION FOR MORAL FACTS	200
God's Nature as the Basis of Morality	200
The Euthyphro Dilemma	203
The Challenge of Ideal Observer Theory	205
PREMISE FOUR: THERE IS NO NON-THEISTIC GROUNDING FOR MORAL FACTS	206
Non-Theistic Theories of Morality	206
Humanity is Small and Ephemeral	212
Humans as Mere Animals	213
Morality and Free Will	215
Atheism and Moral Duties	217
Reductive Moral Naturalism	218
Explanatory Stopping Points	225
SUMMARY OF THE ARGUMENT	229

CHAPTER FIVE — 231

THE CHRISTOLOGICAL ARGUMENT

OVERVIEW OF THE ARGUMENT	231
The Structure of Craig's Argument	231
Criteria for Judging an Explanation	232
The Four Historical Facts	236
THE RHBS HYPOTHESIS	237
Overview of the Hypothesis	237
The model in brief	237
Simplicity and Occam's Razor	241

Key assumptions of RHBS model	241
Postulate One: Removal of the Body	242
Reburial by Joseph	243
Tomb robbery	247
The 'no evidence' objection	250
The production of Jesus' body	251
Postulate Two: Private Hallucinatory Experiences	256
The plausibility of individual hallucinations	256
Would hallucinations have led to belief in a resurrection?	262
The appearance to James the brother of Jesus	270
The appearance to Thomas	271
The appearance to the five hundred	272
Postulate Three: Collective Religious Experiences	274
Expectation and perceptual biases	274
The social construction of miracles	276
The diversity of the appearances	279
Historical examples of public miracles	281
Mass hysteria and psychogenic illness	294
Apparitions of the dead	295
Summary of collective religious experiences	304
Postulate Four: Cognitive, Memory, and Social Biases	305
Memory biases and eyewitness testimony	305
Irrational belief persistence	312
Socialisation effects	316
The role of legendary development	318
Explanatory Scope and Power of the Postulates	319

THE RESURRECTION HYPOTHESIS	322
Overview of the Hypothesis	322
Postulate One: God Exists	324
Postulate Two: God Desired to Raise Jesus	324
Postulate Three: Jesus Desired to Appear to his Followers	328
Explanatory Scope and Power of the Postulates	330
SUMMARY OF THE ARGUMENT	332
CHAPTER SIX	**335**
OTHER ARGUMENTS	
THE LEIBNIZIAN COSMOLOGICAL ARGUMENT	335
THE ONTOLOGICAL ARGUMENT	340
THE ARGUMENT FROM INTENTIONALITY	344
THE UNREASONABLE EFFECTIVENESS OF MATHEMATICS	345
CHAPTER SEVEN	**350**
CONCLUSIONS	
AN OVERALL EVALUATION OF CRAIG'S ARGUMENTS	350
WHAT SHOULD WE BELIEVE?	355
BIBLIOGRAPHY	**359**
ENDNOTES	**374**

James Fodor

CHAPTER ONE
INTRODUCTION

THE PURPOSE OF THIS BOOK

This book does not aim to convert Christians to atheism, or to undermine faith in God. Unlike many of my fellow public atheists, I have no interest in bringing about a general decline in religiosity as such in society. Rather, my purpose in this book is exclusively to evaluate a particular collection of arguments that have been put forward in favour of belief in Christianity. Specifically, I have written this book as a systematic critique of the apologetic work of leading Christian philosopher and apologist William Lane Craig. Though it is all too easy to forget, there is a significant difference between saying that an argument is unsound and asserting that the conclusion of the argument is false. In this book, I make no attempt to disprove or refute the existence of God or the truth of Christianity. My interest in this text is solely in the evaluation of the arguments put forward by Craig.

There are several reasons why I think it is important to carefully consider Craig's arguments. First, these arguments have been widely propagated through both his writings and his many oral debates. The fact that many people hear his arguments and find them (to varying degrees) compelling is itself an important reason for subjecting them to greater scrutiny. Second, a detailed analysis of exactly how and why Craig's arguments fail provides an engaging and important framework in which to sharpen one's critical thinking and analytical skills, and teaches one how to reason about philosophical, scientific, and historical subjects in a more careful, rigorous way than many people are accustomed to. If my readers were to take away nothing more than an enhanced appreciation for and ability to analyse such arguments, I would regard that as a significant success. Finally, and most importantly, Craig's arguments attempt to provide a series of reasons in virtue of which even an atheist or agnostic should, if they are responding rationally, adopt a belief in the truth of certain core Christian doctrines. I, along with many other atheists and agnostics, do not believe that Craig's arguments provide the sort of rational warrant to his conclusions that Craig claims they do. This book, therefore, serves as a means of articulating a rejoinder to Craig's arguments and explains why it is that I do not find his arguments convincing. I do not regard this as a matter of 'winning points' in some sort of intellectual contest, but rather as part of an iterative process of working through a complex set of issues together. As sincere seekers of truth, as I believe we all should be, and given the immense importance of the subject matter under discussion, I regard a careful analysis of Craig's arguments to be a matter of considerable importance.

A BRIEF BIOGRAPHY OF CRAIG

William Lane Craig was born in 1949 into a non-Christian family in Illinois, USA. Craig first became interested in religion during his teen years, when he began to ponder questions like, 'why am I here?' and 'where am I going?' He tried attending a nearby church, but grew disillusioned with what he considered to be their superficial and hypocritical attitude towards faith. Craig's views regarding Christianity changed dramatically at the age of sixteen, when a Christian classmate told Craig that Jesus loved him. Craig says that he found this idea staggering, and this event therefore marked the beginning of a long period of soul-searching and seeking. As Craig explains[1]:

> "My spiritual search went on for the next six months. I attended Christian meetings; I read Christian books; I sought God in prayer. Finally, one night I just came to the end of my rope and cried out to God. I cried out all the anger and bitterness that had built up inside me, and at the same time I felt this tremendous infusion of joy, like a balloon being blown up and blown up until it was ready to burst! I remember I rushed

outdoors – it was a clear, mid-western, summer night, and you could see the Milky Way stretched from horizon to horizon. As I looked up at the stars, I thought, "God! I've come to know God!" That moment changed my whole life. I had thought enough about this message during those six months to realize that if it were really the truth – really the truth – then I could do nothing less than spend my entire life spreading this wonderful message among mankind."

In 1971, Craig completed his undergraduate studies at Wheaton College majoring in communications, and subsequently completed his dual master's theses in Philosophy of Religion and Church History at Trinity Evangelical Divinity School in 1975[2]. Having been originally introduced to Christian apologetics in his senior year of college, upon graduation from seminary Craig travelled to the United Kingdom to complete a doctorate under philosopher John Hick in developing a cosmological argument for the existence of God. Craig's work during this time formed the basis for the much-discussed kalam cosmological argument. Craig completed his Doctorate in Philosophy in 1977, and shortly thereafter commenced a second doctorate program in Theology under Dr. Wolfhart Pannenberg at the University of Munich in Germany, which focused on developing an argument for the historical evidence for the resurrection of Jesus[3]. In 1980 Craig returned to the United States, teaching philosophy of religion for seven years at Trinity Evangelical Divinity School and then for one year at Westmont College, before accepting a position at the Université Catholique de Louvain in Belgium. During this period, Craig completed extensive research on the philosophy of time and God's relationship to time, which is important for defence of his kalam cosmological argument. In 1994, Craig commenced his current role as Research Professor of Philosophy at Talbot School of Theology in California.

In the 1990s, Craig began to engage in regular debates concerning the existence of God and the evidence for the resurrection of Jesus[4]. It is through these debates, widely circulated and discussed online, that Craig built his following and profile. Craig possesses a combination of skills and knowledge uniquely suited to such debates. First, he had extensive experience with the techniques of debate and oratory in high school and college[5], having won the state championship in oratory in high school. Furthermore, Craig's doctoral work on the cosmological argument and later the resurrection argument, in addition to his many subsequent publications on related subjects, meant that he was a world expert in these areas. Many of Craig's opponents lacked the debating experience, the rhetorical skills, or the subject-specific knowledge to seriously compete with Craig in these debates, leading a wide range of Christian and atheist observers alike to praise Craig's debating performance and declare him as the victor in the large majority of his encounters.

In addition to his public debates and scholarly writings, Craig has also written several popular apologetics works, most prominent of which is the book *Reasonable Faith*. Building upon the successes of this work and his increasing public profile, in 2007 Craig founded the website ReasonableFaith.org, which hosts a large number of Craig's articles, in addition to a podcast, links to debate recordings, and forum discussions[6]. Today ReasonableFaith.org is one of the leading evangelical apologetics websites. It is because of his high public profile, as well as the relatively poor response to his arguments thus far provided by atheists and agnostics, that I have decided to focus this book on the arguments of Craig specifically.

THE PURPOSE OF CRAIG'S ARGUMENTS

Craig states very clearly that the primary reason he believes in the truth of Christianity is because of what he believes to be his direct experience of the Holy Spirit[7]:

> *"Fundamentally, the way we know Christianity to be true is by the self-authenticating witness of God's Holy Spirit. Now what do I mean by that? I mean that the experience of the Holy Spirit is veridical and unmistakable (though not necessarily irresistible or indubitable) for him who has it; that such a person does not need supplementary arguments or evidence in order to know and to know with confidence that he is in fact experiencing the Spirit of God; that such experience does not function in*

> this case as a premise in any argument from religious experience to God, but rather is the immediate experiencing of God himself... Thus, although arguments and evidence may be used to support the believer's faith, they are never properly the basis of that faith. For the believer, God is not the conclusion of a syllogism; he is the living God of Abraham, Isaac, and Jacob dwelling within us. How then does the believer know that Christianity is true? He knows because of the self-authenticating witness of God's Spirit who lives within him."

As such, Craig believes that the purpose of rational argumentation and evidence is to strengthen one's belief in God, and to help bring others to knowledge of God. In this respect reason is completely subservient to faith, with Craig stating that[8]:

> "Should a conflict arise between the witness of the Holy Spirit to the fundamental truth of the Christian faith and beliefs based on argument and evidence, then it is the former which must take precedence over the latter, not vice versa."

Craig sometimes expresses this by saying that the witness of the Holy Spirit functions as an 'intrinsic defeater-defeater', such that it automatically overwhelms any potential defeaters or rebuttals that a believer might be confronted with[9]:

> "I have argued the witness of the Holy Spirit is indeed an intrinsic defeater of any defeaters brought against it. For it seems to me inconceivable that God would allow any believer to be in a position where he would be rationally obliged to commit apostasy and renounce Christ. It seems to me rather that in such a situation a loving God would intensify the Spirit's witness in such a way that it would become an intrinsic defeater of the defeaters such a person faces."

Given the foregoing, it is evident that the purpose of the arguments Craig develops is not to help to determine whether Christianity is true, but rather to serve as apologetic tools in the task of furthering Christianity. In particular, Craig believes that apologetic arguments are useful for showing that Christianity is true[10]:

> "We must make a distinction between knowing that it is true and showing that it is true. We know Christianity is true primarily by the self-authenticating witness of God's Spirit. We show Christianity is true by presenting good arguments for its central tenets."

Craig thus judges the success of his arguments by how persuasive they are in this task of showing that Christianity is true. Regarding persuasiveness Craig says[11]:

> "Since we cannot hope to persuade everybody, our aim should be to make our cumulative apologetic case as persuasive as possible. This can best be done by appealing to facts which are widely accepted or to intuitions that are commonly shared (common sense). When we appeal to expert testimony, our authorities should not be partisan but neutral or even anti-Christian."

I do not agree with Craig's view that such 'intrinsic defeater-defeaters' can overwhelm any other possible evidence or arguments against a belief. I believe that we should form our beliefs about the world such that our mental models of reality best account for the phenomena that we observe via our senses. Going into more detail about my views on this subject would lead us beyond the scope of the present volume, however, and so I will not engage in a lengthy critique of Craig's views on this matter. Suffice it to say that Craig's arguments will only be persuasive to others to the extent that they adhere to the generally accepted principles of logic, rationality, and evidence, and it is by these standards that I will attempt to adjudicate the strength of his arguments in this book. Consistent with established practise for persuasive arguments, I will require that his arguments are logically valid, and that the premises are defended on the basis of either generally-accepted facts, or by appeal to widely shared intuitions or experiences. Craig does not claim that his arguments show with certainty that Christianity is true, but rather he claims to develop a cumulative case, in light of which it is considerably more likely that Christianity is true than false. This is then the claim that I will critically analyse in this book – how good are Craig's arguments in establishing that Christianity is probably true?

The Structure of This Book

In his oral debates and published writings, Craig defends four main arguments in favour of the existence of the Christian God. Three of these arguments attempt to establish the existence of a deity, while the fourth attempts to identify this deity with the God of Christianity. Craig thus presents what is in effect a cumulative case for the truth of Christianity. In this section, I will briefly summarise each of Craig's main arguments, and in so doing outline the structure for the remainder of the book.

In chapter two I discuss the kalam cosmological argument. This attempts to show that the universe must have had an absolute beginning in time, and so cannot be eternal in the past. Craig has three main arguments for this: first, that an infinite series of past events is impossible, second, that the present could never be reached following an infinite succession of events, and third, that there is powerful scientific evidence that the universe began to exist. Having presented a case for the beginning of the universe, Craig then argues that anything that has such an absolute beginning must also have a cause of its coming into existence. This cause, Craig argues, must be something that can exist outside time and space (since neither existed at the time of creation), and also be capable of bringing about an effect from an initial changeless state. Craig argues that only a nonphysical agent endowed with free will could function as this sort of cause, and thus such a mind is the best explanation for the original cause of the universe. This agent, of course, Craig identifies as God.

In chapter three I discuss the fine-tuning argument. This attempts to show that various physical constants have been discovered by scientific inquiry to be finely-tuned for the existence of intelligent life, such that if the values of these constants were even slightly different, intelligent life could not exist. Craig argues that the only possible explanations for such fine-tuning are chance, physical necessity, or design. He then argues that chance and physical necessity fail as plausible explanations for various reasons, and therefore design emerges as the only plausible explanation for the fine-tuning of the universe. Such design, however, naturally implies a designer, which Craig identifies with God.

In chapter four I discuss the moral argument. According to this argument, though we can all discern the existence of objective moral values whether we are religious or not, only under a theistic worldview can we make any sense of how such objective moral values could exist. Craig argues that in the absence of a God to serve as the source of morality and the paradigm of goodness, there simply could not be anything that would make objective moral values exist. Without God, morality would simply be an evolutionarily-evolved set of adaptations and preferences conducive for the survival of *Homo sapiens*, but would not have any ultimate objective truth or binding force. Since, however, we all know deep down that objective moral values do exist, it follows that God must also exist to serve as a foundation for such values.

In chapter five I discuss the Christological argument, also known as the argument from the resurrection of Jesus. Craig begins with a set of key facts concerning the death and resurrection of Jesus of Nazareth, which he argues are widely accepted by both religious and non-religious biblical scholars based on substantial textual and historical evidence. Craig then argues that by far the best explanation for these key facts is the hypothesis that God raised Jesus from the dead. Other proposed naturalistic explanations, he argues, suffer numerous problems and have been widely rejected by scholars. The superiority of the resurrection hypothesis over all other candidates therefore provides a strong reason, according to Craig, to believe that God really did raise Jesus from the dead, thereby vindicating the truth of Christianity.

In chapter six I briefly discuss four additional arguments that Craig has defended at various times, but which he has written far less about and devoted much less attention to than his four major arguments. These are the ontological argument, the Leibnizian cosmological argument, the argument from intentionality, and the argument from the unreasonable effectiveness of mathematics.

In chapter seven I provide a summary and some concluding remarks, summarising the strength of Craig's various arguments, and also considering what in the end we ought to believe about these issues.

Each of the chapters is largely self-contained, though occasionally I do refer to certain concepts discussed in a different chapter. The chapters differ in length largely in accordance with the quantity of writing that Craig has produced in defence of each argument. Craig has devoted most of his writing to the kalam and the Christological arguments, and therefore these two arguments occupy the majority of the book. In the chapters discussing the kalam, fine-tuning, and moral arguments, I first introduce the argument and then discuss each major premise of the argument in a separate section. Since the structure of the Christological argument is different to the other three major arguments, in this chapter I first introduce Craig's key historical facts and then devote a section each to the two competing explanations for these facts.

A Note to the Reader

I have attempted to make this book as accessible as possible to people of all backgrounds. Given the breadth of subject matter covered in this book, as well as the inherent difficulty of some of the concepts, this is a goal for which complete success is doubtless impossible. I have wherever possible attempted to avoid the use of jargon, or to explain it clearly when introduced. I also do not assume any prior knowledge about Craig's arguments or the many specific scientific and philosophical concepts they appeal to. My explanations of such concepts, however, are necessarily brief, and readers are encouraged to augment my cursory descriptions by consulting the additional sources that I cite. Readers with little background in philosophy may find certain sections more difficult than others, particularly the discussion of the tensed/tenseless theories of time. To enable such readers to avoid getting bogged down in more detail than is necessary, I have included numerous subheadings to facilitate skimming or skipping of particularly difficult passages.

Since each of Craig's four main arguments could easily be the subject of an entire book by itself, I have not attempted to provide a comprehensive overview of every single supporting argument Craig raises in defence of his arguments, or of all the various objections that have been raised against his arguments over the years. Instead, I endeavour only to discuss what I consider to be the most significant issues and most pressing objections. Often this means bypassing significant discussion of a number of issues that are sometimes raised in response to Craig's arguments, but which I believe are either poor objections, of questionable relevance, or do not address the central topic of dispute. Examples of such exclusions include the 'who created/designed God?' objection to the cosmological and fine-tuning arguments, the objection that virtual particles can come into existence without a cause, discussion of various specific multiverse models purporting to explain fine-tuning, responses to the moral argument based upon cultural relativism or error-theory, discussion about the general unreliability of the

New Testament gospels, and any disputation concerning the key facts Craig defends concerning the death and resurrection of Jesus. Readers desiring further discussion of these issues should consult one of the many sources already available. I should instead focus on other aspects of Craig's arguments which I believe will generate a more robust discussion.

My sincere hope is that readers of this book – Christians, agnostics, atheists, and others alike – will approach the arguments discussed herein with a critical but open mind. By this I mean considering what is being argued fairly and thoughtfully, not merely accepting or rejecting an argument out of hand because one is disinclined to agree with its conclusion, or because it sounds similar to other arguments they have accepted or rejected in the past. Arguments ought to be accepted or rejected based on their merits, and often the merits of an argument can depend importantly upon the particular details of how they are formulated, and exactly what evidence is provided to support them. I thus encourage my readers to approach this book with a careful eye to those details, doing their best to set aside pre-existing biases and as much as possible be objective in their evaluation of the arguments.

James Fodor, January 2017

Chapter Two
The Kalam Cosmological Argument

Overview of The Argument

The kalam cosmological argument is an argument for the existence of God that Craig developed during his doctoral work in the 1970s. 'Kalam' is Arabic for 'word', and is the term that Craig adopted to describe his argument because it is built upon the work of various medieval Islamic theologians[12]. The argument is 'cosmological' in the sense that it attempts to show that God exists in virtue of his role as the creator of the cosmos. The argument therefore appeals to considerations about the origin of the universe, and how space and time came into existence. There are a number of different forms of cosmological argument discussed in the apologetics literature; hence the importance in specifying that here I will be discussing the kalam version of the cosmological argument as opposed to one of the other forms.

The kalam cosmological argument is a sophisticated piece of natural theology, and is by far the argument that Craig has written the most about and received the most responses to. As such, in this section I will not seek to survey every single dispute or issue that has been discussed in relation to the kalam. Rather, I shall focus on what I regard to be the most important and pertinent to evaluating the effectiveness of the argument.

Strictly speaking, the kalam cosmological argument has only two premises and a modest conclusion:

- Premise one: The universe began to exist.

- Premise two: Everything that begins to exist has a cause.
- Conclusion: The universe has a cause.

This argument only concludes that the universe has a cause, saying nothing about the nature of this cause. In his original publication, Craig defines the above as 'the kalam cosmological argument,' and identifies the subsequent question regarding identifying this cause of the universe with a personal God as distinct from the kalam proper[13]. For the purpose of this book, however, I find it more convenient to consider all these issues together, and thereby make the kalam into an argument for God proper. This, after all, is the real reason why the argument is of interest and why Craig developed it in the first place.

In addition to the nature of the cause of the universe, there is another crucial issue which Craig did not include as part of the original kalam argument. After it was published, Craig came to realise that his original formulation of the kalam was dependent upon a particular theory in philosophy of time known as the tensed theory of time, and did not work under its main rival position called the tenseless theory of time. Only under a tensed theory of time can anything truly 'begin to exist' in the sense that Craig is appealing to in the kalam, and thus without assuming the truth of the tensed theory the argument cannot go ahead. In Craig's words[14]:

> *"On a (tenseless theory) of time, the universe does not in fact come into being or become actual at the Big Bang; it just exists tenselessly as a four-dimensional space-time block that is finitely extended in the earlier than direction. If time is tenseless, then the universe never really comes into being, and, therefore, the quest for a cause of its coming into being is misconceived."*

This is not something that Craig discussed in his original work, nor does he typically mention it in his popular debates. Nevertheless, Craig has acknowledged that the kalam is crucially dependent upon a tensed theory of time, and therefore I think it is sufficiently important to include it as an additional implicit premise of the kalam.

As a result of these two considerations, we arrive at what I call the extended kalam cosmological argument, which can be summarised as follows:

- Premise one: Time is tensed, so things can begin to exist.
- Premise two: The universe began to exist.
- Premise three: Everything that begins to exist has a cause.
- Premise four: If the universe had a cause, that cause was a personal creator.
- Conclusion: A personal creator (God) exists.

In this chapter, I shall critically respond to this extended kalam cosmological argument, considering each premise in turn, and critically analysing the arguments that Craig presents in favour of each.

PREMISE ONE: TIME IS TENSED

In order for the kalam cosmological argument to succeed, Craig needs to adopt a very specific assumption about the nature of time. Specifically, he needs to assume the truth of what is called the tensed theory of time. In Craig's own words[15]:

> "The kalam cosmological argument presupposes from start to finish a theory, not of tenseless time, but of tensed time, according to which temporal becoming is an objective feature of the world."

The tensed theory of time stands in contrast to its main competitor, the tenseless theory of time. Each of these theories makes substantially different and conflicting claims about the nature of time. For historical reasons, these competing theories also go by the names A-theory (tensed theory) and B-theory (tenseless theory). Since the terms tensed and tenseless are far more descriptive, I have substituted in parentheses all references to 'A-theory' or 'A-theorist' with 'tensed theory' and 'tensed theorist', and 'B-theory' or 'B-theorist' with 'tenseless theory' and 'tenseless theorist', in all quotations taken from Craig's work. This does not alter the meaning of any of Craig's statements, but does help to avoid the confusion intrinsic to such non-descriptive labels.

While the dispute between tensed and tenseless theories of time can often be subtle and complex, the main difference between the theories lies in their different attitudes to the nature of tense. According to the tensed theory of time, tense is a real and irreducible part of reality. That is, there is an absolute sense in which events are *future*, then become *present*, and finally recede to become *past*. An adherent of tensed time thus would say that the proposition 'World War Two is past' is true, because while this conflict was at one time present, it is now and forever past. It is objectively true that this event *was present*, but *is now past*. The tenseless theory of time, by contrast, denies that tense is a real, irreducible part of reality. That is, there is no absolute sense in which any event is future, present or past. Instead, events can only ever be *earlier than, simultaneous with*, or *later than* some other event. Thus, an adherent of the tenseless theory of time would say that the proposition 'World War Two is past' is either false (because no event is ever past in an absolute sense), or really means something like 'World War Two is earlier than this conversation'. See figure 1 for a diagrammatic depiction of the differences between the two theories.

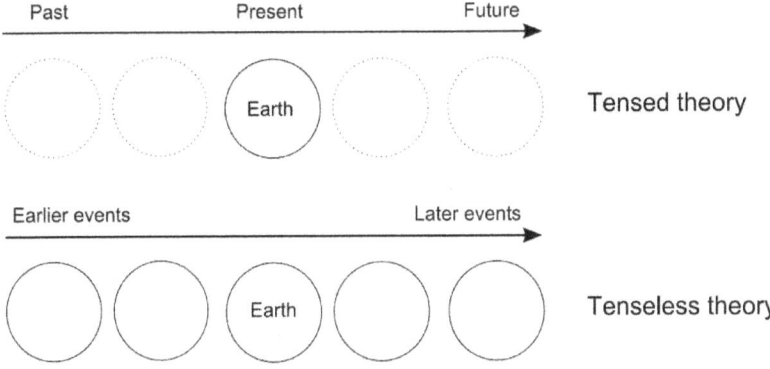

Figure 1. The tensed theory of time (top) holds that tense is an intrinsic part of reality, with only present events existing (represented by solid circles) and past and future events being unreal (represented by dotted circles). The tenseless theory of time (bottom) holds that tense is an intrinsic part of reality, and instead says that events can only be placed in temporal relations of earlier than, simultaneous with, and later than. All events exist alongside one another, but at different times.

To better understand this distinction, imagine a series of markers placed along a one-way street. Each marker is separated in space and so is located at a different spatial location, however everyone would agree that all of the markers are equally real, each existing alongside the others, just at a different spatial location. There is no sense in which any marker is 'forwards' or 'backwards' in an absolute sense, since even if the road has a given direction (as a one-way street), there is no meaningful sense in which objects in any part of the road are simply 'forward'. Rather, all one can say is that some marker is in front of or behind some other marker, or more forward and more backwards. Adherents of the tenseless theory of time say that events in time are structured in much the same way as these markers along the road. That is, just as all the markers exist alongside each other but at different *spatial* locations, so too do different moments of time exist alongside each other but at different *temporal* locations. All points in time are thus just as real as each other, though of course we as finite beings only ever experience one moment of time at once. Likewise, just as there is no sense in which a marker can be 'forwards' or 'backwards', no event can be 'future' or 'past' in an absolute sense. Instead, each event is only earlier than or later than some other event. Adherents of the tensed theory of time, by contrast, think that only the present moment of time (or sometimes the past and the present but not the future) are 'real', while the past and the future (or sometimes only the future) is not real in the same way. Adherents to the tensed theory therefore believe that time is different to space precisely because all moments of time do not exist alongside each other in the way different spatial locations do, but pass from future, to present, to past in a process of 'absolute becoming'.

The tensed theory of time is essential for the kalam cosmological argument because the first premise of the kalam is that the universe began to exist, by which Craig means an absolute coming into existence. If the tenseless theory of time is correct, however, then even if the universe wasn't eternal it still wouldn't have 'begun to exist'. Rather, the universe would simply be temporally extended a finite length in the 'before than' direction. We typically don't think of spatially extended objects as having an 'absolute spatial beginning', a point in space where they objectively 'begin', with each subsequent segment of the object deriving its existence in virtue of the existence of this beginning point. Rather, we typically think of all parts of spatially extended objects as simply existing at once alongside each other. The object thus doesn't have an absolute spatial 'beginning'; it simply has a finite spatial extension in each dimension. To see how spatial and temporal extension work, consider the case of the original World Trade Center twin towers. These structures had a finite spatial extent, from a particular point on the Earth's surface extending upwards some 415 meters. They also had a finite temporal extent, from their completion in April 1973 to their destruction in September 2001. The tenseless theory of time holds that the universe is the same way with respect to its existence in time. Even if there was a first moment of time, this simply represents the part of the universe that is earlier than all other parts, or the part temporally extended farthest in the 'earlier than' direction. Neither this first moment nor any other temporal part of the universe 'began to exist' in an absolute sense, since under the tenseless theory nothing 'begins to exist' in this way. Rather, different entities simply have variable temporal extensions depending upon how long they last. Thus, if the tenseless theory of time is true, nothing ever 'begins to exist' in the way that Craig means (not just 'has a first moment' but actually comes into being), then the first premise of the kalam cannot possibly be true. This is why philosophy of time is so critical to Craig's argument, and why he has written four lengthy books defending his views on time.

In this section I will consider the main arguments that Craig provides in favour of a tensed theory of time and against a tenseless theory. These arguments are as follows:

- The inelimibility of tense from language implies the reality of tense.
- Our direct experience of time shows that time is tensed.
- Relativity theory does not undermine tensed theories of time.
- Tenseless theories of time entail absurd conclusions.

The Inelimibility of Tense from Language Implies the Reality of Tense

Tensed and Tenseless Sentences

A tensed sentence is one that refers to tensed concepts such as 'present', 'past', and 'future'. A tenseless sentence is one that only refers to tenseless relations such as 'earlier than', 'simultaneous with', and 'later than'. Often in everyday discussions of time people are not careful to distinguish whether they are making tensed or tenseless claims (or both), since for most purposes it does not matter. Thus, if I were to say 'my exam is tomorrow', I could be making the tensed claim 'my exam is future' (i.e. it has not yet come into existence), or I could me making the tenseless claim 'my exam is later than my present conversation with you' (i.e. it exists but at later time). Note that both of these formulations seem rather awkward, which is to be expected because they have both been rephrased from sloppy everyday language to more precise philosophical language. The important thing to understand is simply that, while we might typically mix them up in everyday usage, philosophically one can make a distinction between tensed sentences and tenseless sentences.

Craig argues that tensed words and phrases are an indispensible part of human language, such that it would not be possible to remove them from our communication without significant loss of meaning. He concludes that this fact provides strong evidence in favour of the real existence of tensed facts – i.e. that the tensed theory of time is true. Craig summarises his argument as follows (premise numbering altered)[16]:

> "*Premise one: Tensed sentences ostensibly ascribe ontological tenses.*
> *Premise two: Unless tensed sentences are shown to be reducible without loss of meaning to tenseless sentences or ontological tense is shown to be superfluous to human thought and action, the ostensible ascription of ontological tenses by tensed sentences ought to be accepted as veridical.*

Premise three: Tensed sentences have not been shown to be reducible without loss of meaning to tenseless sentences.
Premise four: Ontological tense has not been shown to be superfluous to human thought and action.
Conclusion: Therefore, the ostensible ascription of ontological tenses by tensed sentences ought to be accepted as veridical."

Premise one of this argument states that tensed sentences at least apparently refer to tenses that really exist. This isn't to say that tenses must exist simply because people talk about them. Rather, the point is that at least taken at face value, tensed sentences are making claims about tensed facts that are thought to really exist – people seem to talk about tenses *as if* they really exist. I regard this premise as quite plausible, so I will not discuss it further. By far, the majority of space in Craig's work is spent defending premises three and four, which relate respectively to what are called the 'Old' and 'New' tenseless theories of language. I will begin, therefore, by discussing these tenseless theories of language, and examining whether it is in fact possible to reduce tensed sentences to tenseless ones. I will then consider Craig's second premise, concerning whether we should take tensed sentences as literally describing the way reality is.

The Token Indexical Tenseless Theory of Language

One of the most promising responses to premise three is called the 'token-indexical' tenseless theory of language. According to this theory, tensed sentences are rendered true or false by certain properties of their 'tokens'[17]. A token is a particular instance when a given sentence is uttered. Thus, the same sentence (e.g. 'I am here now') could be uttered multiple times by different people in different times and places, with each specific instance being described as a separate 'token' of the same underlying sentence. The token-indexical theory of language is thus said to be 'indexical' because each statement is interpreted relative to the particular time and place that it was uttered. The purpose of this indexical theory is to be able to specify what makes tensed sentences true in terms of purely tenseless facts, in which case Craig's third premise would be false. For example, a tensed remark such as 'the holidays have already ended' is interpreted in the new tenseless theory of language to mean 'the holidays ended earlier than this statement'. These concepts and distinctions, while subtle, are important to understand for some of the discussions below.

My overall view concerning how to understand tensed sentences, sentences that Craig says are indispensable to human thought and action, is similar to that developed by Oaklander[18], which he summarises as follows[19]:

> "On the new theory as I conceive it, no tenseless sentence can state all the truth conditions, that is, give the complete 'meaning' of a tensed sentence... However, just because no tenseless sentence type or token gives all the truth conditions (read 'meanings') of a tensed sentence type or token, it does not follow that no tenseless sentence truth conditions sentence can state one of the conditions of a tensed sentence. Indeed, a tenseless sentence can state the most important condition of a tensed sentence, namely, its pragmatic condition that accounts for why tensed sentences and beliefs are useful."[20]

In essence, this view holds that statements about time are complex, involving multiple layers of meaning depending on how exactly we interpret them. These different layers of meaning are dependent upon the context in which statements are uttered, and also upon the mindset and beliefs of the person making the statement. Since most people do not have any specific metaphysical views about the nature of time, in most cases everything they wish and need to convey can be expressed perfectly adequately in terms of tenseless indexical statements. In some contexts, however, certain statements will involve unique meanings which cannot be translated in this way. An obvious example is the set of statements made by Craig in defending his tensed theory of time; clearly Craig holds that he is making intrinsically tensed statements that appeal to the existence of tensed facts, and so are not translatable into tenseless sentences. Such untranslatable sentences can be regarded by a proponent of the tenseless theory of time as referring to propositions that are false, because there are no tensed facts to render them true. This position avoids Craig's criticism that some tensed sentences simply cannot be translated into a single tenseless sentence while preserving all aspects of their meaning, since it holds that some aspects of the meaning of tensed sentences are simply false and therefore do not need to be translated into tenseless sentences. To summarise, my position is that most tensed discourse can be translated into indexical tenseless sentences without loss of meaning, while the remaining sentences that cannot be so translated (e.g. Craig's claims about time) are all false. In effect, therefore, my position with respect to Craig's above argument is that most tensed sentences can be reduced without loss of meaning to tenseless sentences, while those that cannot (or the aspects of meaning that cannot be so translated) are superfluous to human thought and action because they are all false.

One objection that Craig raises against a token-indexical account of temporal language is that it leads to the absurd conclusion that two tokens of 'it is now 1980' are not logically equivalent, since they refer to two separate and distinct tokens. Considering the example of two different tokens called R and S, both asserting the statement 'it is now 1980', Craig argues[21]:

"If the only facts stated by R are the tenseless facts given in its token-reflexive truth conditions and similarly for S, then S and R cannot state the same fact, which is absurd."

Essentially, Craig is saying that two different instances of stating 'it is now 1980' must always be asserting the same fact regardless of when and where they are asserted. According to the token-indexical tenseless theory of language, however, two different tokens of the same sentence do not necessary assert the same thing, which Craig regards as an absurd result. Why, however, should we regard this as absurd? We do not regard it as absurd to say that other indexical phrases assert different facts depending upon who says them. Thus, for instance, if the author of this text were to assert 'I am Bill Gates', this would be to assert the proposition 'James Fodor is Bill Gates', which is false. However, if the co-founder of Microsoft and the Gates foundation were to utter a different token of the very same sentence 'I am Bill Gates', he would be asserting the proposition 'Bill Gates is Bill Gates', which is obviously true. The point here is that for indexical phrases, the fact asserted is not determined only by the words that are uttered, but also by when, where, and by whom the utterance is made. The very same sentence, uttered in a different setting or by a different person, can assert a very different fact. As such, there is nothing absurd about saying that the two different tokens of 'it is now 1980' assert different facts. The two tokens R and S are not identical, which is precisely what we mean when we say they are separate tokens, and thus they can refer to different facts. If, however, the two utterances were simultaneous, then they will always share the same truth value (i.e. if one is true the other will always be true), and hence they will be logically equivalent. Two tokens of a proposition can always share the same truth value without the tokens themselves being identical. As such, Craig's objection is based upon misunderstanding the difference between identity in meaning and sharing the same truth value.

Another objection that Craig raises to token-indexical accounts of tensed language concerns their alleged inability to properly capture all aspects of the meaning of tensed sentences. To illustrate this, he quotes the following example[22]:

> "Suppose that the token T of 'the storm is approaching' occurred two months ago, simultaneously with the storm's approach. Since the tenseless truth condition, T's being simultaneous with the approach of the storm, is met, T is true when it occurs. But it is false that T is (present tense) true. Rather T was true, namely, when the storm was approaching.' In order for T to be presently true, a different condition is needed, namely, that T is present."

In other words, proponents of tensed and tenseless theories of time will both agree that the truth of a statement like 'the storm is approaching' depends on when the statement is uttered. They disagree on how to determine whether the statement is true. Craig, being a proponent of the tensed theory, thinks that we need to know more than whether or not this statement was uttered simultaneously with the approach of the storm; he thinks we also need to know whether the time when the storm approaches is *now*, or whether it approached last Tuesday or a century ago. The tenseless fact of the utterance being simultaneous with some weather pattern isn't enough for Craig, as he thinks we also need to know whether that simultaneity is present right now, or occurred in the past. As such, Craig thinks that a token-indexical account of tensed sentences simply misses out a significant component of what makes those sentences true or false. The only way of capturing this component of the sentence, Craig thinks, is to appeal to tensed facts – tenseless token-indexical facts just won't do. Craig clearly expresses this idea in the following passage[23]:

> "We want to know what makes (present-tense) P [a proposition] true. We want to know, not what makes 'Jim races tomorrow' true on June 1, but what makes it true that 'Jim races tomorrow' or that 'Jim is racing'."

In Craig's view, the trouble with token-indexed accounts is that they are only able to say whether a particular utterance (or token) of a sentence is true or false. They have nothing to say about whether the sentence *itself* is true or false. Craig thinks this is a major problem, for, as he says, to know whether or not 'Jim is racing' we shouldn't need to know anything about when this sentence was uttered – all we should need to know is whether or not Jim racing *is happening* now (i.e. this event is *present*), or *did happen* in the past, or *will happen* in the future. Craig thinks that the token-indexical theory of language leaves out a crucial aspect of language precisely because it is unable to account for what makes such sentences true, not in a particular utterance made at a particular time, but *in general*. There is no way for token-indexical theories of language to express whether the event being referred to is present or not, and therefore no way to express all the necessary aspects of temporal discourse.

The problem with this objection is that Craig is begging the question in favour of the tensed theory of time, assuming that tensed facts exist when that is precisely the question under dispute. He is assuming the existence of tensed facts is evident by his remark "we want to know, not what makes 'Jim races tomorrow' true on June 1, but what makes it true that 'Jim races tomorrow'." The proponent of the tenseless theory, however, *doesn't* wish to know what makes 'Jim races tomorrow' true in general (i.e. independent of when that sentence is uttered), because under the tenseless theory there simply *isn't anything* that could make such a sentence true independently of when it is uttered. To see why this is the case, imagine somebody were to say "never mind about whether that particular token of 'Jim is here' is true – what I want to know is whether it is true *in general* that 'Jim is here'." We would regard such a statement as absurd, because it simply doesn't mean anything to ask whether Jim is 'here' unless we have some indexical way of specifying *where* 'here' refers to. As such, the statement 'Jim is here' cannot be said to be either true or false 'in general' – only particular *tokens* of this sentence can be true or false. Likewise, the tenseless theorist does not want to know what makes 'Jim races tomorrow' true or false independently of when that sentence is uttered, since they don't think there is anything that could make such a sentence true without some indexical way of specifying *when* 'tomorrow' is, relative to the time the phrase is uttered. Craig, of course, *does* want to know what makes 'Jim races tomorrow' true or false independently of when that sentence is uttered, and he thinks that what does the job are tensed facts (i.e. whether or not the event of Jim racing will be 'present' tomorrow). This highlights the fact that Craig's objection is question-begging, because his alleged 'problem' with the token-indexical account is only a problem for those who *already* accept the tensed theory of time, and therefore think we should be able to provide 'in general' truth conditions for statements like 'Jim races tomorrow'. For those who reject the existence of tensed facts, tensed sentences like this need not have any 'in general' truth conditions, but can only be sensibly understood in relation to when they are uttered. As such, under the tenseless theory there is nothing left out by token-indexical theories, and so Craig's objection fails.

Craig elsewhere argues that the tensed theory of time is the view of "the man on the street"[24] and therefore he presumably would argue that even if some philosophers have no problem with saying that sentences like 'Jim is racing' have no 'in general' truth conditions, the fact that most non-philosophers *would* have a problem with this would undermine the tenseless theory of language. It is by no means clear to me, however, that the 'man on the street' does hold to a tensed theory of time. After all, more than half of professional philosophers do not sufficiently understand the distinction between tensed and tenseless theories to wager an opinion on them[25], let alone laypersons. Nor is it obvious that, even if most laypersons did hold to a tensed theory of time, this would mean that their use of language should be given preferential treatment – after all, we certainly wouldn't grant this in various scientific fields, where laypersons often use words and concepts in very confused and inaccurate ways. Thus, the attitude that laypersons have with respect to the correct philosophy of time seems to be of little relevance to Craig's argument against tenseless theories of language.

The Problem of Untokened Sentences

A third objection that Craig raises against token-reflexive accounts of the meaning of temporal sentences is that such an analysis makes it impossible to give a meaning to tensed sentences that are not tokened. Craig frames the argument as follows[26]:

> "But now consider (3) 'the era of no linguistic or mental tokens exists'. During most of the history of the universe this seems to have been the case. The token-reflexive theorist must, however, translate (3) as: 4. 'the era of no linguistic or mental tokens exists simultaneous with the time of (3)', which is incoherent. Thus, the token-reflexive theorist seems committed to the rather bizarre position that there can be facts about what existed at some time without there being at that time a corresponding fact about what exists."

Craig's objection is mistaken, however, because it confuses the concept of a fact with the concept of a proposition. He says that during most of the history of the universe it was the era of no linguistic or mental tokens (since there were no people around to think or speak). This is correct – the state of affairs existed in reality such that there were no linguistic or mental tokens. The token-indexical theory, however, is a theory of *the meaning of sentences*, not a theory of truth. To say that 'it was the case that there were no linguistic or mental tokens' is not the same as to say 'the proposition "there were no linguistic or mental tokens" was true'. I do not think this proposition was true because, like Craig, I think that propositions are abstractions which do not exist by themselves, but only in virtue of being instantiated by particular mental or linguistic tokens. Thus, before humans evolved, it was a *fact* that there were no linguistic or mental tokens, because no one was around to think or say such tokens. However, the sentence 'it is the era of no linguistic or mental tokens' was *not true* at that time, because no such sentence existed (who was there to say it?), and non-existent propositions do not have truth values. Craig likewise argues that[27]:

> "It seems obvious that what is expressed by 'there is paper in the desk drawer' would be true even had one not uttered this true token and that what is expressed by 'no language users exist' is possibly true."

The problem here is that 'what is expressed by' a sentence is a proposition, not a fact. Facts are states of affairs that exist in the world independently of our understanding of them, but propositions (at least as far as both Craig and I believe) do not exist by themselves, but are abstractions which require instantiation in some concrete sentence. To see how this works, consider that 'humanity' is an abstract idea which does not exist by itself and is not the same thing as any individual human, but only exists in virtue of being instantiated by particular human beings. In Craig's example, it is not the case that the proposition 'there is paper in the desk drawer' would be true even if no one uttered this token, because without instantiation the proposition *would not exist*, and so would have no truth value. A non-existent statement does not refer to anything and so is neither true nor false. Of course, it may be a fact that 'there is paper in the desk drawer' regardless of whether anyone says that there is, but the fact of there being paper in the drawer is not the same as the proposition 'there is paper in the drawer'. Facts and propositions are not the same thing – propositions can be true or false, while facts can only ever be true. Facts exist all by themselves whether we know about them or not, while propositions require instantiation in some sentence (see figure 2). The token-indexical theory only attempts to give an account of the meaning of temporal *sentences*, and thus the fact that it has nothing to say about the meaning of *non-existent sentences* hardly seems to count as a compelling objection against it.

James Fodor

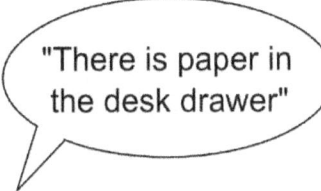

Proposition asserted

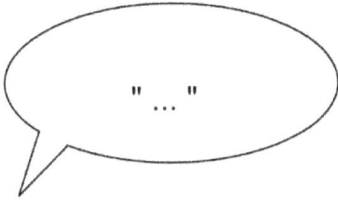

No proposition asserted

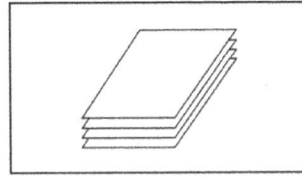

Fact exists: there is paper in the desk drawer

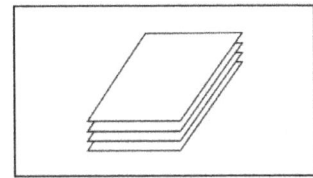

Fact exists: there is paper in the desk drawer

Figure 2. Facts are states of affairs that simply exist (bottom). Propositions about those facts may or may not be asserted (top), but the fact continues to exist in either case.

Tensed Statements as Enablers of Timely Action

Craig believes that tenseless statements (or the tenseless component of temporal statements) are by themselves not sufficient to facilitate timely action. Rather, Craig argues that tensed sentences are necessary for timely action. To illustrate his point, Craig considers the example sentence 'the faculty meeting starts now'. Under a token-reflexive account of the meaning of such tensed phrases, this sentence means 'the faculty meeting starts simultaneous with this utterance'[28]. The problem with this interpretation, Craig says, is that knowing the meeting starts simultaneous with a certain utterance is not enough in order to know when we should leave for the meeting. Craig argues that[29]:

> "One could always believe that these tokens are true; they never change their truth values. But then one will never know when to get up and go to the meeting, since one will never come to believe

27

that '*the time of θ (the meeting) is now*'."

Craig thinks that tensed propositions are thus informative in a way that tenseless ones aren't, because the tenseless proposition 'the meeting starts now' clearly conveys the information that I need to get to the meeting now, whereas 'the meeting starts simultaneously with this utterance' does not. Note that the question here is not whether a tensed sentence can be completely *translated* into a tenseless sentence, but whether the tenseless version of the sentence is sufficient for timely action.

The problem with Craig's objection is that, once again, he is presupposing the existence of tensed facts, and then critiquing a tenseless account of temporal language for failing to account for such facts. Thus, Craig thinks that we need to know the tensed fact 'the meeting starts now' before we can determine that it is time to go to the meeting. To the proponent of a tenseless theory of time, however, knowing that the meeting will commence simultaneously with a knock on one's door, or a particular utterance, or the hand of a clock falling upon a particular letter, is perfectly sufficient in order to determine that it is time to go to the meeting. In order to act in a timely way, all I need to know is at what time I should depart for the meeting. Suppose, for instance, that somebody were to call at my office and say 'the meeting starts two minutes from now'. I would then know to depart simultaneously with that utterance, for doing so would enable me to arrive simultaneously with the start of the meeting. It is not at all clear what is supposed to be lacking in the tenseless account that would prevent me from getting to the meeting on time.

Craig, however, can press his critique further. Suppose now that one week later I reflect back and consider last week's utterance of 'the meeting starts two minutes from now'. It is still (tenselessly) true that leaving my office simultaneously with *that* utterance (the utterance made last week) would allow me to arrive simultaneously with the start of last week's meeting. So why, upon reflecting on this tenseless fact, do I not get up and leave for the meeting once again? Craig thinks that in order to know that we should not *now* get up to go to *last week's* meeting, we need to understand the tensed fact that the meeting is *past*, and so is not happening *now*. Absent this tensed fact, all we have is the tenseless fact that a certain utterance is simultaneous with the start of the meeting, a fact which is always true and hence, according to Craig's reasoning, gives me no information about when I should leave for the meeting. What Craig is missing, however, is that we also have another piece of information at our disposal. When I am thinking about the start of the meeting, I can ask myself 'will my leaving simultaneously with this thought allow me to arrive simultaneously with the start of the meeting?' Obviously if I am thinking about leaving immediately prior to the meeting the answer will be yes, but if I am reflecting back a week later, the answer will be no. Thus, while the start of the meeting is always (tenselessly) simultaneous with the particular utterance 'the meeting starts now', it is *not* always simultaneous with every thought we have about whether I should depart for the meeting. Only those thoughts that are simultaneous with (or slightly earlier than) the start of the meeting will be thoughts that will prompt me to leave for the meeting, for reflecting on the meeting at any other time (e.g. a week later) I will realise that leaving simultaneously with my thoughts about the meeting will not allow me to arrive at the meeting on time. Therefore, under the tenseless account of time I am able to act in a timely manner because of the way in which our thoughts and language indexically pick out the temporal relationships between events that enable us to act at the correct time.

There is therefore no defect in tenseless accounts of time, and no inability to act in a timely manner absent an appeal to tensed facts. The only reason Craig thinks the tenseless theory is lacking is because his account of timely action makes reference to tensed facts (e.g. 'I should leave because the meeting starts *now*'), and tensed facts do not exist according to the tenseless theory. The proponent of a tenseless theory of time, however, is under no obligation to accept Craig's tensed articulation of how we act in a timely way, and as I have just shown, is quite capable of providing an adequate tenseless replacement that is perfectly sufficient for timely action.

Should Tensed Language be Taken as Veridical?

I have now discussed at some length Craig's arguments in defence of premises three and four of his argument for the inelimibility of tense from language, namely that tensed sentences have not been shown to be reducible without loss of meaning to tenseless sentences, and tense has not been shown to be superfluous to human thought and action. I now consider the second premise that Craig needs for his argument to succeed, namely that unless tensed sentences can be shown to be translatable or unnecessary for timely action, we should infer that the tensed facts these sentences refer to really do exist. In defence of this premise, Craig says the following[30]:

> "Unless there are some good reasons to call into question this ascription of ontological tense, then one ought to regard it as correct. Again, this seems quite reasonable. A view of truth as correspondence requires that a true sentence or proposition correspond to the way the world is, and if some tensed sentences are true, then reality must be tensed, since such sentences purport to ascribe ontological tenses."

The correspondence theory of truth would only apply to tensed language, however, if such language were taken to be literally true, as attempting to describe reality directly. Craig does not give any reasons, however, to regard the use of tensed language as committing us to the view that such sentences should be interpreted literally. Indeed, it seems plausible that one of the key points of dispute between tensed and tenseless proponents concerns whether tensed language should be interpreted literally or not. Craig is quite willing to consider the possibility of our temporal discourse being non-literal in other contests, as for instance when he explains why he believes it is acceptable to speak metaphorically of the 'flow' of time[31]:

> "The flow of time is thus metaphorical; but it is so in a 'philosophically important' way, for this way of talking is in some sense 'natural to us' and, at first sight, nearly unavoidable. So long as we separate such metaphorical talk from philosophical discussion, counsels Smart, there is no reason why we should not sing 'time like an ever-rolling stream' with a clear logical conscience."

If Craig thinks it is appropriate for talk about the ostensible 'flow of time' to be interpreted non-literally, and thus not to commit one to the view that time literally 'flows', then why can we not also say that our talk about tensed facts is equally appropriate but non-literal? That is, we could regard tensed propositions as not literally true, but as conveying metaphorical truths about time, or merely conventional ways of speaking which are (as Craig says) 'natural to us' and 'nearly unavoidable'. Indeed, it seems that humans use language like this all the time, such as when we speak of the sun 'rising', or speak of a ball 'wanting' to roll down a hill. Yet another example of an instance where Craig argues for a non-literal interpretation of some set of discourse is with respect to the general theory of relativity. He says, for instance[32]:

> *"In the same way that possible worlds semantics is an illuminating and perhaps indispensable tool for exploring questions of modality, but does not commit one ipso facto to modal realism, so also spacetime methodology can enlighten without implying a spacetime ontology."*

Craig argues that the general theory of relativity should be interpreted in an instrumentalist way, meaning that it is useful for making predictions, but does not describe the actual way reality 'really is'. Thus, the fact that general relativity speaks of the existence of four-dimensional spacetime does not imply that such a thing actually exists, because general relativity should not be taken to be literally true. This example clearly shows that Craig is willing to countenance the possibility that an entire discourse that is untranslatable into an alternate language and has proven to be indispensable in its relevant domain, is nevertheless not literally descriptive of the way reality is. If this can be the case for such a venerable scientific theory as general relativity, as well as for the previous example of our talk of the 'flow' of time, then I see no reason why it should not also be the case for talk involving tensed facts.

Yet another example where Craig rejects the idea that our language commits us to the actual existence of something can be found in his discussion about natural law, where he says[33]:

> *"'The natural law' shouldn't, or needn't, be taken to be a metaphysically heavyweight term but just a convenient way of*

> talking, for example, about the intrinsic value of human persons and what moral obligations/prohibitions we have to fulfil. The overall lesson here is: don't read ontology off of language."

Given these considerations, I think that there is no necessary reason to regard tensed sentences as committing us to the real existence of tensed facts, however untranslatable or useful such language might be. I thus conclude that Craig's argument that we should infer the existence of tensed facts from the ineliminability of tense from language is unsuccessful. He has neither shown that tense is truly eliminable from language, nor that our use of such language in any way commits us to the actual existence of tensed facts.

OUR DIRECT EXPERIENCE OF TIME SHOWS THAT IT IS TENSED

Our Direct Experience of Presentness

Separately from his arguments about tensed language, Craig believes that we directly experience the tensed nature of time. He argues[34]:

> "The reality of tense is experienced by us in a variety of ways which are so evident and so pervasive that the belief in the objective reality of past, present, and future and in the passage of time is a universal feature of human experience."

As a result of such experiences, Craig asserts that "belief in the objectivity of tense and the reality of temporal becoming is a properly basic belief"[35] and speaks repeatedly of how "basic, deeply ingrained, strongly held, and universal is our belief in the reality of tense and temporal becoming."[36] Craig does not, however, provide sufficient justification for such sweeping claims. Primarily his examples consist either of appeals to his own intuitions or experiences, or to various features of our language that (according to Craig's interpretation) seem to presuppose the reality of tense. The latter point about tensed language has already been discussed in the previous section, and I do not believe offers much support for Craig's position. With regards to intuitions and experience of time, I do not think Craig has provided any significant justification for his assertion that belief in tense is so deeply ingrained and strongly held throughout mankind. As Paul Helm aptly says of this claim[37]:

> "It is an empirical claim whose truth seems implausible, and for which Craig offers no evidence. It is surely more likely that people's basic beliefs in this area, proper or not, are an untidy mixture of (tensed) and (tenseless) features."

Even before considering some more specific aspects of temporal experience that Craig believes support the tensed theory of time, I want to raise some objections to this general approach of appealing to alleged direct experiences in defence of particular metaphysical theories. It seems to me that such an approach is fraught with dangers when considering such a general and abstract notion as time, where there is little reason to suppose that human experience is either accurate or complete in outlining all the properties of time. Quantum mechanics provides an example of a field whose findings stand directly in contrast to many of our basic intuitions and direct experiences of the way the world is: we experience space as continuous rather than discrete, objects as possessing a definite location rather than being spread over a region with varying probabilities, and objects as moving smoothly from one place to another rather than suddenly jumping to a new location with some probability. Indeed, our intuitions about space and time are easily shown to be inaccurate even in the most familiar settings. For example, while we perceive a table to be a solid object, in fact it mostly consists of empty space between the atoms. Similarly, while we perceive a motion picture to be a seamless series of moving images, what is actually displayed is a succession of static images with significant gaps of blackness in between too rapid for us to detect. Given that our intuitions and direct experiences of space and motion can be so at odds with the well-established findings of physics, it seems that we cannot be nearly as confident as Craig is that our experiences of the nature of time are always veridical. To assume such is to display an extreme form of naive realism, to suppose that we experience the world just the way it is, that our experiences provide some direct connection with the metaphysical nature of the world. I see no reason to suppose this is the case, and I think the examples I have provided yield good reasons to suppose this is in fact *not* the case. As such, I do not find Craig's strategy of appealing to our direct experiences of time as a particularly compelling method of argument.

Even aside from this general question about the reliability of our experiences of time, Craig's specific claims about the nature of our experiences of time are highly dubious. He argues that[38]:

> *"We experience events as happening presently. Every one of us lives in the present, which we often refer to indexically as 'now'... even if what we see and hear is not present, our experiences of seeing and hearing are observed as present."*

Under Craig's presentist philosophy of time, however, to be present is simply to exist. Thus, Craig's remarks here amount to saying that we experience events when they exist. Even when what we experience does not exist in reality (perhaps because it is past or imaginary), our *experiences* of seeing and hearing that thing are observed to exist. These statements are so trivial that they do nothing whatsoever to substantiate Craig's view that we experience time as tensed. Of course, when we experience things we experience those things to exist – how could it possibly be otherwise? If this is the substance of Craig's claim, it is hard to see how it lends any support to the tensed theory of time, since *any* theory of time will affirm that we observe our own experiences to exist. Furthermore, both tensed and tenseless theories of time agree that all we ever experience is that which is present, or that which is simultaneous with our experiences. Both theories agree that we do not experience anything that is past (earlier than) or future (later than) to our current experiences. The only issue on which the tensed and tenseless theories differ is in the nature of the past and the future, neither of which we experience. Therefore, Craig's appeals to our *experience* of the present are not even capable in principle of establishing the tensed over the tenseless theory of time, since the two theories only disagree about things that we *do not experience*.

Our Differential Attitudes Towards Past and Future

Another argument that Craig raises against the tenseless theory of time is that it is unable to make sense of our differential attitudes towards past and future. Craig (quoting A. N. Prior) outlines this 'thank goodness it's over' objection as follows[39]:

> "*One says, e.g. 'thank goodness that's over!', and not only is this, when said, quite clear without any date appended, but it says something which is impossible that any use of a tenseless copula with a date should convey. It certainly doesn't mean the same as, e.g. 'thank goodness the date of the conclusion of that thing is Friday, June 15, 1954,' even if it be said then. (Nor, for that matter, does it mean 'thank goodness the conclusion of that thing is contemporaneous with this utterance'. Why should anyone thank goodness for that?)*"

Craig contends that only under a tensed theory of time does it make sense to feel relief that a bad event is over, because only then can the unpleasant event objectively be said to have ceased to exist and have receded into the *past*. Under the tenseless theory of time, by contrast, Craig argues that there is simply nothing to be relieved about, because the unpleasant event still exists (tenselessly) just as it always has. Of course, the event is simultaneous with some events in our life and not with others, but it seems to make no sense to be relieved because an event is contemporaneous with (for example) Friday the 16th, unless we also know that this date is *past*. Thus, Craig thinks that tensed facts and beliefs are necessary in order to make relief (and similarly anticipation or dread) intelligible and rational.

The issue here is not of our experience of unpleasant events per se, but rather of our *attitudes* towards past or future unpleasant experiences. We have different attitudes towards unpleasant future events than we do towards unpleasant past events, and Craig thinks this can only make sense if reality is tensed and past events are truly 'over and done with' while future events are 'yet to come'. Under the tenseless theory of time, unpleasant events are never truly past or future, but simply earlier than or later than our reflections about these events. The problem then becomes: why should it be rational to hold a different attitude to an unpleasant event occurring *later than* my reflection about the event, compared to an unpleasant event occurring *earlier than* my reflection about the event, if there are no tensed facts? It seems to me, however, that this is simply a brute fact about what it is to be a

Unreasonable Faith

temporal being – we have an irreducibly different attitude towards 'earlier than' events compared to 'later than' events because we experience these events differently. The tenseless theory of time does not deny that there is an inherent direction (called anisotropy) to time, and thus there is no problem in affirming that we have different attitudes towards one direction compared to the other. Craig has also argued that an intrinsic anisotropy in time does not imply temporal becoming, however this is irrelevant as the tenseless theorist does not accept the reality of temporal becoming. The point is not that the anisotropy of intrinsic difference between 'earlier than' and 'later than' restores some form of temporal becoming. Rather, it is simply that this difference provides a distinction in virtue of which differential attitudes towards earlier and later events can be justified, which is all Craig can require.

If this is unsatisfying, Craig must acknowledge that his presentism (which is the view that only the present exists) provides no greater insight into our differential attitudes towards past and future. Craig says that under the tensed theory of time the rationality of feeling relief is "grounded in the reality of temporal becoming,"[40] even though under his account it is totally unclear what the real difference is supposed to be between non-existent future events and non-existent past events. Since under presentism both past and future are equivalent in their non-existence, it is unclear in virtue of what one could differentially regard past compared to future events. Of course, Craig will argue that future events *will exist* whereas past events *did exist*. In a subsequent section I argue that Craig has trouble providing an account of what these tensed terms actually mean, but even aside from that, we can still ask in virtue of what these two varieties of non-existence warrant our differential attitudes towards past and future events? At the end of the day it seems that Craig has nothing further to say other than that it is natural and appropriate for us to prefer unpleasant events to be the 'past' form of non-existent rather than the 'future' form of non-existent. This is just a brute fact with no further explanation. This, however, is no better than the answer provided by the proponent of the tenseless theory.

Thus, contrary to Craig's presentation of the matter, the proponent of the tenseless theory does not think that we experience relief because some painful event is earlier than some arbitrary event in our life history. Rather, they think that we experience relief when some painful event is earlier than *our recollecting or imagining* that event. We do so because, in virtue of the irreducible difference between the 'later than' and 'earlier than' relations, it is proper and appropriate for temporal agents such as ourselves to have differing attitudes to events which stand in each of the two relations relative to the time when we recollect or contemplate such events. This is no worse an explanation than that provided by Craig, in which he appeals to a similarly basic and unexplained preference for the one type of non-existent events (future) over another type of non-existent events (past).

Our Experience of the Reality of Temporal Becoming

Craig also argues that the reality of temporal becoming is an obvious aspect of our perception of temporal experience[41]:

> "*The reality of temporal becoming is even more obvious to us than the existence of the external world itself. For in the inner life of the mind we experience a continual change in the contents of consciousness, even in the absence of any apprehension of an external world.*"

He also quotes with approval Richard Taylor, who has said[42]:

> "*It cannot be denied that things in time seem to pass into, through, and out of existence. That can be our datum or starting point, and if metaphysics declares this to be an illusion, then it is up to metaphysics to show that it is.*"

It seems to me, however, that these statements conflate our experience with one particular metaphysical interpretation of such experience. In the words of Oaklander[43]:

> "*(Tenseless theorists) are not attempting to defeat the experience of time, but rather they are attempting to explicate what are the ontological commitments of that experience. Craig packs into the experience an ontology that assumes what needs to be proves and then criticizes (the tenseless theory) for trying to eliminate a (tensed) ontology that is given to us in experience.*"

It is simply not the case that we experience things 'coming into' and 'going out of' existence. What we experience is things coming into and going out of our *awareness*. Whether or not this means they also come into and go out of existence is not something we can determine based on direct personal experience – this is a metaphysical position that goes beyond what we directly experience. If Craig disputes this distinction, I would challenge him to specify what it is about his personal experience of temporal passage that allows him to discern specifically that things *cease to exist* when they pass out of his awareness. Unless we say that only things we are aware of exist, then we cannot infer that our personal experience of an object or event passing out of our awareness means that it has passed out of existence.

To illustrate our alleged experience of the reality of temporal becoming, Craig uses the specific example of the statement 'I wish it were now 1968' to illustrate how we can clearly understand the idea of the 'now' being differently located. Craig argues that, even though such wishes are impossible to fulfil, all of us clearly entertain them from time to time and know what we mean when we do. Craig thinks this supports a tensed theory of time, because such wishes make sense under the tensed theory but not under a tenseless theory. The reason why Craig thinks that the tenseless theory cannot make sense of a statement such as 'I wish it were now 1968' is because such a statement obviously refers to a tensed fact, namely the 'location of now'. Tenseless theorists deny the existence of tensed facts, and so obviously such a wish cannot be taken at face value under the tenseless theory. Craig also thinks that all tenseless attempts to capture the meaning or rephrase the wish without using tensed language fail. He argues[44]:

> "*The best that the (tenseless theorist) can do to make sense of such experiences is to misconstrue the wishes into (tenseless) substitutes, for example, 'I wish that the events of the world were reconstituted in such a way that things appear to be exactly as they were in 1968', 'I wish that I had not made the decisions which I did in 1968', 'I wish that Christmas were celebrated on the seventeenth of December instead of the twenty-fifth', 'I wish that this event had occurred earlier than it does', and so forth. These ersatz-wishes are clearly not what we are*

expressing in our original wishes! The (tenseless theorist) seems obligated to say that our real wishes, which are probably the universal experience of mankind, are just irrational."

Craig likewise argues that to wish it was 1968 is not to wish that we had different perceptions[45]:

"I am not wishing to have different perceptions-I could go to a hypnotist for that-I want it to be 1968, not just appear to me to be 1968."

What strikes me from such passages is Craig's firm conviction that all people who entertain wishes like 'I wish it were 1968' have a single definite meaning in mind when they do so, and that this meaning is the same for all instances of such wishes. Yet there seems no reason at all to make this assumption – indeed, quite clearly many people think and say such things with many different things in mind, or even multiple conflicting things. Some people *do* wish they could make different choices, while other people *do* wish for different perceptual experiences, and still others *do* wish particular states of affairs were the way they were at an earlier time rather than the way they are at a later time. Craig denies that *he* is wishing for any of these things, but that is to be expected given that he is convinced of the truth of the tensed theory of time, and thus regards wishes like this as expressing irreducibly tensed facts. As such, no matter what interpretation of these wishes the tenseless theorist tries to give, Craig can always claim 'but that's not what I'm wishing for'. The tenseless theorist should thus obviously say that what Craig specifically wishes for, interpreted in terms of tensed facts, is conceptually confused because there *are no* tensed facts. Contrary to Craig's repeated claims, this does *not* mean the tenseless theorist thinks that Craig's wish is *irrational*, only that his wish is informed by a mistaken metaphysical belief. It seems therefore that the tenseless theorist has a perfectly adequate account of such wishes. They acknowledge that such wishes are not monolithic in their meaning, but reflect a diversity of intentions depending on the person in question and their particular desires, as well as their understanding of time. Some of these meanings can be rephrased using tenseless language that is perfectly consistent with a tenseless theory of time, as in the examples given above. Those wishes that remain untranslatable, since like Craig's they depend upon the existence of tensed facts, are simply conceptually confused because they are based on a false theory of time. This does not make them irrational, simply misconceived.

A final example Craig gives to illustrate the reality of temporal becoming is the experience of waiting. He argues that waiting does not involve simply the elapse of an interval of time as the tenseless theory would say, but rather it involves "the notion of the passage of time, which one lives through until the expected event occurs."[46] Craig's only argument as to why a tenseless account of waiting is unsatisfactory is that waiting requires an awareness of temporal succession, and thus we would not say that a comatose person is awaiting their recovery. This is an odd objection, for the tenseless theorist can fully endorse the position that awareness of time is necessary for one to be considered 'waiting'. Under the tenseless theory, however, to wait is simply to occupy a succession of temporal positions during which one is experiencing (perhaps subconsciously to some degree) anticipation or dread for an event which will occur later than one's experiences during the waiting period. Craig would deny this is a satisfactory account of waiting because he believes that waiting involves an essentially tensed aspect. As we have seen, however, this is just another case of Craig conflating our experience with his preferred account of the nature of such experience.

If Craig wishes to show that our experiences are inconsistent with a tenseless of time, he needs to show specifically which aspect of our experience cannot be accounted for such a theory. Yet he never does this; all he can ever say is that tenseless accounts fail because they don't incorporate the tensed aspect of our experiences. Yet of course they don't, as after all tenseless theorists deny the reality of any tensed facts. Unless Craig wishes to simply beg the question, he needs to provide clear examples from shared temporal experience that the tenseless theory cannot account for. Craig needs to describe experientially what it is exactly that tenseless theories of time cannot account for, without doing so in a manner that already presupposes the reality of tensed facts. I do not believe that Craig is able to do this, and therefore I do not think that any of his examples of our 'direct experience' of the reality of tense are compelling arguments in favour of the tensed theory of time.

RELATIVITY DOES NOT UNDERMINE TENSED THEORIES OF TIME

Special Relativity and the Tensed Theory of Time

One important consequence of Einstein's special theory of relativity is that whether an event is past, present, or future depends upon one's 'frame of reference', meaning one's velocity relative to other objects or events[47]. This means, for example, that someone on Earth may disagree with someone travelling in a very fast rocket about whether two particular supernova explosions occurred at the same time or not. This is not the result of any problems with measuring devices; rather it stems from the fact that, according to special relativity, space and time *themselves* are altered when the velocity of an observer approaches the speed of light. These processes of the alteration of space and time are respectively known as length contraction and time dilation. The details of special relativity are beyond the scope of this book – what is important for our purposes are the implications relativity theory has for the philosophy of time. In particular, if it is the case that the pastness, presentness, or futurity of an event varies depending upon one's frame of reference, then this seems to cast significant doubt upon a presentist theory of time. Presentism is the specific form of tensed theory of time that Craig defends. According to presentism, to be present is simply to exist, and only what is present exists. The past and future, under this view, are unreal and do not exist. However, if what is present depends upon one's frame of reference, then it follows that what exists also depends upon one's frame of reference. The implication of this is that each reference frame corresponds, in a sense, to a 'different reality'. This presents far too radical and fragmented a view of the world to be acceptable to most philosophers, Craig included. As such, there appears to be a conflict between special relativity and presentism. If special relativity is true, there is no real 'objective becoming', and thus the tensed theory of time is false.

Craig's response to this attack on presentism involves first distinguishing between the mathematical structure of the theory of special relativity, which is firmly established and empirically supported, and its philosophical interpretation, which is not so firmly established. Craig then argues that the standard interpretation of special relativity, whereby all reference frames are considered to be equivalent and therefore there is no absolute or preferred reference frame, is in fact inferior to Craig's preferred alternate interpretation. He argues that the standard interpretation of special relativity depends upon the assumption that because there are no experiments one can perform or observations one could make in order to distinguish which frame of reference was 'really' in motion, that therefore there is no preferred reference frame, and therefore all reference frames are equivalent. To illustrate this attitude, Craig quotes Max Born[48]:

> "'A conception has physical reality only when there is something ascertainable by measurement corresponding to it in the world of phenomena.' With respect to distant simultaneity he advises, 'the quantitative physicist... sees no meaning in the statement that an event at A and an event at B are simultaneous, since he has no means of deciding the truth or the incorrectness of this assertion.' Since Einstein showed that there is no means of determining absolute time, 'this signifies that absolute time has no physical reality'."

Craig criticises this approach as deriving from an outmoded metaphysical position known as logical positivism, which holds that only statements which are either true by definition (like those in mathematics) or empirically verifiable (like those in the natural sciences) have any real meaning. According to logical positivism, all other statements should be rejected as meaningless. Positivism has been almost universally rejected in philosophy, and Craig argues that we should therefore revisit the idea that just because special relativity shows that there is no measurable difference between reference frames, it therefore follows that no absolute space or time exist. Craig says[49]:

> "With the failure of positivism, the (tensed theorist)... is quite free to make, with Newton, a distinction between physical time and space (clock and rod measurements) and metaphysical time and space (ontological time and space independent of physical

measures thereof). (Special relativity) is a theory about physical time and space and says nothing about the nature of metaphysical time and space. Questions dealing with the latter are philosophical in nature and must be dealt with as such."

Instead of the conventional interpretation of special relativity, in which space and time are united in a single entity called 'spacetime' and in which there is no preferred frame of reference, Craig defends what he calls a 'neo-Lorentzian' interpretation of relativity. According to this interpretation, which he argues is equally consistent with all the empirical observations, there *is* a preferred reference frame, motion relative to which leads to the relativistic effects of time dilation and length contraction. Craig argues that this interpretation is well suited to a tensed theory of time, because it permits reconciliation of the empirical successes of special relativity with the objective temporal becoming in a preferred frame of reference necessary for the tensed theory of time.

Only a small minority of contemporary physicists accept a Lorentzian interpretation of special relativity. One of the reasons for this is that it proposes the existence of an absolute frame of reference which the standard spacetime interpretation has no need for, and thus the spacetime interpretation is deemed simpler in accordance with Ockham's razor. Another reason for the widespread rejection of the Lorentzian interpretation is that it requires that all laws of nature be modified when one is in motion relative to the preferred frame of reference, in just such a way as to make it impossible to detect the preferred frame, even though there is no particular reason given and no mechanism provided for why this should be so or how this occurs. Craig does not regard these objections as decisive, and considers them outweighed by the advantages offered by the Lorentzian interpretation with respect to its consistency with the tensed theory of time.

I will not go into any further detail here into the debate between spacetime and Lorentzian interpretations of special relativity, because I do not regard the issue as central to the question at hand, which concerns the plausibility of tensed versus tenseless theories of time. Even if Craig's Lorentzian interpretation is shown to be a failure, he can simply adopt the position that relativity theory describes only physical time, and as such we cannot make any inferences about metaphysical time on the basis of relativity theory.

The General Theory of Relativity

Nearly all of Craig's writing on relativity theory has focused on explicating the relevance of special relativity for the philosophy of time, and demonstrating that special relativity has not actually *proven* that no privileged reference frame exists. Granting Craig this point for the sake of argument, I wish to focus instead on what I regard as a much more powerful argument in favour of the tenseless theory of time based on the general theory of relativity. While the special theory of relativity is primarily about how time and space are affected by the relative motion of observers in different reference frames, general relativity is primarily about how the matter and energy within space alters the shape of space and time. General relativity constitutes the most developed theory form of the idea that space and time are inextricably linked in a four-dimensional matrix called 'spacetime'[50]. As Craig acknowledges[51], taken at face value this four-dimensional conception of spacetime is very conducive to a tenseless theory of time, since all points of time exist tenselessly alongside the three spatial dimensions. This four-dimensional spacetime, however, cannot be reconciled with a tensed theory of time, since if all moments of time exist alongside each other there is no room for objective temporal becoming. Even more importantly, Craig's neo-Lorentzian interpretation is not relevant to general relativity[52]:

> "*A crucial point of general relativity is that the 4-dimensional space-time with non-zero curvature is not dispensable anymore. Contrarily to the Minkowskian case, general relativity is not susceptible of a global Lorentzian formulation.*"

This fact leads me to present the following argument from general relativity in favour of the tenseless theory of time:

- Premise one: The general theory of relativity treats spacetime as intrinsically united into a single entity called 'spacetime', the warping of which generates the effects of gravity.

- Premise two: This theory has generated many novel predictions, which have subsequently been experimentally verified to an exceptionally high degree of precision.
- Premise three: The best explanation for the successful predictions of general relativity is that treatment of space and time as combined into four-dimensional spacetime is at least approximately correct.
- Premise four: If the four-dimensional spacetime description is at least approximately correct, then the tensed theory of time is an untenable theory.
- Conclusion: The tensed theory of time is an untenable theory.

Somewhat more cautiously, I could rephrase the argument to assert that the tensed theory of time is rendered implausible to the degree that the predictions of the general theory of relativity are confirmed by experiment. This argument is therefore an inference to the best explanation, the same form of argument that Craig uses in his arguments from fine-tuning and for the resurrection of Jesus. The argument does not assert that the general theory of relativity *proves* that presentism cannot be true. Rather, it asserts that the spacetime framework of the general theory of relativity provides a simple and coherent explanation for a wide range of phenomena that cannot be explained under a tensed theory of time, and this greater explanatory power provides strong reason to regard the tenseless theory of spacetime that general relativity utilises as a correct description of reality.

Evaluating this argument, we must consider each premise in turn. The first premise is undeniable, since the theory of general relativity treats space and time as united into a single four-dimensional manifold which can be curved and distorted in various ways under the influence of matter and energy (see figure 3). In the formalism of general relativity, time is just one of the four dimensions of the spacetime manifold, all of which 'exist' alongside each other. As Craig acknowledges, there is simply no room for temporal becoming in such a model. If taken literally, therefore, it seems to preclude the possibility of a tensed theory of time, and as such premise four is also quite firmly established. Premise two appeals to the multiple independent predictions made by

Unreasonable Faith

general relativity that have subsequently been confirmed experimentally. Some of the most important of these confirmations are given below:

- The Hafele-Keating experiment: general relativity predicts that time passes more rapidly in weak gravitational potentials compared to strong gravitational potentials. This prediction has been verified by comparing the times measured on atomic clocks kept on the Earth's surface to those flown on high altitude aircraft.

- Shapiro time delay[53]: signals sent to distant targets take longer to reach their destination and return to the source when they pass near a massive object (like a star) than they do in the absence of the massive object. This is another manifestation of gravitational time delay, but is an independent means of detection which further confirms the predictions of general relativity.

- Gravitational redshift[54]: electromagnetic radiation has been observed to be redshifted, or have its wavelength increased, when emitted from within a strong gravitational field. The effect is predicted by Newtonian gravity, but again the magnitude of the effect is only correctly predicted by general relativity. This phenomenon is yet another observational confirmation of gravitational time dilation.

- Gravitational lensing[55]: massive objects such as distant galaxies have been observed to bend light in a way that can produce multiple images of the same background object. This effect is predicted by Newtonian gravity but the magnitude of lensing is only correctly predicted by general relativity.

- Gravitational waves[56]: gravitational waves are waves in the curvature of spacetime that are predicted by general relativity to propagate through spacetime at the speed of light. They have recently been observed by very sensitive experimental detectors, which measure the periodic variation in distance as gravitational waves pass through the detector.

- Equality of inertial and gravitational mass[57]: gravitational mass, defined as the ability of an object to exert a gravitational force, and inertial mass, defined as the ability of an object to resist changes in its velocity, are predicted by general relativity to be identical. For decades, increasingly sophisticated tests have still failed to find any difference between inertial and gravitational mass, thereby yielding strong support for Einstein's principle of equivalence.

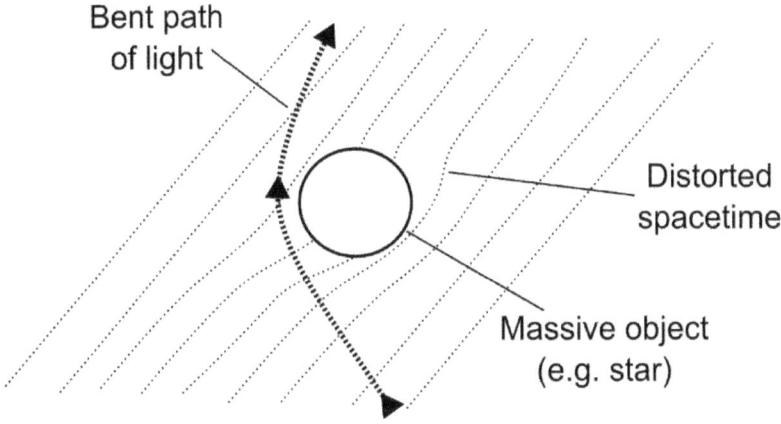

Figure 3. In the general theory of relativity, massive objects distort the shape of four-dimensional spacetime, represented here by a budge in the two-dimensional sheet surrounding the central object. This distortion bends the paths of light rays and other particles passing near the massive object, leading to various effects that can be experimentally detected as tests of the theory.

On the basis of the above, therefore, I consider premise two to have been very firmly established. The most controversial premise of my argument will therefore be premise three, that the best explanation of the empirical successes of general relativity is that the four-dimensional spacetime described by the theory really exists. Craig will attempt to avoid this conclusion by appealing to alternative interpretations of general relativity. His problem, however, is that he simply does not have an alternate interpretation that is able to account for all the empirical observations while avoiding the existence of four-dimensional spacetime.

To my knowledge, Craig has never specifically addressed the issue of gravitational time dilation and how to reconcile it with a tensed theory of time. Appealing to a Lorentzian interpretation of special relativity will not help here, because gravitational time dilation is a distinct phenomenon not present in special relativity. Regarding the detection of gravitational waves and connection to his preferred Lorentzian interpretation of special relativity, Craig argues that[58]:

> "In the Ligo experiment laser beams are similarly measured along the two arms of (an)... interferometer device. The interference patterns produced by the beams indicate that the two arms change length due to the gravitational waves. This is precisely what Lorentz would have expected. Our physical measuring devices are distorted by causal forces acting upon them... On the tenseless interpretation gravitational waves are taken to be ripples in the geometry of spacetime. They would be like wrinkles on a sheet. On a tensed theory, they would be radiation propagating through space at a finite velocity."

These statements, however, are simply not satisfactory as an explanation for the explanatory successes of general relativity. Saying that our physical measuring devices are being 'distorted by causal forces acting upon them' does not constitute providing an alternative theory which is capable of accurately predicting the nature and magnitude of such distortions without reference to the four-dimensional spacetime manifold of general relativity. Craig simply has nothing to say about what these causal forces might be or why they would have the effect they do. His proposed 'explanation' is pure speculation which is explanatorily vacuous, for there is no reason why under a tensed theory of time gravitational waves should exist at all. By contrast, the general theory of relativity predicted their existence nearly a century before they were actually detected. Their existence in general relativity is a natural consequence of the treatment of space and time as an integrated four-dimensional manifold. Craig cannot simply ignore this fact and then pretend that gravitational waves are only ripples in space, rather than ripples in spacetime as general relativity actually states. As a result of these considerations, I conclude that Craig has no alternative explanation to provide for gravitational waves.

More generally, Craig has argued that general relativity can be interpreted instrumentally, meaning that it is useful for making predictions but does not actually describe the way reality really is. In defence of this he asserts that "most physicists are apparently content to take the theory instrumentally, interpreting spacetime curvature as a geometrical representation of gravitation."[59] This is quite an odd position for Craig to take given his elsewhere hostile remarks regarding the poor philosophical sophistication of many physicists[60], and particularly given his strong opposition to the prevailing interpretation of the special theory of relativity. It is unclear, therefore, why Craig trusts the philosophical interpretation of physicists concerning general relativity but not with anything else. More importantly, this response simply is not relevant to the argument I have presented, for whatever physicists might think (and generally physicists are little interested in philosophical interpretations of their theories) it is nevertheless the case that the explanatory power general relativity provides with respect to the various lines of evidence discussed above, constitutes strong evidence in favour of the approximate truth of the theory. These phenomena were only predicted (or the magnitude of the effect correctly predicted) as a result of a theory which treats space and time as part of a connected four-dimensional entity whose shape is warped by the presence of matter and energy. If Craig wishes to deny that time really has this structure, it is not sufficient to simply assert that general relativity can be interpreted 'instrumentally' – he needs to provide some comparably good explanation as to why we should observe all these phenomena in a universe where time is tensed and the four-dimensional spacetime manifold described by general relativity does not in fact exist. Absent such an explanation, I think I have presented a strong argument for the likely truth of the tenseless theory of time based on the empirical successes of general relativity.

Further Responses to General Relativity

Unable to provide an explanation for the findings of general relativity, Craig instead effectively adopts the approach of arguing that other considerations which indicate against the realistic interpretation of general relativity outweigh whatever support gravitational time dilation (etc) provides for it. One such argument Craig gives is that[61]:

> "A realist interpretation of spacetime actually obscures our physical understanding of nature by substituting geometry for a physical force, thereby impeding progress in connecting gravitational theory to particle physics."

To support this claim Craig provides a quote from Steven Weinberg[62]:

> "I believe that the geometrical approach has driven a wedge between general relativity and the theory of elementary particles. As long as it could be hoped, as Einstein did hope, that matter would eventually be understood in geometrical terms, it made sense to give Riemannian geometry a primary role in describing the theory of gravitation. But now the passage of time has taught us not to expect that the strong, weak, and electromagnetic interactions can be understood in geometrical terms, and too great an emphasis on geometry can only obscure the deep connections between gravitation and the rest of physics."

Craig seems to be misrepresenting what Weinberg is saying, however, as Weinberg does not explicitly say anything about gravity *not* being a product of the geometry of space, only that we should not push the analogy too far and assume that *all forces* can be understood in this way. More importantly, this quote dates before the surge in work on quantum gravity over the past few decades, including loop quantum gravity and string theory. The approach of such methods typically involves quantising a spacetime manifold (or something similar) in a way which makes it consistently treatable by both quantum mechanical and general relativistic approaches. As typical for science, advances in our understanding are unlikely to be the result of drastic rejection of previously well-established theories, but by building upon them and extending their results to higher levels of generalisability. This is especially pertinent in the case of general relativity, which has been so well established by experiment that it is essentially inconceivable for it not to be correctly describing reality to a significant extent. Craig's argument that a geometric understanding of gravity thereby impedes progress in providing a quantum theory of gravity is therefore totally without foundation.

Another argument that Craig gives against spacetime realism is that we have good grounds for thinking that time can exist independently of space. He says[63]:

> "A series of mental events alone is sufficient to set up a temporal sequence. Thus, if we imagine God's counting down to the moment of creation: '3, 2, 1, Fiat lux!' then the beginning of spacetime would be preceded by a metaphysical time associated with the mental events of counting which would be wholly independent of space. Whether such a count-down can be beginningless or whether metaphysical time must itself have also had a beginning need not concern us here; the point is that physical events having spatial co-ordinates are clearly not a necessary condition of temporal events."

In assuming that it is possible for minds to exist not merely in the absence of a physical body but also in the absence of any space at all, Craig is making quite a big leap. Such a claim goes well beyond what might reasonably be established by typical arguments for substance dualism, which simply establish at most that there is more to the mind than the activity of the brain. Of course, Craig is right that there is nothing obviously *logically impossible* about his scenario of a mind existing and marking time without space; however, the question is not whether it is *logically necessary* that spacetime exist, but merely about whether it *actually does exist* in the real world. As such, the mere *possibility* of a totally non-spatial mind does not establish anything other than that it is *conceivable* that spacetime might not exist. Unless Craig can provide actual reasons for thinking that such minds really do exist or have existed, these thought experiments provide no reason at all to doubt the existence of spacetime. As such, I conclude that Craig's objection does nothing to undermine the support for spacetime realism.

Craig also presents the argument that we should be suspicious about the realism of four-dimensional spacetime because spacetime intervals take imaginary values over time-like intervals. Here he quotes Christensen who says[64]:

> "This is disturbing in the first place because imaginary numbers seem like a paradigm of a convenient conceptual fiction... The serious question, however, is not whether there are imaginary numbers – numbers being a peculiar lot of entities to begin with – but whether there could really be such a thing as mathematically imaginary physical quantities... No one doubts the convenience of computing with such quantities, even in an eminently practical field such as electrical engineering; but in the end the imaginary parts of the result are discarded. Could it be otherwise in SR, rationally?"

This concern is strange since as noted in the quote itself, imaginary numbers occur in many applications in science and engineering, for example in quantum mechanics where they appear in Schrödinger's equation. Scientists do not regard the presence of imaginary values as indicating anything impossible or non-physical, just so long as any quantities that are actually *observable* are measured in real numbers. In quantum mechanics, the wavefunction can take imaginary values but it is never observable, only the square of the wavefunction (which is always real-valued) is observable. Similarly, in general relativity the spacetime interval is never observable; only proper time and length intervals are observable, and these are always real numbers. Spacetime intervals can take imaginary numbers, but they are never something we can observe directly, and so just as wave functions in quantum mechanics, this does not in any way indicate that the theory cannot describe reality.

Although Craig himself says little about this possibility, other presentists have argued that presentism and general relativity can be reconciled by positing the existence of a 'preferred foliation' of spacetime[65]. Essentially this can be visualised as a spacelike 'slice' of spacetime consisting of all the moments that are 'present'. Objective temporal becoming would therefore consist of the successive coming into and going out of existence of different preferred foliations of spacetime. The four-dimensional spacetime manifold of general relativity would therefore be retained, except that only a single slice of it (the preferred foliation) would actually exist at any particular moment in time. One problem with this interpretation is simply that it posits the existence of a preferred foliation for which we have no evidence, and therefore represents a more complex interpretation than the usual interpretation which does not recognise any particular foliation as preferred. This might not seem like much of a problem, but it should be noted that an application of Ockham's razor is the only argument Craig gives for rejecting polytheism in favour of monotheism with respect to the cause of the universe[66]. Thus, if the simplicity argument is so effective in that instance, it would seem also to be applicable in this instance as a means of rejecting the unnecessarily postulate of a preferred foliation. There are, furthermore, various technical problems in defining a preferred foliation given the existence of rotating black holes and an accelerating rate of cosmic expansion, both of which violate the strict conditions necessary for a preferred foliation to be possible[67].

More importantly, even if a preferred foliation did exist, it would simply not provide the sort of 'present' that Craig requires for his theory of time to work. In particular, the general theory of relativity states that massive objects distort the shape of space and time. This would still hold even if a preferred foliation did exist, because it is an essential component of general relativity, and the only way to account for the various observational confirmations I describe above. Under a tensed theory of time, however, time is not conceived of as the dimension of a manifold that can be curved and bent by matter. Rather, time is conceived of as the successive coming into being of new moments of time through the process of objective temporal becoming. It simply makes no sense to say that time as temporal becoming is distorted by massive objects. How are massive objects supposed to affect the process of temporal becoming? Under general relativity the reason time dilation occurs, for example, is because time-like paths through spacetime are literally made longer (at least as we measure them) as the result of the bending of spacetime by massive objects. In a tensed theory of time, however, there is nothing about time that can bend, and thus no way for time dilation effects to be produced. As such, the existence of a preferred foliation, even if it could be established, simply does not provide the sort of theory of time that Craig requires for presentism.

As a result of these considerations, I conclude that even if the special theory of relativity does not necessarily pose a strong challenge for presentism, the general theory of relativity does pose such a challenge. Craig simply does not have any way of accounting for the empirical successes of general relativity that is consistent with his presentist philosophy of time, and as a result the general theory of relativity constitutes powerful evidence in favour of the tenseless theory of time.

THE TENSELESS THEORY OF TIME LEADS TO ABSURD CONCLUSIONS

The Alleged Absurdities of Perdurantism

Craig argues that the tenseless theory of time implies the truth of perdurantism, a doctrine which he thinks is absurd. Perdurantism is the view whereby objects possess temporal parts analogous to the spatial parts we are all familiar with. Thus, an object like a rock possesses one part that existed yesterday, one part that exists today, and one part that will exist tomorrow. The proponent of the tenseless theory of time would say that all these temporal parts exist tenselessly, and correspond to different parts of the rock at different times during its existence. Under the tenseless theory of time, objects are conceived as four-dimensional entities with extension throughout time as well as space. Since Craig thinks that perdurantism is extremely implausible, he argues that if the tenseless theory of time implies perdurantism then this should be considered strong evidence against the plausibility of the tenseless theory of time. In responding to this argument, I will consider each of his objections to perdurantism in turn.

First, Craig notes that there are various difficulties associated with defining precisely what is meant by a 'temporal part', and how to fix the boundaries of four-dimensional objects. Craig states[68]:

> "I do not know if these difficulties pose insuperable obstacles for the perdurantist; but he does need to address them more fully."

This is obviously true, for perdurantism is a controversial and complex position, and like many in philosophy there are difficulties in precise formulation. One possible route, which Craig himself acknowledges as likely to allow the perdurantist to "most plausibly make sense of his contention"[69] is to adopt a spacetime ontology whereby space and time are essentially connected together as posited in general relativity. In this case, it seems that at least in principle the problem of defining the boundaries of objects and the nature of temporal parts is no different to that of defining the boundaries and nature of spatial parts, since time and space are linked together and are fundamentally unified. As I discuss in the section on general relativity, I believe that the evidence for general relativity is very strong, and therefore there is good reason to believe that space and time are intrinsically linked together, and that as a result objects do possess temporal as well as spatial parts.

Second, Craig argues that perdurantism implies a metaphysically counter-intuitive and bizarre account of change. In particular, he argues that in order for there to be genuine change in the perdurantist scheme, it must be the case that change is viewed as a relation between tenselessly existing temporal parts of the entity in question. The entity as a whole cannot change, because four-dimensional entities simply have a fixed four-dimensional shape and fixed characteristics which exist tenselessly. As Craig says[70]:

> *"In terms of its intrinsic properties (an object O) has a changeless, four-dimensional shape which is bent at one end and straight at the other. No temporary intrinsics (i.e. properties that change over time) here... What of O's instantaneous (spatio-)temporal parts? The same is true of them: not one lasts more than the instant at which it tenselessly exists; therefore, none ever changes in its intrinsic properties... there are no temporary intrinsic properties on perdurantism."*

Craig thus argues that perdurantism cannot accommodate for the changing properties of an entity, since in the tenseless theory of time either an entity has a property that applies throughout its existence, or properties apply only at particular time-slices of the entity's existence. Nowhere in this analysis, however, does Craig think there is any 'genuine change'. The problem with this analysis is that Craig insists on interpreting the notion of change in a tensed sense. Obviously a four-dimensional object that exists over some particular region of space and time does not possess any properties which change in the tensed sense of 'coming into' and 'going out of' existence, because all temporal parts of the object exist tenselessly alongside one another. The supporter of the tenseless theory of time, however, need not accept this as the definition of change. They may instead regard change as occurring when some property of an entity extends over only part of that entity's temporal existence. Temporary properties could thus also be described as 'partial properties', in the sense that they only apply to specific temporal part of the object. Just as a road might be curved along part of its length but straight along another part, so too might a key be bent for one part of its temporal extension, but not for the part of its temporal extension after the time when it is straightened. When the notion of a 'temporary property' is understood this way, perdurantism is completely consistent with the existence of change.

According to perdurantism, change can be considered to consist of the fact that later temporal parts of an object have different properties compared to earlier temporal parts. There is no need for the perdurantist to be committed to the view that each temporal part of an entity is a new object that inexplicably comes into being at successive moments of time. Craig speaks of a piece of chalk that "I hold in my hand at this second" as being a "wholly different object from the piece of chalk I held in my hand a second ago"[71]. To speak this way, however, is to apply tensed concepts to a view which rejects such concepts as invalid. The perdurantist need only hold to the view of change I outlined above, which has no requirement for objects to be divided into temporal parts which enter into and exit out of existence. Craig, of course, will reject this as not being 'real change', but if this objection is to have force he must develop an argument that does not depend upon saddling the perdurantist with metaphysical positions they need not be committed to. I conclude, therefore, that perdurantism is able to account for temporary intrinsic properties and change in a way that entails none of the absurdities alleged by Craig.

Third, Craig borrows the following argument from Van Inwagen against perdurantism[72]:

"Let D be Descartes, D- be that temporal part of Descartes stretching from 1596-1649, and L be the last year of his life.

James Fodor

Descartes could have lacked L. There are therefore possible worlds in which D- exists and L does not. Now D and D- are not on the perdurantist view identical. But if Descartes had died one year earlier than he did, then D and D- would have been identical. But if D and D- could therefore have been identical, then there are two things that could have been one thing. This not only violates the modal principle about identity (if x and y are identical then they are necessarily so), but also violates the principle of the Transitivity of Identity. Therefore, Descartes is not a perduring (entity)."

The problem with this argument resides in the statement 'if Descartes had died one year earlier than he did, then D and D- would have been identical'. This is false because these two parts do not share all properties in all possible worlds – in some worlds D and D- are the same length, while in others (those in which Descartes lived for a longer or shorter time than he actually did) they are different lengths. The so-called 'modal principle of identity' that Van Inwagen mentions states that two entities are only identical if they share all properties in all possible worlds. Since D and D- do not share all properties in all possible worlds, they are not identical. All that can be said is that if Descartes had died one year earlier then in *that particular* possible world, and in that world *only*, D would have been coextensive with D-. That does not entail that the two must be identical any more than 'next Saturday' and 'the 27th of August' are identical because in some possible worlds (i.e. in some circumstances) they refer to the same day. Furthermore, the astute reader may note that there is nothing essentially temporal about this argument. We could replace D and D- with B and B-, where B is the empire state building and B- is all floors of the empire state building minus the top floor, and make exactly the same argument about B and B- being possibly being identical and thus implying the exact same absurdity. This equivalency clearly illustrates that there is something wrong with the argument, and as I have argued the problem is that two objects being equivalent in one possible world does not imply the identity of those two objects in all possible worlds. As a result, this argument against perdurantism fails.

Finally, Craig argues that perdurantism is inconsistent with the phenomenology of personal consciousness. He argues[73]:

> "*On the perdurantist view, persons are not what we normally take them (or ourselves) to be: self-conscious individuals who act and react with other things in space and time. Such individuals are just temporal parts or stages of persons. Persons are temporally extended objects which have no consciousness and, hence, no intelligence, volition, or emotion, no interactions, no agency, no moral responsibility, no aesthetic intuition, virtually none of the distinctive properties which we normally associate with personhood.*"

The problem with this argument is that Craig is misrepresenting and poorly characterising what perdurantism entails about personal identity. Under perdurantism, persons are properly understood to be temporally extended, four-dimensional entities, which exist in a particular defined region of space and time. It does not follow from this, however, that the people we meet and interact with are 'not persons'. Rather, they are not the *whole person* or the entirety of a person, but only a small temporal part of that person. Saying that somebody isn't actually a person unless they are the whole entirety of the person is equivalent to saying that the part of the street along which your house is located is 'not a road' because it is not a whole separate road unto itself, but merely part of a larger road. We regularly speak of a whole entity even though we only ever see or interact with a part of it. For example, we might say 'that is the Empire State Building' even if only a small portion of it can be seen, or that we have 'visited China' even if we have only been to a single city in that very large country. The position that persons are temporally extended also fits naturally with various commonsense aphorisms, such as that you only know somebody when you have 'walked a day in their shoes' (i.e. experienced a larger temporal portion of the person in question). We regularly recognise that persons are complex beings and that you don't really 'know someone' unless you have seen them in various circumstances and environments. These observations seem to fit very well with the metaphysical position that persons are temporally as well as spatially extended, and thus I see no absurdity in this view.

Regarding Craig's argument that the temporal parts of persons cannot be conscious or experience emotion, this is simply an absurd extrapolation which does not at all follow from the position of perdurantism. Each temporal 'slice' of a person is conscious of thoughts and perceptions that are simultaneous with that temporal part of the person. They are obviously not conscious of *everything* that any part of the entire four-dimensional person is conscious of at any point in its temporally extended existence, but that doesn't mean they aren't conscious of *anything*. The four-dimensional self as a whole is also conscious, but this consciousness takes the form not of some sort of super-consciousness of the entire four-dimensional person in its entirety, but rather is simply a way of saying that the temporal parts of the person are conscious of their own simultaneous happenings. This is perfectly consistent with our phenomenological experience, since there is no part of us that is conscious of anything except what is immediately before our senses and minds. A temporally extended person is thus said to be conscious if some temporal part of them is. This is consistent with the fact that we would say that somebody is a 'conscious person' even if at that particular moment they happened to be asleep or in a coma. Craig's objection that spatially-extended persons cannot be conscious therefore fails to detract from the plausibility of perdurantism, and does nothing to undermine the tenseless theory of time.

The Removal of Temporal Relations from Tenseless Time

Craig believes that tenseless theories of time are unable to provide any account as to why the temporal dimension of four-dimensional spacetime is really time at all. He argues[74]:

> *"Despite the protestations of (tenseless theorists), there seems to be no reason to regard that dimension which is treated by the (tenseless theory), now stripped of all tense, as time – and therefore the (tenseless theory) cannot be a correct theory of time... What the (tensed theorist) wants to know is why, on the (tenseless theory), those relations which are said to obtain among putatively temporal particulars deserve to be called 'earlier than' or 'later than', why these relations so labelled should be thought*

> to be temporal at all? After all, these relations, as usually understood by (tenseless theorists), furnish no basis for structurally distinguishing one direction in time from the other nor for specifying a direction to time. Moreover, even a spatial continuum can be constructed which is anisotropic, based on purely spatial relations. So why should we regard the... tenseless dimension or its ordering relations as temporal?"

Craig further argues that under a tensed theory of time it is possible to provide a reductive account of the meaning of terms like 'earlier than' and 'later than' in terms of the more fundamental process of absolute becoming. By contrast, Craig thinks that a tenseless theory of time cannot offer any equivalent such account of what terms like 'earlier than' or 'later than' mean, or why the 'time dimension' referred to by tenseless theories of time is really time at all. He asks a hypothetical proponent of a tenseless theory[75]:

> "What entitles you, having stripped time of all its tense-determinations, to assume that what remains is really time? Why should we regard those relations obtaining between tenselessly existing events... as earlier than/later than rather than as some atemporal relations analogous to the less than/larger than relations obtaining between the members of the natural number series? Indeed, why think that any such relations exist at all, in addition to the relations which obtain between, say, the points on a spatial line?"

Here Craig is arguing that tenseless theorists have no justification for thinking that the de-tensed ordered series of events is really a temporal series at all, any more than the ordered series of natural numbers. The problem with this objection is that Craig speaks as if tenseless theorists began with a series of events and then just arbitrarily declared that this series represented a temporal series. The tenseless theory of time is not just some random act of theorising in this way – rather it is an attempt to make sense of the same set of pre-theoretic assumptions and ideas that tensed theories of time considers. Paul Helm explains the problem with Craig's objection as follows[76]:

James Fodor

> "What's odd here is that Craig's arguments fail to reckon with a basic fact about the (tensed/tenseless) dispute, namely that each arises from a common set of pre-theoretic conceptions of time, which each then attempts to theorize about. We all have a pre-theoretical understanding of time and temporal locutions such as earlier than, later than, yesterday, tomorrow, past, future, indicating our recognition of a temporal series. The question is then, which theory makes best sense of this recognition? Craig sometimes gives the impression that the (tenseless theory) is a freestanding construction with no roots in pre-theory."

Far from free-standing, the tenseless theory of time is justified on the basis that it provides a more satisfactory explanatory model of the nature of time. In particular, as I argued above it is more consistent with the results of general relativity, and avoids the problems associated with the problem of the extent of the present (which I discuss below). The superiority of this model of time thereby grants justification for treating time as an ordered series of events in the way tenseless theorists do. Asking how a series without tense can be a temporal series is thus question-begging, for the tenseless theorist regards the foregoing as strong evidence *against* the reality of tense, and thus the correct account of time will not feature any tense determinations. Understood in this way, Craig's objection loses its force since proponents of the tenseless theory of time have a perfectly sound justification for their position.

Regarding the four-dimensional spacetime found in relativity theory, Craig remarks[77]:

> "If physical reality is conceived to be a tenselessly existing Minkowski spacetime consisting of three spatial dimensions and one temporal dimension, then the difference in sign associated with one of its dimensions could at best serve only as evidence that that dimension is temporal, but not as grounds for that dimension's being temporal."

This response is misplaced, however, since it is not the difference in sign of the temporal dimension in the spacetime metric used in relativity which makes that dimension temporal as opposed to spatial.

Rather, the four-dimensional treatment of space and time is adopted as a descriptive model, and the success of the numerous predictions made by that model, its wide explanatory power, constitutes evidence in favour of the hypothesis that the model correctly describes the way time really is. Thus, it is the underlying structure of time that serves as the grounds for the fourth dimension of spacetime being regarded as temporal. This is similar to Craig's argument that the underlying fact of temporal becoming is the ground for the truth of tensed facts. The only difference, I argue, is that Craig's proposed theory of time has weak explanatory power, whereas that offered by general relativity his much greater explanatory power, and therefore we have much better reasons to regard it is correctly describing the world.

Presentism and the Difference Between Past and Future

Craig also argues that the tenseless theory of time cannot provide a basis for the directionality of time, why time proceeds from past, to present, to the future. Craig admits that this objection is only relevant if tensed theories of time prove superior by providing such a reductive analysis of temporal relations when tenseless theories cannot. Craig argues that tensed theories of time *are* able to provide a reductive account of temporal relations in terms of the process of absolute becoming as follows[78]:

> "To be earlier than = to be more past or less future than. To be later than = to be more future or less past than."

According to Craig, this definition "succeeds admirably in giving a reductive analysis of earlier than/later than in terms of tensed facts alone"[79]. As Oaklander has argued[80], however, this definition appeals to some essential difference between an event being 'past' compared to an event being 'future'. This is a problem because presentism does not provide any basis for distinguishing between 'past' and 'future' in this way. According to presentism, to be present is simply to exist, while past and future events do not exist. What, then, is it that distinguishes non-existent past events from non-existent future events that could make one past and one future? What distinguishes the claim 'Billy will be taller next year' from 'Billy was shorter last year'? Obviously, one is a statement about facts which *will be* true, and the other is a statement of facts that *were* true. But what, on Craig's account, makes the difference between 'will be' and 'were', given that both refer to states of affairs that do not exist? In other words, what is the part of reality that actually exists (i.e. the present) that makes it the case that one moment of time has already elapsed while the other has yet to elapse?

Craig attempts to answer this question by providing the following definitions[81]:

> "A future-tense statement is true iff there exists some tensed actual world at t in which the present-tense version of the statement is true, where t has not elapsed by the present moment.
>
> A past-tense statement is true iff there exists some tensed actual world at t in which the present-tense version of the statement is true, where t has elapsed by the present moment."

The trouble with this account is in using the language of worlds that exist at particular times t that have or have not yet elapsed, Craig seems to be describing a tenselessly existing series of events which are successively actualised as each becomes present. However, this will not do, since as Oaklander points out, "this is the moving present theory of time that the metaphysic of presentism sought to avoid[82]." Craig responds that[83]:

> "My characterization of presentism in terms of possible worlds is not meant to explain why only the present exists or to found the objectivity of temporal becoming, but simply to provide a language in which to formulate such notions."

If this is the case, then it seems Craig's attempt to provide a reductive account of pastness and futurity in terms of temporal becoming is unsuccessful. What then is the fundamental difference between past and future? After all, under presentism a past state of affairs and a future state of affairs are alike in both being non-existent, so there is nothing that exists to provide a grounding for saying that the past event 'has already elapsed' while the future event 'has yet to elapse'. In response to this further question Craig says that[84]:

> "Ultimately what makes the (past or future tensed) statements true is that reality was or will be as the statements describe; when the time comes, for example, a sea battle is going on, and therefore the statement made the day before, 'There will be a sea battle tomorrow', was true. There are tensed facts corresponding to what tensed statements assert, but past- and future-tense facts exist because of the present-tense facts which did or will exist."

Thus, Craig says that ultimately past-tense statements are true "because a purely present-tense fact – a battle is being fought at Waterloo – did obtain, and the ontological basis of that fact was a battle"[85]. In other words, past-tense statements are true because of present-tense facts which did exist. Yet here Craig is apparently admitting that there are no actually-existing facts which make past and future-tensed statements true, as under presentism to say that the basis of past-tensed statements is present-tensed facts that *did exist* is precisely to say that these facts *no longer exist*, and so there is nothing that *currently exists* to make past-tense statements true. Under Craig's presentism, therefore, there is nothing that actually exists which is able to distinguish non-existent past events from non-existent future events.

Craig's attempted explanation of tenseless facts in terms of the process of temporal becoming is a failure. All he has succeeded in doing is providing an account of the phrases 'earlier than' and 'later than' in terms of the phrases 'did exist' and 'will exist', while being unable to provide an account as to what actually exists in the real world that distinguishes between the latter two phrases. Under presentism, after all, there just *isn't anything* that did exist or will exist, because neither past nor future events exist. Craig's attempted reduction only succeeds in accounting for two somewhat mysterious concepts in terms of two at least equally mysterious concepts, and thus fails as a reductive account of the directionality of time. I therefore conclude that Craig's attempted reduction fails to offer any conceptual insight or advantage over simply accepting 'earlier than' and 'later than' as primitive notions, and fails as an argument for the tensed theory of time.

The Problem of the Extent of the Present

While Craig criticises the tenseless theory of time for leading to absurd conclusions, there is a major unsolved problem with Craig's presentist theory of time, in that Craig fails to offer a convincing response to what is called the problem of the extent of the present. The relevant question here is, if all that exists is what is present, then what exactly counts as being 'present'? Is it the present second, the present minute, the present year, or something else? Since Craig's entire philosophy of time is predicated upon the unique existence of the present, Craig needs to be able to provide an answer to this if his theory is to make any sense. One possibility is that the present consists of a single infinitesimally small, instantaneous moment. Craig rejects this option, arguing that this would result in various paradoxes[86]. More importantly, such a position would also conflict with his argument that an actual infinite cannot exist (since there would be infinitely many past instants), and also his belief that time forms through successive addition (since instants are not discrete units that are added one after the other). As such, this view would fatally undermine both of Craig's key arguments in defence of the premise that the universe began to exist, and so is not a feasible alternative when used in conjunction with the kalam cosmological argument.

A second possibility is that time could consist of 'temporal atoms', with the smallest possible length of time sometimes referred to as a 'chronon'. A chronon would not be instantaneous but would instead have a finite duration, and this duration would represent the smallest possible temporal duration, with no smaller division of time possible even in theory. While Craig does not explicitly reject this option, he is clearly somewhat uncomfortable with some of the counterintuitive implications of such a theory of time. In particular, such an atomic theory of time gives rise to a certain paradox of motion, which Craig describes as a 'peculiar result'[87]. More importantly for our purposes, the atomic theory of the present is inconsistent with Craig's understanding of the nature of metaphysical time. That is, while physical time could potentially have a smallest possible unit, Craig thinks that it is possible for time to come into existence if God were to simply begin counting one, two, three, etc. That is, Craig thinks that metaphysical time could exist without any corresponding physical time, purely as a result of the mental process of God. If this is the case, however, then surely it would be possible for God to take an action or think a thought in any arbitrarily small interval between existing events. For example, between the count of one and two God could make a subsidiary count of however many prime numbers he wanted to. This, however, would negate the possibility of a smallest possible unit of time, since for any temporal division God could always make a yet smaller temporal division within it. As such, it seems that if Craig wishes to maintain the view that metaphysical time could be created simply by mental processes of God, then he cannot adopt the view that the extent of the present is determined by a smallest atomic unit of duration, since God's mental activity could not be restricted to a smallest temporal unit in this way.

Cognizant of such problems, Craig thus resorts to a third theory of the extent of the present which he calls the 'non-metrical' present. According to this theory, "the extent of the present depends upon the extent of the entity described as present... the duration stipulated to be present will be an arbitrary, finite duration centred on a conceptually specified instant[88]." This interval, Craig believes, exists independently of and prior to any conceptual divisions we may apply to the interval, or any metrification we apply to the interval. As he explains[89]:

> "Any temporal interval which is contextually taken to be the present interval is susceptible of being conceptually divided into shorter temporal phases which will be past, present, and future respectively. For example, in certain contexts it is appropriate to refer to the present minute; but if we wish to narrow our consideration of what is going on now, we are at liberty to divide the minute into seconds and to focus on the present second. The present minute can thus be analyzed into a past phase composed of seconds earlier than the present second, a present phase which is the present second, and a future phase composed of the later seconds remaining in the minute. This process of narrowing can be continued indefinitely, with the present instant as a conceptual limit, so that there is no minimal temporal interval which is now."

In response to the objection that this iterative division of the present into ever finer subdivisions will eventually reduce the present into a single infinitesimal instant (and so correspond to the first option discussed above), Craig replies[90]:

> "*An interval is present if any phase of it is present... an interval may be present simpliciter even though we can divide it into sub-intervals which are not every one present. Thus, the present minute is qua minute present simpliciter, but if we divide it into seconds, then only one second is qua second present simpliciter. If any sub-interval of an interval is present, then the whole interval is as such present.*"

This conception of the present consisting of an interval of variable length depending upon how it is conceptually analysed, however, is patently absurd. This absurdity is clearly manifest if we simply substitute 'exists' for 'present' in Craig's previous remarks. Such a substitution is legitimate since, according to Craig[91], "to be present is simply to exist." Carrying out this substitution thus yields, for instance, the statement 'the extent of what exists depends upon the extent of the entity described as existing'. This statement seems to imply that we can change what exists simply by changing the scope of what we choose to describe or refer to. Likewise, we have the statement 'any temporal interval which is contextually taken to exist... is susceptible of being conceptually divided into shorter temporal phases which will not exist, exist, and not exist', where we have also substituted 'past' and 'future' for 'not exist' in accordance with Craig's view that past and future are simply (again quoting Prior) "two particular species of unreality[92]." The absurdities mount when we consider that Craig says that any interval is present (and therefore exists) when any portion of it is present, from which it follows that simply by mentioning or referring to any arbitrarily long period of time, we are able to bring that entire interval and all its constituent events into existence. Indeed, since the present instant obviously exists, and since the present instant is clearly part of the longer interval comprising the entire time from the present instant back to the Big Bang, then it follows from Craig's position that this entire time period must be present, and hence exist. Craig's presentism thus collapses into the 'growing block' theory of time, whereby the present and all past events exist, but not future events. Paul Helm summarises these absurdities in the following passage[93]:

> "*Given the claim of the (presentist) that only the present is real, if I refer to the present aeon as 'the present aeon' that aeon is real. Do I, in deciding to refer to 'the present aeon' confer reality on it? Creatio ex nihilo indeed! How can Craig claim that only the present is real when the present might be an age? Does not the present age have past and future features? Are these equally real simply in virtue of designating a stretch of time 'the present age'? Do things persist through stretches of the present age, as they seem to? Craig often excoriates conventionalism in others while seeming to embrace it here. At this point, is not his presentism in danger of unravelling?*"

In order for Craig's presentism to represent a viable theory of time, he needs to be able to provide an explanation as to which interval of time exists objectively as present and which periods of time outside of the present are part of the non-existent past and future. Otherwise he is left with a completely absurd ontology whereby what exists can vary from the present nanosecond to the entire duration of the universe, depending upon what we refer to our take as being present in a given context. Since there are no such options available to Craig that do not conflict some aspect of the kalam cosmological argument, I conclude that Craig has no coherent answer to the problem of the extent of the present, and thus no viable theory of time with which to undergird the kalam.

SUMMARY

Given the foregoing discussion, I do not believe that Craig has succeeded in demonstrating that time is tensed. His arguments based on the inelimibility of tense from language are largely question-begging in that they assume time is tensed, and then require a theory of language to accommodate this alleged fact. All such arguments also assume that our use of language is a reliable guide to what exists, an assumption which Craig rejects when applied to other cases. Craig fails to show that any of our direct experiences support the tensed theory of time, largely because tensed and tenseless theories differ only in respect to the reality of the past and the future, neither of which we directly experience. The various absurdities that Craig alleges arise in the tenseless theory of time are either not real absurdities, or arise only as a result of misstating the claims of the tenseless theory. Finally, I argued that the theory of general relativity provides strong evidence in favour of the tenseless theory of time, and that Craig's presentist theory of time is plagued by his inability to provide a cogent answer to the problem of the extent of the present. With such a poor justification for his first premise, Craig's kalam cosmological argument is already on very shaky ground.

PREMISE TWO: THE UNIVERSE BEGAN TO EXIST

In this second key premise of the kalam cosmological argument, when Craig refers to 'the universe', he says that he is referring not just to the part of the universe that we can currently see and interact with (what cosmologists call the 'observable universe'), but to all of material reality that exists as part of space and time. In saying that the universe 'began to exist', Craig means that this totality of material existence had an absolute beginning at some time in the finite past, 'before' which there was no time and no universe.

Craig presents three distinct arguments in favour of his contention that the universe began to exist:

- The impossibility of an actual infinite.
- The impossibility of forming an actual infinite by successive addition.
- Empirical evidence for a beginning of the universe.

The first two of these arguments are philosophical, while the third appeals to the findings of modern scientific inquiry. Since Craig believes that each of his arguments stands largely independently of the others, I will address each of them in turn.

AN ACTUAL INFINITE IS IMPOSSIBLE

An actual infinite is something that is infinitely large, and exists fully and totally in reality all at once. It is distinguished from a potential infinite, which simply refers to any situation where something can increase or grow without limit (forever), but which at any given time is always finite. Thus, Craig believes that the future is a potential infinite, since time could continue forever without end, even though at any given moment in time only a finite number of events would ever have elapsed. By contrast, an actual infinite is already 'all there', existing in totality and as a whole. If the universe never began to exist, but had existed forever in the past, then Craig argues this would amount to there being an actually infinite number of past events, since all these past events must have already elapsed in order to reach the present.

Craig's primary method of defending his premise that the universe began to exist is by arguing that an actually infinite past cannot exist, since an infinite past would entail various absurdities. Craig here is not arguing that an actual infinite is logically inconsistent, as he says that "viewed *in abstracto* (i.e. abstractly), there is no logical contradiction involved in any of these enormities[94]." Rather, he contends that when applied to concrete situations in the real world, the concept of an actual infinity leads to absurd results. Thus, even if they are not logically impossible, actual infinities cannot exist in reality. His argument can be summarised as follows:

- Premise one: It is impossible for an actual infinite to exist in reality.

- Premise two: An infinite temporal regress of events is an actual infinity.

- Conclusion: The universe cannot be eternal in the past.

Cantor's Arithmetic

Cantor was a mathematician who introduced a formalism for working with infinite quantities in mathematics. Called transfinite arithmetic, Cantor's results are widely regarded as providing a logically consistent and mathematically sound basis for carrying out operations like addition and multiplication of infinite sets. Sometimes the results of transfinite arithmetic can be very counterintuitive. For example, under Cantor's system the size of the set of all natural numbers $\mathbb{Z} = \{1,2,3,..\}$ is the same as the size of the set of all odd numbers $\{1,3,..\}$, even though there are clearly two natural numbers for every odd number. In set theory, the cardinality of a set refers in essence to the size of that set. For example, the set $\{1,2,3,5\}$ has a cardinality of four, because it has four elements. Cantor wanted to find a way of describing the cardinality of the set of natural numbers $\mathbb{Z}$. Obviously, there are infinitely many natural numbers, so the cardinality of $\mathbb{Z}$ cannot be any number in $\mathbb{Z}$ itself. Cantor therefore used the symbol $\aleph_0$ (pronounced 'aleph-nought') to denote the size of the set of natural numbers. This symbol $\aleph_0$ refers to an actually infinite discrete number of things, and so does not have the same meaning as the symbol ∞, which is typically used in mathematics to refer to infinity as a potential limit.

Craig does not dispute that Cantor's arithmetic is logically or mathematically consistent; rather his argument rests on the idea that these results only describe *abstract* mathematical quantities, not anything that exists *in reality*, since the actual existence of any infinite quantities would lead to absurd conclusions.

The Problem of Hilbert's Hotel

The main thought experiment that Craig presents in arguing for the impossibility of the existence of an actual infinite is known as Hilbert's hotel, a hypothetical infinitely large hotel with infinitely many rooms. Craig thinks that the very idea of such a hotel is absurd for a range of different reasons, and as such an actually infinite hotel like this could not possibly exist in reality[95]. The paradoxes he discusses include the following:

- If the hotel was initially full, but then a new guest arrived, the new guest could be accommodated by moving person one into room two, person two into room three, etc, thereby creating a vacant room without increasing the number of rooms in the hotel, even though previously all the rooms were full.

- After such a new guest arrives, the number of guests in the hotel is the same as before, even though one more guest has moved in. This applies even if infinitely many more guests arrive.

- If all the rooms are initially full and then the guests in every odd numbered room depart, then there would still be infinitely many people in the hotel (the guests in every even numbered room), even though infinitely many guests just left, and even though the hotel is now only half full. Further, the proprietor could then move the person in room two into room one, the person in room four into room two, and so on, thereby refilling all the rooms without a single new guest having to enter the hotel.

- The proprietor of the hotel could begin with a full hotel with an infinite number of guests, move the occupant of room two into room one (thereby doubling the occupancy of that room), then move the occupants of rooms three and four into room two, and so on, resulting in a hotel that was still completely full with infinitely many guests (as before), but now with two guests in each room instead of one, all without any new guests checking into the hotel.

Craig argues that, while consistent with the results of Cantor's arithmetic and so not logically contradictory, these scenarios indicate that Hilbert's hotel is absurd and hence cannot possibly exist in the real world. Craig also argues that the only absurd thing about Hilbert's hotel is the fact that it is supposed to be infinite, and not (for instance) the fact that it is a hotel. Thus, from the fact that Hilbert's hotel is absurd and could not possibly exist, Craig thinks we can conclude that an actual infinity cannot exist in reality. It is important to note that it is obviously *physically impossible* for Hilbert's hotel to exist in our universe, since the finite observable universe is insufficiently large to hold an infinitely large hotel. Furthermore, an infinitely extended object would be unable to maintain causal connections with itself owing to the finite velocity of the speed of light, meaning that the proprietor of the hotel would not be able to move about infinite numbers of guests in the way Craig describes. Craig's point, however, is not the obvious one that Hilbert's hotel is *physically* impossible, but rather the much stronger claim that Hilbert's hotel is absurd and therefore *metaphysically* impossible.

That is, Craig thinks that Hilbert's hotel could not exist in *any* possible universe, not even in one with very different conditions and laws of physics to our own.

I am in agreement with Craig, along with essentially all philosophers who have considered the matter, that Hilbert's hotel is bizarre, counterintuitive, hard to understand, and intuitively seems like it could not exist. I disagree with Craig, however, in that I do not think that Hilbert's hotel can be shown with any confidence to actually be *absurd*. As a result, I do not believe it is metaphysically impossible in the way Craig argues.

Suppose therefore we imagine a very different universe in which travel and communication are instantaneous, and in which we can have a hotel that is finite in volume but infinite in capacity since the guests (and hence the rooms) are non-physical and so take up zero volume. It is my view that Hilbert's hotel *would* be possible in such a universe. Such a hotel could have an infinite number of guests, and would still have an infinite number of guests even if some guests left. If half the guests left, the hotel would be half empty, but could become full again if the proprietor moved around all the guests as described previously. Craig thinks these results are absurd, but I think we can make perfect sense of such scenarios. In the case of an infinite hotel, to be 'full' simply means that every room is occupied by at least one guest, while to be empty (i.e. not full) means that at least one room has no guest. The proprietor of our hypothetical hotel is at leisure to distribute his infinite guests across the infinitely many rooms as he pleases. If he puts one guest in each room, then the hotel is full by this definition. Likewise, if he places two guests in each room it is also full. On the other hand, if he places all the guests in only a single room, or only places a guest in every second room, then hotel is not full because at least one room remains empty. As Craig acknowledges, there is no contradiction in any of these statements. Where, then, is the absurdity supposed to arise? Finite hotels must either gain or lose a guest in order to change between being full or empty, but this simply isn't how infinities work. An infinitely large hotel can go from being full or empty simply by re-arranging guests among existing rooms. Craig, of course, will nevertheless say that this is absurd, but he gives no argument or explanation why - it is simply his opinion that the results seem too strange. Certainly, an infinite hotel such as this *would* be very strange to us, because we are not used to reasoning with infinite quantities. That something seems counterintuitive or even bizarre, however, does not imply that it is truly absurd or impossible. Since Craig is making the claim that such a hotel is absurd, it is he who needs to articulate precisely what the absurdity is, and why such a hotel could not possibly exist in any imaginable universe.

Even if, however, we thought that Hilbert's hotel *was* absurd and therefore is metaphysically impossible, it does not at all follow that no actual infinite can exist in reality. Hilbert's hotel is but one specific instance of an actual infinity, and the impossibility of a single instance does not imply the impossibility of any other instance of a general class. As Landon Hedrick argues, this is especially so given that Craig's Hilbert hotel at most shows that an infinite number of discrete objects cannot exist, and it is not clear that events or moments of time are objects in this manner[96]. Craig thinks that he is warranted in making a general inference on the basis of this specific case, arguing that[97]:

> "If a (denumerably) actually infinite number of things could exist, they could be numbered and manipulated just like the guests in Hilbert's Hotel. Since nothing hangs on the illustration's involving a hotel, the metaphysical absurdity is plausibly attributed to the existence of an actual infinite."

This statement, however, is quite obviously incorrect. It ignores the possibility that there may be types of actual infinities which are not manipulable in the way the guests in Hilbert's hotel are. Remember that in all the alleged absurdities of Hilbert's hotel, the key to Craig's demonstrating an apparent absurdity is some ability to change, shuffle, move around, or manipulate infinities into different arrangements. What he ignores is that there may be actual infinities that cannot be manipulated in this way, and on which his argument would therefore have no purchase. A pertinent example of such an actual infinity would be that constituted by an infinite temporal sequence of events. If time is tensed in the way Craig thinks it is, then moments of time obviously cannot be moved about, rearranged, or manipulated in the way hotel guests could be. As Wes Morriston argues[98]:

> "It is metaphysically possible for the guests to be moved. It is not metaphysically possible for events to change their temporal locations. So the disanalogy between a Hilbert's Hotel and a beginningless series of events remains in full force."

In response, Craig has said the following[99]:

> "Let's suppose Hilbert's Hotel is a hotel where, say, all the rooms are locked so that people can't move out of them. Or maybe there are no doors to the rooms so that you have an infinite number of rooms, one person in each room, but there are no doors. I said you can still imagine what it would be like for a person in room 1 to be in room 2, and the person in room 2 he could be in room 4, and you will generate the same absurdities. You don't have to actually go through the trouble of moving the people physically."

While in this modified case the Hilbert's hotel example may be more relevant, it does seem that Craig is here backing away from his earlier claim that 'if an actually infinite number of things could exist, they could be numbered and manipulated'. This altered scenario is, at least to my mind, also considerably less counterintuitive than Craig's original scenarios. Whether one shares this assessment or not, most of Craig's alleged absurdities in both versions of his Hilbert hotel thought experiments derive from two fundamental axioms that we unthinkingly accept with respect to finite quantities, but are inconsistent when applied to infinite quantities. These axioms are described by Blake McAllister[100]:

> "i. Cantor's Principle of Correspondence. If one-to-one correspondence exists between two sets, then the number of members in each set is equal.
> ii. Euclid's Maxim. The number of members in a set is always larger than the number of members in any of its proper subsets."

Demonstrating the incompatibility of these two axioms when applied to infinite sets is straightforward. The set of all odd integers, for example, is a proper subset of the set of all integers, but nevertheless the two can be placed in one-to-one correspondence with each other. Thus, the Principle of Correspondence indicates that the two sets are the same size, while Euclid's Maxim indicates that the set of integers should be larger. Therefore fundamentally, in appealing to the Hilbert's hotel thought experiment, Craig is arguing that it is obvious that both of these axioms must always hold in the real world. If this is true, it follows that infinitely large sets of real-world entities cannot exist. By contrast, Cantor's transfinite arithmetic rejects Euclid's Maxim, and thus is able to generate a consistent mathematical treatment of infinite sets, with the side effect of generating some of the counterintuitive results that Craig presents in his Hilbert's hotel problem. Whether these results are sufficiently counterintuitive to justify declaring an actual infinite impossible is, as Craig himself admits "to a considerable degree subjective"[101]. While Craig says that he finds them "sufficiently troubling," plausibly this is largely attributable to a lack of familiarity with the properties of infinite sets. As McAllister has said[102]:

> *"If Craig's thought experiments do not seem intuitively absurd to an individual, as seems to be the case with many philosophers, then he has not offered any independent reason for why that individual should believe the situation to be absurd... It seems reasonable to assume that someone familiar with the branch of trans-finite mathematics could view Craig's thought experiments as merely drawing out intriguing implications of actual infinites in the real world."*

As such, it does not seem to me that the problems of Hilbert's hotel provide any compelling reason for someone who does not share Craig's intuition about the 'absurdity' of the results to conclude that an actual infinite cannot exist.

Subtraction of Infinite Quantities

In addition to the previously discussed alleged absurdities of Hilbert's hotel, Craig presents another objection to the possibility of the existence of an actual infinite. His argument is that while in Cantor's system of transfinite arithmetic inverse operations such as subtraction are prohibited or left undefined, in the real world there would be nothing preventing, for example, an infinite number of guests from actually checking out of Hilbert's hotel. This inability to account for the real possibility of subtraction of infinite quantities, Craig argues, shows that actual infinities cannot exist in the real world.

This argument is fallacious, however, because it exhibits a misunderstanding of the meaning of subtraction. To solve the equation $X - Y = Z$, for example, is just to ask what number added to Y will give X? The reason such an operation cannot be defined in transfinite arithmetic is because when dealing with infinite sets this question has no unique answer. For example, if both X and Y are equal to $\aleph_0$ (aleph-nought, the 'size' of the set of natural numbers), then Z could be any number from 0 up to $\aleph_0$ and still satisfy the relation, since by the way transfinite arithmetic works, $\aleph_0 + 1 = \aleph_0, \aleph_0 + 2 = \aleph_0, ..., \aleph_0 + \aleph_0 = \aleph_0$ (loosely this means adding anything to infinity still leaves you with infinity). Thus, in Cantor's arithmetic subtraction is prohibited for good reason, because it cannot be defined in a *general* way that yields a single definite answer. It is still possible, however, to meaningfully answer questions involving *specific* instances of removing items from infinite sets. For example, the set of natural numbers $\mathbb{Z} = \{1,2,3,...\}$ has cardinality $\aleph_0$, and if all the odd numbers are removed, the remaining subset (the even numbers) still has cardinality $\aleph_0$. We can therefore say that $|\{\mathbb{Z} \text{ with odds removed}\}| = |\{\mathbb{Z}\}|$. By contrast, if we take the set of natural numbers and then remove the subset of all numbers greater than 100, the resulting set has a cardinality of 100. Thus, in any *specific case* of removing particular elements from an infinite set, we are able to determine the cardinality of the set that is left over, which is called the relative complement, denoted $A \backslash B$. Craig's argument fails because he does not appreciate the difference between $|A| - |B|$ and $|\{A \backslash B\}|$. The former refers to the difference in the size of sets A and B and involves the operation of subtraction which is undefined for infinite sets. The latter, however, refers to the size of the relative complement of sets A and B and *is defined* and can be carried out even for infinite sets. It is only this latter operation that is required for real-world operations involving specific infinite sets. After all, in the real world we never observe 'subtraction' in the abstract – what we observe are specific instances of taking some items away from a set of some others, and determining the size of the set that is left over. This problem with Craig's argument has also been noted by Louis Swingrover[103]:

> "In each operation... Craig describes the production of the relative complement of one well-defined set in another... However he proceeds to characterize each operation as if it were the subtraction of an undefined infinite quantity from an undefined infinite quantity and the cardinality of the resultant set as if it were the difference between the two undefined quantities, which is different in each case. This equivocates between the relative complement of one set in another and the difference between their cardinalities. The contradictions cannot be reached if the equivocations are not made: The relative complement of a well-defined transfinite set in another well-defined transfinite always yields a unique result."

In any real-world case involving a specific (even infinite) number of guests checking out of a hotel, therefore, the size of the set of guests remaining at the hotel would always be uniquely defined. As such, the fact that the abstract notion of 'subtraction' is not defined for infinite sets does nothing to undermine the possibility of an actual infinity existing in reality.

Spatial and Temporal Intervals

One common objection to Craig's argument against the possibility of an actual infinity is that every spatial and temporal interval already consists of an infinite number of points. Craig retorts that[104]:

> "This familiar objection gratuitously assumes that space and time are composed of real points and instants, which has never been proven."

In this response, however, Craig once again shifts the burden of proof, since *he* is claiming that no actual infinities can exist, and therefore it is up to *him* to demonstrate that space and time, plausibility infinitely divisible, are not in fact so divisible. Craig goes on to describe his preferred model of spatial and temporal intervals as follows[105]:

"If one thinks of a geometrical line as logically prior to any points which one may care to specify on it rather than as a construction built up out of points... then one's ability to specify certain points, like the halfway point along a certain distance, does not imply that such points actually exist independently of our specification of them... Time as duration is then logically prior to the (potentially infinite) divisions we make of it. Specified instants are not temporal intervals but merely the boundary points of intervals, which are always nonzero in duration."

This position meets with a number of difficulties. First, if neither space nor time are composed of points, it is very mysterious how we are able to 'create' a division at any arbitrary point by the act of, for example, sweeping our hand in an arc and stopping at any arbitrary location, or stopping a stopwatch at any arbitrary time. There is no limit to the precision at which this can be done (at least none we know of), and therefore we seem capable of arbitrary 'creating' a division in time or space at any point we wish, at any time. How we are able to exercise such apparently magical power over the structure of space and time itself, given that such points do not already exist prior to our intervention, is quite inexplicable. Second, Craig's view meets with various absurdities when considering the question of the 'extent of the present', which I discussed in a previous section. There I argued that Craig's notion of a temporal interval existing 'prior to' any events that exist in that interval is completely absurd, and must collapse either into a tenseless theory of time or a view that only the present instantaneous instant exists. The former case is inconsistent with the kalam's dependence upon the tensed theory of time, while the latter case is inconsistent with Craig's premise that the temporal series of events is formed by successive addition.

Craig has also presents the 'Grim Reaper paradox' as an argument against the possibility of time being composed of individual instants. The paradox is stated as follows[106]:

"You are alive at 12:00 p.m. Grim Reaper 1 will strike you dead at 1:00 p.m. if you are still alive at that time. Grim Reaper 2 will strike you dead at 12:30 p.m. if you are still alive then. Grim Reaper 3 will strike you dead at 12:15 p.m., and so on.

Such a situation seems clearly conceivable but leads to an impossibility: you cannot survive past 12:00 p.m. and yet you cannot be killed at any time past 12:00 p.m."

Craig thinks that this scenario should be possible if time was composed of instants, but since it leads to a contradiction, we should conclude that time cannot be composed of instants. The problem with this argument is that it incorrectly identifies the reason for the contradiction as lying with the absurdity of time being composed of instants. Instead, the contradiction is a result of the specified situation describing a logically impossible scenario. To see why, note that the situation specifies two key facts: 1) for every Grim Reaper there is another Grim Reaper who arrives in half the time, 2) you will be killed by the earliest Grim Reaper. Since each Grim Reaper is a distinct entity, we can assign each of them a label in accordance with number of minutes after 12pm they arrive: Grim Reaper 1 is assigned 60, Grim Reaper 2 is assigned 30, then 15, 7.5, 5.25, and so on. This set of labels is not arbitrary, but based on the fact that each Grim Reaper must arrive after a determinate number of minutes. In formal notation, this set of possible arrival times (which we will call A) is denoted by $\left\{\frac{60}{2^n} : n \in \mathbb{Z}_{\geq 0}\right\}$. The first postulate about Grim Reapers is therefore equivalent to saying that for each number in our set A, there is also a number in that set equal to half its size. The second postulate, however, states that there is a smallest number in the set A, corresponding to the number of minutes after 12pm that the Grim Reaper who kills us arrives at. This stands in direct contradiction with the first postulate, if for each element in set A there is another element equal to half the first, then it is impossible for A to have a smallest member. The Grim Reaper problem, therefore, effectively states that you will be killed by the grim reaper that bears the smallest number in a set that has no smallest number. By this analysis, we see that the Grim Reaper paradox in fact describes not a paradoxical situation but a logical impossibility. As such its impossibility has nothing to do with the impossibility of time consisting of instants, but simply because the situation it describes is self-contradictory.

A modified form of the Grim Reaper argument involves an infinite number of Grim Reapers which appear at random in the interval between 12pm and 1pm[107]. As there are infinitely many reapers, for any reaper appearing at time t there will always be will appearing before t. It follows that no individual reaper could be the first to appear, and thus no individual reaper could actually make the killing blow. At the same time, it seems absurd to say that you could survive this situation, since it only takes a single reaper to kill you, and by assumption there are infinitely many reapers appearing during this interval. Since (unlike the previous version) there is nothing logically impossible about an infinite number of reapers appearing in this way, the question arises as to how to resolve this apparent contradiction – what is it that makes this situation impossible? Craig seems to think that the only answer is that time must not be infinitely divisible, which would entail that there was a first instant after 12pm at which a first reaper could appear. Perhaps, however, it is not actually possible for the reapers to randomise their arrival times in this way. Alternatively, noting that the Grim Reapers would have to be immaterial in order to act within infinitesimal time spans (no material object could do that), we could reject the possibility of immaterial Grim Reapers interacting with a physical embodied person. Overall, therefore, even this modified thought experiment has no clear implications concerning whether time could be composed of infinitesimal instants. It clearly describes an impossible situation, but what exactly is the cause of this impossibility, and therefore whether temporal intervals can be infinite, remains an open question, and hence a potential counterexample to Craig's argument that actual infinites cannot exist.

Is an Infinite Regress of Events an Actual Infinite?

Craig's argument that if the universe had no beginning then the past would be actually infinite[108] is hard to reconcile with his presentist philosophy of time, according to which the past does not exist. In particular, it seems that if Craig argues the past cannot be actually infinite, then he must also say that the future cannot be infinite, which seems like an absurd conclusion. Craig has responded that the past is already completed and so would be an actual infinite, while the future is yet to come and therefore is only a potential infinite. Craig, however, believes that God knows everything that can be known, including the outcome of all future events. Since Craig believes that the future is a potential infinite (i.e. it will go on forever without end), it seems to follow that God must know an infinite number of things about the future. Craig has responded that God's knowledge is not propositional, and thus cannot be divided up into infinitely many discrete units. This response, however, seems to unduly focus on the question of whether God's knowledge consists of propositions. Even if God's knowledge is non-propositional, it still must be the case that God knows an infinite number of *facts* about the future. Unlike propositions, facts are not abstractions or mentally existing entities, but are sates of affairs which exist in the real world.

We may consider, for example, that if God exists then he must know how many praises Craig will sing on his first day in heaven, how many he will sing on the second day, and so on for infinitely many future days. Even if God knew nothing of the future, there would still be infinitely many future-tensed facts concerning events that had yet to happen. Even though the future *events* have yet to occur, and thus according to Craig's presentist philosophy of time do not exist, there are still infinitely many *facts* about events that *will occur*, one concerning each distinct event. Craig cannot respond that facts about the future merely are a *potential* rather than an *actual* infinite, with the total number of future praises being indefinite, since there is *now* a future-tensed fact concerning each praise that *will* eventually be said. Furthermore, given that he is omniscient, God must know about each of these infinitely many future praises in complete detail, and God's knowledge of what is to come cannot be left 'indefinite'. God must therefore currently know an actually infinite number of facts about an infinite number of future praises. Morriston summarises the situation as follows[109]:

> "*For any n, praise number n will be said. There is a completely determinate fact of the matter about when it will be said, by whom, with what words, and in what precise manner. Nothing has been left 'indefinite' or 'indeterminate'. The correct answer to the question, How many praises will be said?, can only be, infinitely many...*
> *If there are truths about the future, then presentists cannot dodge questions about the number of events that will occur in*

scenarios like the ones I have proposed. If there is – now – a complete body of truth about an endless series of discrete and successive events, each of which will occur, presentists cannot avoid answering the question, How many will occur?... The non-existence of past events does not prevent us from asking how many have occurred. Nor should the non-existence of future events prevent us from asking how many will occur. In neither case will 'indefinitely many' do as an answer."

In response to this line of criticism Craig has said the following[110]:

"If the series of future praises goes on forever, there will never be uttered an actually infinite number of praises. Rather, infinity serves merely as the limit which you endlessly approach but you never arrive at. The number of praises is always finite but it is always increasing toward infinity as a limit... you can't say that about the past. For the past to be potentially infinite, it would have to be finite but growing in a backward direction. That is to say, growing in the earlier-than direction to be the mirror image of the future. And that is crazy. The past isn't growing backward in the earlier-than direction. It is moving forward in the sense that with the present event more and more events are being added to the past."

Craig's remarks here, however, simply miss the point. The argument is not that one day there will have been uttered an infinite number of praises. Rather, the argument is that it is *now* the case that there are infinitely many future-tensed facts about praises that will be uttered in the future. This is exactly analogous to how there would be infinitely many past-tensed facts about how many praises had already been said, if the past was actually infinite. This is similar to the mistake Craig makes when he argues that[111]:

"An infinite temporal progress of events does not entail that an actually infinite number of (future) events will occur. There never will occur an actually infinite number of events, since it is impossible to count to infinity. The only sense in which there will be an infinite number of events is that the series of events will increase toward infinity as a limit."

It is true that every event in the future will occur a finite amount of time from the present, since as Craig says it is impossible to count to infinity. However, this is in no way inconsistent with there being an actually infinite number of events that will occur in the future. This is equivalent to saying that, while every natural number has a finite difference from any other natural number, there are also infinitely many natural numbers (see figure 4). No individual future event is infinitely distant from the present, such that from some future vantage point we will be able to look back and say 'since then, infinitely many events have occurred'. Nevertheless, it is also true that the number of future events that will occur is infinite (what else could it be?). Craig's attempts to defend this portion of his argument continually fail to appreciate this distinction.

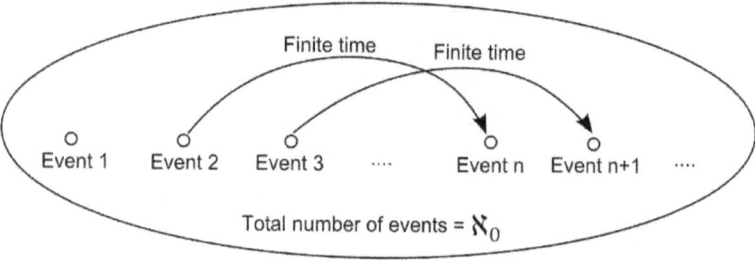

Figure 4. The temporal distance between any two events (for an arbitrarily large value of n) is always finite, even if the total number of events is infinite.

The real trouble for Craig is in trying to establish a difference between the status of the past and the future. Under presentism both the past and the future are equivalent in that they do not exist, and so the analysis of the status of past-tensed facts must be the same as the analysis of future-tensed facts. Thus, either neither constitutes an example of an actual infinity, in which case Craig's argument that the past cannot be actually infinite fails, or they both constitute actual infinites, in which case the possibility of an actually infinite past is proven by the acknowledged possibility of an actually infinite future. In order to avoid this bind, Craig must find some way of affirming that past events actually exist in reality while future events do not. In one attempt to draw this distinction he argues that[112]:

> "It is far from clear that the presentist is unable to draw a meaningful distinction between the actuality of the past and the potentiality of the future. Future events have not as of yet been actualized, whereas past and present events have been actualized."

Craig's grouping of past and present events in this way, however, is highly misleading. For as a presentist, Craig argues that the past and future are alike in not existing, while only the present exists. He is unequivocal in stating, for instance, that "past entities do not exist"[113]. Thus it is not correct to say that present events are like past events in that both have been actualised. Rather, according to Craig's view past events have already been actualised and have since gone out of existence, present events have been actualised and now exist, and future events have yet to be actualised and not come into existence. When presented in this, more accurate manner, it remains unclear as to what exactly past and present events are supposed to have in common that distinguishes them from future events that makes them more 'actual'. Under presentism, the past has gone out of existence, and so is just as unreal as the future.

In a second attempt to draw a distinction between past and future Craig claims that[114]:

> "When we say that the number of past events is infinite, we mean that prior to today $\aleph_0$ events have elapsed. But when we say that the number of future events is infinite, we do not mean that $\aleph_0$ events will elapse, for that is false."

This statement, however, is simply mistaken. Under presentism, a future event is simply an event that has not yet elapsed. If events continue to occur without end into the future, then clearly the number of events that have not yet elapsed is $\aleph_0$, for there are infinitely many of them. Craig's appeals to the objectivity of temporal becoming are simply irrelevant, for the fact is that the number of events yet to elapse is infinity large, the same as the number of events in an infinite past.

There just isn't anything under a presentist philosophy of time that is 'growing' in the direction of the future – the present exists, while past and future events do not. Thus, if he describes past events as 'actual', he must likewise say that future events are 'actual'. Craig's responses now become rather desperate. He claims that "the series of events that have not yet happened"[115], under a presentist theory, "in no sense exists"[116]. If this is true, how can God know about (as he surely must) each and every praise that will be uttered in the future? If there is no series of events that will occur, it seems there could not be anything in the future that God can know about. Yet clearly this is wrong, as even if there will never be a future time when infinitely many praises have been said, it is nevertheless the case that the number of future-tensed facts about future events which God knows is actually infinite. There is nothing potential about this infinite, for it is now true that God presently has knowledge of an actually infinite number of praises that will be said.

At this point, Craig's attempts to distinguish past from future become truly baffling[117]:

> "The perfect tense of 'has happened' covers every time up through the present and so includes every event past and present. Everything that has happened has been actualized... The actual world thus includes both what does exist and what did exist. But events which have yet to take place, being pure potentialities, are, on a tensed view of time, not part of the actual world... The ontological distinction between the past-present on the one hand and the future on the other is especially perspicuous in 'growing block' views of time... A proponent of the kalam argument who accepts the growing block view has no difficulty in differentiating the actuality of the past from the potentiality of the future. My claim is that the tenseless existence of the past block of events is not a necessary condition of the past's actuality. Even if past events do not exist, they are still part of the actual world in a way that future events are not, since the actual world comprises everything that has happened." (My emphasis)

It seems that Craig is truly grasping at straws here; he needs the past to be unreal in order to be consistent with his presentist philosophy of time, but at the same time needs the past to be more real than the future in order for his argument against the possibility of an infinite past to succeed. Faced with this dilemma, Craig is forced to endorse the absurd notion that past events can be part of the actual world despite not actually existing! Compare these remarks with what Craig says when defending presentism in a different context[118]:

> "On a presentist ontology, past and future events/things/times are not real or existent and, hence, do not exemplify properties like pastness or futurity. Hence, there can be no question of an entity's trading in futurity for presentness or cashing in presentness for pastness. Rather entities come to be and pass away absolutely, so that the only temporal entities there are are the present ones."

Here there is no hint of any distinction between the existential status of past and future events, things, or times, and an unequivocal statement that neither exists. This is because when outlining and defending presentism as a philosophy of time, it is convenient for Craig to emphasise the unreality of past and future alike. When defending the kalam, however, such positions become inconvenient, and thus Craig attempts to escape his self-imposed quandary by arbitrarily asserting that non-existent past events are still somehow part of the actual world in a way that future events are not. Nor do Craig's appeals to the 'growing block' theory of time help in this context, for as Landon Hendrick notes[119]:

> "Craig could, I suppose, renounce presentism and start endorsing a view that he's previously said was incoherent. Otherwise, I can't see how the growing block theory is going to offer any comfort to Craig, who remains a presentist."

There is simply no way out of this predicament. Under Craig's presentist philosophy of time, past and future are placed squarely in the same category of non-existent things. Since Craig is firmly committed to presentism in order to establish the tensed theory of time needed for the first premise of the extended kalam argument, he is unable to defend the view that the past series of events constitutes an actual infinity.

THE IMPOSSIBILITY OF FORMING AN INFINITE BY SUCCESSIVE ADDITION

In addition to his argument that no actual infinite can exist in reality, Craig also presents a second, independent argument for the finitude of the past. According to this argument, the past must be finite because the present has been reached by the successive addition of each moment in time to the immediately preceding moment. Such a method of sequential addition, however, cannot ever give rise to an actually infinite series, for then the present would never actually be reached. As such, the temporal series of past events must be finite. This argument can be summarised as follows[120]:

- Premise one: It is impossible to form an actually infinite series by successive addition.

- Premise two: The temporal series of past events is a collection formed by successive addition.

- Conclusion: The temporal series of past events cannot be actually infinite.

Counting to Infinity

The most fundamental argument Craig provides against the possibility of forming an actual infinite by successive addition is that, however long one 'counts' or continues to accumulate, there will still always be an infinite amount left to go. For example, the difference between one and infinity is the same as the difference between any finite number and infinity – namely infinite. As such, the amount remaining to count is never diminished, and no progress towards reaching infinity is ever made. Another way of putting this is that every finite number is succeeded by another finite number, so whenever we start from a finite beginning and add a finite increment, we must get a finite result[121]. There is simply no way to turn a finite series into an infinite series by adding finite quantities to it.

The problem with this argument is that it only establishes that one cannot turn a finite set into an infinite set by successive addition, not that it is impossible for an infinite set to be formed through successive addition. In Craig's examples it seems that he implicitly assumes the

James Fodor

existence of some sort of starting point which is then removed to an infinite distance. Craig rejects the notion that he assumes an infinitely distant starting point, retorting that[122]:

> "It is surprising that a number of critics, such as Mackie and Sobel, have objected that the argument illicitly presupposes an infinitely distant starting point in the past and then pronounces it impossible to travel from that point to today... But, in fact, no proponent of the kalam argument of whom we are aware has assumed that there was an infinitely distant starting point in the past."

Nevertheless, I think it is clear that Craig's examples *do* in fact rely on such an assumption. First, he states that[123]:

> "Given any finite number n, $n + 1$ equals a finite number. Hence, $\aleph_0$ has no immediate predecessor."

By this Craig means that the infinite value $\aleph_0$ can never be 'reached' by adding to any finite number, since there is no number x such that $x + 1 = \aleph_0$. This is true, but only establishes the impossibility of attaining an infinite result by adding to a finite starting point. He then argues that the result still holds even if infinite time were somehow available to perform the addition, since[124]:

> "Regardless of the time available, a potential infinite cannot be turned into an actual infinite by any amount of successive addition since the result of every addition will always be finite. One sometimes, therefore, speaks of the impossibility of counting to infinity, for no matter how many numbers one counts, one can always count one more number before arriving at infinity. One sometimes speaks instead of the impossibility of traversing the infinite. The difficulty is the same: no matter how many steps one takes, the addition of one more step will not bring one to a point infinitely distant from."

Here again, Craig speaks of adding and counting, operations which require starting values to act upon. Addition is only possible if we have a number that we are adding to, and that number in this instance must clearly be finite, as otherwise we would already have the actual infinite that Craig is saying cannot be formed. So once again, all that Craig's example shows is that adding a finite number to another finite number will never yield an infinite number, which is not in dispute. What Craig needs to show is not that adding two finite numbers always results in a finite result, but that it is impossible for an actual infinite to form by successive addition.

Even when he explicitly turns his attention to the question of whether it might be possible to form an actual infinity "by never beginning but ending at a point, that is to say, ending at a point after having added one member after another from eternity,"[125] Craig still falsely assumes the existence of an infinitely distant beginning. This is evident from his remark[126]:

> "If one cannot count to infinity, how can one count down from infinity? If one cannot traverse the infinite by moving in one direction, how can one traverse it by moving in the opposite direction?"

The problem with this analogy is that counting is an operation that requires a beginning. One cannot just 'count'; one always has to count by *starting somewhere*. Hence Craig finds that in order to apply a counting analogy to the series of temporal events, he must use absurd phrases like 'count down from infinity', as if infinity were a number from which we could commence counting. As Craig says, infinity has no successor or predecessor, so it is simply impossible to count either up or down 'from infinity'. The problem thus has nothing to do with what direction we imagine counting in. Rather, the problem lies in Craig's insistence on using the language of counting when such terms are only applicable if we have something finite to start our count with. In the case of forming an actual infinite by successive addition, however, not only is there no *finite* starting point, but no starting point *at all*. Counting analogies, therefore, simply are not applicable.

Craig's fundamental difficulty seems to be that he insists on describing or conceptualising the process of forming an actual infinite by successive addition as literally an additive or counting process, which must start somewhere and then count up. This is clearly not how infinite time could work, as Craig's examples show. Rather, a better way of describing how infinite time would operate is that there exists a process of continuous and eternal temporal becoming. Each moment continues from the previous moment and inexorably gives way to the next moment in time, a state of affairs which has always been (i.e. has been at every past moment of time). For every past moment, there was a moment of time before that. Time has always been passing, each moment giving way to the next, for an infinite length of time that has no beginning. It is *this* conception of a beginningless past that Craig needs to refute, not the absurd notion that involves counting up from some starting point.

Zenoian Considerations

Zeno was an ancient Greek philosopher who famously argued that motion is impossible. His argument was that in order to get from one place to another, one must first traverse half the distance, but in order to traverse half the distance one must traverse half of that half (i.e. one quarter of the distance), but to do that one has to traverse one eight of the distance, and so on. There would be no end of intervals one has to cross, and thus no hope of ever reaching one's destination. Craig argues that the reason an actual infinite cannot be formed by successive addition is analogous to the reason Zeno gave for why motion is impossible, namely that before any interval can be traversed there is some prior interval that must be traversed, and hence it seems no interval could be traversed at all. Craig expresses this idea as follows[127]:

> *"Before the present event could occur, the event immediately prior to it would have to occur; and before that event could occur, the event immediately prior to it would have to occur; and so on ad infinitum. One gets driven back and back into the infinite past, making it impossible for any event to occur. Thus, if the series of past events were beginningless, the present event could not have occurred, which is absurd."*

Evidently realising that proving the impossibility of motion would be to prove rather too much, Craig attempts to distinguish his argument from Zeno's argument by asserting that while the intervals in Zeno's thought experiment were potential and unequal, those of

Unreasonable Faith

Craig's argument are actual and equal. While it is true that the intervals in Zeno's thought experiment were of progressively diminishing size, nevertheless it is clear from Zeno's case that it is in fact possible to traverse an infinite number of intervals, since what Zeno says about having to traverse half the distance, and a quarter of the distance, etc, is perfectly correct. The key feature of Zeno's apparent paradox is not that the intervals are of diminishing length, but that there are infinitely many of them. If, then, it is possible to traverse an infinite number of intervals of diminishing length, why should it not also be possible to traverse through an infinite number of intervals of the same length, given infinite time? Craig also responds that the claim that one must pass through an infinite number of intervals "already assumes that the whole interval is a composition of an infinite number of points, whereas Zeno's opponents, like Aristotle, take the line as a whole to be conceptually prior to any divisions[128]." If, however, two objects are separated by a given distance, then a person traversing that distance must first cross half that distance, regardless of whether we regard the interval or the points of which it is comprised as 'conceptually prior'. Thus, it is not at all clear that Craig is able to distinguish his arguments from those of Zeno, since the two distinctions he draws are of dubious relevance.

Even if we accept that Craig's argument is relevantly different from Zeno's and so does not lead to the absurd conclusion that motion is impossible, nevertheless it remains unclear what the force of Craig's argument is supposed to be. Craig is correct to say that an infinite past implies that for every event that occurs, there must have been an event that occurred prior to (and thus before) that event. But from this he jumps straight to asserting "one gets driven back and back into the infinite past, making it impossible for any event to occur." He does not explain how every event having a prior event would imply that it would be impossible for any event to occur. If the past is infinite, then events have always been occurring, one succeeding another. There have always been infinitely many past events, with every event in the past preceded by a previous event. The answer to Craig's question[129] – "How can an actually infinite series of congruent temporal intervals successively elapse?" – is therefore simply 'one at a time, each event after the previous event, continuing eternally without beginning'. Craig obviously has a strong intuition against this possibility, but I do not believe his Zenoian-style arguments succeed in showing it to be absurd or impossible.

Coordinated Events

Another argument that Craig presents against the possibility of forming an actual infinite by successive addition is his appeal to what he calls 'coordinated events'. He considers a situation where the planets have been orbiting our sun for an infinite time, with Saturn completing one orbit for every 2.5 orbits completed by Jupiter. In relation to this scenario, Craig says[130]:

> *"If they have been orbiting from eternity, which planet has completed the most orbits? The correct mathematical answer is that they have completed precisely the same number of orbits. But this seems absurd, for the longer they revolve, the greater becomes the disparity between them, so that they progressively approach a limit at which Jupiter has fallen infinitely far behind Saturn. Yet, being now actually infinite, their respective completed orbits are somehow magically identical. Indeed, they will have 'attained' infinity from eternity past: the number of completed orbits is always the same."*

As Craig correctly states, the number of orbits completed in this situation will be the same for both planets, and further they will always have completed the same (namely an infinite) number of orbits. Craig is clear elsewhere to emphasise that he is not arguing that there is any *logical* contradiction in this state of affairs. Rather his point is that it is absurd to think that such a state of affairs could have come about through an iterative process of absolute temporal becoming, with one moment of time giving way to the next.

My response to Craig's argument is simply to ask why we should expect hypothetical processes that have been operating for an infinite period of time to accord with our intuitions about what seems strange or even absurd. The situation, as I see it, can be described as follows: the planets have both been orbiting the sun for an infinite amount of time, and thus their total number of orbits is the same, infinite in both cases. For every orbit they complete, there is always a previous orbit completed immediately prior, and at every orbit in their history, they have always already completed an infinite number of orbits, so there is no time when they had only completed a finite number of orbits. As I noted previously, Craig admits there is no logical contradiction in this picture, and argues based only on his own intuition that the state of affairs seems absurd. Many others who have considered problems such as this, however, simply do not see the absurdity, even if they acknowledge that the situation is contrary to our normal experience of how coordinated processes such as this work, nevertheless our intuitions are expected to be unreliable when applied to cases so far outside our experience, namely infinite processes. This appeal to a sense of absurdity, however, is the only real argument Craig has as to why the orbital example he provides could not come about.

The Tristram Shandy Paradox

Tristram Shandy is a hypothetical man who writes his autobiography so slowly that it takes him a whole year to write about a single day. Suppose Shandy never aged nor grew tired of his task, and could write for as long as he wished nonstop. Suppose now that he had been writing for eternity at this rate of one day per year. On the basis of this thought experiment, Craig argues[131]:

> "If Tristram Shandy has been writing for 1 year's time, then the most recent day he could have recorded is 1 year ago. But if he has been writing for 2 years, then that same day could not have been recorded by him. For since his intention is to record consecutive days of his life, the most recent day he could have recorded is the day immediately after a day at least 2 years ago. This is because it takes a year to record a day, so that to record 2 days he must have 2 years. Similarly, if he has been writing 3 years, then the most recent day recorded could be no more recent than 3 years and 2 days ago. In other words, the longer he has written the further behind he has fallen...the beginningless, infinite series of days which he has recorded are days which lie at an infinite temporal distance from the present."

Craig objects, however, that this is absurd because one cannot traverse an infinite distance in this way, as it is impossible for an event that was once present to recede to an infinite temporal distance. On this view, even if Shandy never began writing, nevertheless the most recent day that he recorded was once present, and has now receded infinitely distant into the past[132]. Craig claims this is cannot be, since[133]:

> "It is impossible to traverse the temporal interval from an infinitely distant event to the present, or, more accurately, for an event which was once present to recede to a point infinitely temporally distant."

Obviously, it is not possible for a once present event to recede to an infinite temporal distance, as this would be equivalent to beginning at zero and counting up to infinity. How, then, can we say that Shandy must be writing about events that occurred in the infinite past? The answer, as Robin Small has shown, is that it is actually impossible to establish a correspondence between days to write about and years in which Shandy could have written about them, since for any given day he might be writing about, we realise that since Shandy is infinitely far behind, he cannot have gotten up to that day yet, and therefore must be writing about the previous day[134]. The way in which the Shandy paradox is specified, therefore, makes it impossible for Shandy to have been writing for an infinite length of time. Craig thinks that this means that the past cannot be actually infinite, because there is nothing paradoxical about Shandy writing as slowly as he does. Here Craig is mistaken, however, since quite evidently supposing that Shandy writes so slowly *does* lead to paradoxical outcomes if we also assume that he has been writing for infinitely long. Just because the situation is non-paradoxical in the finite case doesn't mean that the infinite case is only paradoxical because infinities cannot exist. Rather, it could be that only *this particular situation* (or a relevant class of similar situations) cannot be extrapolated into an infinite past. There is, in fact, good reason to think this is so, since the paradox vanishes if instead we propose that Shandy takes only one day to write about a whole year, since then it is perfectly possible to establish a correspondence between days to write and years to write about. Nor can Craig reply that if the past was infinite then somebody could just start writing their autobiography in the way specified, since then there would be a starting point to the writing, which violates the key assumption that Shandy has always been writing in this way. As such, I conclude that this version of Shandy's paradox only shows that certain classes of events cannot be extrapolated back into the infinite past. Craig is not justified in extrapolating from this to argue that therefore *no* process or class of events *at all* could be extrapolated into the infinite past.

Elsewhere, Craig considers a different version of the Shandy paradox. Rather than assuming that Shandy gets infinitely far behind and so could never possibly finish, Craig drops the assumption that Shandy can never finish writing and asks if he does finish writing today, why he did not finish writing yesterday or the day before[135]? He argues that this should be possible since he has had infinitely long to write it, and thus one can place the number of years he has been writing in a one-to-one correspondence with the number of days he has had to write about. Every day should have a time when it was written about, and Shandy should be finished with his autobiography. But this is absurd, because clearly he cannot simultaneously have finished and be infinitely far behind. Craig concludes that this paradoxical situation proves that time cannot be infinite in the past.

The problem lies in Craig's assumption that Tristram Shandy will finish writing his autobiography if and only if the days he is writing about and the years he has to write about it can be placed in a one-to-one correspondence. Even if such a correspondence existed, all this would show is that both sets (of days and years) are the same size, namely infinite. In order to answer the separate question of whether he has finished or not we cannot simply look at the sizes of the sets in question. This would work for finite sets, but will not work for infinite sets precisely because of their differing properties. In order to answer a question like 'when, if ever, will Sandy finish his autobiography?', it is not sufficient to consider the size (cardinality) of the sets of days and years. Rather, it is necessary to look at the specific details of the situation. In this situation, it is clear that he could not possibly ever finish writing, as every day he gets further and further behind. Unless we permit Shandy to write about events that have not yet occurred[136], if Shandy ever finishes writing then it cannot be the case that there is a one-to-one correspondence between days that he must write about and years in which he is able to write about that corresponding day. As Graham Oppy clearly explains[137]:

> "Given that Tristram Shandy takes a year to record a day, and that he can only record a day after it happens, it follows – without any considerations about how long he has been writing (whether from eternity past or not) – that there is no year in which he could have recorded that day... Craig is just wrong when he claims that 'what the Tristram Shandy story really tells us is that an actually infinite temporal regress is absurd'. For... this story is trivially inconsistent."

Since there is simply no way that Shandy could ever finish his autobiography, Craig's question as to why he did not finish earlier has no sensible answer. Indeed, the situation is little different from the example given above of the number of orbits completed by Saturn and Jupiter. Clearly Saturn will never be able to 'catch up' to Jupiter in orbiting the sun because it orbits more slowly, even though both have orbited for the same (infinite) number of times. Such situations are obviously counterintuitive because the experiences that shape our intuitions about such matters do not include examples of infinitely reoccurring events such as these. It does not follow, however, that such situations are absurd or impossible.

Finishing an Infinitely Long Count

Craig argues that arriving at the present moment after infinite time in the past is analogous to a man who claims to have been counting down from negative infinity for eternity, and just at this moment to have reached zero. Craig thinks this is impossible[138]:

> "We could ask, why did he not finish counting yesterday or the day before or the year before? By then an infinite time had already elapsed, so that he has had ample time to finish. Thus, at no point in the infinite past should we ever find the man finishing his countdown, for by that point he should already be done!"

This scenario, Craig argues, shows that a situation where one never begins but still reaches an end is impossible, and as such it is not possible for the sequence of events in the universe to have had no beginning, but somehow still reach an end in the present moment. The trouble with this argument, however, is exactly the same as the problem with Craig's appeal to the Tristram Shandy paradox. Namely, it appeals to the logically contradictory notion that it is possible to count down 'from infinity'. Counting is an operation which begins with some set and progressively adds or removes a set number of elements (in this case a single element) each time. Such an operation, however, is impossible to perform on a set that is initially infinitely large (i.e. starting 'from infinity'), since infinity has no finite predecessor or successor. The situation Craig describes is simply logically contradictory – there are simply no numbers to count in this situation. A slightly different way of putting this is that infinity does have a predecessor, namely itself. If a man really did begin counting down 'from infinity', his count would look like: 'infinity minus one is infinity, minus one is infinity, minus one is infinity...' Thus, he would be counting forever without ever getting anywhere, and would never reach zero.

Some may argue that I have just proven Craig's point, by showing that it is indeed impossible to count down from infinity, and so it is likewise impossible to reach the present after traversing an actually infinite number of past events. The problem with this argument is that it is not the case that arriving at the present is analogous to having counted down from infinity, since counting requires a starting point, but the infinite series of temporal events did not have and does not need a starting point. Events have always been transpiring, giving way to the next moment in time, for an infinitely long time. The present moment came about after the immediately prior moment, which in turn came about following the moment immediately before that, and so on. There is no end to this backward chain of events, since there was no beginning of time and events have always been occurring. This in no way, however, implies that there must have been some infinitely distant 'starting point' that we have in some sense been 'counting down from'.

Some of the confusion here may derive from a conflation between the two claims 'there is an infinite number of past events' and 'there is a past event infinitely temporally removed from the present'. The former does not imply the latter, just as the existence of infinitely many numbers does not imply the existence of a number infinitely large. Thus, for any time in the past, there is a finite temporal distance between that time and the present time, and a person counting down from that date to the present would be able to do so and terminate as usual, for they would only have a finite number of days to count.

Is the Temporal Series of Events Formed by Successive Addition?

In this section, I have been responding to Craig's argument that it is impossible to form an actual infinite by successive addition. For this even to be relevant to the kalam cosmological argument, however, it must be the case that, as Craig says "the temporal series of events is a collection formed by successive addition"[139]. This, however, makes quite strong assumptions about the nature of time. In particular, Craig assumes that time is not continuous, growing forward from one instant to the next like a sprouting plant with no discrete 'steps' from one moment to the next. If this were the case, moments of time would not accumulate by a discrete process of addition, but rather by a continuous process of growth. This would entail either that time was composed of an infinite number of infinitesimal points, or that it was composed of a finite number of intervals existing independently and 'logically prior' to any divisions or points they might be divided into. As I argued previously, however, this latter possibility is simply incoherent. Thus, if Craig is to argue that time is formed of discrete moments accumulated by a process of addition, he must first provide an argument as to why time could not 'grow' continuously in the way just mentioned. The two main arguments that he provides in defence of this assumption is the 'grim reaper paradox', and the impossibility of the existence of an actual infinite, both of which I have already shown to be flawed. As such, I find that Craig has not provided sufficient reason to justify this crucial assumption that the temporal series of events is formed by successive addition, and so his second argument against the impossibility of an infinite past is unsuccessful.

Craig attempts to circumvent this problem by arguing that even if time does have the structure of the real numbers, nevertheless the series of past events is still formed by successive addition. He argues[140]:

> *"If we take, for example, the collection of past seconds in the history of the universe, such a collection has been formed by the successive addition of seconds, even if those seconds can themselves be divided into infinitely many sub-intervals."*

This response, however, clearly cannot be right, since if time increases continuously from one infinitesimal moment to the next, then intervals of the length of one second are not added all at once, but progressively 'grow' until they reach completion and the next second is begun. Thus, between one second and the next there has already been traversed an infinite successive of temporal instants. Indeed, if time does have the structure of the real numbers, then the number of instants in the interval of one second is actually the same as the number of instants from eternity past up to the present. It is completely arbitrary for Craig to divide time up into equally sized 'events' and claim that while infinite numbers of instants are possible within these 'events', the total number of such events must be finite. If time fundamentally 'grows' in a continuous fashion, then successive addition is simply not the appropriate framework to analyse the passage of events. Craig's analogy is inapplicable to the situation in which he applies it.

Craig also faces a problem with the language of this premise, since under his presentist ontology of time there is in fact no such thing as 'the temporal series of events'. The only event Craig believes to really exist is the present, all past events having ceased to exist when they ceased to be present. Thus, there simply is no real referent to which the phrase 'the temporal series of events' can apply. At best Craig could argue that this collection is an abstraction, something we could imagine in our minds as being the collection of all past events. This collection, however, neither exists in the mind-independent world, nor is it formed by successive addition, since when we imagine the set of all past events, we think of it all at once, but by thinking of each past event one at a time. As such, under Craig's own theory of time there simply is no 'temporal series of events' that has formed through successive addition. According to Craig, all that exists in the real world is the present, so there is only ever one real moment of time, never an infinite collection of temporal moments.

Given the foregoing considerations, I conclude that Craig has not adequately defended his premise that 'the temporal series of events is a collection formed by successive addition'. As such, even if it is impossible to form an infinite series by successive addition, it does not necessarily follow that the past must be finite, since Craig has not established that time operates by a process of successive addition. This concludes my discussion of Craig's philosophical arguments in defence of the premise that the universe began to exist. In the next section, I turn to the empirical evidence to which Craig appeals as establishing the beginning of the universe.

THERE IS POWERFUL EMPIRICAL EVIDENCE FOR A BEGINNING OF THE UNIVERSE

The Big Bang Theory

Craig argues that, in addition to the philosophical arguments for the beginning of the universe, there is also powerful scientific evidence for an absolute beginning. To understand Craig's argument, some initial background knowledge of cosmology is necessary. According to the Big Bang theory, which has been the dominant theory in cosmology since the 1960s, the universe began to develop from a hot, dense point about 13.7 billion years ago, since which time it has been expanding and cooling. The Big Bang theory is supported by a wide range of empirical evidence, including the rate of expansion of the universe, the presence of the cosmological microwave background radiation, and the relative abundance of hydrogen and helium throughout the universe. The details of this evidence are not important for our purposes; suffice it to say that such evidence has led to the theory being widely accepted as an accurate description of the development of our universe.

The Big Bang theory itself, however, is not actually a theory of the origin of the universe. The theory makes no claims as to what happened at the 'very beginning' or the 'moment of creation' itself, but rather describes the evolution of the universe from very early times. This limitation is a result of the fact that the current Big Bang theory is based on the hypothesis that the universe has been expanding throughout its existence. Extrapolated back into the past, this leads to a state where all matter and energy in the entire universe was compressed into a single infinitely small point at a finite time in the past. However, at the very high energies and small distances that become relevant in the early universe, our current physical theories break down. Specifically, the theory of quantum mechanics (which is applicable at very small scales) and the theory of general relativity (which is applicable when considering extremely high energies and masses) both simultaneously become applicable. This is a problem because these two physical theories, while highly successful in their respective domains, are fundamentally incompatible. Various attempts to combine quantum mechanics and general relativity have been proposed, for example the widely publicised string theories, but all face their own distinct problems, and none are currently widely accepted. Thus, the current state of knowledge concerning the very early universe is limited by our inability to make any significant predictions about the behaviour of the universe during its earliest period of existence, when quantum mechanics and general relativity were both important. This is why the Big Bang theory does not, strictly speaking, provide a theory of the actual beginning of the universe itself, only its evolution beginning at times when it becomes possible to apply current physical theories.

Craig is well aware of these limitations in current cosmological knowledge, and as such he has developed his empirical argument for the beginning of the universe by appealing to certain results which, he claims, show that the universe as a whole had an absolute beginning, irrespective of what exactly happened at the moment of the Big Bang. That is, Craig is primarily interested in appealing not to the Big Bang theory itself, but to certain other results which he claims support his contention that the universe could not have existed for an infinite period of time. His basic approach is as follows. First, Craig appeals to a particular cosmological theorem named after its originators as the Borde-Vilenkin-Guth theorem (or Borde-Guth-Vilenkin theorem). Craig argues that this theorem proves that, under certain conditions, the universe must have had an absolute beginning regardless of what occurred at the moment of the Big Bang. Second, Craig considers the various assumptions that this theorem relies upon, successively arguing that various attempts to describe the early universe without these assumptions either fail, or still lead to an absolute beginning. Craig thus concludes that the Borde-Vilenkin-Guth theorem provides strong scientific support for his premise that the universe began to exist. Note that Craig does not argue that his theorem proves that God exists, only that it lends support for a key premise in his argument for the existence of God. In the following sections I will critically examine Craig's claims, arguing that the Borde-Vilenkin-Guth fails to provide any significant evidence in favour of Craig's contention that the universe began to exist.

The Borde-Vilenkin-Guth Theorem

Craig argues that the Borde-Vilenkin-Guth theorem provides strong evidence that the universe, or indeed the multiverse (if such a thing exists), had an absolute beginning. Indeed, in recent debates and publications this theorem has featured very prominently in Craig's presentation of his kalam cosmological argument. Given its importance, I will take some time to describe carefully what the theorem says. The original paper presenting the theorem is very short, and I encourage any readers with even basic knowledge of undergraduate-level maths and physics to read it for themselves. Here I will do my best to explain the theorem in simple terms. Taken from the paper itself, the result that Borde, Vilenkin, and Guth prove is that[141]:

> *"Null and timelike geodesics are, in general, past-incomplete in inflationary models... provided only that the averaged expansion condition... holds along these past-directed geodesics."*

Let me define some of the jargon in this statement. A geodesic is simply the shortest line between two points on a curved surface. Geodesics are important in cosmology because the general theory of relativity holds that light and matter follow geodesic paths (i.e. the shortest route) in curved four-dimensional spacetime. Different types of objects follow different types of geodesics, with photons (i.e. light) travelling along what are called null-geodesics. In addition to describing the paths that objects travel along, geodesics can also be used to describe the distance between two points in spacetime. Loosely speaking, two events at different points in time are said to be separated by a timelike geodesic. A geodesic is said to be 'past-incomplete' if it is not infinitely long in the past direction. Thus, the statement 'timelike geodesics are past-incomplete' means essentially that the time interval between the present and any event in the past must always be finite. The 'averaged expansion condition' refers to the condition of the theorem, which is that it only applies when the universe is expanding throughout its existence on average, as is generally thought to be the case in most modern cosmologies (or 'inflationary models' as they are called in the quote).

To summarise, the Borde-Vilenkin-Guth theorem states that tracing every time path in the universe back into the past will always eventually terminate at some beginning, with no infinitely long time paths being possible (see figure 5 for a diagrammatic representation of this idea). This applies so long as the universe is on average expanding over its history, which is the contemporary mainstream view in cosmology. As such, there is no possible way that an expanding universe (or multiverse) could be infinitely old in the past.

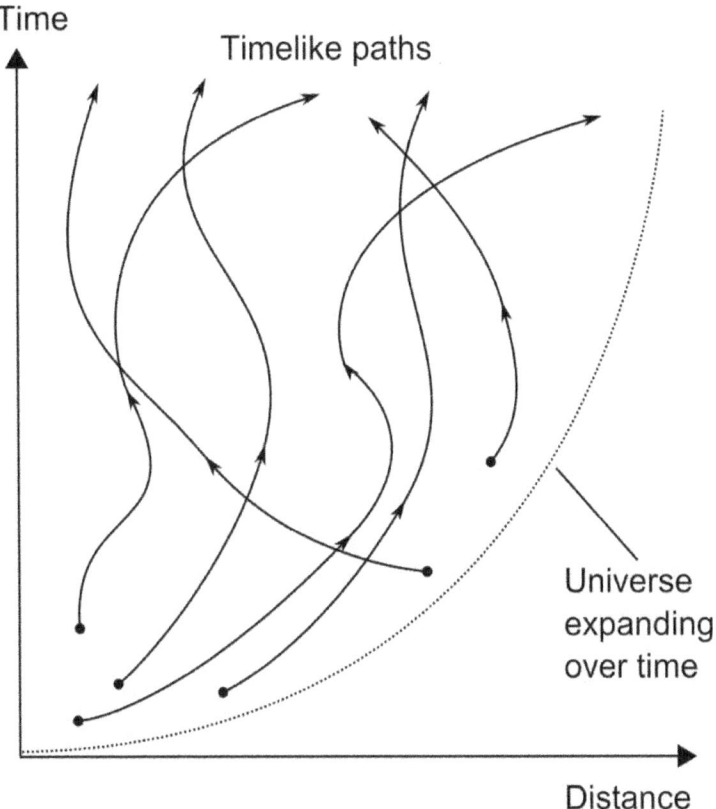

Figure 5. This diagram shows various timelike paths through spacetime, with all three spatial dimensions represented as a single dimension along the horizontal axis, and time shown on the vertical axis. The expansion of the universe over time is indicated by the dotted curve on the right. The Borde-Vilenkin-Guth theorem states that all such paths must terminate after tracing them back a finite length (as shown by the black circles), and so cannot extend infinitely far into the past.

On the relevance of the theorem for the kalam cosmological argument, Craig says[142]:

> "*The Borde-Guth-Vilenkin theorem proves that classical spacetime, under a single, very general condition, cannot be extended to past infinity but must reach a boundary at some time in the*

> *finite past. Now either there was something on the other side of that boundary or not. If not, then that boundary just is the beginning of the universe. If there was something on the other side, then it will be a region described by the yet to be discovered theory of quantum gravity. In that case, Vilenkin says, it will be the beginning of the universe. Either way, the universe began to exist."*

What Craig does not seem to realise, however, is that his own metaphysical commitments preclude him from using the fact that 'timelike geodesics are past-incomplete' (which is what the theorem proves) to infer 'the universe had an absolute beginning a finite time in the past' (which is what he wants to show). These two statements are not equivalent: the first refers to a spacetime interval, and the second refers to a period of duration of metaphysical time. In order for Craig's desired conclusion to follow, he would need to assume that the spacetime intervals described in the theorem are in fact the same thing as the metaphysical time he talks about in his philosophical writing. At the very least, he must argue that the finitude of the one implies the finitude of the other, though if the two descriptions of time do not refer to the same thing it is unclear why this should be the case.

This position that there is a close connection between physical and metaphysical time, however, stands in stark tension with Craig's remarks about the philosophy of time in his other published works. Craig has repeatedly and emphatically emphasised the importance of distinguishing the concept of time in physics (especially relativity theory) from the conception of time he appeals to in his philosophical arguments. Thus, he emphasises the difference between "physical time and space (clock and rod measurements) and metaphysical time and space (ontological time and space independent of physical measures thereof)"[143]. In particular, he argues that one should[144]:

> *"Distinguish metaphysical time from physical or clock time and maintain that while the former is (tensed) in nature, the latter is a bare abstraction therefrom, useful for scientific purposes and quite possibly (tenseless) in character, the element of becoming having been abstracted out."*

Craig is very sceptical about the relevance of findings about physical time to philosophy, stating that "(special relativity) is a theory about physical time and space and says nothing about the nature of metaphysical time and space"[145], and "we must not forget that relativity theory concerns physical time only, not metaphysical time."[146] This seems to present Craig with a major problem – if relativity theory describes physical time only and says 'nothing' about metaphysical time, then how can Craig infer that past metaphysical time is finite from a result about the finitude of past physical time? Indeed, Craig explicitly acknowledges the fact that a beginning in one type of time does not imply a beginning in the other[147]:

"If we draw a distinction between metaphysical time and physical time as Newton did, it is quite evident that a beginning of the latter does not imply a beginning of the former. God in metaphysical time could be quite active prior to creation (perhaps creating angelic realms) and could bring physical space and time into being after having existed without their being co-existent with Him."

In discussing the various notions of time used in different fields of physical inquiry (thermodynamics, special relativity, general relativity, etc), Craig notes the many differences in properties these notions have from each other and from time as used in natural language, and as a result concludes[148]:

"It is difficult to resist the conclusion that all of these operationally defined 'times' are not really time at all, but just various measures of time suitable for their respective fields of inquiry."

In regard to the spacetime manifold that is the subject of special and general relativity, Craig says[149]:

"Minkowski's four-dimensional, mathematical space serves as a convenient calculational and diagrammatical aid... but says absolutely nothing about ontology... the four-dimensional continuum should therefore be regarded as a useful tool, and not as a physical 'reality'... Minkowski's spacetime is at best a representation of physical time and space as described by the

Unreasonable Faith

> *equations of (special relativity) and cannot pretend to imply a four-dimensional ontology."*

All of this then raises the question as to what metaphysical significance Craig can place on the Borde-Vilenkin-Guth theorem. It seems impossible for Craig to appeal to the Borde-Vilenkin-Guth theorem as establishing anything of significance about the origin of the universe or the finitude of time if he believes physical time is distinct from metaphysical time, and the operationalised 'times' used in physics are not really time at all. At the very most, all the theorem shows is that one measure of physical time used in one particular theory, which Craig thinks should be interpreted instrumentally anyway, must have a beginning. To infer from this that the universe therefore must actually have an absolute beginning is simply impossible given Craig's views about time. Craig's inconsistent attitude about the philosophical implications of physical theories has been noted by Mauro Dorato, who in a review of Craig's book *Time and the Metaphysics of Relativity* states that[150]:

> *"(Craig) seems to oscillate between two contrasting philosophical positions. According to the first, 'relativity physics... is not necessarily saying anything that is relevant for the metaphysician', a claim that tends to be advanced whenever evidence coming from physics is against his metaphysical views. The second position is that physics 'confirms' certain metaphysical and theological views over others, a claim that is put forth whenever evidence for the existence of a privileged frame (coming for instance from cosmic time or quantum non-locality) seems more reassuring. If this impression is well-founded, Craig's book is essentially guided by an apologetic attempt and opportunistically uses physics and metaphysics for his purpose."*

The problem goes beyond the issue of interpretation of physical time and its role in scientific theories, because the way time is treated in the Borde-Vilenkin-Guth theorem is totally at odds with Craig's views about the nature of time. In the paper, time is treated as a continuous variable that can be integrated over. This makes no sense at all under Craig's presentism, since he does not believe time has the structure of real numbers, nor does he believe that different moments of time co-exist in a way that it would make sense to sum (integrate) over them. Craig believes that time consists of a series of non-metrical intervals of 'present', one constantly replacing the other as the objective temporal progression of time passes on, as per the tensed notion of objective becoming. Given this understanding, it is simply absurd to integrate over a timelike geodesic to produce a result for the maximum possible length of a proper time interval. Such a result is metaphysically meaningless given that time is not continuous and consists of non-metrical present moments. Such a result might have instrumental value, but given Craig's commitments it is ontologically totally confused and uninterpretable. Thus, given Craig's own arguments, the Borde-Vilenkin-Guth theorem is absolutely worthless in establishing the absolute ontological beginning of the universe.

In response to Graham Oppy[151] raising the possibility of some sort of mathematically-describable metaphysical time existing prior to the beginning of physical time, Craig responds[152]:

"I must confess that I have no idea at all what Oppy is talking about. Such a purely mathematical extension is physically impossible, so that the entities of that prior regime are presumably abstract objects which cannot by their very nature stand in causal series. In any case, Oppy's postulation of a prior regime of temporally ordered contingent causes is an exercise in metaphysics, and to advert to metaphysics at this point just is to admit that the scientific evidence supports (the absolute beginning of the universe)."

This response is completely inadequate, since what Oppy is talking about is fundamentally the same as what Craig himself has spoken at length about in the passages I quoted above, namely that what science has to say about physical time has little to no bearing on metaphysical time, and that therefore the beginning of one need not imply the beginning of the other. To advert to metaphysics is not, as Craig says, to admit that the scientific evidence supports an absolute beginning of time, but rather to simply *agree with Craig himself* in his assertion that scientific findings have no necessary bearing on the beginning metaphysical time.

Closed timelike curves

One interesting way in which the absolute beginning of the cosmos could be avoided in spite of the Borde-Guth-Vilenkin theorem is through the existence of what are called closed timelike curves (CTCs)[153]. Though the details are complex, the essential idea is that certain solutions of the equations of general relativity permit models in which the timeline loops back upon itself to allow the universe, in Gott and Li's words, "to become its own mother"[154]. One problem with such proposals is that they allow for the possibility of time travel, which raises a host of philosophical and physical problems. Following a brief analysis Craig concludes[155]:

> *"While it is true that no one has been able definitively to rule out CTCs, the evidentiary burden lies upon those defending the viability of such spacetimes and models predicated upon their reality."*

Once again, Craig shifts the burden of proof. Since *he* is making the claim that the universe began to exist, and in particular that this claim is supported by empirical evidence such as the Borde-Guth-Vilenkin theorem, it is incumbent upon *him* to provide reasons to reject proposed models like closed timelike curves which cast doubt on his desired conclusion. Craig does argue that these models cannot actually describe the real world, calling them "metaphysically absurd"[156] as a result of the various time travel paradoxes they potentially permit. More importantly, however, closed time loops are inconsistent with Craig's presentist philosophy of time, since once the present ceases to exist it cannot ever return to being present by forming a loop in time. Thus, although I regard the existence of closed timeline curves as an open theoretical question, their existence is not especially important in the evaluation of Craig's argument. For the kalam cosmological argument to succeed, the tensed theory of time must be correct, in which case the possibility of closed timelike curves is ruled out automatically on purely philosophical grounds.

Quantum Cosmology

In addition to its explicit assumption of a universe that is an average expanding, the Borde-Vilenkin-Guth theorem also implicitly depends upon the ability to describe the universe in terms of a curved spacetime manifold, where geodesics and other essential concepts can be meaningfully defined. As noted previously, however, the validity of such approaches breaks down at very early times of the universe when the effects of quantum mechanics become important. As Sean Carroll explains, this means that the theorem in effect states that the part of the universe we can describe classically is past-incomplete[157]. It remains possible, therefore, that a beginning could be circumvented by some model of the universe incorporating the effects of quantum mechanics.

Vilenkin and Hawking have both proposed quantum models by which the universe is posited to have come into being as a result of a quantum fluctuation. Craig argues that such models cannot avoid an ultimate beginning because "the initial metastable state can have had only a finite lifetime"[158]. A metastable state is one that is only stable temporarily, but like an ornament perched precariously on a high shelf, is eventually expected to fall (or 'decay') into a lower, more stable energy state. Craig's argument is that unstable quantum states always have a finite lifetime, since if there is any non-zero probability of the fluctuation occurring, this initial metastable state can only have a finite lifetime. As such, even if the universe did form as a result of some quantum fluctuation from an unstable initial state, this metastable state cannot have existed for an infinite period of time, so the initial fluctuation causing the beginning of the universe must have occurred at a finite time in the past.

One problem with this response is that the concept of classical time is not well defined in quantum scenarios such as this, and so as Vilenkin says "we do not know what the right questions are"[159]. Thus, it is premature of Craig to say that quantum states must have a finite lifetime since we can't even yet construct a clear definition of what a 'lifetime' might mean in such contexts. A second problem with Craig's argument is that it is theoretically possible for randomly decaying metastable states to have a finite lifetime. Consider, for instance, the normal distribution with its characteristic bell curve shape (figure 6). If we regard the horizontal axis as representing time, then the probability of an event occurring between negative infinity and zero time is equal to exactly half. Strictly speaking, an event is only guaranteed to occur after an infinitely long interval if its probability of occurring over some finite interval is constant with respect to the time parameter, as occurs for example in the uniform distribution. If it were possible to define some sort of time parameter during which a quantum state could exist and if the probably of decay increased over time in accordance with the normal distribution, or some similar function, then it would be possible for the metastable quantum state to exist for an infinite amount of time. A time-variable probability of decay is unusual, and it is true that we have no knowledge in current physical theories of a process that would work in this way. However, Craig is arguing that the universe *must* have had an absolute beginning, and so it is incumbent upon him to show that other possibilities are ruled out. Since we truly have no idea what physics govern this very early period of the universe, it seems grossly premature for Craig to claim that a quantum fluctuation from a metastable state could not explain the origin of the universe.

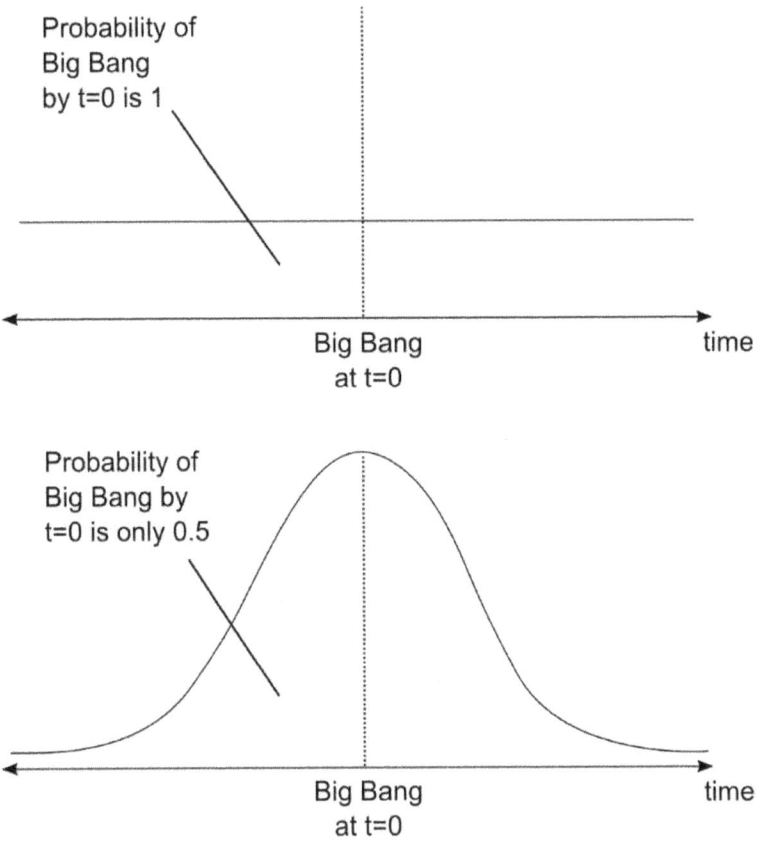

Figure 6. For a decay process with a constant probability over time (top), the probability of a decay occurring at some time during the infinitely long interval $-\infty < t < 0$ is equal to 1, and so as Craig says is certain to occur. For a decay process with a probability that increases over time in accordance with a normal bell curve distribution, however, the probability of decay occurring during the infinitely long interval $-\infty < t < 0$ is only equal to 0.5.

Craig may instead argue that such a quantum fluctuation is *possible*, but given its unusual properties and the lack of precedent for such a mechanism, it is not a very good explanation for the origin of the universe. This objection is only relevant, however, if Craig can provide a *more* plausible explanation for the origin of the universe that does not appeal to unusual or unprecedented mechanisms. As I argue in the discussion of premise four, however, Craig's proposal appeals to an immaterial mind and the theory of agent causation, both of which are completely alien to modern scientific theory, and even more unusual and unprecedented than the quantum fluctuation explanation. Also, the fact that we lack a rigorous scientific theory for such a decay process is irrelevant, since here I am simply raising the possibility in a philosophical context, as an alternative to Craig's equally non-scientific, philosophical explanation of an immaterial mind as the cause of the universe.

The Second Law of Thermodynamics

In addition to the cosmological evidence for the beginning of the universe, Craig also argues that the second law of thermodynamics provides strong empirical evidence that the universe began to exist at a finite time in the past. To understand Craig's argument, it is necessary to understand the concept of entropy. In physics, entropy is a measure of the number of microscopic states that a given macroscopic system can be arranged in, and is often loosely described as a measure of 'disorder'. There are, for instance, a vast number of different ways in which the gas molecules in the air could be arranged so as to fill evenly the space of my study, and thus the macroscopic state of 'the air in my study is evenly disbursed throughout the room' has relatively high entropy. By contrast, there are many fewer ways in which all the air molecules could be crowded together in one corner of the room, since each is now restricted to a corner of the room instead of being able to be at any point in the room. As such, the macroscopic state of 'all the air in my study is bunched in one corner of the room' has very low entropy.

The second law of thermodynamics is a key principle of physics which states that in a closed system (that is, one with no external energy input), entropy always increases over time. Since the universe is usually considered to be a closed system (meaning there is no energy input from outside the universe), it follows that entropy should increase over time in the universe as a whole. As such, Craig argues that an infinitely old universe should feature maximally high levels of entropy, such that the universe should now be in a "cold, dark, dilute, and lifeless state"[160]. That is, since entropy increases over time, if the universe had been around for an infinite amount of time, there should be no further possible ways in which entropy could still be increased, as every possible event that could increase entropy would already have occurred. This, however, is not the way we observe the universe to be, since we observe many processes involving entropy reduction that are still ongoing, such as the formation of stars, the gravitational collapse of galactic clusters, and the chemical reactions that support life. Craig therefore concludes that since entropy isn't at a maximum state, the universe cannot be infinitely old, and hence the universe must have had an absolute beginning – a finite time in the past.

There are two main problems with this argument. First, Craig's argument assumes that the universe is a closed system, and hence there is no external source of energy outside the universe. Certainly this is true under naturalism, since the universe (in this context) is simply the totality of all physical things that exist in spacetime. However, Craig has not established that naturalism is the only possible alternative to theism. There may be some other form of non-physical entity which exists outside the universe providing an external source of energy, or through some other means operates to prevent the continual increase in entropy. Since Craig is attempting to argue that the universe had a beginning, he needs to provide a reason for rejecting this possibility if his appeal to the second law of thermodynamics is to work in the way he intends. To put it another way, all Craig's appeal to the second law of thermodynamics could potentially show is that naturalism (and hence a closed universe) is inconsistent with an infinitely old universe. It does not therefore follow that the universe began to exist, because he does not consider any other non-natural explanations for the present non-maximal entropy state of the universe.

The second major problem with Craig's argument is that he assumes that the universe is not in a maximal entropy state. Certainly, it is clear that the *observable universe* is not in a maximal entropy state, for as mentioned above we observe many processes still operating that increase entropy. However, it does not follow that the universe *as a whole* (i.e. the totality of physical existence) cannot be in a maximum entropy state. Our observable universe could be part of a spontaneous fluctuation away from the overall equilibrium maximum entropy state of the universe as a whole. This general possibility has been considered by a number of cosmologists and is the subject of ongoing research. Craig has argued that various particular models to explain how this fluctuation could come about face various practical problems. The fact that we have not yet established a complete model of how such a process of fluctuation could occur, however, does not imply that such a process could not have occurred, especially given how relatively new such theorising is, and how little empirical data is available to constrain such theories. For Craig's argument to work, he must make the inference that because the part of the universe we observe is not in a maximal entropy state, we should conclude that the universe as a whole is also not in such a state. Such an inference, however, extrapolates far beyond the empirical evidence we currently have, and requires a strong claim about matters which are still highly uncertain and poorly understood.

Craig may respond that the probability of our observable universe having begun as a random fluctuation from a pre-existing universe in a state of maximal entropy is so exceptionally low that this would be effectively impossible. Undoubtedly, it is true that the initial entropy of the very early universe was so low that it would be effectively impossible for events like this to occur within our observable universe. To determine how likely such an event would be to occur in the universe as a whole, however, we would need to know the size of the entire universe. While the size of the observable universe is known, we have no idea how large the universe as a whole may be – indeed it may be infinite in extent. As such, we simply do not know how often we should expect fluctuations of the size of our observable universe to occur in the universe as a whole, and therefore we cannot conclude that a fluctuation of this size is too improbable to have occurred. There is also a more technical problem with this response, relating to an assumption in entropy probability calculations that all microstates are equally probable. This assumption has been successful when applied within our observable universe, but since it is only an assumption we cannot simply extrapolate its application to the universe as a whole with any confidence that it will still remain valid. As a result of these considerations, I conclude that while the reason for the low-entropy state of the observable universe is an open question in contemporary cosmology, I think that Craig is grossly premature in arguing that we must infer that the explanation is that the universe as a whole must have had an absolute beginning.

Finally, it should also be noted that as with Craig's appeal to the Borde-Vilenkin-Guth theorem, the second law of thermodynamics at best shows that the *physical* universe began to exist, but says nothing about whatever nonphysical events or causes may have proceeded the beginning of physical time and space. While Craig dismisses such a distinction as "altogether mysterious," this response is utterly bizarre given that Craig himself discusses this distinction at length[161], as I have shown previously. Overall, while I actually find Craig's appeal to the second law of thermodynamics to be the strongest of all his arguments for a beginning of the universe, it is still not nearly as conclusive an argument as Craig asserts.

SUMMARY

I do not believe that Craig has succeeded in showing that the universe must have had an absolute beginning. His argument against the impossibility of an actual infinite is largely based upon intuitions about the absurdity of Hilbert's hotel, intuitions which many others who consider the scenario do not share. This argument is furthermore fatally undermined by the fact that Craig's presentist philosophy of time prevents him from consistently asserting both that the past is an actual infinite without implying that the future is also an actual infinite. Craig's second philosophical argument that an actual infinite cannot be formed by successive addition is similarly unpersuasive in its appeals to allegedly absurd situations, and also stands in tension with his presentist philosophy of time. The appeal to scientific evidence is doomed to failure as a result of Craig's own insistence that the physical time studied by science can tell us nothing useful about the metaphysical time that he is concerned with in his arguments, in addition to making various other assumptions in areas such as quantum cosmology where our knowledge is lacking and uncertainty is still great. Given all these considerations, I conclude that Craig has failed to show that the universe had an absolute beginning.

PREMISE THREE: EVERYTHING THAT BEGINS TO EXIST HAS A CAUSE

The third key premise of Craig's extended kalam cosmological argument is 'everything that begins to exist has a cause'. This is an essential premise because Craig is seeking to establish a cause of the beginning of the universe that is transcendent (i.e. outside the universe). For such a cause to exist, it is not enough simply for the universe to have a beginning – that beginning must also have a cause outside the universe.

Craig presents three arguments to defend this premise:

- 'Nothing comes from nothing' is a self-evident metaphysical principle.
- If something can come from nothing, why only universes?
- This principle is verified by extensive experiential examples.

In some of his more recent debates, Craig has weakened this premise to simply state that 'if the universe began to exist, it had a cause'. This weaker principle is easier for Craig to defend, and also is sufficient for his argument since it is not irrelevant if (for example) certain subatomic particles can begin to exist without a cause, which may be the case under certain interpretations of quantum mechanics. Since the arguments Craig presents in defence of this weaker version of premise three are essentially the same as those he presents in defence of the stronger form, in this section I will simply discuss the stronger form of the argument. I will, however, avoid discussion of whether or not quantum events can be uncaused, which Craig and I both agree is largely irrelevant to the question of whether the universe as a whole could have begun without a cause.

James Fodor

THAT NOTHING COMES FROM NOTHING IS A BASIC METAPHYSICAL PRINCIPLE

On Popping Out of Nothing

Craig thinks that it is profoundly obvious that it is not possible for something to come from nothing. Regarding this principle he declares that it "is rooted in the metaphysical intuition that something cannot come into being from nothing"[162]. Similarly, he says that it is simply ridiculous to suggest that anything could "just pop into being uncaused out of nothing." While I agree with Craig that the notion of something 'popping into being from nothing' is absurd, I believe that in using this sort of language Craig is describing the situation in a misleading manner. In particular, I do not believe it is correct to assert that denying that 'everything that begins to exist has a cause' entails affirming that 'things can pop into being uncaused out of nothing'.

First, it is not claimed that the universe 'popped' into being. The word 'pop' implies there was some void or space into which a universe is able to 'pop'. One is asked to imagine a vast chasm which is initially empty and into which the universe 'pops'. This, however, runs contrary to the notion that there is nothing at all – not even a space or void – that existed outside of the universe into which it could 'pop'. The universe did not 'pop into' anything; it simply began at a finite time in the past. The other problematic aspect of Craig's formulation of the phrase 'out of nothing' is the implication that there was a time before the beginning of the universe. The concept of 'popping' only makes sense if the 'pop' is considered in relation to some prior time of stillness, the stillness then being disturbed in the subsequent 'pop'. This characterisation of the beginning of the universe, however, is misleading because *time itself* only began with the beginning of the universe, so there was no time 'before' the universe existed. There was no 'popping into existence', just a beginning, and no 'coming from nothing', simply an absence of any cause. Craig might object that the absence of a cause is just what he means by 'popping into being out of nothing', however my point is precisely that this way of phrasing it is misleading. Craig uses this phrase because it is obviously absurd to say that something can 'pop into being from nothing', even though (as I have just argued) the uncaused beginning of the universe is not equivalent to this. Even Craig seems to tacitly acknowledge the inadequacy of this language when he says[163]:

> "Locutions like x's 'popping into existence' or 'springing into existence' were attempts on my part to express in ordinary language the objective reality of temporal becoming. Again, it just seems to me obvious that things do not begin to exist in this sense without a cause."

Another phrase that Craig uses is 'being coming from non-being'. For example, he says[164]:

> "We are asking whether the whole of being could come out of non-being; and here a negative answer seems obvious."

Once again, however, in using such language Craig is misconstruing the question. The issue is not whether being can 'come from' non-being. As Craig says, such a notion is absurd. Indeed, I would go further and say it does not even make sense to say that being (or anything at all) can 'come from' non-being, for the use of the phrase 'come from' implies the existence of something out of which something else can come, much as the word 'pop' implies something into which a thing can pop. Non-being is not some entity with minimal properties (e.g. it is not a cosmic vacuum); it is the complete nonexistence of anything at all. To say that the universe 'came from' non-being would be to say that there was a state of non-being which pertained before the universe came into being, a state which then led to (or caused) the beginning of the universe. But this is absurd because there was no state before the beginning of the universe: no time, no existence, and no causes – nothing at all. Craig himself supports this conception of non-being when he says[165]:

> "If absolutely nothing existed prior to the Big Bang-no matter, no energy, no space, no time, no deity – then it seems impossible that anything should begin to exist."

Craig seems to be imagining an absolute void of nothingness existing, and then the universe coming (or 'popping' as he says) into existence at the very beginning of time. Of course, this is an absurd picture, but the absurdity results from the mischaracterisation of the situation, not the absence of a cause. A causeless beginning does not imply a 'coming from nothing' since the latter, as I have argued, implies a something that the universe came from, and a prior state to which the 'coming' refers, neither of which pertain to this case.

Considering the question in this way, it becomes much less clear to me what is so absurd about space and time beginning to exist a finite time ago with no antecedent cause. On this understanding, the universe simply 'began', starting off in motion. There was no space, no time, no causation, nothing whatsoever 'before' this event. There was no prior empty or void state of non-being that the universe 'came from'. The hypothesis is simply that *at the very beginning of time, the universe was already there*. No cause was needed for the existence of the universe at the very beginning of time. This is in no way inconsistent with the process of objective temporal becoming, because this process implies only that one moment of time goes out of existence bringing the next moment into existence. Contrary to what Craig says, it does not imply that the very first moment of time must have come into existence from a prior void of nothingness. Rather, the initial moment of time simply *started off as existing*, being the very first stage in the process of temporal becoming. Craig speaks as if there must have been a time before when it didn't exist, but that is not what is being claimed. Once again, all that is being claimed is that at the very beginning when time began, the universe existed without cause. At least to me, this does not seem an obviously absurd possibility. Much of the absurdity derives from Craig's misleading phrasing of the situation in terms of 'popping' and being 'coming from' nonbeing. Nothing of the sort could have happened, for there was no 'prior state' into which the universe could 'pop', no antecedent state of non-being that 'gave rise' to the universe. At the beginning of time, the universe was just *already there*.

'Beginning to Exist' and the Tensed Theory of Time

Craig has stated that when he says something 'begins to exist', what he really means is the following[166]:

> "x comes into being at t ≡ x exists at t; t is either the first time at which x exists or is separated from any time t*<t at which x existed by a non-degenerate, temporal interval; and x's existing at t is a tensed fact."

We can summarise this by saying 'anything that begins to exist in the sense of a tensed fact has a cause'. I have already discussed at length Craig's arguments in favour of the tensed theory of time, concluding that they are unsound, and that in fact a tenseless theory of time represents our best candidate for a model of time. In this case, Craig's third premise becomes irrelevant since nothing 'begins to exist' in this tensed manner. However, even if my arguments against the tensed theory of time fail, we can actually use Craig's very own third premise to construct an argument against the tensed theory. Such an argument would look something like the following:

- Premise one: Everything that begins to exist in a tensed-sense has a cause.
- Premise two: The universe had no cause.
- Conclusion: The universe did not begin to exist in a tensed-sense.

I am not saying that this argument should be rationally compelling to all readers, since I cannot give conclusive arguments in defence of premise two. Rather, my point is to show that incorporating the tensed theory of time into the very meaning of 'beginning to exist' renders it possible to use Craig's premise that 'everything that beings to exist has a cause' as a *reductio ad absurdum* against the tensed theory of time. In other words, if we think that assuming the truth of the tensed theory of time leads to implausible conclusions about what must happen at the beginning of time (for example if we regard transcendent causes as implausible), then that constitutes a reason for rejecting the tensed theory of time itself. Building in the very notion of the tensed theory of time into the definition of 'beings to exist', therefore, substantially weakens the plausibility of the premise that the universe 'began to exist'.

James Fodor

The Reliability of Metaphysical Intuitions

Craig argues that[167]:

> *"Our conviction of the truth of the causal principle is not based upon an inductive survey of existents in spacetime, but rather upon the metaphysical intuition that something cannot come out of nothing."*

Craig's appeal to metaphysical intuition and notions that he regards as 'obvious', however, is deeply problematic when it comes to considering the origin of the universe. This is because these intuitions are formed with reference to cases and scenarios which all involve events that are temporal and occur during time. Extrapolating this to the beginning of time itself seems to represent, at the very least, a considerable leap concerning which we should not accord a high degree of confidence. Certainly, many capable philosophers who have considered this argument do not share Craig's intuition. This does not prove that Craig is wrong, but I believe it should at the very least temper one's confidence in such intuitions. Metaphysical intuitions, after all, have a very poor track record of reliability in the history of philosophy and science, as the near universal agreement with Aristotle's intuition that the Earth was stationary (among many other examples) clearly demonstrates.

These considerations notwithstanding, Craig thinks that we *can* be confident in such extrapolation of our intuitions. He argues[168]:

> *"What is the relevant difference between something's coming into existence within time and something's coming into existence at the beginning to time? If the universe could not come into existence uncaused at t, where t is preceded by earlier moments of time, why think that if we were to annihilate all moments earlier than t, then the universe could come into existence uncaused at t? How could the existence of moments earlier than an uncaused event be of any possible relevance to the occurrence of that event? Indeed, given a dynamic or tensed view of time, every moment of time is a fresh beginning, qualitatively indistinguishable from a first moment of time, for when any moment is present, earlier moments have passed away and do not exist.*

Thus, if the universe could exist uncaused at a first moment of time, it could exist uncaused at any moment of time."

This response is mistaken on at least two grounds. First, since time comes into existence with the universe (as Craig himself thinks is the case), then assuming that there was a first moment of time, it is logically impossible for this first moment to occur at any time other than $t = 0$. To say otherwise would be to assert that time (and thus the universe) began to exist *after* the beginning of time (i.e. after $t = 0$), which is logically contradictory. This fact alone constitutes a very important difference between the universe beginning to exist at the beginning of time, and something within the universe beginning to exist in time.

Second, it is obviously incorrect to say that under the tensed theory of time every moment of time is a 'fresh beginning, qualitatively indistinguishable from the first moment of time'. If this were true, then literally everything that begins to exist would come into existence without a cause. Since each moment of time would constitute an entirely new beginning unconnected to any previous moments of time, it follows that anything that existed at any moment of time would have simply sprung into existence totally uncaused. Obviously this is false; each moment in time exerts a causal influence upon the next moment in time, thus providing a means by which different moments in time are casually related to each other and hence explaining the continuity of the world – this is why things don't just appear at one moment and disappear in the next for no reason. I also note that Craig's argument here seems to imply that no object or person persists over time, with everything in some sense forged anew at each moment of time – this contradicts Craig's belief in the persistence of the soul. Given these considerations, it becomes quite obvious how the first moment in time is distinct: it bears causal relations to the future, but not to the past, for there is no past relative to that first moment. The very first instant of time, lacking any causal effects exerted by (or connections to) previous moments of time, is thereby distinct in a very important way. This is why it is plausible that the first moment of time, and the first moment alone, could have begun to exist. As such, I conclude that there are very significant and pertinent differences between the beginning of time as a whole and the beginning of things within time, and as such we should exercise considerable caution in extrapolating intuitions developed from the latter and applying them to reasoning about the former.

IF UNIVERSES COULD COME FROM NOTHING THEN SO COULD ANYTHING

Craig argues that if universes can come into being without a cause, then there is no reason why *anything* shouldn't come into existence without a cause. He writes[169]:

> "Second, if things really could come into being uncaused out of nothing, then it becomes inexplicable why just anything or everything does not come into existence uncaused from nothing. Why do bicycles and Beethoven and root beer not pop into being from nothing? Why is it only universes that can come into being from nothing? What makes nothingness so discriminatory?"

Here Craig repeats his mistake of speaking of nothingness as if it were a substance. The hypothesis in question is not that the universe 'came from nothing' as if 'nothing' was some sort of entity in its own right. Rather, the hypothesis is that the universe began without a cause. Thus, rather than ask 'why is it that only universes can come from nothing?', a better way of phrasing this question is 'why is it that if the universe was able to begin to exist without a cause, entities like bicycles and Beethoven cannot also begin to exist without a cause?' It seems, however, that there is a very obvious answer at hand. Namely, that if something is to begin without a cause, it surely must be the sort of thing that is not *already known* to have specific causes of its coming into being. We already know that bicycles are brought into existence by people making them, that life forms derive from earlier forms of life, that planets form from collapsing clouds of dust and gas, and so on. Since we already know that all of these things require particular causes to be brought into existence, it is not possible for them to begin to exist without a cause. Very simply, Craig is arguing that if *some* entity can begin without a cause, then *any* entity must be capable of so doing. But this simply is a fallacy – there is no reason why only certain types of entities (namely those that do not require one) could begin to exist without a cause. Bicycles and Beethoven are obviously not these sorts of entities.

Wes Morriston ably expresses this objection as follows[170]:

> "We know where tigers and such come from, and that just isn't the way it happens. Now contrast the situation with regard to the beginning of time and the universe. There is no familiar law-governed context for it, precisely because there is nothing (read, 'there is not anything') prior to such a beginning. We have no experience of the origin of worlds to tell us that worlds don't come into existence like that. We don't even have experience of the coming into being of anything remotely analogous to the 'initial singularity' that figures in the big bang theory of the origin of the universe. The intuitive absurdity of tigers and the like popping into existence out of nowhere does not entitle us to draw quick and easy inferences about the beginning of the whole natural order."

Craig's response to this objection is to argue that if causation "derives solely from the causal powers and dispositions of things that actually exist" then there cannot be any "constraint placed on things' springing uncaused out of nothingness into being. After all, there is nothing there to be constrained"[171]. Here Craig speaks as if his opponents imagine that 'nothingness' has some sort of power or impetus to bring into being anything and everything that it possibly could, and only the existence of some causal process is able to act as a 'constraint' to stop this from happening. This, however, is *exactly the opposite* of what is being argued. Rather, the idea is that entities like bicycles and tigers *only* come into being when the necessary and sufficient causal prerequisites are present; absent such causes, it is *impossible* for them to come into being. Nothing needs to exist to 'constrain' them from coming into being out of nothingness; rather certain things need to be present in order to cause them to come into being. The universe as a whole, by contrast, is plausibly not an entity of this sort. The claim is therefore that it may be possible for universes (or quantum singularities that go on to bring universes into existence) to come into being without a cause. Craig thinks this is implausible, asking[172]:

> "Why is it that only a certain kind of particle, say, can come into being uncaused at the first moment of time? Obviously, we cannot say that nothingness has a peculiar disposition to

producing such particles, as so saying reifies nothingness and invests it with properties."

Yet again, Craig misses the point that it is not a property of 'nothingness' by which only certain kinds of entities can come into existence without a cause. Rather, it is simply that these entities do not require the specific causal prerequisites to come into being that most entities do. In other words, most things require specific causes to make them come into being. Quantum singularities (or similar) that mark the beginning of the universe, however, plausibly *do not require such causes*, and thus are able to come into being uncaused. This is purely a fact about certain types of entities, not about the 'discerning powers of nothingness'.

Craig's final response to this argument clearly manifests his inconsistent standards[173]:

"What we want to know is why the entities have these odd essential properties, which are, after all, not qualities of the entities in question but more like arbitrarily asserted predications."

The naturalist, however, can plausibly say precisely the same thing of Craig's appeal to God as an uncaused first cause. Why does God have these odd essential properties? Craig's answer is, presumably, because they are essential to his nature. Yet this is exactly what the naturalist says of the nature of an initial universe-causing quantum singularity (or similar). Indeed, Craig is attempting to argue that God exists on the basis that *only* a disembodied mind could have the right properties to bring the universe into being from nothing, and that only by positing an entity with these properties can the beginning of the universe be explained. Once again, this is exactly what the naturalist is doing. By proposing that the initial quantum singularity (or similar) came into being without a cause, they are postulating a special kind of entity with this unusual property in order to explain how the universe came into being. Craig, of course, does not think such an entity is as plausible as the existence of an uncaused, immaterial mind. He has not, however, given any reasons to think this is the case, and nor can we simply extrapolate from our experiences with objects *within* the universe to infer that the universe as a whole requires a cause, since both the divine and naturalistic hypotheses refer to entities well outside our range of experience. As such, I conclude that Craig's arguments against the possibility of an uncaused initial state of the universe are unsuccessful.

I also note that that Craig's very same argument can, with appropriate modifications, be applied against Craig's own position that entities which exist timelessly (e.g. God) do not require a cause. One could ask: if God can exist timelessly without a cause, then why not anything? Why not bicycles or Beethoven or root beer? Of course, Craig is likely to reply that bicycles and Beethoven and root beer are intrinsically *temporal* entities, and so are simply not the sorts of things that could exist timelessly. God, by contrast, is an immaterial soul who according to Craig can exist outside of time. Of course, this is exactly the same reasoning I used to argue why the universe, but not bicycles or Beethoven, could begin to exist without a cause. The question then comes down to whether an immaterial soul existing outside of time is the only 'special' sort of entity that would not require a cause. I do not believe Craig provides sufficient reason to think this is the case, and during the discussion of premise four I provide some potential examples of entities which may plausibly be regarded as 'special' in that they could exist without requiring a cause.

We Have Strong Evidence in Favour of This Principle

Craig thinks that the principle 'everything that begins to exist has a cause' is overwhelmingly confirmed by everyday and scientific experience. It seems, however, that this is not quite true, for our experience is of many *particular things* having a cause. Craig wants to make an inductive inference based on these particular instances to a general principle that *everything that begins to exist* must have a cause. This is, of course, a perfectly valid form of inference, however it is a fallible one, and particularly suspect if the case we are attempting to describe is significantly different to the cases used to make the generalisation. Considering the question concerns the origin of the universe, it seems like this is precisely such a case of drawing inferences outside of our range of observations, since there is a significant difference between events that occur in time and the beginning of time itself. In particular, the beginning of time was not preceded by any prior moment of time, whereas every subsequent moment of time does have such a preceding moment. This means that all the moments of time that we have observed are known to be causally connected to previous moments in time, thereby potentially explaining why everything we observe to begin has a cause. This property will not hold, however, of the first moment of time. We therefore have reason to regard the beginning of time as something significantly different to the events we observe that occur in time, and therefore we should be extremely cautious about drawing any inferences about the former on the basis of the latter.

We may also note that, if time has the structure of the real numbers and if the beginning of the universe represents the boundary of time but is not itself an event, then we can quite easily understand the beginning of the universe. Under this interpretation, every event is caused by some preceding event, so no event has ever occurred without a cause. Just as there is no smallest real number, there is no first event, for every event that occurred had a previous event to cause it. If we imagine moving backwards in time and perceiving the chain of causes, there would never be an end or limit to the chain, even though the universe was still finitely old. Craig, of course, would not accept such an explanation because he rejects the existence of actual infinities, and also rejects that time has the structure of the real numbers. For those not convinced by his arguments for these positions, however, this explanation provides what I think is quite a compelling account for the origin of the universe at a finite time in the past, without the need to postulate an uncaused beginning.

Premise Four: If the Universe Had a Cause, That Cause Must be Personal

The first three premises of the extended kalam cosmological argument attempt to establish that the universe had a cause which brought it into being. By itself, however, this is not sufficient to constitute an argument for the existence of God, since nothing has yet been said about the nature of this cause. As such, the final stage in Craig's argument is to establish that the cause of the universe must have been *personal*. By personal, Craig effectively means an immaterial mind with volition and immense causal power – that is, a personal creator God. To establish this conclusion, Craig first argues that the cause of the universe cannot have been any material cause, such as a particle or energy field. He then argues that ruling out material causes leaves no other plausible option than an immaterial personal cause. Finally, Craig also argues that only an immaterial free agent is capable of initiating the beginning of time from timelessness, as it is the only entity with the right metaphysical properties or powers. In this section, I will examine each of these three arguments in turn.

THERE ARE NO OTHER PLAUSIBLE CANDIDATES

A Material Cause of the Universe

Craig believes that the cause of the beginning of the universe could not have been material, meaning that it could not have been the sort of thing studied by physics as part of the natural world. One argument he gives in favour of this position is that[174]:

> "Whatever is material involves incessant change on at least the molecular and atomic levels, but the uncaused First Cause exists in a state of absolute changelessness."

This argument is misplaced, however, since whatever material state might have caused the beginning of the universe is hardly likely to have been atomic or molecular in nature, since atoms and molecules did not even exist until sometime after the Big Bang.

A more plausible candidate for a material cause of the universe is some sort of quantum fluctuation from an infinitesimally small region of spacetime, as has recently been proposed by Vilenkin. According to such models, the universe 'tunnelled into being' from an instable quantum state, thereby triggering the Big Bang and hence the beginning of time. Craig thinks that such models cannot explain the ultimate origin of the universe because unstable quantum states cannot exist timelessly. He says[175]:

> "*But neither can it (the initial quantum gravity region) exist literally timelessly, akin to the way in which philosophers consider abstract objects to be timeless or theologians take God to be timeless. For this region is in a state of constant flux, which, given the indiscernibility of identicals, is sufficient for time.*"

'The indiscernibility of identicals' is a philosophical principle according to which two separate and distinct entities cannot share all properties in common, for if they did they would be indiscernible from one another and thus identical to each other – in other words, they would in fact be the same entity. Craig's purpose in appealing to this principle is to argue that if two moments in time are the same in every way, then these moments are identical and so actually constitute the same moment of time. Conversely, Craig believes that in order to exist outside of time, an entity must be completely changeless, since if it ever underwent change then there would be two distinct moments where it possessed different properties, and thus it would not exist outside of time. Craig's key argument, therefore, is to say that quantum systems are in a constant state of flux, and therefore they cannot exist timelessly. God, by contrast, is not in a state of flux but is always the same, and therefore he *can* exist timelessly.

Whether the mere existence of any sort of change is sufficient for the passage of time is a controversial philosophical position which I shall not discuss in detail here. Instead, I want to focus on Craig's claim that an initial quantum state could not have existed timelessly because such states exist in constant flux. It is certainly true that, in our current understanding of quantum mechanics, quantum systems always exist in constant flux and cannot exist timelessly in the way Craig believes the cause of the universe must have existed. The major problem with this as an argument against the possibility of a material cause of the universe, however, is that we also know that the origin of the universe was *not* the result of the operations of the laws of quantum mechanics as they are currently understood. In particular, it is known that existing quantum theories must be replaced with a quantum theory of gravity to describe the very early universe. Since so little is known about very early times in the history of the universe, there may well be other modifications that need to be made to current physical theories in order to properly describe the very beginning. Craig himself recognises this when he describes such quantum theories as "so problematic and underdeveloped"[176]. We simply do not have a physical theory capable of describing the very early universe, and as such it is invalid for Craig to apply existing quantum theories to a situation in which we know they are inapplicable, and then infer from this that the cause of the universe could not have been material. The fact is that, as evidenced by the bourgeoning field of quantum cosmology, the appropriate physical description of the very early universe is still an *open question*, and as such Craig is unjustified in prematurely rejecting the possibility of a timeless material cause of the universe.

Furthermore, even if a physical, scientific description of the origin of the universe cannot currently be provided, it is still possible to develop *philosophical* accounts of the cause of the universe in terms of material entities. Craig himself, of course, does not offer a scientific account of the cause of the universe, but only a philosophical one, so he can hardly criticise a materialist account on this basis. As an example of what such an account might look like, we can imagine that the beginning of the universe may have been caused by a new type of particle or field which is capable of existing changelessly outside of time. This 'primeval atom,' as we may call it, would have been the cause of the beginning of the temporal universe by giving rise to the Big Bang. Craig will doubtless describe this scenario as 'speculative', but I do not see how it is any more so than Craig's theistic explanation. We do not have any direct evidence for either account, with both proposed causes having been *inferred* on the basis of the chain of reasoning Craig has outlined. Since *Craig* is the one who is attempting to argue that the beginning of the universe constitutes evidence for God's existence, *he* therefore bears the burden of proof to show that other possibilities are either implausible or ruled out altogether. Craig may assert that a timeless material state is considerably less plausible than a timeless immaterial agent, however it is unclear what basis Craig has for such a judgement. Furthermore, as I argue below, I believe there are good reasons for regarding Craig's proffered agent-based explanation as implausible, and as such an atemporal material cause is rendered more plausible in comparison.

Possible Non-Material, Non-Personal Causes

Craig outlines several properties that, on the basis of his argument, he believes can be deduced about the nature of the cause of the universe. The first cause must obviously be causeless, since Craig's whole argument is directed towards establishing a first cause of the universe which itself has no prior cause. Since the first cause is itself causeless, it cannot have begun to exist, as if it did then by premise three of the extended kalam cosmological argument it would need to have a cause. Existing without a beginning and being itself the cause of time, the first cause must therefore be timeless, existing outside of time. The cause must also be changeless, since (according to Craig) change implies the passage of time. Thus, as a result of this reasoning we arrive at three properties that the first cause must have: it must be changeless, causeless, and timeless[177]. As I discussed in the previous section, Craig also thinks the first cause could not be material, since no material entity can exist changelessly.

Craig argues that there are only two candidates that meet all four criteria of being changeless, causeless, timeless, and immaterial: abstract objects and disembodied minds. As Craig says[178]:

> *"No other candidates which could be suitably described as immaterial, beginningless, uncaused, timeless, and spaceless beings come to mind. Nor has anyone else, to our knowledge, suggested any other such candidates."*

This statement is demonstrably mistaken, as it is almost trivially easy to provide counterexamples to Craig's assertion. There are, in fact, many other candidates that meet the criteria Craig outlines (immaterial, beginningless, and uncaused). Though I suspect there may be others that are less well-known, I will briefly outline a few candidates that I am familiar with below.

The Dao is a complex concept from Chinese philosophy which has a number of meanings. It can refer to a 'way', a path of action, and also a metaphysical principle or force of nature. Lawrence Fagg describes the Dao as[179]:

> "The mysterious quiet that pervades all nature... There is an apparent aspect manifested by the order of the universe and an absolute aspect which is the Essence from which the order arises... The world and all its creatures emerge from and return to the Absolute Dao, which is ineffable and timeless."

The Dao is certainly not a physical law or abstract principle – it has real ontological substance. At the same time, it is clearly non-personal, and so differs dramatically from the disembodied mind Craig wishes to appeal to.

Brahman is the ultimate supreme deity in many forms of Hindu belief. Brahman is "the only Absolute Reality: beginningless, endless, changeless, ineffable, and beyond good and evil, time, space, the universe, and causation"[180]. As Haridas Chaudhuri explains [181]:

> "The term 'Brahman' etymologically means the Great, the Supreme. It sums up the Hindu view of the nature of ultimate reality. Brahman is the cosmic principle of existence, the ultimate unifying and integrating principle of the universe. It has two inseparable aspects or modes of existence: nirguna and saguna, impersonal and personal, indeterminable and self-determining."

Exactly how Brahman is to be understood, and the degree to which it should be understood as personal, varies between schools of Hindu philosophy. For our purposes, what is important is that Brahman is clearly quite distinct from the monotheistic notion of a God, and is not (or at least not merely) a disembodied mind. Furthermore, it is clearly understood to be immaterial and timeless. Whether Brahman has causal powers is a complex question, since Brahman is typically understood to subsume and transcend everything, so (as noted above) there is no sense in which Brahman can cause anything outside of itself, nor cause itself to change. Nevertheless, Brahman is also considered to be the ultimate ontological ground of all being, and is clearly not thought to be causally impotent in the way abstract objects are. Thus, while it may not neatly fit into the ontological categories specified by Craig, it nevertheless seems to me that Brahman provides a possible alternative to Craig's dichotomy.

In recent decades, various physicists and philosophers have made the argument that information, rather than matter or energy, forms the fundamental basis of reality. John Archibald Wheeler has famously said[182]:

> "Every it – every particle, every field of force, even the spacetime continuum itself – derives its function, its meaning, its very existence entirely – even if in some contexts indirectly – from the apparatus-elicited answers to yes or no questions, binary choices, bits."

This case has been made more recently by Paul Davies, who argues that[183]:

> "We have both philosophical and scientific reasons to doubt the adequacy of this widely accepted doctrine of materialism. In the history of Western philosophy, as we will see, it has turned out to be notoriously difficult to formulate a viable concept of matter. And physics in the twentieth century has produced weighty reasons to think that some of the core tenets of materialism were mistaken."

Norbert Wiener has likewise said[184]:

> "Information is information, not matter or energy."

We see therefore that theorists like Wheeler and Davies clearly regard information as both immaterial and causally efficacious.

In the Sāṃkhya school of Hindu philosophy, there is a concept known as *guṇa* which refers, in part, to a quality, virtue, or attribute, but is also thought to represent the three interacting strands or 'threads' of reality. The three *guṇas* are called: *sattva* (goodness, existence), *rajas* (passion, activity), and *tamas* (darkness, inertia)[185]. The manner in which they behave combines some of the properties of a physical force with some of the properties of an agent, as William J. Johnson describes[186]:

> "Prior to the evolution of the universe, these three guṇas exist in a state of perfect equilibrium or unmanifest potentiality

> *(pradhāna); but once their balance is upset by the influence of puruṣa, they manifest themselves in the evolutes, which make up the variegated world. Thereafter, it is the predominance, or otherwise, of particular guṇas in material nature (including the mind) which constrains beings to act in particular ways."*

In response to all of the above proposals, Craig might argue that the examples fail to meet his criteria. He could argue, for instance, that the Dao is not capable of exerting causal effects, that Brahman is really just a form of personal being, and that information is either physical or an abstract object. He could continue to maintain that a personal agent is the only truly immaterial, timeless, causal entity available to furnish an explanation for the origin of the universe. One problem with such a response is simply that it seems to be factually mistaken – Brahman and the Dao, for instance, are regarded by many as being neither material nor personal, and thus lying outside Craig's narrow dichotomous classification. Furthermore, such a strategy is also susceptible to what I regard as the fundamental flaw of this line of reasoning, namely that the concepts in question are far too vague and poorly characterised for the sort of process of elimination to work. There are so many competing conceptions of what it means to be 'material', what it means to be 'timeless', and what it means to be a 'cause', as well as varying interpretations of the Dao, Brahman, God, etc., that by selecting a suitable combination of definitions one could arrive at nearly any desired conclusion. This is similar to the criticism levelled of Craig's position by Sean Carroll in their debate, when he declared that "theism is not well defined"[187]. Indeed, it seems to me that none of these concepts are very well defined, and as such Craig is unjustified in his misleadingly precise categorisation of possible causes. In sum, since Craig has failed to provide any reasons to reject these or other possible immaterial causes of the universe, and nor has he established a sufficiently clear categorisation scheme such that he can decisively eliminate them as distinct proposals, he has not succeeded in establishing that an immaterial agent is the only possible cause of the beginning of the universe.

James Fodor

FREE AGENCY IS THE ONLY WAY FOR CHANGE TO COME FROM CHANGELESSNESS

The Alleged Need for Agent Causation

Craig believes that only a free agent can bring about a temporal effect from an initial timeless state. He makes this argument by asking[188]:

> *"If the necessary and sufficient conditions for the production of the effect are eternal, then why is not the effect eternal? How can all the causal conditions sufficient for the production of the effect changelessly existent and yet the effect not also existent along with the cause? How can the cause exist without the effect?"*

In responding to these questions, we need to understand precisely what Craig is asking. Clearly, he cannot be asking why the effect did not exist sooner than it did, since the effect came into existence at the earliest possible time, namely the first moment of time. Likewise, Craig's question as to how the cause exists 'without the effect' is irrelevant because the cause never does exist without the effect. That is, there is no moment of time when the cause exists but the effect does not, for the cause exists outside of time. Thus, it seems the only thing Craig could be asking is how it is possible for a timeless cause to bring about a temporal effect at all. The answer to this question, however, seems to be entirely straightforward – it just does. That is, the timeless entity exercises its causal power and brings about the temporal effect. This scenario only poses a dilemma if we suppose that there is something absurd or impossible about a timeless cause bringing about a temporal effect. But why should we think this is the case? Craig does not provide any reason. Indeed, Craig says that[189]:

> *"Presentness should be construed as a mode of existence, a temporal as opposed to a timeless mode of being."*

Thus, being timeless and being present are just two different modes of existing, distinguished by the fact that the former does not stand in any temporal relations to other moments in time, while the latter does. What reason do we have for thinking that an entity that

137

does not stand in any temporal relation to other moments of time (and hence is timeless), cannot be the cause of an entity that *does* stand in temporal relation to other moments of time (and hence is temporal)? Craig does not provide any such reason, and therefore I think there is simply no reason to regard this as paradoxical.

Nevertheless, let us suppose for the sake of argument that there *is* actually something paradoxical about the notion of a timeless cause bringing about a temporal effect. We now consider why Craig thinks that agent causation is the only possible solution to this paradox. Craig believes that agent causation is the "best way out of this dilemma," arguing that[190]:

> *"Because the agent is free, he can initiate new effects by freely bringing about conditions which were not previously present. For example, a man sitting changelessly from eternity could freely will to stand up; thus, a temporal effect arises from an eternally existing agent."*

In Craig's view, three criteria must be met in order for an effect to be brought about by an agent cause: the agent must have the desire to bring about the effect, must have the power to do so, and also must take some sort of action, some exercise of causal power, in order to bring about the effect. According to Craig, God timelessly possessed both the desire and power to bring about the creation event, however God's exercise of his causal, creative powers to actually bring about the effect of creation only occurred at a finite time in the past, and was not exercised timelessly 'from eternity'[191]. The change constituted by this exercise of causal powers brought about the beginning of time and brought God into time as a temporal being. Craig's argument thus hinges on the fact that an agent must perform some action, undertaking some exercise of causal powers, in order to bring about their desired effect.

There is, however, a major problem with Craig's line of argument. God's act of exercising his causal powers is clearly not timeless, as it is something that begins to exist along with the beginning of the universe. By the third premise of the extended kalam, therefore, this exercise of causal powers would need to have a *cause*. So what could this cause be?

Clearly the answer cannot simply be 'the agent's ability and intention to bring about the effect', because Craig has already argued that an agent bringing about an effect requires something beyond this, namely an exercise of causal powers. If we say that the agent's exercise of causal powers was in turn caused by a prior exercise of causal powers, we run into an infinite regress which Craig regards as impossible[192]. Craig responds to this dilemma as follows[193]:

> "We should not say that in agent causation the agent causes his causing of some effect. Partisans of agent causation typically say that the agent's causing some effect is not an event requiring a cause, either because it is not itself an event, but just a way of describing an agent's causing an event, or if it is an event, then it is not further caused... neither alternative requires revision of (premise 3), which concerns, not events, but substances which come into being."

It is unclear, however, how exactly it can be the case that God exercising his causal powers is *not* an event, since Craig says elsewhere[194]:

> "There must be an exercise of (God's) causal power in order for the universe to be created. That entails, of course, an intrinsic change on God's part which brings Him into time at the moment of creation."

Surely an 'intrinsic change that brings God into time', and also brings about the beginning of the universe, constitutes an event, since a change in the properties of an entity has taken place. Furthermore, Craig also endorses the position that "an event is just the coming to be of some thing or things"[195]. God's action of exercising his causal powers and creating the universe, however, would presumably constitute a 'thing' that 'comes into being' – after all, if it is not a thing or an event, then what is it? As such, it seems that by his own definition, God's exercise of his causal powers should count as an event that requires a cause.

Craig's only recourse at this point is to argue that an instance of an agent exercising their causal powers is a unique and special type of occurrence that does not operate according to any laws or principles. In explaining how this might be, J.P. Moreland (whom Craig references) states[196]:

> "In libertarian acts, agents are unmoved or first movers. They do not first undergo a change before they can cause a change. Rather, agents, qua substances, directly cause their volitions by virtue of possessing and exercising their power to do so. Since an exercise of power is not a change undergone by an agent (nor a coming-to-be of a substance), it is not an event with a beginning in the sense relevant to the causal principle, even though there was a time before and after which the agent caused his volitions. Besides coming into existence, only changes (internal or relational) need a cause."

This response appears, however, to be little more than special pleading. Surely an act of volition undertaken by an agent implies a change from the agent being in a state of not exercising a causal power to being in a state (or passing through the state) of exercising that power. If not, then it seems there just isn't anything for the agent to do in exercising its causal powers. Without some sort of change or transition taking place in the process of exerting their causal powers, either the agent has no way of effecting their desires and causing a change in the world, or their exercise of power is simply coextensive with the agent. If, however, undertaking an act of volition entails a change, then it seems there must be a cause of this change from inaction to action. The cause of this cannot simply be the agent themselves, since the effect would then occur timelessly and eternally with the agent. It seems therefore that agent causation does not succeed in helping Craig avoid the problem of how a temporal effect can be brought about by a timeless cause. The only way Craig can get his account to work is by arbitrarily asserting that there is no change involved in an agent exercising their causal powers, and thus no cause of such a change is required. If, as I have argued, this assertion cannot be sustained, then I conclude that agent causation offers no advantages over other types of causes in accounting for the cause of the universe.

In addition to this problem with agent causation, the notion that only the coming into being of substances requires a cause also fatally undermines the kalam cosmological argument for the simple reason that the universe is not a substance; rather it is simply the totality of space, time, and everything they contain. It is a category error to assert that a collective term for the totality of all substances is *itself* a substance. Thus, if only substances that come into being require a cause, the universe needn't require a cause as it isn't a substance. Perhaps Craig could argue that according to the position known as spacetime substantivism, the spacetime continuum is itself a substance that came into being at the beginning of the universe. This view, however, stands in tension with Craig's firmly presentist view of time, according to which time is not a substance that began to exist but rather simply refers to the temporal process of absolute becoming. It therefore seems that if spacetime substantivism is true, the tensed theory of time is false and so the kalam fails, while if spacetime substantivism is false, the universe is not a substance that requires a cause, and so the kalam fails anyway. Even if the universe *is* a substance, this would still not rescue Craig's argument because some prior event could simply be the cause of the universe coming into being. As long as this initial event does not constitute a 'substance coming into being', it evades Craig's second premise and thereby provides an explanation for the origin of the universe – the coming into being of the substance of 'the universe' was caused by a prior event, which itself had no cause since events (according to Craig) do not require causes. We can therefore conclude that Craig's redefinition of premise three to apply to only substances but not events means that the universe need not have been caused by a timeless entity outside the universe, but could have been caused by any prior event (if the universe is a substance) or nothing at all (if the universe is not a substance). Either way, the kalam cosmological argument is fatally undermined.

The Plausibility of Substance Dualism

A major problem with Craig's appeal to a nonphysical mind as the cause of the universe is that we have no widely-accepted examples of such a mind. If no such minds are known to exist, then Craig is appealing to nothing more than a theoretical possibility, a possibility whose plausibility is diminished to the degree that the posited entity is distinctly different from anything that is known to exist. Craig, however, believes that we are in fact intimately familiar with examples of immaterial minds exhibiting agent causation – namely our own minds. This line of argument of course avoids the criticism that immaterial minds are a hitherto unknown entity, but only at the cost of giving rise to a host of new difficulties. In particular, Craig must defend the controversial position that human minds are immaterial, a position known as substance dualism.

Craig has presented a number of arguments in favour of substance dualism, which it will be worth considering briefly. First, he argues that substance dualism is self-evident[197]:

> "Through introspection a person is directly aware of the fact that (1) he is an immaterial center of consciousness and volition that uses his body as an instrument to interact with the material world; (2) he is the owner of his experiences and he is not identical to a bundle of mental experiences; and (3) he is an enduring self who exists as the same possessor of all his experiences through time. This direct awareness shows that a person is not identical to his or her body in whole or in part or to one's experiences, but rather is the thing that has them. In short, one is a mental substance. Physicalists and property dualists could, of course, simply deny that people are aware of these things. They would also owe us an account of why people are tricked into thinking that they are, in fact, aware of them."

In response to Craig's assertion that the immateriality of the mind is obvious and self-evident, it should be noted that the overwhelming majority of philosophers are not adherents of substance dualism[198], and therefore it seems that the obviousness of its correctness is not nearly as great as Craig says. Examining his argument in more detail, it is unclear how Craig thinks he is able to tell that he is not identical to a bundle of mental experiences, or that the centre of his consciousness is immaterial. For example, while it is widely recognised in philosophy that sensations like pain or seeing a colour are self-evident, it is not clear how Craig can infer directly from introspection that such experiences entail that his mind is immaterial. How exactly does this manifest in his experience of pain or seeing colour? Craig does not give us any account of how he can determine this. Instead, he attempts to shift the burden of proof onto those who doubt the truth of substance dualism, even though it is *he* who is claiming knowledge about the nature of the mind, and therefore *he* who bears the burden of proof. Furthermore, even if we agree that people are 'tricked' into thinking that they are directly aware of being immaterial minds, one needs only to point to the myriad of other ways in which our introspective sense or experience of the world is misleading. We experience time as 'flowing' when it does not (as Craig himself agrees), we experience the Earth as flat when it is not, we experience the sun as rising and setting when it is the Earth that rotates (an idea people ridiculed for centuries as being directly contrary to our experience of a stationary Earth), we experience physical objects as solid and impenetrable when in fact they are comprised of fluctuating fields and mostly empty space, and we experience movies as continuous motion when in fact they are static images interspersed with darkness for half of the time. In so many ways our direct experiences can be misleading about the true nature of things. Given this, it is unclear why Craig places such an enormous degree of trust on how his conscious experiences seem to him, especially when many other thoughtful people do not report their experiences in the same way.

Craig's second argument in favour of substance dualism is that as humans, we experience an irreducible first-person vantage point through which we see the world. He then argues that this is inconsistent with a physical view of the mind because[199]:

> *"According to physicalism, there are no irreducible, privileged, first-person perspectives. Everything can be exhaustively described in an object language from a third-person perspective... But no amount of third-person descriptions capture Tom's own subjective, first-person acquaintance of his own self in acts of self-awareness."*

One problem with this argument is that it misstates the position of physicalism. All that physicalists necessarily hold is that the mind is no more than the product of the physical brain. Craig thinks this is inadequate because, in his words[200]:

> *"'I' refers to one's own substantial soul. It does not refer to any mental property or bundle of mental properties one is having,*

nor does it refer to anybody described from a third-person perspective."

It is quite possible, however, to hold that first-person experiences are purely the product of the physical brain, and yet also affirm that these experiences cannot be fully described in terms of third-person descriptions alone. The first is a statement about what *exists* in the world, while the second is a statement about our ability to objectively *describe* that world. There is nothing inconsistent about holding to the view that subjective experiences are solely the product of physical processes, while denying that all aspects of the experiences so generated can be fully captured by third-person descriptions. To hold this combination of views is simply to assert that certain aspects of first-person experience cannot be fully described by language, because all linguistic descriptions rely on abstractions and approximations which are never capable of capturing the full first-person experience of awareness in all its richness. A second problem with Craig's argument is that it is unclear how Craig can reconcile his statements about the existence of irreducibly subjective experience with his belief in the existence of an omniscient deity who possesses all knowledge. Surely an omniscient God would be able to perceive and objectively know all details of the first-person experiences of each human being without having to actually *be* that person. The objectivity of God's perspective is, after all, precisely the motivation behind Craig's moral argument. If this is true, and God can objectively understand first-person experiences from a third-person perspective, then Craig's argument for substance dualism fails.

A third argument Craig gives in favour of substance dualism is that physicalism and other alternatives imply determinism, which Craig says is self-refuting. He argues that, in order for rational agents to exist and rationally endorse any proposition, three criteria must be met[201]:

"First, humans must have certain mental features true of them. They must have genuine intentionality, they must be capable of having thoughts and propositions in their minds, they must be capable of having awarenesses of the things they claim to know as well as of the contents of their own minds... Second, in order

to rationally think through a chain of reasoning such that one sees the inferential connections in the chain, one would have to be the same self present at the beginning of the thought process as the one present at the end... Finally, rationality seems to presuppose an agent view of the self and genuine libertarian freedom of the will. There are rational 'oughts'. That is, given certain evidence, one 'ought' to believe certain things... But ought implies can. If one ought to believe something, then one must have the ability to choose to believe it or not to believe it."

Craig believes that under physicalist determinism, each of these three criteria is violated, and thus the proposition of determinism would be self-refuting. The problem with this argument is that most physicalists fully embrace existence of intentionality or free will; they simply think that such phenomena are ultimately a product of the physical brain. Craig's argument would only be sound, therefore, if he could show that such physicalist understandings of intentionality and free will were faulty or unreasonable. Since he does not attempt to do so, this fails as a compelling argument against physicalism.

Not only do Craig's arguments for the plausibility of substance dualism fail, but there are also several key reasons for thinking that substance dualism is highly implausible. The first of these is called the problem of interaction, and can be formulated by considering how the immaterial mind is able to interact with the material brain. Craig's answer is effectively to avoid the question by arguing that we can know *that* such interaction occurs without needing to know *how* it takes place. Craig also says that the mind is likely to interact 'directly' with the brain such that there is no intervening mechanism, and thus nothing to explain. Neither of these responses, however, can be reconciled with the current state of scientific knowledge. The function of the brain is the result of the electrochemical impulses of billions of specialised cells called neurons. If the immaterial mind interacts with the brain, then it must do so by affecting neurons in some way. But how could it possibly do this? Does it introduce an electrical charge or a new chemical species into the system, violating conservation of charge and energy? If so, such interaction must be detectable if it is to have any effect on physical systems. This then raises the question as to why no credible evidence of such interaction has ever emerged despite more than a century of research into scientific psychology and neuroscience. Furthermore, electrical or magnetic stimulation of specific brain regions is known to cause subjects to reporting particular sights, sounds, tastes, and smells. If sounds and tastes etc. are purely mental properties, as Craig believes, then why can they be trigged by electrodes activating particular neurons? What could an electrode or a magnet possibly do to an immaterial mind such that it would elicit specific and reproducible types of mental phenomena? While the scientific understanding of how the physical brain gives rise to the mind grows steadily every year, no progress at all has been made since the time of Descartes in the seventeenth century in explaining how an immaterial mind could possibly interact with a physical brain. This longstanding problem, therefore, constitutes a powerful argument against substance dualism.

The second problem is often called the problem of many minds. If the mind is separate and distinct from the body, how does a single immaterial mind stay causally associated with one and only one brain? What form of interaction keeps it bound to one and exactly one mind, instead of having causal interactions with other brains? There seem to be no plausible answers to these questions that do not rely on mere assertion. Craig offers two responses to this problem. The first is to argue that[202]:

> "Since dualism allows for the possibility of many minds in one body, and since such a state actually occurs in cases of demon possession, then the dualist allowance of this possibility is a virtue, not a vice."

Such a response may be compelling to those who believe in the reality of demonic possession, but for those of us who do not, and especially those who regard the ancient practice of attributing mental illness to demon possession as barbaric and profoundly ignorant, such a response will be unlikely to hold much weight. Craig's second response is to argue that the soul and body might be intimately connected. He says[203]:

> "If some version of substance dualism in the tradition of Aristotle or Aquinas is correct, then the soul (perhaps by using

DNA molecules) is what makes the body and gives the body its nature (e.g., your body is human because it is informed by a human soul). The soul provides the form or essence of the body; the body is dependent on the soul for its coming into being and not vice versa."

Such a view is totally at odds with modern scientific theories regarding genetics and the causal pathways of human development, which simply leave no room for the action of an immaterial soul. Indeed, were such causal influences to exist then scientific investigation would almost certainly have detected some trace of them by now. Instead, science has shown and continues to show that the form of the human brain and body is determined by one's genetic inheritance and its interaction with various stimuli from the environment. There is simply no place in the modern scientific understanding of human development for the sort of intimate causal connection Craig proposes.

The third and final problem concerns the explanatory impotence of substance dualism. Materialist approaches to the mind, which study mental activity in terms of physical and chemical causes, utilising signal-response, information-theoretic, and other such scientific paradigms, have yielded immense insights into the structure and function of the mind[204]. We now know a great deal about memory encoding and retrieval, language acquisition and encoding, visual processing, motivation, attention, methods of decision making, and many more. Much, of course, remains to be learnt, but I argue that these materialist-based paradigms, which treat the mind and brain as a deterministic physical system, have been extremely productive and dramatically enhanced our understandings of the mind and brain. By contrast, it is not clear what insights a substance dualist perspective has yielded about the workings of the mind. In treating the mind as a mysterious black box which interacts directly and without antecedent physical causes, substance dualism is a position that simply has no explanatory potency to make any contribution to our understanding of how the mind works. Of course, as a theory, it does not necessarily claim to be able to do this, however, the explanatory impotency of substance dualism compared to scientific materialist approaches constitutes a strong reason for favouring the former over the latter.

As a result of the failure of Craig's arguments in favour of substance dualism and the powerful arguments against its plausibility, we have strong reasons to reject Craig's reasoning by analogy that the cause of the universe could be an immaterial mind broadly similar to those possessed by humans. This, of course, does not show that an immaterial mind could not nevertheless have been the cause of the universe. In appealing to such a cause, however, Craig is postulating the existence of a wholly new type of entity that is not otherwise known to exist. This means we have no greater reason to think the cause of the universe is an immaterial mind than we do to think it is any other sort of timeless entity which we may postulate, such as those various candidates I discussed in the previous section. Thus, even if the first three premises of the extended kalam argument are true, an immaterial mind is but one of many possible causes of the universe, without any particularly strong reason for preferring one over any of the others. As an argument for the existence of a creator God, therefore, the kalam is a failure.

SUMMARY OF THE ARGUMENT

The extended kalam cosmological argument attempts to establish the existence of God by arguing that an act of divine creation is the only way to account for the origin of the universe. In order for this argument to succeed, Craig needs to establish four things: that time is tensed and so things can 'begin to exist' in an absolute sense, that the universe 'began to exist' in this absolute sense, that everything that begins to exist requires a cause, and finally that if the universe had a cause then this cause must be personal. From these four premises, it follows that a personal creator (i.e. God) must exist. An analysis of the kalam then hinges primarily upon how well Craig has been able to establish each of these four key premises. I have argued that Craig's arguments in favour of each of these premises are weaker than Craig asserts, and face powerful objections. Most importantly, Craig faces serious difficulties in developing a single set of positions that allow him to defend all four premises in a consistent manner.

Craig's arguments in favour of a tensed theory of time force him to adopt a purely instrumentalist interpretation of general relativity, such that the theory tells us nothing about the nature of metaphysical time. It also leads him to adopt a presentist position, according to which only the present exists, with past and future being unreal. These positions, however, undermine the arguments that he gives in defence of the premise that the universe began to exist. Craig's philosophical arguments for the impossibility of an infinite past conflict with his presentist position that the past does not exist and so does not constitute an 'actual infinite', his feeble attempts to argue that the nonexistent past is somehow more 'real' than the nonexistent future notwithstanding. Likewise, his philosophical arguments for the impossibility of forming an actual infinite by successive addition conflict with the fact that his presentist philosophy forces him to regard the present as an infinitesimal instant, meaning that time does not progress by successive addition but by continuous growth. Craig's attempt to avoid this problem by arguing that the present consists of a primitive interval that varies in duration depending upon what we are interested in referring to, leads to the absurd conclusion that what exists varies according to what we refer to, and so must be rejected. Finally, Craig's appeal to the Borne-Vilenkin-Guth theorem to establish that the universe must have had a beginning contradicts his instrumentalist interpretation of general relativity, since this theorem (and indeed essentially all of modern cosmology) adopts a four-dimensional spacetime, tenseless framework for analysing time, a framework Craig thinks does not accurately describe true metaphysical time. As a result of these conflicts, Craig is unable to simultaneously defend his first and second premises in a consistent manner. As I noted above, I believe that this fundamental inconsistency is due to the fact that Craig only properly considered the issue of tensed versus tenseless theories of time after he had already completed his initial work on the kalam[205], rendering it impossible to fully reconcile his original arguments with the positions he later adopted regarding the philosophy of time.

Craig's defence of the kalam also suffers from his excessive appeal to pre-analytic intuitions which many others who consider his arguments do not share. This includes Craig's conflation of his experience of time with his preferred philosophical account of that experience, his claim that the truth of the tensed theory of time is an obvious properly basic belief, his claim that the use of tensed language provides evidence that time actually is tensed, his extrapolation of everyday experience about causation to the beginning of space and time, his argument that the premise 'everything that begins to exist has a cause' is so obvious that it needs no argument, his various arguments in defence of substance dualism that appeal to intuition and direct experiences, and his appeals to intuition about the absurdity of various alleged 'paradoxes' involving actual infinities. In every one of these cases, there is ample room both to dispute the universality of Craig's intuitions and experiences, and also the philosophical relevance or interpretation of those intuitions or experiences. Craig can become quite dismissive of those who do not share his intuitions or interpretations of experience, sometimes describing them as "irrational"[206] or in believing things that are "literally worse than magic"[207]. Nevertheless, it seems to me that all of these are weak points of Craig's argument, and significantly undermine its overall strength.

The above remarks notwithstanding, it is nevertheless the case that Craig's first three premises are at least plausible. While Craig's arguments are highly problematic, it is quite plausible that the universe began to exist, and that this beginning had some sort of cause. The real object of the extended kalam cosmological argument, however, is not merely to establish that the universe had a cause, but to argue that this cause must have been a personal being. It is in this fourth and final premise where the argument is at its weakest, for Craig simply presents very few firm reasons to think the first cause must have been personal. His attempted dismissal of any material cause on the grounds that we know of no timeless material entity fails precisely because we do not know enough about the conditions of the very early universe to say whether a timeless material object is possible or what other properties it might have, and thus Craig's rejection of this possibility is far too premature. Likewise, Craig's bold assertion that there are no other possible immaterial entities other than abstract objects or immaterial minds flies in the face of the clear fact that a wide range of possible such entities have been seriously considered in philosophical and theological discussions. Even if there is no particular reason to think such entities are responsible for causing the beginning of the universe, Craig's attempted argument by process of elimination is not valid since he ignores most of the possible candidates. Craig's appeal to an immaterial mind also faces the difficulty of giving an account of how libertarian agent causation could work which does not result in God's act of exercising his causal powers being classed as an event which begins to exist, and therefore requires a cause. Craig's responses to this problem are arbitrary and underdeveloped, and seriously undermine the force of his argument. Finally, Craig's appeal to an immaterial mind faces a dilemma: either Craig rejects substance dualism about human minds, in which case no other cases of immaterial minds are known to exist and Craig must appeal to a purely hypothetical entity to explain the origin of the universe, or on the other hand, Craig appeals to substance dualism with respect to human minds, in which case he faces many powerful objections to this position. In either case, his argument that the cause of the universe must be an immaterial mind is significantly weakened.

Overall, I think the extended kalam cosmological argument is unsuccessful. Craig does not succeed in providing sufficient reason to think that all of the premises are true. Further, we have good reason to think that the first and fourth premises are not true. Fundamentally the problem arises from the complexity of the argument; Craig must appeal to so many distinct philosophical positions and address so many separate issues that the argument collapses under its own complexity.

Chapter Three
The Fine-Tuning Argument

Overview of the Argument

Craig argues that the fine-tuning of the universe for the existence of intelligent life is powerful evidence in favour of the existence of a designer God. He defines fine-tuning as follows[208]:

> "The physical laws of nature, when given mathematical expression, contain various constants (such as the gravitational constant) whose values are not determined by the laws themselves; a universe governed by such laws might be characterized by any of a wide range of values for these constants. In addition to these constants, moreover, there are certain arbitrary physical quantities, such as the entropy level, which are simply put into the universe as boundary conditions on which the laws of nature operate. They are therefore also independent of the laws. By 'fine-tuning' one means that small deviations from the actual values of the constants and quantities in question would render the universe life-prohibiting or, alternatively, that the range of life-permitting values is exquisitely narrow in comparison with the range of assumable values."

Elsewhere Craig specifies that he is not just talking about any sort of life, but specifically about "intelligent, interactive life,"[209] and henceforth for the remainder of this chapter when I talk about 'life' it should be understood that I am referring to embodied, intelligent life such as exemplified by human beings, but by no means limited to only this particular form of intelligent life.

Craig argues that the best explanation for the fine-tuning of the constants of nature for life is that the universe was designed by God specifically in order to permit the existence of intelligent life. Craig also rejects the major alternative explanations to design, namely chance and physical necessity, as being implausible or incomplete. We can therefore summarise Craig's argument as follows:

- Premise one: The universe is fine-tuned for the existence of embodied, intelligent life.

- Premise two: The only explanations for this fine-tuning are chance, physical necessity, or design.

- Premise three: Neither chance nor physical necessity are plausible explanations for fine-tuning.

- Conclusion: Fine-tuning can only be plausibly explained by design (i.e. God)

Much has been written concerning the chance and physical necessity explanations for fine-tuning, so in this chapter I will discuss each of these possibilities only briefly, arguing that they are at least more plausible explanations than Craig acknowledges. The core thrust of my argument, however, is directed against the first premise that the universe is fine-tuned for the existence of life. I will argue that the evidence Craig presents is far too weak to establish this contention, and that in fact we do not have particularly strong reasons for believing that this premise is true.

PREMISE ONE: THE UNIVERSE IS FINE-TUNED FOR INTELLIGENT LIFE

Craig often speaks of fine-tuning as if it is a well-established scientific discovery, when in fact the existence of fine-tuning as defined by Craig is not at all established by current scientific evidence. While many scientists have expressed various opinions about the concept of cosmic fine-tuning, as I shall explain below, most of these statements are either sweeping claims made well beyond the available evidence, or have been misinterpreted and misapplied by proponents of the fine-tuning argument.

THE EVIDENCE FOR FINE-TUNING

The key evidence Craig presents for the existence of fine-tuning consists of a series of observations that, if certain physical constants in the laws of nature were even slightly different, intelligent life would not be possible. Craig states this as follows[210]:

> "The world is conditioned principally by the values of the fundamental constants α (the fine structure constant, or electromagnetic interaction), α_G (gravitation), α_w (the weak force), α_s (the strong force), and m_n/m_e (the ratio between the mass of a proton and the mass of an electron). When one assigns different values to these constants or forces, one discovers that the proportion of observable universes, that is to say, universes capable of supporting intelligent life, is shockingly small. Just a slight variation in some of these values would render life impossible."

In order to consider the strongest from of Craig's argument, I will in this chapter also refer to some of the writings of philosopher Robin Collins, who has written extensively on the subject of fine-tuning. I do so because Craig himself has written relatively little on the fine-tuning argument, and much of what he has written is concerned with responding to the 'chance' and 'physical necessity' explanations I mention above, with very little time spent outlining the actual evidence for the existence for fine-tuning itself. Craig has, however, specifically endorsed and praised Robin Collin's work on the fine-tuning argument, describing him as "the finest exponent of the fine-tuning argument today"[211]. As such, I shall assume that Collin's approach essentially represents the line of argument that Craig would also adopt.

Collins seeks to establish the existence of fine-tuning by first considering various physical constants of nature, then determining the life-permitting range of each (holding the laws of physics and other constants the same), and finally comparing this to the range of possible values of the constant for which we can determine whether the universe is life-permitting or not (he calls this the 'epistemically illuminated range'). The epistemically illuminated range is always finite, Collins argues, because every physical theory is only valid over a limited range, outside of which the theory breaks down and becomes unable to make any predictions. This fact avoids certain technical problems with some versions of the fine-tuning argument which attempt to assign probabilities over infinite ranges. Collins then argues that each subinterval of a given size should be accorded equal probability (i.e. a uniform distribution over possible values), in accordance with a form of the principle of indifference. Basically, the idea is that since (prior to actually measuring their values) we have no reason to think any particular value of the constants is more likely than any other, we should assign equal probability to all the values in the epistemically-illuminated region. Collins is also careful to emphasise that the probabilities he is concerned with are epistemic probabilities, describing the relative likelihood that particular states of affairs pertain according to our current limited knowledge. He is not talking about a probability distribution over different metaphysical or logically possible values of constants, but rather a flat probability distribution indicating our complete lack of knowledge concerning what the values might have been.

Given this setup, Collins defines fine-tuning as follows[212]:

"Let C be a constant that is fine-tuned, with C occurring in the simplest current formulation of the laws of physics. Then, by the definition of fine-tuning, $Wr/WR \ll 1$, where Wr is the width of the life-permitting range of C, and WR is the width of the comparison range, which we argued was equal to the width of the EI (epistemically illuminated) range."

In other words, a particular physical constant or initial condition is fine-tuned for life if the life-permitting range of that constant is much smaller than the range of values of that constant for which we can tell whether the universe would be suitable for life or not. Put simply, fine-tuning exists if the life-permitting range Wr is much smaller than the range of possible values WR. Since, as Collins and Craig argue, physics has demonstrated that this ratio is very small for a number of key physical constants and initial conditions, therefore it follows that the universe is fine-tuned for the existence of life.

This formulation of the fine-tuning argument is particularly useful because it allows me to very simply state the crucial underlying flaw of the argument. Namely, we currently have essentially *no idea* what the width of the life-permitting range Wr is, and therefore no way to determine whether Collin's criterion for fine-tuning (Wr/WR $\ll$ 1) holds or not. The reason why Craig and Collins both think that the range of Wr has been established to be very small, while I claim that it has not, comes down to an inconsistency in how Craig and Collins use the word 'life' compared to how physicists studying fine-tuning use the word. I explain the nature of this inconsistency in the next section.

THE POSSIBILITY OF OTHER FORMS OF LIFE

The first point to be made is that, as Craig and Collins both clearly state, the relevant class of life to consider is not merely carbon-based intelligent life, but embodied intelligent life of any form. The key reason for this is that small probabilities such as those countenanced by the fine-tuning argument are only relevant when they are considered relative to an independently-given pattern[213]. For example, while it is overwhelmingly unlikely that any particular individual will win the lottery, *somebody* must win. This means that we cannot infer from the fact that Mr. Smith won the lottery that the draw must have been rigged, if the only reason we selected Mr. Smith for consideration in the first place was because he turned out to be the winner. In such a case, we have no independently-given pattern, but we have simply picked out whoever happened to be the winner. Regardless of who ended up winning, we could *always* point to that person and claim an absurd improbability of that person winning, even though it is certain that some person would be the winner. Only if we predict that Mr. Smith will win *before* we are aware of the identity of the actual winner can we say that we have an independently given pattern against which to compare the outcome, and thus that an improbable event has occurred.

Applied to the case of fine-tuning, it is clear that the only reason carbon-based life is selected for discussion is because that is the form of life we (humans) are – there is no independently given pattern that provides a reason to focus on this form of life. The appropriate independent pattern is the much more general category of intelligent, embodied life, which possess a number of characteristics that render it of clear interest even absent knowledge of what type of life actually exists (if any) in the universe. Another way of putting this is that, while the theist can plausibly claim that it is likely that God would have reasons to create embodied, intelligent life that was capable of entering into a relationship with him, no equivalent reason can be given as to why God would have a particular reason for creating carbon-based life over any other possible form of life. If the concern is to explain why specifically *carbon-based* life is able to exist in the universe, then Craig's proposed theistic design hypothesis is equally unable to provide an explanation as any of the naturalistic explanations he rejects, since we have no explanation as to why God would want to create specifically carbon-based life as opposed to any other kind of life. As it is, both Craig and Collins seem to recognise this point, for they both speak of the probability of the universe supporting intelligent life in the abstract, and not of carbon-based life specifically.

If the above analysis is correct and what concerns us is the probability that the constants of physics would result in a universe that permits the existence of *some form* of intelligent life, then for the fine-tuning argument to hold we must be able to establish with reasonable confidence that the range of life-permitting values is small relative to the range of possible values. The fundamental problem with this, however, is that we have *no idea* what the range of life-permitting values is. The cases that Craig and Collins cite show that the range of life-permitting values for *carbon-based life* is small; however, this tells us almost nothing about the probability of *some form* of intelligent life being possible. To make this determination we would need to know the minimal requirements for the existence of life, and then determine whether these requirements can be met under each possible combination of values of the physical constants. In fact, however, we do not even know what the minimal requirements for the existence of carbon-based life are, much less what the requirements might be for any form of life of any sort. It is perfectly conceivable that totally alien forms of life might be possible living on neutron stars, in gas giants, or even made from particles or agglomerations of particles that cannot exist in our universe. Craig might retort that such possibilities are 'sheer speculation', but it is he who claims to know that such forms of life are either not possible or extremely unlikely. This is despite the fact that we simply do not know what would or would not be possible given different values of the physical constants, and thus can make no sensible predictions concerning the probably of alternate forms of life existing. I therefore conclude that Craig is without justification in his claim that life would almost certainly not exist were the constants of nature even slightly different, for we simply have no idea what sort of physics or biology would be possible with different physical constants.

Craig does not believe that the possibility of alternate forms of life undermines the fine-tuning argument[214]:

> "Laymen might think that if the constants and quantities had assumed different values, then other forms of life might well have evolved. But this is not the case. By 'life' scientists mean that property of organisms to take in food, extract energy from it, grow, adapt to their environment, and reproduce. The point is that in order for the universe to permit life so defined, whatever form organisms might take, the constants and quantities have to be incomprehensibly fine-tuned. In the absence of fine-tuning, not even atomic matter or chemistry would exist, not to speak of planets where life might evolve!"

Elsewhere he is even more emphatic[215]:

> "That is why it is not a good objection to say, 'if the constants and quantities had different values, there might be different kinds of life that would have evolved'. We are not talking about the forms of life that exist, but just life – period! In order for life in any form to exist, on this definition, you have to have this exquisite fine tuning of the constants and quantities"

Despite Craig's confident claims, he is simply incorrect in claiming that it has been established that no alternate forms of life could exist without fine-tuning. The scientific research into fine-tuning has almost entirely focused on the implications that different fundamental constants would have on the development of carbon-based life, including determining whether star formation, the formation of atoms, and the lifespan of the universe are all in alignment with what is necessary for carbon-based life to develop. However, this approach assumes that intelligent life must take the form of carbon-based life living on rocky planets. Scientists have made this assumption because it is the only form of life we know anything about, and the only one concerning which we can make any scientific statements. The fact is, however, that we have no reason to think that this is the only possible form of life, or that totally strange and alien life-forms could not exist if the constants of physics were different. The criteria that Craig has given for life – taking in food, extracting energy, growing, adapting, and reproducing – are so generic that we simply have no idea whatsoever as to whether totally different entities satisfying these criteria might be possible under various combinations of physical constants. This is compounded by the fact that the laws of nature are sufficiently complex such that all the various phenomena they give rise to (such as life forms) cannot be simply predicted from an analysis of the underlying laws alone. This means that we can only make predictions about what would happen to carbon-based life if the constants of the universe were changed. Extrapolating this to all forms of life in the abstract is totally outside the range of what we can know. This is not to say that intelligent life would be possible under all possible combinations of physical constants, only that we simply do not know what proportion of such combinations could support some form of intelligent life, and thus the probabilistic claim at the heart of the fine-tuning argument is not sufficiently justified.

When during a debate with Craig, physicist Sean Carroll made a similar argument about the possibility of other forms of life, Craig responded by citing a long list of scientists who all had published in defence of fine-tuning[216]. Such a response, however, is only relevant if the definition of life these scientists use in their analysis of fine-tuning is sufficiently similar to that used by Craig in his discussion of the topic. However, as I have argued above, and show in further detail below, physicists who publish about fine-tuning do *not* use Craig's absurdly generic definition of life, since we have no idea under what conditions such life is possible. Rather, physicists are only concerned about fine-tuning with respect to biochemically-based life living on rocky planets; that is, life similar to us. The fact that many physicists believe in this form of fine-tuning should be of very little comfort to Craig, for it says nothing about the wider sort of fine-tuning that he needs to establish in order for his argument to cogent.

Craig's apparent willingness to grossly extrapolate from the form of life that we are familiar with to any form of intelligent life is all the more puzzling when one considers that elsewhere he appeals to the 'cognitive limitations' that human beings are under with respect to discerning divine plans. In discussing the problem of evil, for instance, Craig says[217]:

> *"Our cognitive limitations, such as our confinement in space and time... prevent our discerning the ultimate outcome of specific events."*

Such cognitive limitations, however, would presumably also significantly impede our ability to make judgements as to what forms of life would be possible if the constants of nature were different. After all, we only exist in the universe as it is, and can only do experiments and make observations with the physical constants that actually exist. Sean Carroll has described such problems as follows[218]:

> *"We know very little about the conditions under which complexity, and intelligent life in particular, can possibly form. If, for example, we were handed the Standard Model of particle physics but had no actual knowledge of the real world, it would be very difficult to derive the periodic table of the elements, much less the atoms and molecules on which Earth-based life depends. Life may be very fragile, but for all we know it may be ubiquitous (in parameter space); we have a great deal of trouble even defining 'life' or for that matter 'complexity', not to mention 'intelligence'. At the least, the tentative nature of our current understanding of these issues should make us reluctant to draw grand conclusions about the nature of reality from the fact that our universe allows for the existence of life."*

As a result of such considerations, I regard Craig's claim that we can make confident judgements about the likely existence of alternate forms of life as highly implausible. Contrary to what Craig asserts, science has not established that the universe is fine-tuned for the existence of intelligent life.

James Fodor

EXAMINING MARTIN REES' SIX NUMBERS

To demonstrate that when physicists talk about fine-tuning they are referring to fine-tuning for carbon-based biochemical life, and not for any form of life fitting Craig's very generic definition, I will consider each of the six examples presented in Martin Rees' book *Just Six Numbers*, which is one of the main sources Craig draws from in developing his fine-tuning argument. There are, of course, other sources that Craig cites in defence of the existence of fine-tuning, however many of them address the same or similar examples. Since Rees' is one of the most prominent scientific descriptions of fine-tuning and one of the most widely-cited, I believe a detailed consideration of its core claims will be sufficient to highlight the inaccuracy of Craig's interpretation as to what science has established regarding fine-tuning.

The first of the six constants that Rees considers is called N, the ratio of the strength of the strong nuclear force to the gravitational force. Rees says[219]:

"Gravitation is feebler than the forces governing the microworld by the number N, about 10^{36}. What would happen if it weren't quite so weak? Imagine, for instance, a universe where gravity was 'only' 10^{30} rather than 10^{36} feebler than electric forces. Atoms and molecules would behave just as in our actual universe, but objects would not need to be so large before gravity became competitive with the other forces. The number of atoms needed to make a star (a gravitationally bound fusion reactor) would be a billion times less in this imagined universe. Planet masses would also be scaled down by a billion... This would in itself preclude stable planetary systems, because the orbits would be disturbed by passing stars... But what would preclude a complex ecosystem even more would be the limited time available for development. Heat would leak more quickly from these 'mini-stars'... Instead of living for ten billion years, a typical star would live for about 10,000 years. A mini-Sun would burn faster, and would have exhausted its energy before even the first steps in organic evolution had got under way. Conditions for complex evolution would undoubtedly be less favourable if (leaving everything else unchanged) gravity were

161

> stronger... *The converse, however, is that an even weaker gravity could allow even more elaborate and longer-lived structures to develop... But it is only because it (gravity) is weak compared with other forces that large and long-lived structures can exist. Paradoxically, the weaker gravity is (provided that it isn't actually zero), the grander and more complex can be its consequences."*

From this passage, it is clear that Rees is assuming that life must take the form of organic life forms living on a planet orbiting a star; he even explicitly mentions 'organic evolution.' This is a far cry from Craig's claim that fine-tuning refers to any form of life capable of consuming energy and reproducing. Furthermore, this particular example fails to support the notion of 'fine-tuning' as such, because only values of N significantly less than 10^{36} are ruled out, and indeed Rees claims that larger values of N would actually allow more time for complexity to develop. Thus, even by Rees' own argument N isn't fine-tuned by Craig's definition, since its value does not need to fall into an extraordinarily narrow range even for carbon-based life to form, it simply must be over a certain minimum level.

The second of Rees' constants is ϵ, the fraction of the mass of four protons that is released as energy when these protons fuse into a helium nucleus. Regarding this constant he says[220]:

> "There turn out to be delicate effects, sensitive to this number, in the synthesis process that transforms hydrogen into the rest of the periodic table. The crucial first link in the chain – the build-up of helium from hydrogen – depends rather sensitively on the strength of the nuclear 'strong interaction' force... If the nuclear 'glue' were weaker, so that ϵ were 0.006 rather than 0.007, a proton could not be bonded to a neutron and deuterium would not be stable. Then the path to helium formation would be closed off. We would have a simple universe composed of hydrogen, whose atom consists of one proton orbited by a single electron, and no chemistry. Stars could still form in such a universe (if everything else were kept unchanged) but they would have no nuclear fuel. They would deflate and cool, ending up as dead remnants. There would be no explosions to spray the debris

back into space so that new stars could form from it, and no elements would exist that could ever form rocky planets. At first sight, one might have guessed from this reasoning that an even stronger nuclear force would have been advantageous for life, by making nuclear fusion more efficient. But we couldn't have existed if ϵ had been more than 0.008, because no hydrogen would have survived from the Big Bang. In our actual universe, two protons repel each other so strongly that the nuclear 'strong interaction' force can't bind them together without the aid of one or two neutrons... If ϵ were to have been 0.008, then two protons would have been able to bind directly together. This would have happened readily in the early universe, so that no hydrogen would remain to provide the fuel in ordinary stars, and water could never have existed... The actual mix of elements would depend on ϵ, but what is remarkable is that no carbon-based biosphere could exist if this number had been 0.006 or 0.008 rather than 0.007."

Again, it is clear that Rees' analysis is focused upon carbon-based life existing on rocky planets powered by stars burning hydrogen as nuclear fuel. This is the form of life with which we are familiar, but it would be a profound exhibition of lack of imagination to claim that *only* life of this sort is capable of meeting Craig's much broader definition for what counts as life. Rees does say, however, that for certain values of ϵ only hydrogen atoms would exist, and hydrogen does not undergo the sort of complex chemistry necessary for life to exist. Thus, we might conclude that if only hydrogen atoms existed then no form of life at all would be possible. Such reasoning, however, presumes that life must be based upon chemical reactions. There is no reason in principle why life, defined using Craig's very abstract definition, could not exist on the basis of the effects of the strong or weak nuclear forces, or even based on manifestations of electromagnetism different to anything we would recognise as chemistry. Since we know essentially nothing about what the universe would be like or what complex behaviours might emerge under these conditions, it is equally as speculative to say that we know that life could *not* develop under such conditions as to say that it could – the fact is that we simply do not know.

Rees, however, does not make this argument, as here he is clearly only interested in talking about carbon-based life as we know it, not any form of complex life as envisaged by Craig.

Rees' third number is Ω, the ratio of the actual density of the universe to the critical density. This constant, Rees argues, is fine-tuned as being very close to 1[221]:

> "Ω may not be exactly one, but it is now at least 0.3. At first sight, this may not seem to indicate fine tuning. However, it implies that Ω was very close indeed to unity in early eras. This is because, unless expansion energy and gravitational energy are in exact balance (in which case Ω is, and remains, exactly equal to unity), the gap between those two energies widens: if Ω were to start off slightly less than unity in the early universe, eventually the kinetic energy would completely dominate (so that Ω becomes very small indeed); on the other hand, if Ω were substantially more than unity, then gravity would soon get the upper hand and bring the expansion to a halt... If (the expansion) were started too fast, then the expansion energy would, early on, have become so dominant (in other words, Ω would have become so small) that galaxies and stars would never have been able to pull themselves together via gravity and condense out; the universe would expand forever, but there would be no chance of life. On the other hand, the expansion must not have been too slow: otherwise the universe would have recollapsed too quickly to a Big Crunch. Any emergent complexity must feed on non-uniformities in density and in temperature.... Without being to the slightest degree anthropocentric in our concept of life, we can therefore conclude that a universe has to expand out of its 'fireball' state, and at least cool down below 3000 degrees, before any life can begin. If the initial expansion were too slow to permit this, there would be no chance for life."

We first note that Rees' discussion once again assumes that life requires gravitationally-bound structures such as stars and galaxies, which is certainly true for carbon-based life, but not at all clear given Craig's much broader definition. Regarding the alleged fine-tuning of Ω, Rees himself explains that the initial value of Ω being very close to one is now generally thought to be the result of an inflationary period very early in the universe, in which the universe expanded many times faster than the speed of light. This would result in a value of Ω in the observable universe very close to one regardless of what its value was initially (see figure 7), and thus explains the apparent 'fine-tuning' of this constant in the present. This inflationary epoch itself does not require fine-tuning, since a wide range of possible durations and rates of inflation are consistent with the final end result of a value of Ω very close to one. As Rees explains[222]:

> *"The concept of inflation has been boisterously debated ever since it was first proposed twenty years ago. It has been through many variants, based on different assumptions about how the pressure, density and so forth behaved under conditions far beyond anything that we can study directly. But the general idea will surely retain its appeal unless a better one comes along. At the moment, if offers the only credible explanation for why our universe is so large and so uniform. It suggests why the universe is expanding at such a seemingly fine-tuned rate, so that it could heave itself up to dimensions of ten billion light-years."*

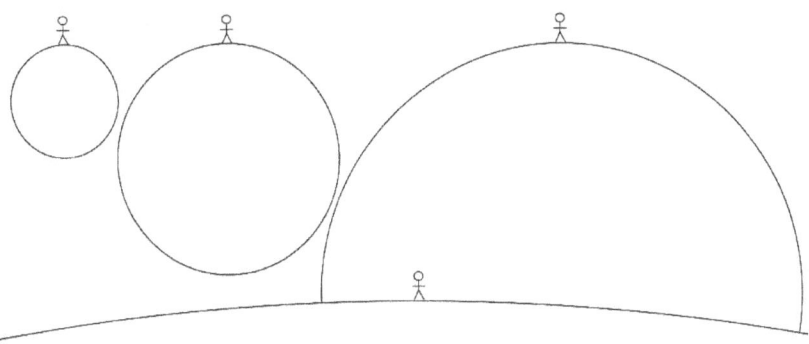

Figure 7. As the radius of curvature increases, an observer seeing only a small localised portion of the shape perceives it as being closer to exactly flat. This occurs regardless of the initial value of the curvature.

Rees does not discuss the effect of altered values of his fourth constant λ, the energy density of dark energy, on the existence of life, and as such it has no bearing on the fine-tuning argument.

Rees' fifth number is Q, the binding energy of galaxy clusters. Regarding this constant he says[223]:

> "Its value is crucial: were it much smaller, or much bigger, the 'texture' of the universe would be quite different, and less conducive to the emergence of life forms. If Q were smaller than 10^{-5} but the other cosmic numbers were unchanged, aggregations in the dark matter would take longer to develop and would be smaller and looser. The resultant galaxies would be anaemic structures, in which star formation would be slow and inefficient, and 'processed' material would be blown out of the galaxy rather than being recycled into new stars that could form planetary systems. If Q were smaller than 10^{-6}, gas would never condense into gravitationally bound structures at all, and such a universe would remain forever dark and featureless, even if its initial 'mix' of atoms, dark matter and radiation were the same as in our own. On the other hand, a universe where Q were substantially larger than 10^{-5} - where the initial 'ripples' were replaced by large-amplitude waves - would be a turbulent and violent place. Regions far bigger than galaxies would condense early in its history. They wouldn't fragment into stars but would instead collapse into vast black holes, each much heavier than an entire cluster of galaxies in our universe. Any surviving gas would get so hot that it would emit intense X-rays and gamma rays. Galaxies (even if they managed to form) would be much more tightly bound than the actual galaxies in our universe. Stars would be packed too close together and buffeted too frequently to retain stable planetary system."

Yet again, Rees' remarks clearly show that he is talking about the possibility of life that is dependent upon gravitationally bound structures, especially planets. We do not, however, know whether life defined in accordance with Craig's very broad conception would necessarily require gravitationally bound structures in order to exist. To say that we know that such life is impossible is pure speculation, and not part of Rees' argument.

Rees' sixth and final number D is the number of macroscopic spatial dimensions in the universe[224].

"One consequence of a three-dimensional world is that forces like gravity and electricity obey an inverse-square law, such that the force from a mass or charge is four times weaker if you go twice as far away... Orbits in our Solar System are stable, in the sense that a slight change in a planet's speed would only nudge its orbit slightly. But this stability would be lost if gravity followed an inverse-cube (or steeper) law rather than one based on inverse squares. An orbiting planet that was slowed down – even slightly – would then plunge ever-faster into the Sun, rather than merely shift into a slightly smaller orbit, because an inverse-cube force strengthens so steeply towards the centre; conversely, an orbiting planet that was slightly speeded up would quickly spiral outwards into darkness... There is therefore a problem with more than three spatial dimensions. Could we then live in a world where there were less than three? The best argument here is a very simple one: there are inherent limitations on complex structures in 'flat-land' (or, indeed, on any two-dimensional surface). It is impossible to have a complicated network without the wires crossing; nor can an object have a channel through it (a digestive tract, for instance) without dividing into two."

As in several of the previous cases, Rees' discussion of the reason why life would not be possible with more than three spatial dimensions concerns the instability of planetary orbits in this condition. Once again, this is relevant for carbon-based life of the sort found on Earth, but it is far less clear that any form of life would require stable planetary orbits in order to exist. His arguments against the possibility of two-dimensional life are more wide-ranging, however they are also not based upon any actual findings from cosmology or physics, nor do I think they are very persuasive. Conway's game of life is a famous computer simulation of a two-dimensional grid of cells, each of which can be in one of two states (usually called 'alive' and 'dead'). The simulation evolves according to very simple rules, such that each cell changes state only in accordance with the state of the cells that surround it. Despite this very simple setup, the game of life can exhibit amazingly complex behaviours, including periodically repeating and self-replicating patterns (see figure 8 for an example)[225]. I am not claiming that the game of life is actually alive. Rather, my point is that given the dynamic complexity that is possible with even such very simple rules, it seems quite conceivable to me that two-dimensional intelligent life could exist in a universe with only two dimensions. Arguing that two-dimensional life could not exist because wires could not cross or digestive tracts could not exist is yet another instance of presuming that any form of life must look something like carbon-based life.

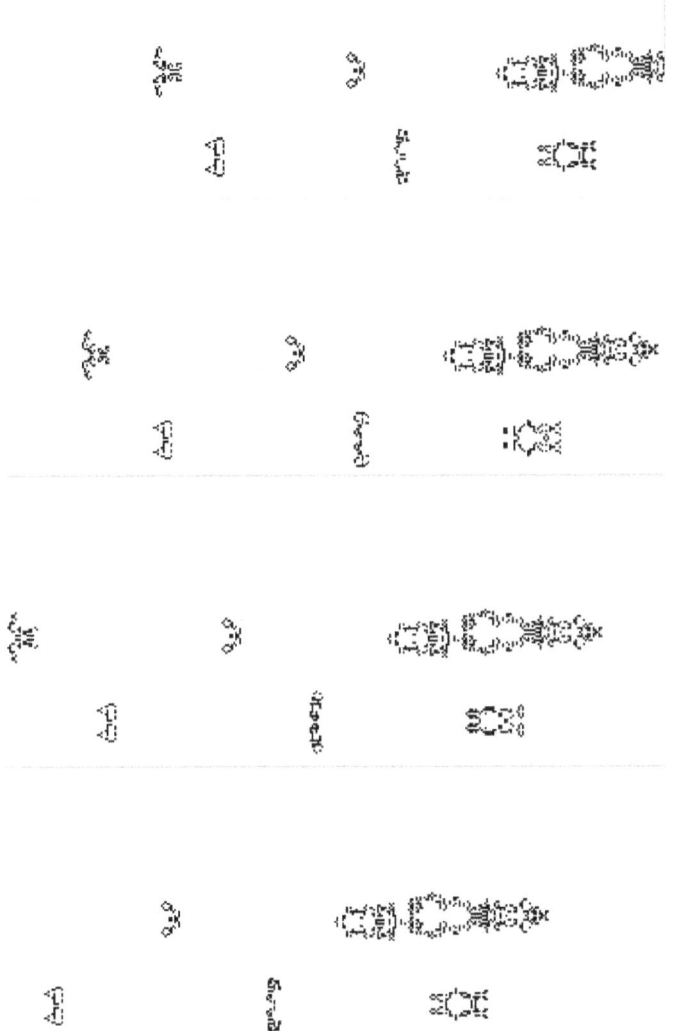

Figure 8. Four images each 16 frames apart from a simulation of Conway's game of life[226]. Each black or white dot represents a square that can be 'alive' or 'dead', and whose state evolves over the simulation in accordance with very simple rules. The self-perpetuating 'spaceship' structures shown here are emergent properties of the simulation that were not programmed in at the outset.

Given this detailed analysis of the claims made by Martin Rees, I think it is safe to conclude that the sort of fine-tuning physicists typically study refers to fine-tuning for carbon-based life living on rocky planets orbiting long-lived stars – that is, life more or less as we know it. Some physicists are likely to be explicit that this is what they mean by 'fine-tuning' than others, but regardless we should not be surprised at this focus because science is only the business of making claims about physical laws and the phenomena they give rise to. Scientists spend little time talking about how things would be different if the laws of nature where changed, precisely because we have so little ability to investigate or test such theories. Thus, while the fine-tuning of the universe for carbon-based life is generally accepted and widely evidenced, this is not the case for the much more generic definition of life used by Craig and Collins. It is precisely this sort of generic fine tuning that Craig needs, however, in order for the fine-tuning argument for the existence of God to work.

The Dimensionality Problem

In addition to the foregoing discussion, there are two further reasons for thinking that fine-tuning for life in general should not be inferred from the existence of fine-tuning for carbon-based life. The first of these reasons I term 'the dimensionality problem', and relates to a discrepancy between what is needed to establish fine-tuning and the argument Craig actually defends. Craig and Collins both consider the fine-tuning of only one (or occasionally two) physical constants at once – recall Collins' definition of a constant as being fine-tuned when $Wr/WR \ll 1$. The amount that any single physical constant can be varied while still sustaining life, however, is not particularly relevant to the broader question of how likely it is that the universe as a whole would be life-sustaining. Instead, what needs to be determined is the proportion of the entire 'phase space' of possible combinations of physical constants that can support the existence of intelligent life. To understand the concept of 'phase space', we can imagine that there are only three independent fundamental constants, and then imagine three mutually perpendicular axes, each of which would represent the possible values of a single constant. These axes would map out a three-dimensional volume which would be the phase space for possible physical constants. Exactly one point inside the phase space will correspond to the current combination of the three values for these constants as we find in our universe. This combination of values could then be said to be fine-tuned if the total volume of all the possible values capable of supporting life is very small in comparison to the entire volume of the cube. Dividing this 'life-supporting volume' by the total volume of the phase space then allows us to calculate the probability that a life-supporting set of constants would occur purely by chance, assuming all the constants are randomly selected – this being the actual probability we are interested in. Considering a single parameter at a time only allows us to map out a line in three-dimensional space. The volume of a line, however, is always exactly zero, and therefore considering only a single parameter does not allow us to make any meaningful statement about what proportion of the volume as a whole is life-permitting. The calculations that Craig and Collins provide based on one or two constants only are thus not sufficient to establish the claim they wish to make.

The problem is in fact worse than is made apparent in my example of the cube, because in fact the number of physical constants and initial conditions that Craig and Collins claim to be fine-tuned for life is much larger than this, with at least eight different constants or initial conditions being mentioned in their writings. While Craig and Collins seem to think that providing more examples of independent physical constants that require fine-tuning strengthens their argument, it actually has the opposite effect by making it more difficult to credibly establish the relevant probabilities. That is, if there were only three constants that could vary then we would only need to investigate a three-dimensional phase space, but with eight independent physical constants we must consider eight-dimensional phase space (which cannot be visualised but can still be described mathematically). Only by varying all eight constants at once and mapping out an eight-dimensional region could we make estimates about the relative proportion of the overall phase-space that is life-permitting. To put it another way, each additional independent physical constant and initial condition that is added to consideration increases by a multiplicative factor the number of

Unreasonable Faith

possible ways in which the constants might be arranged so as to support life. Furthermore, the more physical constants we have to vary the more degrees of freedom are available, and thus the more likely it becomes that somewhere in the phase space is a set of constants that can support forms of life totally alien and unfamiliar to us, based upon new particles or combinations of matter that simply cannot exist in our universe. For example, if the epistemically illuminated range for each constant comprises ten percent of the total range of possible values (see figure 9), then the fraction of phase space that is accessible to our knowledge considering only two constants is $0.1^2 = 0.01$, or one percent of the total. However if we increase the number of constants considered to eight, then the total fraction of phase space that is epistemically accessible falls to $0.1^8 = 0.00000001$, or ten billionths of the total. Exotic forms of life are conceivable even with varying only a single physical constant, but the more constants can be varied and the more the behaviour of the laws of physics changed, the greater is the number of possibilities for such life to form.

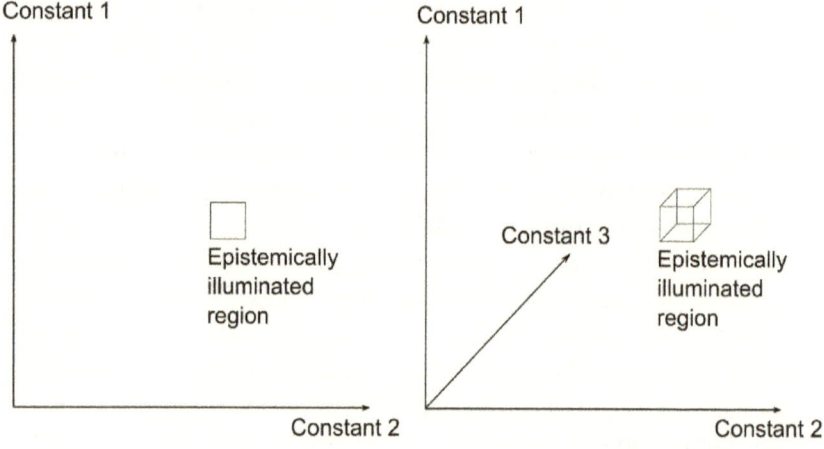

Figure 9. If an epistemically illuminated region comprises ten percent of the total possible range for two different constants (left), the total epistemically illuminated area comprises one percent of the total area of possible combinations of values. If the same situation pertains for three constants (right), then only

one tenth of one percent of the total volume of possible values is in the epistemically illuminated region. This problem worsens the more dimensions are added.

ins himself recognises the possibility of the existence of such exotic forms of life in the remark[227]:

> "If a new physics applies, however, entirely new and almost inconceivable effects could occur that make complex life possible, much as quantum effects make the existence of stable atomic orbits possible, whereas such orbits were inconceivable under classical mechanics."

He does not, however, explain how we are still able to make any confident judgements concerning which combinations of fundamental constants may support intelligent life given this possibility of the effects of 'new physics'. Indeed, Collins' response to the problem of 'multiple constants' is totally inadequate. He argues that we can treat different constants as independent, and so simply multiply their respective probabilities for falling within the life-permitting range. He justifies this approach as follows[228]:

> "When will two constants be independent in this way? Those will be cases in which the factors responsible for C1's being life-permitting are effectively independent of the factors responsible for C2's being life-permitting. For example, consider the case of the fine-tuning of the cosmological constant (C1) and the fine-tuning of the strength of gravity (C2) relative to the strength of materials... The life-permitting range of gravity as it relates to the strength of materials does not depend on the value of the cosmological constant... This means that the joint probability of both gravity and the cosmological constant's falling into their life-permitting ranges is the product of these two probabilities... This same analysis will hold for any set of fine-tuned constants in which the life-permitting range for each constant is independent of the values the other constants take in their respective EI ranges: e.g., the set consisting of the fine-tuning of the strong nuclear force needed for stable nuclei and the previously discussed example of the fine-tuning of gravity."

What Collins ignores here is that we can only make a judgement about whether the fine-tuning effect of one constant is independent of the effect of another constant if we assume that current physical theories are still applicable. This, however, is obviously a questionable assumption since precisely the point of the exercise is that we are changing constants of nature and thereby changing the manner in which the laws of physics operate. The more the value of any constant is changed from its current value, the less confident we can be that we can accurately predict the behaviour of the new system. This is especially true because different aspects of physics are rarely so independent in the way that both Collins and Craig assert. Even using Collins' own example, the gravitational and cosmological constants are closely related in that both affect the rate of expansion of the universe and the operation of forces determining at what rate various elements are produced following the Big Bang. Collins says that he is only talking about the force of gravity as it relates to the strength of materials, but the trouble is that the laws of physics simply don't work that way. One cannot simply isolate one effect of a constant in one particular application and ignore all the other effects that changing the constant would have, since all the laws of physics are connected and interact with each other. We can certainly imagine varying physical constants separately, but when we do so we must be willing to acknowledge that we should have little confidence in applying current physical models to predict the results.

Collins' 'independence' argument also presumes that we know the conditions under which life are possible and simply need to determine whether altering a particular physical constant will render such conditions achievable or not. As I have discussed at some length, however, we do not even accurately know the conditions under which carbon-based life can exist, let alone the conditions under which any form of intelligent life at all is possible. Altering a single physical constant and then comparing this to a fixed set of conditions for the existence of life is simply absurd. If, to use one of Craig's examples, the force of gravity were much stronger and therefore the universe collapsed into a single black hole in a relatively short period of time, we could not simply conclude that life would be impossible because we do not know what forms of life might be possible in a universe with much stronger gravity nor how long they might take to develop. Though the universe might only exist for a fraction of a second, perhaps a form of life could exist which would take only fractions of a second to develop. We cannot, after all, simply assume that the timespans typical of our own universe would apply if some of the physical constants were dramatically different. Nor could we even argue that gravity does not interact with the other forces of nature and so can be considered separately, since we do not know if this assumption would still hold if gravity were many times stronger than it currently is. Since we have no ability to make accurate predictions about such things, I think it is unreasonable to treat physical constants as independent in the way that Craig and Collins do. As such, the dimensionality problem even further hampers our ability to say anything meaningful about the overall probability of a random set of physical constants being life-permitting.

THE REPRESENTATIVENESS PROBLEM

Distinct from the issue of dimensionality, the second additional problem which faces Collins' formulation of the fine-tuning argument is what I call the 'representativeness problem'. As I explained above, Collins seeks to estimate the probability that an arbitrary set of physical constants would be capable of supporting life by considering only values that fall in the 'epistemically illuminated' region, which is the range of constants that we can make predictions about. Craig likewise speaks of a local subset of possible universes when he says[229]:

> "There are simply a vastly greater proportion of more life-prohibiting universes in our local area of possible universes than there are life-permitting universes."

Collins and Craig then infer that if only a small fraction of the epistemically illuminated region is life-supporting, then only a small fraction of the total phase space will be life-supporting. Collins justifies this inference as follows[230]:

> "Thinking in terms of reference classes, the justification for restricting our reference class to the EI (epistemically illuminated) region is similar to that used in science: when testing a

hypothesis, we always restrict our reference classes to those for which we can make the observations and calculations of the frequencies or proportions of interest – what in statistics is called the sample class. This is legitimate as long as we have no reason to think that such a restriction produces a relevantly biased reference class."

While Collins is correct regarding the scientific use of samples to infer properties of larger populations, he is completely wrong about when it is legitimate to infer facts about a population from a given sample. Good scientific methodology does not simply *assume* that any sampling method is legitimate until given reason to think it is biased. Rather, good practise assumes that any sampling method is likely to result in sample biases *unless* we have good reason to think that the method in question samples more-or-less randomly from the underlying population. This is why randomised trials are so prevalent in science, because selecting one's sample randomly is generally the best way to ensure that it represents the underlying population in an unbiased way. If the sample upon which one bases one's inferences is biased (that is, it looks different to the population as a whole), any inferences one makes about the population will be inaccurate, perhaps wildly so (see figure 10).

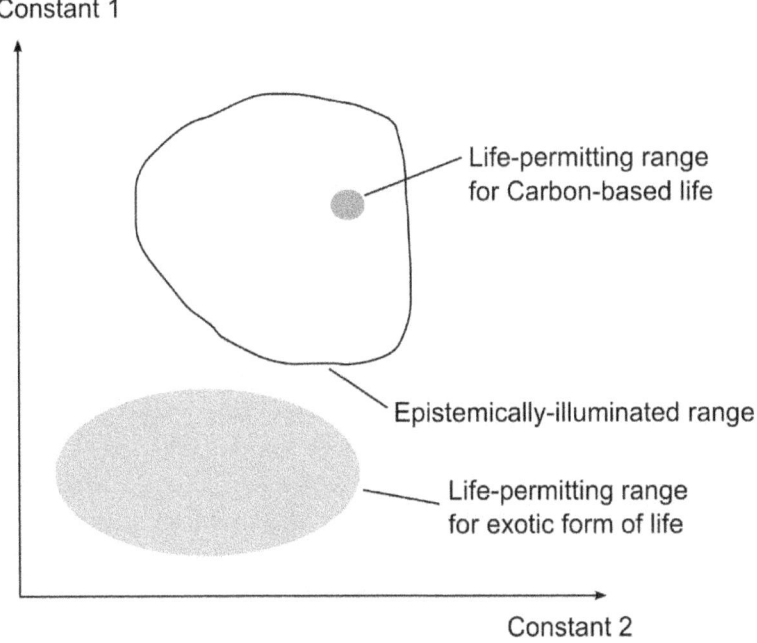

Figure 10. The proportion of the epistemically illuminated region for which known forms of life can exist may be dramatically different than the proportion of the total region for which any form of life can exist, since we do not know what lies outside the epistemically illuminated region.

In the case of fine-tuning, Collins does not give any reasons for thinking that the epistemically illuminated region constitutes a representative sample of the total population of possible combinations of constants. This alone is sufficient to undermine his claim that we can determine the existence of fine-tuning with any confidence. I also believe, however, that there are good reasons to think that the sample we have is in fact *unrepresentative* of the whole space of possible constants. In mathematics, certain systems of equations exhibit what is called chaotic behaviour. The defining feature of such systems is that for certain critical values of their parameters they exhibit a phenomenon called sensitive dependence upon initial conditions, meaning that even very tiny changes in the initial values put into the equation can result in wildly different results. It is quite possible that the laws of physics also exhibit chaotic behaviour with respect to which values of the constants are conducive to the existence of intelligent life. This of course can only be a conjecture, since we do not know what other forms of life are possible or what would happen if the constants of physics were changed. But given the high degree of complexity of the laws of nature, including coupled second-order partial differential equations with many free parameters, it is certainly plausible that systems of this sort could exhibit chaotic behaviour. This means that even very small changes in these constants would be expected to disrupt the equilibrium and thus render the universe incapable of supporting life. Larger changes in the values of these constants, however, may well find a new equilibrium point at which a similar or quite different form of intelligent life was possible. The key point here is that if the laws of nature do exhibit this sort of sensitive dependence to initial conditions, the observed 'fine-tuning' reported by Craig and others is *exactly what we would expect to see* even if, as a whole, the proportion of phase space conducive to life was quite large. In other words, if the physical constants exhibit this sort of chaotic behaviour then the *local* epistemically illuminated region is expected to be very different from the *global* distribution of possible life-permitting combinations of physical constants, thereby making it impossible for us to draw conclusions about the latter solely on the basis of the former. An illustrative example of such behaviour is shown in figure 11.

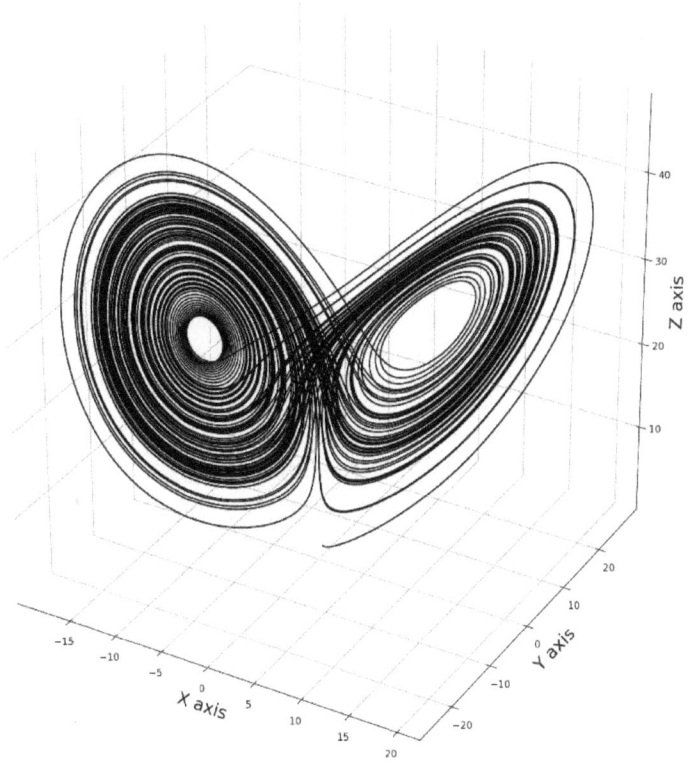

Figure 11. An illustration of a Lorenz attractor, the lines of which map out the solution to a set of nonlinear equations[231]. I use this as an analogy, imagining that each axis represents a physical constant and black lines represent life-permitting combinations. The purpose of this illustration is to show that for chaotic systems the solutions can be wildly and unpredictably dispersed, so that even if the immediately neighbouring space around one solution is unfavourable, the total portion of the space that yields favourable solutions may be much larger.

Given the foregoing discussion, I conclude that Craig and Collins have failed to establish that the universe is fine-tuned for the existence of intelligent life. At most they have established that relatively small changes in the values of various physical constants would render carbon-based life impossible. This in itself, however, says nothing about whether the universe is fine-tuned to be capable of supporting intelligent life of any form, which is necessary for fine-tuning to work as an argument for the existence of God. To make this determination, Craig would have to provide good reason to think that the proportion of physical constants phase space that is conducive to the existence of life is small relative to the total possible phase space. In considering only the variation of one or at most two constants at once, however, we are not able to make any inferences about the volume of phase space, given the possibility of unknown and unpredictable exotic forms of life. This difficulty is compounded by the likelihood of the laws of physics exhibiting sensitive dependence to the values of the physical constants with respect to their ability to support intelligent life, meaning that we have reason to think that the small epistemically illuminated region surrounding the current values of the constants may not be representative of the entire space. Therefore, we cannot simply extrapolate from the fine-tuning of physical constants with respect to the existence of carbon-based life to fine-tuning with respect to the existence of any form of intelligent life.

PREMISE TWO: THE EXPLANATION OF FINE-TUNING IS EITHER CHANCE, NECESSITY, OR DESIGN

The second premise of Craig's fine-tuning argument is that there are only three possible explanations for the existence of fine-tuning: chance, physical necessity, or design. Whether this premise is true depends upon how broadly one understands the notion of 'physical necessity'. Craig seems to use the term to apply to any mechanistic explanation as to why the physical constants have the values they do, as opposed to other possible values. The idea seems to be that if there is a mechanistic explanation for why the constants have some value they do, then the values of the constants are thereby physically determined and hence necessary. Understood in this way, the 'physical necessity' option actually encompasses a wide range of possible explanations, including any attempt to explain the values of the constants in terms of the operation of more fundamental physical laws. Physical necessity in this sense is not the same as logical or metaphysical necessity, but only means that given the laws of physics as they are, the constants had to have their current values. It is not to say that the constants *must* have had their current values in any possible world, even ones with different laws of physics or initial conditions, nor is it to say that the existing set of constants is the only logically consistent set. As such, while possibilities outside of Craig's three options are conceivable (for example the operation of some non-physical but impersonal force or principle), for our purposes it seems reasonable to focus on the three options that Craig outlines as the major contending classes of explanation for fine-tuning.

PREMISE THREE: CHANCE AND PHYSICAL NECESSITY ARE NOT PLAUSIBLE EXPLANATIONS

CHANCE AS AN EXPLANATION

To explain fine-tuning as the result of 'chance' is effectively to say that there is no reason for the constants having the values they do; it was simply due to luck. This is not a plausible answer if our universe is the only one to exist, for if the constants are indeed fine-tuned then the odds against this occurring by chance would be so astronomically low as to be effectively impossible. In order to overcome this problem, advocates of the 'chance' explanation typically appeal to the concept of a multiverse. A multiverse is a hypothetical collection of a very large number of universes, which all exist alongside of but independently from one another. If each universe has different values of physical constants, then the existence of this ensemble of universes would greatly increase the chances that at least one of them would have the combination of physical constants necessary for intelligent life. Both Craig and Collins, therefore, devote considerable space to discussing various proposals for the existence of a multiverse with varying values of the physical constants. Particular focus is given to various proposals for a multiverse based on current theories of inflationary cosmology, since in Collins' words[232]:

"The one based on inflationary cosmology conjoined with superstring theory is by far the most widely discussed and advocated, since this is the only one that goes beyond mere speculation."

Craig and Collins both present a number of specific objections to such multiverse theories, including that they themselves would require fine-tuning, and that they would predict that the most common sort of universe we would find ourselves in would be much younger and smaller than our current universe. While I acknowledge the validity of many of these criticisms, I regard it as premature to make any firm claims about the likely composition of the multiverse when there is so much that we do not yet understand about our own universe, let alone the possibility of other universes.

The major problem with Craig's responses to the multiverse hypothesis concerns not his analysis of any particular model, but in the fact that Craig falsely infers that the failure of any existing model to provide a fully satisfactory account of the multiverse implies that the very concept of a multiverse should be rejected as a possibility for explaining fine-tuning. Even if we have no satisfactory description of how such a multiverse could form or what it could look like, it does not follow that there *cannot* be any such multiverse, or even that such a multiverse is unlikely. Not only is the study of such theories barely in its infancy, but more importantly it is not even necessary for the opponent of the fine-tuning argument to present a scientific model for a multiverse, since Craig does not require that the explanation for fine-tuning be scientific. His proposed explanation for fine-tuning, namely an intelligent designer, does not offer any scientific or mechanistic cause for how the existing universe and its 'fine-tuned' constants came about; it only states *that* such a creator would be able to create a finely tuned universe, not *how* they did so. As such, all a competing account need do is explain why it is that we find ourselves in a universe with finely-tuned constants, even if it cannot provide a precise mechanism by which this occurs. The existence of a multiverse consisting of many universes each with different combinations of physical constants provides an explanation for fine-tuning, as even though the probability of any *single* universe being suitable for life is very low, the probably of *some* universe in the entire ensemble being life-permitting is much greater. We, of course, live in one of these few life-permitting universes alongside many lifeless universes. This explanation accounts for the fine-tuning of the universe just as well as does Craig's proposed explanation. The fact that no specific scientific model for such a multiverse has yet proven successful does not undermine its explanatory power because Craig's account likewise lacks a scientific explanatory mechanism. Craig does not seem to agree with this, demanding that[233]:

"If the Many Worlds Hypothesis is to commend itself as a plausible hypothesis, then some plausible mechanism for generating the many worlds needs to be to be explained."

Craig, however, does not apply this same principle to his own preferred explanation of intelligent design, for when Richard Dawkins asks for an explanation of the cosmic designer that explains how it is possible for a disembodied mind to design and create a universe, Craig responds[234]:

"In order to recognize an explanation as the best, one needn't be able to explain the explanation. In fact, so requiring would lead to an infinite regress of explanations, so that nothing could ever be explained and science would be destroyed! So in the case at hand, in order to recognize that intelligent design is the best explanation of the appearance of design in the universe, one needn't be able to explain the Designer."

This is clearly a case of special pleading, arbitrarily applying different criteria to different proposed explanations of the same phenomenon. If we do not need an explanation of the designer for intelligent design to be the best explanation for fine-tuning, then likewise we should not require an explanation of exactly how a multiverse came into being or how it operates in order to infer that the existence of a multiverse is the best explanation for fine-tuning. As such, Craig's 'mere speculation' criticism and list of specific arguments against particular multiverse proposals are simply not relevant, as they concern only the details of particular models and not to the concept of a multiverse as a whole.

The only argument that Craig advances against the multiverse hypothesis in general is that it is *ad hoc*, meaning that there is no reason for thinking that such a multiverse exists except for the fine-tuning it is supposed to explain. This response, however, could just as easily be directed against Craig's preferred explanation of intelligent design. Even if we think (on the basis of some other argument) that the universe was created by some sort of deity, it does not follow that this deity would necessary have any purpose or reason to create a universe suitable for embodied intelligent life, or that this God would fine-tune the constants of physics in order to create such a world. The only reason to suppose that God would want to create embodied, intelligent life through a finely-tuned universe is the very fact of fine-tuning it is supposed to be explaining, which is no different than the multiverse hypothesis. God, after all, is omnipotent, and therefore is able to create as many embodied agents as he wishes regardless of whatever constants of nature he may have put in place. To see this, consider that in the case of the resurrection of Jesus, Christians believe that God raised a man from the dead despite the fact that the universe he created has laws that (in the normal course of events) make it impossible for a dead man to come back to life. God is able to do this, Christians believe, because he is all-powerful and so not limited by the laws of physics. If we believe that God can act in this way in one case, why should he not similarly create intelligent life even in a universe where such life (in the normal course of events) would not be able to exist? God is simply not bound by the laws of physics, since he himself creates those laws. As such, even if a God did exist who wanted to create embodied intelligent life, it doesn't follow that he would necessarily have any reason to create a fine-tuned universe, since he could create such life regardless of the laws of physics. The cosmic designer hypothesis, therefore, only explains why life exists, not why the constants of nature are fine-tuned for the existence of such life.

Craig may respond that God generally works through the operation of natural laws, the resurrection of Jesus and other miracles being the exceptions that prove the rule. This amounts to claiming that God has a reason to bring about his ends through the operation of natural laws, except in the cases where he chooses not to (e.g. the resurrection of Jesus). The problem is that this position is *ad hoc*, because there is no reason why we should expect God to act in this way, apart from the very fact of fine-tuning the theory is supposed to explain. In other words, the only reason we have for thinking that God would need the universe to be fine-tuned for life (as opposed to the creation of life being a miraculous intervention) is because we observe the universe to be finely-tuned. Thus, proposing that God finely-tuned the universe for life is no less *ad hoc* than proposing the existence of a multiverse in order to explain fine-tuning. Craig may find the design hypothesis more plausible, but that is only to be expected given his philosophical and theological allegiances, and does not constitute an argument as to why one is objectively a better explanation than the other. It does not seem to me that Craig has provided any compelling argument for this position.

Physical Necessity as an Explanation

Craig argues that the fine-tuning of the universe is not due to physical necessity because as far as we know the values of the physical constants are independent of the laws of nature, and therefore could have been different. Of course, this is only to say that *so far as we know* there is no deeper law that determines the values of physical constants. Craig cannot infer from this that there definitely is no deeper law, or cannot be a deeper law; any such inference is mere speculation. We simply do not know whether there is a deeper law which determines what the constants must be. Of course, the fact that there *might* be a deeper law does not itself constitute an explanation for fine-tuning. All it means is that an explanation may not turn out to be necessary if the values are fixed by some deeper law that itself is metaphysically necessary, and thus (in Craig's view) not itself in need of further explanation. Nevertheless, Craig cannot give any reason as to why this is unlikely to be the case – we simply do not know. Physicists continue to search for a deeper 'theory of everything', and so the 'deeper law' possibility remains a live option.

SUMMARY OF THE ARGUMENT

The fine-tuning argument attempts to establish that the best explanation for the fine-tuning of various physical constants for the existence of intelligent, embodied life is that the laws of physics were designed by a creator. There is undoubtedly something intuitively compelling about this argument. After all, we can imagine a wide range of possible universes in which life could exist, and this leads naturally to the question of why our life-permitting universe exists, and not one of the many possible non-life-permitting universes. The existence of a God with an interest in creating conditions suitable for the existence of intelligent life seems to provide a very natural explanation for this outcome. While I do think there is some validity to this sort of reasoning, the trouble comes in attempting to make the argument rigorous. I believe that the efforts of Craig and Collins to do so are ultimately unsuccessful, leaving the fine-tuning argument far less powerful than Craig claims.

I have contended that the single greatest problem with Craig's version of the fine-tuning argument is that he has not presented sufficient evidence that the physical constants of nature are 'fine-tuned' for life to the degree of precision he claims. I showed how his argument that such fine-tuning is an established scientific fact is based upon a misinterpretation of what physicists have actually found, which is only that small deviations in the values of physical constants would render carbon-based life of the sort that we know impossible. Craig's claim that science has shown that the universe is fine-tuned for the existence of any sort of embodied life is simply not correct, since it is not known under what conditions life can exist when it is defined so broadly. I also showed how Craig's argument faces the dimensionality problem, whereby the overall probability of the physical constants being life-permitting cannot be determined simply by examining each constant in isolation since they interact in complex ways. Finally, I argued that Craig has failed to provide sufficient justification for assuming that what Collins calls the 'epistemically illuminated' region of the space of possible values of physical constants is representative of the phase space as a whole. All these considerations greatly weaken the case for the existence of fine-tuning, and render it implausible for Craig to claim that it has been shown that the physical constants of nature are finely-tuned to an extremely high degree of precision for the existence of intelligent life. In fact we have no idea how finely-tuned the parameters are, since we do not know under what conditions life (broadly defined) is possible, nor what sorts of physics would be possible if the values of the constants were very different.

A final problem with Craig's fine-tuning argument is that he too readily dismisses the possibility of explaining fine-tuning by appeal to a multiverse. While many of Craig's specific criticisms of particular physical models for a multiverse are valid, he overlooks the fact that it is not necessary to provide a physical mechanism for how a multiverse could produce fine-tuning. Rather, all that is required is to show that the existence of a multiverse would be sufficient to explain fine-tuning if it existed. This is a principle that Craig himself applies to his own preferred explanation of intelligent design, but then arbitrarily refuses to apply to the multiverse hypothesis. His responses to particular models for a multiverse are thus beside the point, for they do not show that a multiverse as such is impossible. Since they both lack mechanisms or explanations as to how they could work, the design and multiverse hypotheses should both be either rejected or seriously considered on their merits – applying different criteria to each is arbitrary and unjustified. As such, Craig has failed to show that chance is not a plausible explanation for fine-tuning. Overall, therefore, while the fine-tuning argument retains some degree of persuasive force, it is a much less compelling argument for the existence of God than Craig claims it to be.

CHAPTER FOUR
THE MORAL ARGUMENT

OVERVIEW OF THE ARGUMENT

Craig argues that the existence of objective moral values is evidence for the existence of God. His moral argument can be summarised as follows:

- Premise One: If God does not exist, then objective moral values do not exist.
- Premise Two: Objective moral values do exist.
- Conclusion: God exists.

By the term 'objective moral values', Craig means moral facts whose truth is independent of whatever anyone thinks about them. He gives the following example[235]:

> "To say that there are objective moral values is to say that something is right or wrong independently of whether anybody believes it to be so. It is to say, for example, that Nazi anti-Semitism was morally wrong, even though the Nazis who carried out the Holocaust thought that it was good; and it would still be wrong even if the Nazis had won World War II and succeeded in exterminating or brainwashing everybody who disagreed with them."

It is important to emphasise that Craig is *not* arguing that belief in God is necessary in order to know what is right or wrong, nor is he arguing that atheists are incapable of leading morally good lives. Craig describes this as a distinction between moral epistemology and moral ontology[236]:

James Fodor

"The claim that moral values and duties are rooted in God is a metaethical claim about moral ontology. It is not fundamentally a claim about moral linguistics or about moral epistemology. It is fundamentally a claim about the metaphysical status of moral properties, not a claim about the meaning of moral sentences or about the justification or knowledge of moral principles... the theist will agree quite readily... that we do not need to know or even believe that God exists in order to discern objective moral values or to recognize our moral duties."

In defence of his first premise that objective moral values cannot exist without God, Craig's key argument is that absent a perfect divine being to act as the source of morality, there cannot be anything which serves as the ontological foundation of moral values. I will discuss this issue in greater detail later in this chapter, but given that his argument hinges so critically on this notion of determining the grounding for moral values, I think it is helpful to reformulate Craig's argument to make more explicit some additional assumptions and steps of reasoning that he is making. My reformulation of Craig's argument can be summarised as follows:

- Premise One: If there are objective moral facts, they must have some sort of ontological foundation.
- Premise Two: Objective moral facts exist.
- Premise Three: God provides an objective ontological foundation for moral facts.
- Premise Four: Without God there cannot be any ontological foundation for objective moral facts.
- Conclusion: God exists.

I will now proceed to consider each of these four premises in turn. By far the most important and controversial premise, and also that for which I thinks Craig's arguments are the weakest, is premise four, and it is this premise that I devote the majority of the discussion to.

Note that throughout this chapter I will use the terms 'moral values' and 'moral facts' interchangeably. By either term I mean moral states of affairs which pertain in the objective, external world. Thus, to say that 'rape is wrong is a moral fact' or 'it as an objective moral truth that rape is wrong' means that 'rape being wrong refers to some state of affairs in the world which pertains objectively and independently of our apprehension of it'. As far as I can tell, this is consistent with Craig's usage of these terms.

PREMISE ONE: MORAL FACTS REQUIRE GROUNDING

While Craig is clear that he believes objective moral facts require 'grounding', as Wes Morriston notes, he is often rather vague as to exactly what he means by this. He has, however, endorsed an account by Mark Murphy, according to which Y grounds the existence of X when Y is more ontologically basic than X, and also explains X's existence. So, for example[237]:

> "If we ask ... about whether language has a foundation or grounding, we are likely to appeal to persons and their interaction as more ontologically basic and as explaining the phenomenon of language."

In asserting that moral values must have an ontological grounding, Craig is asserting that if moral facts exist then they must do so only in virtue of something that exists more fundamentally. Murphy describes this as providing an 'informative identification' of morality with something more basic.

It is not clear, however, that moral facts *do* require any further foundation beyond themselves. Moral facts may simply be irreducible brute facts which are true all by themselves, not true in virtue of any other facts that are more fundamental. For example, the fact that "electrons have a charge of -1" is not true in virtue of any other fact about reality, nor is it true by definition (for they might easily have a different charge). Instead, it is simply a brute fact – there is no answer to the question 'in virtue of what is true', other than to say, 'it simply is!' Some philosophers think that moral facts (or at least the most basic, fundamental moral facts) are also like this. For example, a proposition like 'causing unnecessary harm is morally wrong' is not true in virtue of anything else; it is simply a brute fact true by itself. After all, any explanation of a fact must *eventually* terminate at some stopping point, so what is wrong with terminating moral explanations in terms of basic moral facts? Wes Morriston articulates this position as follows[238]:

> "Why are love and justice and generosity and kindness and faithfulness good? What is there in the depths of reality to make them good? My own preferred answer is: Nothing further. If you like, you may say that they are the ultimate standard of goodness. What makes them the standard? Nothing further. Possessing these characteristics just is good-making. Full stop. Is there some problem with this? Some reason to press on, looking for a 'deeper' answer that only theism can provide? It's not obvious that there is. No matter what story you tell about the ontological ground of moral value, you must at some point come to your own full stop."

Note that to say that moral facts are fundamental is not to say that moral values exist as some sort of platonic abstraction such as numbers or sets. Craig sometimes confuses these two issues, as for instance when he says[239]:

> "Atheistic Moral Platonists affirm that objective moral values do exist but are not grounded in God. Indeed, moral values have no further foundation. They just exist. It is difficult, however, even to comprehend this view. What does it mean to say, for example, that the moral value Justice just exists? It's hard to know what to make of this. It is clear what is meant when it is said that a person is just; but it is bewildering when it is said that in the absence of any people, Justice itself exists."

To assert that moral facts are fundamental is simply, as Wes Morriston says, to affirm that virtues like kindness and justice, or acts that increase the flourishing of conscious creatures, are simply good in themselves. They are not good in virtue of some other property that they hold, nor does the fact that they are good have or require some further explanation. This is not to say that there is some ethereal thing called 'justice' which exists apart from any particular act or person. Acts of justice aren't good because they somehow embody the abstract object of 'justice'. Rather, they are simply good because they are just, and that is the end of the explanation. In conflating the two issues of moral Platonism (the view that abstract objects like 'justice' exist) and the view that moral facts are foundational (do not exist in virtue of anything beyond themselves), Craig is confusing the issue and thus attacking a straw man. As Morriston explains[240]:

> "The pertinent issue here isn't whether uninstantiated moral properties can exist. It is whether – in a Godless universe – goodness is present in whatever instances of love and justice might exist in that universe. So far, then, Craig has done nothing to show either (a) that love and justice could not be instantiated in a Godless universe or (b) that goodness would not be present if they were."

Craig says nothing about this issue, but simply presupposes the impossibility of some moral facts being brute facts. He assumes without argument that moral facts cannot be brute facts, but must exist in virtue of something more fundamental. This is all the more puzzling since he does discuss the possibility of irreducible brute facts (or basic facts) elsewhere in his work, and so it is unclear why the concept could not be applied to the case of moral values. Furthermore, Craig also believes that knowledge of moral facts and morally good behaviour are both possible regardless of the status of moral values, and so it does not even seem that such grounding serves any practical or functional purpose. I conclude that Craig has offered no reason to accept his first premise that moral values require any further grounding outside themselves.

PREMISE TWO: OBJECTIVE MORAL FACTS EXIST

Craig's main argument for the existence of objective moral facts is intuitive and experiential: we all just know that moral facts exist, as we directly apprehend them from our experience. Craig says[241]:

> "Objective values do exist, and deep down we all know it... There's no more reason to deny the objective reality of moral

James Fodor

values than the objective reality of the physical world. Actions like rape, cruelty, and child abuse aren't just socially unacceptable behaviour – they're moral abominations."

The position that Craig is endorsing here is known as moral realism, the view that there are objective moral facts. Craig is arguing that we directly perceive the truth of moral realism in the same way that we directly perceive the existence of the external physical world. Although I am personally sympathetic to moral realism, I do not believe Craig's argument for this view is very persuasive. In this section, I will therefore consider several problems with his argument for moral realism, and consider some of the implications this has for his moral argument as a whole.

COGNITIVISM AND NON-COGNITIVISM

Craig uses the language of truth and falsity in discussing moral values, and in doing so he implicitly presupposes the truth of a position called moral cognitivism. Moral cognitivism is a theory in metaethics according to which moral statements are propositions with truth values. It stands in contrast to non-cognitivist theories which deny that moral statements are propositions, instead holding that they are variously injunctions, emotive expressions, or something else entirely. According to such non-cognitivist views, the phrase 'rape is wrong' really means something like 'don't rape!' (an injunction) or 'boo on rape!' (an emotive expression), neither of which are propositions that can be true or false. That Craig presumes the truth of moral cognitivism is important because his demand for a foundation of the existence of moral facts becomes irrelevant if moral facts do not actually exist. While Craig thinks that is it just obvious that 'rape is wrong' and that this is something we can directly apprehend, directly apprehending that 'rape is wrong' is not the same as directly apprehending 'it is objectively true that rape is wrong'. That is, while we directly perceive morality in relation to our actions and the actions of others, we don't directly perceive the truth of moral cognitivism itself. To argue otherwise is to confuse our moral perceptions with one particular theoretical account of them, a mistake I argue Craig makes repeatedly in his writings (see for example my

193

discussion of his arguments for the tensed theory of time). Many moral non-cognitivists would agree that 'rape is wrong', but would not agree with Craig's theoretical account as to what such a statement means (see figure 12 for an illustration of this). To establish this requires further philosophical discussion and reflection on what we mean exactly when we make moral judgements.

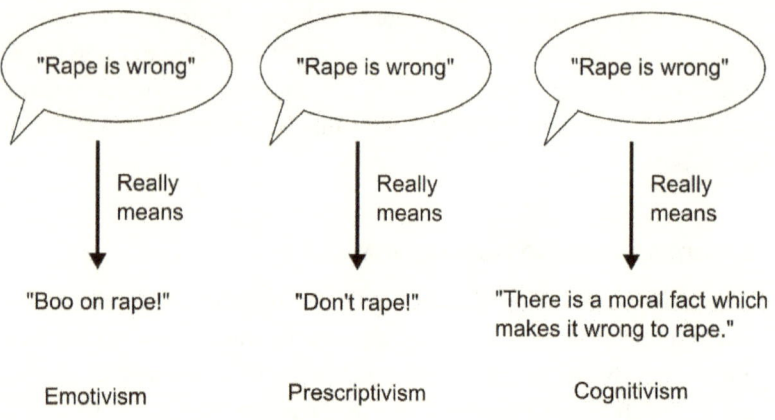

Figure 12. Diagrammatic representation of the way in which different metaethical systems provide different interpretations of the meaning of the exact same moral statement.

Evidently recognising this, Craig has provided reasons for rejecting non-cognitivism theories, arguing that they "fail to do justice to the nature of morality[242]." He offers three main arguments in support of this contention. First, he argues that moral judgements can be made in the absence either of any emotive reaction occurring or any injunction being made, which implies that morality cannot consist purely of emotional reactions or the issuing of commands. To support this, he provides the example[243]:

> "One can form the judgment 'Killing rats is wrong' without feeling or commanding anything."

The idea behind this objection seems to be that moral judgements can be made simply by thinking about them, without making any actual emotive expressions or issuing any commands. The problem with this objection is that non-cognitivists typically argue only that moral *statements* are emotional expressions or injunctions, not that internal moral judgements or thoughts are also emotional expressions or injunctions. Craig is thus attacking a straw man, as under such theories making a purely internal moral judgement could easily be understood as recognising that one would be disposed to a particular emotive reaction or likely to issue an injunction when the relevant circumstance comes about. So, for example, forming the purely internal judgement 'killing rats is wrong' would under emotivism amount to consciously recognising that one reacts negatively to the killing of rats. Craig may think that this is not what *he* is doing when he makes an internal moral judgement, but that is simply to restate without argument his opposition to non-cognitivist theories of ethics.

Second, Craig argues that non-cognitivist theories of morality make moral disagreement impossible, for according to these theories neither party to a disagreement is actually making an assertion, and thus nobody can be right or wrong. Craig says this is implausible, since we observe that moral disagreement is widespread. The trouble with this argument is that seems to be adopting an unduly narrow conception of disagreement, whereby two people disagree only if they affirm mutually contradictory propositions. It is quite plausible however, that many things we would typically describe as disagreements would not fit this definition. Two authorities issuing contradictory commands, for example, are clearly in disagreement, even if neither asserts any actual proposition. If non-cognitivism is true, moral disagreement obviously does not take the form of assertion of different propositions, but the assertion of mutually conflicting injunctions or wildly different emotional reactions. Thus, the problem here is Craig's overly narrow conception of moral disagreement, and not the inconsistency of non-cognitivism with the existence of moral disagreement.

Third, Craig argues that moral judgements can stand in logical relation to one another, but injunctions and emotive expressions cannot stand in logical relation to one another, so clearly moral values cannot be injunctions or emotive expressions. All this argument seems to establish, however, is that an adequate logical theory for non-cognitivist moral theories has not yet been devised. This should not come as especially surprising considering the theories in question have not been around for very long. Furthermore, modal and temporal logics, to which Craig frequently appeals in his writings about the nature of time, God's omniscience, the ontological argument, and in many other instances, were devised only a few decades ago. Prior to that, we lacked an adequate theory for how possibility statements stood in logical relation to one another. At present there are many other forms of logic that are being developed, and no reason to suppose that one could not also be developed which would apply to non-cognitivist moral claims. Some attempts have already been made to develop such a theory, against which Craig offers various criticisms. My point here is not to defend any particular account of non-cognitivist moral logic, but rather that the current non-existence of such a theory does not show that no such theory is impossible, or that moral injunctions etc. cannot stand in logical relationship to each other.

Overall, I conclude that Craig has provided insufficient justification for his rejection of non-cognitivist theories of morality, and thus lacks a sufficient basis for his claim that objective moral values exist. This is important because Craig's primary argument for the existence of moral facts is that all morally-competent persons can directly apprehend that, for example, 'rape is wrong'. Under non-cognitivist theories of ethics, however, this statement does not constitute a proposition, and so one can agree that 'rape is wrong' without thereby committing oneself to the existence of objective moral truths. As such, Craig's failure to show that non-cognitivist theories of morality are false means that he fails to establish his key second premise that objective moral values exist.

RELATIVISM AND UNIVERSALISM

Craig says that for moral values to be objective they must be right or wrong 'independently of whether anybody believes it to be so'. Obviously by 'anybody' Craig must mean 'anybody apart from God', since Craig's account of morality is dependent on the judgements of God,

James Fodor

and presumably God is 'somebody'. The idea seems to be that it is not sufficient merely for some individuals or groups of people to believe that something is right or wrong; rather there needs to be some objective sense in which facts of rightness and wrongness are independent of parochial human opinion. Behind this is an assumption that if God believes something to be right or wrong, then it really is objectively right or wrong. Human opinion is deemed to be subjective and insufficient to ground morality, while divine judgement is considered objectively transcendent. While this premise is likely quite intuitive to Craig, it is nevertheless an additional assumption that he does not really defend in any depth. In particular, others have argued that truly objective morality requires a standard independent of anyone's opinion – including God. I discuss this issue at more depth in the subsequent section covering premise three of Craig's moral argument.

Craig's Mutually-Conflicting Arguments

If, as Craig says, it is intuitively obvious to every morally competent person that objective moral values exist, then it seems plausible that this is a belief too entrenched to be shaken simply by the inability to provide a philosophically robust grounding for objective moral values. If this is the case, then Craig's efforts to establish the existence of objective moral values may undermine his efforts to establish the premise that if God does not exist, then objective moral values do not exist. We can see this by applying a technique that Craig himself uses in responding to the problem of evil, which he justifies by quoting the philosophical adage[244]:

"One man's modus ponens is another man's modes tollens."

We first consider Craig's original moral argument:

- Premise 1a: Objective moral values exist.
- Premise 2a: If God does not exist, then objective moral values do not exist.
- Conclusion a: Therefore, God exists.

Now consider now an inverted form of Craig's argument:

- Premise 1b: Objective moral values exist.
- Premise 2b: God does not exist.
- Conclusion b: Therefore, God is not necessary to ground objective moral values.

Since the first premise is identical, and Craig believes is very strongly confirmed in our experience, which of the above two arguments we accept will depend solely upon whether one regards premise 2a or 2b more plausible. Since, as I argue below in my discussion of premise four, Craig's arguments for premise 2a are quite weak, anyone who thinks that God's nonexistence is at least somewhat likely should judge the second argument more plausible than the first. In order to avoid this objection, Craig would need to show not just that premise 2a is more likely to be true than not, but also that it is more likely true than premise 2b. Craig may well believe he has does this by his other arguments for the existence of God, however those like me who are generally unpersuaded by Craig's other arguments are liable to reject Craig's claim to have shown that premise 2a is more plausible than premise 2b. As such, by the second argument given above they are perfectly rational to conclude that God is not necessary to ground objective moral values, even if they cannot actually present any specific non-theistic foundation for moral values.

POSSIBLE DEFEATERS OF OUR MORAL EXPERIENCE

Craig regards the truth of moral realism as a properly basic belief, something that he is justified in affirming without any argument. Even if we accept that this is the case, Craig himself acknowledges that properly basic beliefs can be overturned if subject to sufficiently strong defeaters. Thus, our direct experience of the truth of moral realism could be defeated if it was shown to contradict even more readily apparent beliefs, or a sufficient number of slightly less apparent beliefs. Yet another possible variation of Craig's moral argument is therefore possible:

- Premise 1c: God does not exist.

- Premise 2c: If God does not exist, then objective moral values do not exist.
- Conclusion c: Therefore, objective moral values do not exist.

Since the second premises (2a and 2b) are the same, whether one accepts conclusion a or conclusion c will depend upon whether one regards premise 1a or premise 1c as more likely. If one is inclined to think the existence of God quite improbable, then it is reasonable to reject the existence of objective moral values and conclude that God does not exist. To do so is not equivalent to embracing moral nihilism, but rather could constitute a reason for embracing a non-cognitivist understanding of morality as discussed above. As Stephen Law has argued[245]:

> "I agree objective moral values exist up until I am shown reason to believe the first premise (if atheism is true there is no objective morality) is true (which Craig never supplied). At that point, the rational thing for me to do, given overwhelming empirical evidence there's no god (as Craig defines god), is to give up on moral realism... I might not like that conclusion very much. And it is counterintuitive. But, hey, sometimes we have to give up what seemed intuitively obvious, such as that the earth does not move, in the face of powerful evidence to the contrary."

As a result of these considerations, I conclude that Craig's formulation of the moral argument is very sensitive to the prior assumptions one brings to the table concerning the relative plausibility of different propositions. Those who regard the existence of God as somewhat or very likely are liable to be persuaded by Craig's argument, while those who regard God's existence as relatively unlikely will quite rationally reject one of Craig's premises and therefore find his argument unpersuasive. This is the case even if, as Craig asserts, the belief in objective moral values is a properly basic belief, since this still leaves two alternate argumentation paths available depending upon the plausibility assigned to the other premises. Thus, even before considering Craig's discussion of the foundation for moral values, his argument is not robust to those who are not already predisposed to accept Craig's conclusion.

Premise Three: God Provides a Foundation for Moral Facts

God's Nature as the Basis of Morality

Craig believes that Christian theism can provide a sound grounding for objective moral values in the form of a position known as divine command theory. Under the view defended by Craig, something is morally good if it is commanded by God, while something is morally bad if it is forbidden by God. God's commands exist objectively independent of what anybody thinks about them, and so supply an objective basis for moral values. Craig also argues that God's commands are not arbitrary, but "flow necessarily from his moral nature"[246]. Thus, Craig ultimately grounds moral values by 'informatively identifying' them with certain attributes of God, such that a statement like 'rape is wrong' is ultimately true because of some particular attributes of God's character. Furthermore, the moral duty to not commit rape exists in virtue of God's issuing the command to not rape. Craig argues that God provides the perfect moral paradigm for us to emulate, and acts as the standard and grounding of moral value[247]:

> "God's own holy and perfectly good nature supplies the absolute standard against which all actions and decisions are measured. God's moral nature is what Plato called the 'Good'. He is the locus and source of moral value. He is by nature loving, generous, just, faithful, kind, and so forth."

While this theory may sound intuitively plausible on first blush, closer examination reveals this is sorely lacking as a foundation for morality. Although Craig describes God as 'loving, generous, just, etc.', he cannot argue that God's nature is good *because* God possesses these traits, for if so then the ultimate foundation of morality would lie in characteristics or values external to God. He would be asserting that attributes such as lovingness, generosity, justice, etc., were more fundamental than God's nature, and thereby the goodness of God's nature pertains only because it accords with these independently existing, more basic properties. This would undermine Craig's argument that

God is the ultimate locus and source of moral values. As Wes Morriston explains[248]:

> "The trouble is that this makes it look as if love and generosity and justice and the rest are doing all the work in the proffered account of moral goodness, leaving God no significant role to play."

Instead, Craig has to argue that the dependence is the other way around, that lovingness, generosity, justice, etc. are good *because* these are attributes of God. Yet this view faces the problem that it entails that generosity, justice, etc., are *only* good because they are attributes of God, meaning that if God did not exist or embodied different properties, then these attributes would not be morally valuable. However, this is inconsistent with what we know about morality, namely that such things are valuable in themselves, irrespective of the existence of God. This is a point that Craig himself seems to recognise, as illustrated in the following passage[249]:

> "A judgment is moral only if it makes reference to proper human flourishing, human dignity, the welfare of others, the prevention of harm and the provision of benefit."

If (as I think it should be) this criterion is accepted as constitutive of moral judgements, then it poses significant problems for Craig's attempt to ground morality in God. Under his account moral facts are true in virtue only of whether they refer to aspects of God's nature, totally irrespective of whether or not they relate to human well-being or suffering. Craig could of course argue that concern for human well-being is intrinsic to God's nature, however this would still incorrectly identify what makes a judgement moral as whether it refers to God's nature, this being more primary or fundamental than whether the judgement has anything to do with human well-being. Craig therefore says that[250]:

> "The theist can agree that God forbids rape because it is bad; and it is bad because it is incompatible with God's nature."

I contend, however, that our moral experience clearly shows that this is simply not correct. Rape is not wrong 'because it is incompatible with God's nature'; it is wrong because it causes grievous and unjustified harm to the victim. Since it posits what I think is clearly an incorrect explanation for the truth of moral claims, I believe that Craig's account is deeply implausible, and would require significant arguments in its favour in order to overcome such implausibility. I do not believe, however, that Craig is able to provide such arguments.

There is a second problem with appealing to God's nature as the locus of moral value. This issue is illustrated by the following passage, where Craig states[251]:

> "The Good is determined paradigmatically by God's own character. Just as a meter was once defined paradigmatically by the length of an iridium bar housed in the Bureau des Poids et des Mesures in Paris, so moral values are determined by the paradigm of God's holy and loving character."

There is, however, a strong disanalogy between God and the meter stick. In the case of the meter stick, it is the length of the stick which defines the length of the meter, while it is merely stated as 'God's character' or 'God's nature' that determines the standard of morality. This by itself is unsatisfactory, since 'God's nature' includes a wide range of properties which are not moral in nature, such as being all-powerful, immaterial, personal, and all-knowing. It seems incorrect to say that God's being immaterial is relevant to providing a grounding for moral values, just as the iridium bar's being made of iridium was irrelevant to it providing a standard for measurement of the meter. Thus, I think Craig must argue that God's *moral nature* or *moral properties*, rather than his nature as a whole, is what serves as the grounding for moral values. This formulation, however, raises the problem as to what it is about certain properties or aspects of God's nature that make them distinctively 'moral'. For example, why is God's characteristic of being 'kind' something that serves to ground the existence of objective moral values, while his characteristic of being immaterial does not? Obviously, it can't be that 'lovingness' is a moral virtue which exists independently of God, since this would undermine Craig's argument of God's nature being the ultimate source of moral value. Craig's position thus seems unable to explain why particular characteristics of God, and only those, are 'good-making', without appealing to external criteria or standards of goodness. As Wes Morriston argues[252]:

> "Craig says that God's moral nature is the ultimate standard of goodness. But what is God's moral nature? By way of explanation, Craig says that God is essentially 'loving, generous, just, faithful, kind, and so forth'. But this raises more questions than it answers. If God's moral nature consists in these properties, one has to wonder what role the existence of a deity who possesses these wonderful properties is supposed to play in Craig's moral ontology."

As a result of these difficulties, I believe that Craig's attempt to ground moral values in God's nature fails.

THE EUTHYPHRO DILEMMA

Originally proposed by Plato, the Euthyphro dilemma has often been put forward as an objection against divine command theories of ethics. The dilemma is posed by the question:

Is something good because it is commanded by God, or does God command it because it is good?

Either option seems problematic for the theist. If something is good only because it is commanded by God, then goodness becomes ultimately arbitrary, since if God had commanded us to rape and kill then these would become 'right'. On the other hand, if God commands something because it is good, then there must be some standard or basis for morality outside of and independently of God, thereby making God's commandments unnecessary for grounding morality. Craig is able to avoid this dilemma because he advocates a form of what is called modified divine command theory, according to which nothing is good independently of God, but only in virtue of divine commandments. Such commandments, however, are not arbitrary, since they derive from and are grounded in his good and loving nature.

While Craig's theory avoids the classical form of the Euthyphro dilemma, I believe that it is vulnerable to an altered from of the dilemma, what is often called the arbitrariness objection. Under Craig's account, moral facts are dependent upon particular attributes of God's character. It follows that if God's attributes were different, then certain moral facts would be different – e.g. if God lacked a disposition against cruelty, or was not kind, then cruelty would not be morally wrong and kindness would not be morally good. Thus, according to Craig's account, propositions such as 'if it wasn't against God's nature, then cruelty wouldn't be morally wrong' would be true. Yet it is obvious that such statements are clearly false – cruelty would still be wrong even if God's nature were different, because cruelty is wrong in and of itself. As Wes Morriston explains, this is such an absurd consequence as to render Craig's account of the grounding of morality extremely implausible[253]:

> "Could Craig get away with saying that love and generosity and justice and faithfulness and the rest are good-making only because there is a God who is loving and generous and faithful (etc.) to the maximum possible degree? This alternative seems incredible to me. It implies that if there were no God who perfectly exemplified them, these properties would count for nothing. A person could be as fair-minded and loving and generous and faithful as you please and still fail to be morally better than a cruel and malicious person. Why would a discerning and consistent atheist have to think a thing like that?"

Craig's response to this problem is to avoid the issue by arguing that God's nature is necessary (i.e. it is the same in all possible worlds), and thus conditionals of the form 'if God's nature were different' have an impossible antecedent. Craig argues that conditionals with impossible antecedents are essentially nonsense and have no bearing on the matter of the grounding of morality. He compares them to nonsensical questions like[254]:

> "If there were a round square, its area would equal the square of one of its sides."

I think, however, that Craig is clearly wrong about this, as it is quite easy to give examples of conditionals with impossible antecedents that nevertheless are perfectly meaningful to assert. The fact that some counterfactuals with impossible antecedents are simply incoherent doesn't imply that *all* such counterfactuals are. For example, all mathematical theorems are true necessarily. Yet it is perfectly reasonable to say, "if the theorem P=NP is true then cryptography would be much more difficult" or "if the theorem P=NP is not true then many difficult computational problems will never be solved quickly." The reader need not be concerned if they don't know what the theorem P=NP refers to; the point is that these statements are perfectly meaningful and are exactly the sort of things that computer scientists say when discussing this problem, even though one of these statements has an antecedent that is logically impossible.

Indeed, if we apply Craig's dictum against conditionals with impossible antecedents consistently, this would rule out the key premise of Craig's very own moral argument that 'If God did not exist, objective moral values would not exist'. After all, Craig affirms that God's existence is metaphysically necessary[255], and therefore it is impossible for the antecedent of this proposition to be fulfilled. I think it is clear that Craig is stuck in a bind here: if impossible conditions are ruled out, then his moral argument must be completely reformulated, while if they are allowed, then his account is rendered grossly implausible by affirming statements like 'if God's nature was different, killing would be morally right'. As such, Craig's modified divine command theory is still subject to the arbitrariness horn of the Euthyphro dilemma.

THE CHALLENGE OF IDEAL OBSERVER THEORY

Yet another problem for Craig's moral argument is that his formulation of the foundation of objective moral values lends support for a metaethical theory known as ideal observer theory. According to this view, an act is right or wrong depending upon whether it would be approved of by a fully moral observer with access to all the relevant information. The important point is that all that matters is what such an entity would endorse *if they existed* – whether or not they *actually exist* is not important. As Morriston explains[256]:

> *"Even by his lights, there must be a fact of the matter about what a being possessing a perfect moral nature would command if there were such a being. Once again, it turns out that the*

> *actual existence of God makes no difference to the ontological foundation of morality."*

Since all that Craig requires is that objective moral values have some grounding, this reasoning constitutes a rebuttal to Craig's claim that the actual existence of God is necessary for providing a foundation for moral values. This is because all that is needed is that there be some fact of the matter, or some state of affairs, corresponding to what such a being would endorse. If this is the case, then objective moral values have a foundation regardless of whether God actually exists or not.

PREMISE FOUR: THERE IS NO NON-THEISTIC GROUNDING FOR MORAL FACTS

Uncharacteristically, Craig does not provide any clear or coherent argument in favour of his crucial premise that moral facts cannot be grounded outside of God. Instead he makes several brief and apparently unrelated arguments, provides quotes from various philosophers, asks questions, and criticises particular statements made by various atheists defending the existence of objective moral values. This lack of cohesion in Craig's argument renders it effectively impossible to present a summary of or response to Craig's case in any cogent order. Instead, I will address various remarks and responses that he has made individually, attempting when possible to identify connections and interrelations between them.

NON-THEISTIC THEORIES OF MORALITY

Craig argues that if atheism is true, there can be no ontological foundation for moral values. He writes[257]:

> *"If God does not exist, then what is the foundation for moral values? More particularly, what is the basis for the value of human beings? If God does not exist, then it is difficult to see any reason to think that human beings are special or that their morality is objectively valid."*

Likewise he asks[258]:

> "*If there is no God, what reason is there to regard human flourishing as in any way significant?*"

Questions like this abound in Craig's discussion of the moral argument, unfortunately with relatively little in the way of clarification as to exactly what chain of reasoning Craig is attempting to construct to establish his desired conclusion. The way he phrases his argument as a series of questions is especially odd given that, in discussing the problem of evil with Michael Payton, Craig retorted that "asking a question isn't an argument"[259]. Nevertheless, we may infer from his remarks that Craig believes that no atheistic account of objective moral values has been developed or can be developed which is able to provide satisfactory answers to these questions. In particular, he believes that only by appealing to God can an objective ontological grounding for moral values be provided, as in an atheistic universe there would simply be nothing suitable in virtue of which moral propositions would be true, and thus there would be nothing to establish an objective difference between right and wrong.

Obviously, if God does not exist then God cannot serve as the foundation for objective moral values. But what argument does Craig give for the assertion that nothing else can serve this role? One of his common strategies is to appeal to the remarks made by various atheist scientists and philosophers. For example[260]:

> "*Richard Dawkins' assessment of human worth may be depressing, but why, on atheism, is he mistaken when he says, 'there is at bottom no design, no purpose, no evil, no good, nothing but pointless indifference... We are machines for propagating DNA... It is every living object's sole reason for being'?* Atheist philosophers who are humanists do not seem to have faced squarely the consequences of their naturalism. *For example, humanist philosopher Paul Kurtz insists that human flourishing is 'the be-all and end-all' of human life, while affirming like Dawkins that 'the discoveries of Copernicus and Darwin... have [undermined] the belief that we are fundamentally different from all other species'.*"

Elsewhere, Craig appeals to quotations apparently affirming his key fourth premise from Bertrand Russell, Friedrich Nietzsche, Richard Taylor, Fyodor Dostoyevsky, and many others. Yet it is unclear what such appeal to authority is supposed to achieve in this context, since one can equally well cite many examples (often from the very same figures Craig quotes) of atheists affirming that objective moral values in no way depend upon God. As Walter Sinnott-Armstrong aptly says[261]:

> *"(That objective moral values exist) implies nothing about God, unless objective values depend on God. Why should we believe that they do? Because Russell, Ruse, and Nietzsche say so? But their claims are denied by many philosophers, atheists as well as theists. Even Russell and Ruse themselves denied these claims at other times in their careers. So Craig needs a reason to believe some authorities rather than others."*

The problem with Craig's argument, however, is not only that he selectively quotes some philosophers while ignoring others. Despite claiming that no non-theistic foundation of morality is possible, Craig completely ignores the large number of metaethical theories concerning the foundation of objective moral values that have already been developed and widely discussed in the philosophical literature. Prominent among such theories are the following:

- Railton's reductive naturalism[262]: moral propositions are true in virtue of objective facts concerning the maximal fulfilment of idealised desires, which are what individuals would want themselves to desire if they had access to all the relevant information.

- Jackson's moral functionalism[263]: a reductive analysis of moral discourse which holds that the truth of moral propositions is based upon non-moral properties which collectively account for the various functions that moral terms play in the complex conceptual scheme that we call 'morality'.

- Cornell realism[264]: a non-reductive account of morality which holds that properties like 'rightness' supervene on a range of different non-moral properties depending upon the situation. Thus, there is no single thing that makes moral propositions true, but a wide range of facts and properties corresponding to the diversity of ethical circumstances we can experience.

- Discourse ethics[265]: building upon Kant's deontology – in this theory moral facts are true in virtue of universalisable presuppositions that underpin discourse between persons.

- Contractualism[266]: ethics is based upon certain norms or rules of behaviour which, if not always accepted in the real world, nevertheless could not reasonably be objected to if they were to be agreed upon from an informed and unbiased vantage point.

- Ethical intuitionism[267]: moral propositions are true in virtue of simple irreducible non-natural properties that cannot be defined in terms of biological or sociological properties.

- Buddhist ethics[268]: actions are morally right insomuch as they contribute to accumulation of good karma and facilitate exit from the cycle of rebirth.

Regarding non-naturalistic, non-theistic accounts of the nature of morality, philosopher Kevin Scharp makes a very similar point[269]:

"There are literally dozens of theories of moral values and moral duties that are objective, not naturalist, and make no appeal to gods. For example, G. E. Moore, Sir William David Ross, Christine Korsgaard, Thomas Scanlon, Derek Parfit, Philippa Foot, David Enoch, Russ Shafer-Landau, Rosalind Hursthouse, John McDowell, Jonathan Dancy, H. A. Prichard, Roger Crisp, Joseph Raz, Jean Hampton, and Rey Wedgwood. That's just a few. Therefore, until he's refuted every single one of these theories, he needs to stop using the moral argument. The lesson for everybody else: Stop assuming that atheists cannot accept that there aren't objective moral values. All it demonstrates is that you know nothing about ethics."

Such lists point to the fact that, rather than there being *no* non-theistic foundation for morality as Craig says, the problem is in fact exactly the opposite – there are *too many* contending theories and little agreement among philosophers as to which provides the best account of morality. Despite this plethora of theories, Craig has not written anything specifically responding to any of them. In response to this list Craig has retorted[270]:

> "But simply providing a list, as Dr. Scharp does, does nothing to show their (the theories') explanatory adequacy; that these are good theories or plausible theories. In fact we know that most of them can't be because they are contradictory with each other."

This is clearly a totally inadequate response, equivalent to an atheist declaring that all religions must be false because there are so many and they contradict each other, thereby dismissing them all without even bothering to investigate any of them. Furthermore, the fact that all of these theories cannot be true is irrelevant, since any one of them being true would be sufficient to undermine Craig's moral argument, and the existence of many well-developed philosophical theories increases the chances that at least one of them is (approximately) correct. If Craig wants to do what he describes as "serious metaphysics[271]," then he must engage with these theories and show why they cannot serve as a foundation for objective morality. Simply ignoring them demonstrates a lack of serious engagement with the literature, and thus critically undermines Craig's argument. Furthermore, it is not enough for Craig to argue that we don't have sufficient reason to believe that any particular such theory of morality is true, for this would be to make only an epistemological claim that he insists is irrelevant to his argument. Instead, he must demonstrate that none of these theories can provide a plausible foundation for objective moral facts. Since he makes no effort to do so, I believe that Craig has given very little reason for accepting his crucial fourth premise.

Craig has offered the following reason to accept a version of the divine command theory of ethics[272]:

> "The critic must be asking, 'Why believe your theory?' The answer is, 'because it makes the best sense of objective moral values and duties'. It is the most plausible ethical theory out there."

This, of course, is precisely the same argument that a proponent of any theory of morality will make, that their preferred theory best accounts for moral values and duties and is thus the best ethical theory. Craig cannot justifiably make the claim that his preferred theistic theory of ethics is better than all the others, since as I noted previously he makes no effort to discuss any of the other metaethical theories that have been proposed in the philosophical literature. Craig also exhibits an inconsistent attitude in accepting such reasoning as a sufficient justification for divine command account of morality, but refusing to accept this as a legitimate reason for accepting a reductive naturalistic account of morality. Thus, if overall explanatory power is not a sufficient justification for a metaethical theory, then Craig must abandon this mode of defending divine command ethics. On the other hand, if overall explanatory power is deemed to be sufficient, then Craig must demonstrate that his preferred theory outstrips the various other specific theories discussed in the philosophical literature. Since Craig does not offer any such comparative analysis of the competing metaethical theories, his claim to have superior explanatory power is completely without foundation.

Further highlighting the underdeveloped and flimsy nature of Craig's moral argument is the fact that the view that only God can provide any sort of foundation for objective moral values is a fringe view held by only a tiny minority of philosophers. Indeed, over half of philosophers are both atheists and moral realists, with many philosophers adopting other positions which also place them in opposition to Craig's argument[273]. Even in a book containing responses to one of his debates that was edited by two theists and included contributions from four theists and three atheists, only *one* of those seven contributors agreed (more or less) with Craig's thesis that God is necessary to ground morality[274]. Other prominent theists such as Richard Swinburne have explicitly rejected Craig's formulation of the moral argument as unsound. Further, while Craig has published widely about the cosmological and resurrection arguments, he does not, to my knowledge, have a single publication in any academic journal defending his views about metaethics or advancing his moral argument. As a result of these considerations, I conclude that Craig's argument that there can be no atheistic foundation for moral values is poorly developed and faces the powerful objection that it simply fails to address the relevant philosophical ideas. In the following sections I shall consider some further, more specific arguments that Craig gives in defence of his position that without God objective moral facts could not exist.

HUMANITY IS SMALL AND EPHEMERAL

In addition to his appeals to authority, Craig also argues that humans cannot have moral value in a Godless universe since they are so small and ephemeral[275]:

> "But if there is no God, what reason is there to regard human flourishing as in any way significant? After all, on the atheistic view, there's nothing special about human beings. They're just accidental by-products of nature that have evolved relatively recently on an infinitesimal speck of dust called the planet Earth, lost somewhere in a hostile and mindless universe and doomed to perish individually and collectively in a relatively short time."

It is unclear, however, what any of these facts has to do with the question of morality. Of what relevance is the size of the universe or the means by which humans came about to the question of morality? The fact that human beings will (presumably) only exist for a very short cosmic time is especially irrelevant given that on Craig's view of time the only thing that exists is the present, and so it hardly makes sense to say that whether or not morality exists is somehow dependent upon future states of the universe which don't actually exist. Wes Morriston expresses these objections aptly when he says[276]:

> "I fail to see why anyone should move from these premises to the conclusion that there is nothing special about human beings... That we are the 'accidental by-products' of mindless natural processes, or that we haven't been around very long, or that we won't be around all that much longer, or that we are tiny in comparison with the universe is entirely beside the point. What matters to our worth is what we are – not how we got here or how long we will be here."

James Fodor

HUMANS AS MERE ANIMALS

Craig argues that under naturalism, human beings are 'merely' animals, and since animals do not have moral value or duties, neither do humans. In his words[277]:

> "On the naturalistic view, human beings are just animals, and animals have no moral obligations to one another. When a lion kills a zebra, it kills the zebra, but it does not murder the zebra. When a great white shark forcibly copulates with a female, it forcibly copulates with her but it does not rape her — for there is no moral dimension to these actions."

The response to this objection is so straightforward that it is unclear why Craig even makes this argument. Human beings are unique among animals in the degree to which we are able to comprehend the consequences of our actions on the well-being of other creatures, and rationally deliberate concerning how we should behave and what constitutes a 'good life'. Humans are thus a special type of animal – we are rational agents, greatly surpassing the ability to which other animals can perform such feats. As such, there is nothing mysterious about the fact that a lion killing a zebra is not murder while a human killing another human is. It is essentially the same reason why it is not considered criminal when children or mentally disabled persons commit actions which would otherwise be considered crimes – they lack the capacity to understand the consequences of their actions or to deliberate as rational agents, and therefore they are not considered culpable.

Craig also argues that under naturalism "there's nothing special about human beings" since there is nothing morally significant that makes humans any more valuable than other animals[278]:

> "But if man has no immaterial aspect to his being (call it soul or mind or what have you), then he is not qualitatively different from other animal species. For him to regard human morality as objective is to fall into the trap of specie-ism. On a materialistic anthropology there is no reason to think that human beings are objectively more valuable than rats."

Craig, however, nowhere defends his key assumption that an

immaterial soul is necessary for distinguishing human beings from other animals. As noted above, human beings possess a great many properties that other animals do not, including the ability to use language to gain much greater insight into the desires and preferences of others, a much higher capacity for empathy, the ability to produce art and science, a much higher complexity of social organisation, ability to pursue rational plans in pursuit of long-term interests, the ability to develop virtues, ability to perform philosophical reflections on our place in the cosmos and the good life, and the ability to understand the consequences of our actions on the well-being of others. Since it is these sorts of properties that make human beings distinctively morally valuable, it is not clear what relevance the existence or non-existence of an immaterial soul has to the issue. As Wes Morriston argues[279]:

> "If one were to draw up a list of things that make us special, it would probably include things like these. Humans are (or can be) self-conscious, capable of rational reflection and deliberation, of making plans and carrying them out. They fall in love, they have children, form family bonds, and care for one another. Some of them write poems or compose symphonies or discover proofs of deep mathematical theorems... Non-human animals share some, though by no means all, of these characteristics; and none are shared by rocks. So why aren't characteristics like these – all of which could be found in a Godless universe – sufficient to make us 'special'?"

Regarding the importance of an immaterial soul Morriston continues[280]:

> "What difference would the presence of an immaterial soul make, anyway? As far as I can see, it could make a moral difference only if having one is necessary for having properties like those I have already emphasized – self-awareness, a capacity for rational reflection, and so on. Clearly, Craig has his work cut out for him here. First, he needs to show that these special-making features cannot be possessed by beings with material minds. Second, he needs to show that they would be possessed by beings having immaterial minds. And third, he needs to show that

immaterial minds could not emerge in the ordinary course of nature but must be implanted by God."

As to the charge that the naturalist is engaging in speciesism, Craig here attacks a strawman. The claim is not that human beings are morally special because they are members of the species *Homo sapiens*. Rather, the claim is that human beings are morally special because they embody, to a much greater extent than any other known creatures, various morally significant properties. Thus, a focus on human beings is not, as Craig has said an instance of "speciesism, an unjustified bias in favour of one's own species"[281], since it is based (or should be based) not on humans per se, but on objective characteristics, abilities, and properties which human beings uniquely embody. Sentient aliens and artificial intelligences, should they achieve similar levels on these measures, would also be accorded comparable moral value to human beings. As it stands, however, human beings are the only known entities to exhibit the properties necessary for personhood (though the great apes and some other species may exhibit some degree of personhood). Persons are moral agents capable of understanding the consequences of their actions and appreciating their place in the moral order, and thus have unique moral value and responsibility in virtue of exactly these abilities.

Morality and Free Will

Craig has argued that libertarian free will is essential to morality. He says[282]:

> *"If there is no mind distinct from the brain, then everything we think and do is determined by the input of our five senses and our genetic make-up. There is no personal agent who freely decides to do something. But without freedom, none of our choices is morally significant. They are like the jerks of a puppet's limbs, controlled by the strings of sensory input and physical constitution. And what moral value does a puppet or its movements have?"*

We can summarise this argument as follows:

- Premise one: Only libertarian free agents can be morally responsible or have moral value.

- Premise two: Under materialism, human beings are not libertarian free agents.

- Conclusion: Under materialism, human beings are not morally responsible and lack moral value.

While premise two of this argument is widely accepted, it is also important to note that many philosophers, theists and non-theists alike, would also argue that even if theism is true, human beings are still not libertarian free agents. As such, if this argument is to succeed Craig needs to provide some argument to establish that humans are in fact libertarian free agents. I discussed some of Craig's arguments in defence of substance dualism under premise four of the kalam cosmological argument, highlighting their various flaws and shortcomings. The first premise of this argument, the principle that only libertarian agents can be held morally responsible is exceptionally controversial and widely disputed by many philosophers. The philosophical position known as compatibilism holds that humans still have free will, and so can be held morally responsible, even if all their actions are ultimately determined by genetic and environmental causes. Craig thus needs to show that compatibilism is false, which he makes no effort to do, simply asserting that 'without freedom, none of our choices is morally significant'. A recent survey found that some 60% of philosophers accepted or leaned towards compatibilism, while only 14% supported libertarian free will, placing Craig's view in the clear minority[283]. This does not mean it is automatically false, but does highlight the importance of engaging with the question in a rigorous manner, something Craig makes no effort to do.

Regarding Craig's comparison of human actions to the limbs of a puppet, this analogy is inapt because no one thinks that a puppet can be morally responsible for its actions. By contrast, very many philosophers, both theists and atheists, believe that humans can be morally responsible for our actions even absent libertarian free will. Thus, the fact that Craig can cite one example of an entity that lacks libertarian free will and also cannot be held morally responsible for its actions does not entail that *any* entity which lacks libertarian freedom must also lack the ability to be held morally responsible. There are many obvious differences between human beings and puppets: unlike puppets, human beings can think abstractly, make plans about the future, feel empathy for others, and understand the consequences of its actions for the pain and pleasure of other people. The fact that these competencies are essential for holding somebody morally responsible is evident from the fact that humans lacking these abilities (e.g. young children and the mentally disabled) are not held accountable for their actions. Humans are thus morally culpable not because they have libertarian free will but because they possess these crucial characteristics, all of which are abilities that exist totally independently of whether or not humans have libertarian free will. As such, there are ample respects in which humans differ from puppets which make no reference to free will, and Craig's analogy fails. As a result of these considerations, I conclude we have no reason to accept his argument that morality requires libertarian free will.

ATHEISM AND MORAL DUTIES

One final argument that Craig makes against the possibility of naturalistic theories of ethics is that even if they can provide a foundation for objective moral *values*, they cannot offer any foundation for objective moral *duties*. This argument is rather odd given that typically at least some moral values are thought to entail moral obligations, while Craig seems to believe the two are completely separable. Nevertheless, it seems that a reductive moral naturalist can ground objective moral duties very easily by positing that a person has a moral obligation to do what contributes most to, or detracts least from, total human flourishing. This, of course, would entail that moral duties would vary between persons according to their circumstances and abilities, as seems eminently reasonable.

Such an answer does not satisfy Craig, who says that[284]:

> *"We are left wondering why, on naturalism, we have a duty to promote human flourishing and an obligation not to detract from it."*

This statement, however, is yet another instance of Craig shifting the burden of proof, for what Craig initially required is an account of the foundation of moral duties. Having provided such an account, the atheist does not need to show that the account is correct, since it is *Craig* who is making the positive argument and claiming that the atheist *cannot* offer such an account, and thus it is he who needs to show that any proffered account is defective and that his preferred account of moral duties is superior. The atheist could just as easily turn Craig's question back at him and ask in virtue of what we have a moral duty to obey God's commandments. Presumably Craig would respond that such a duty is owed to God in virtue of the fact that he is the ultimate standard of moral goodness and source of moral values. The atheist, however, could similarly say that moral duties are owed to human beings and other conscious creatures in virtue of the fact they possess intrinsic moral worth and thereby embody moral value. Each response, of course, assumes the correctness of its own perspective on morality, thus illustrating that if Craig is unsatisfied with the naturalist's answer, his answer is nevertheless no better.

REDUCTIVE MORAL NATURALISM

An atheistic theory of morality is simply a theory that describes the foundation for objective moral values without making any reference to a personal God. In a previous section I noted that Craig has not offered any specific responses to the numerous such theories that have been discussed in the philosophical literature, and thus his assertion that 'there just aren't any atheistic theories of morality' is simply false. There is, however, one moral theory that Craig does discuss in some detail, a version of reductive moral naturalism defended by Sam Harris. In this section, I shall consider Craig's responses to Harris' account, as well his arguments against the plausibility of reductive moral naturalism in general.

Sam Harris has developed a popular moral theory which attempts to provide a naturalistic foundation for objective moral values. The basic idea of Harris' theory is that some action or outcome is moral to the degree to which it is conducive to the well-being or flourishing of conscious creatures. Although Harris' account is not especially philosophically sophisticated and has some problems, it is to my knowledge the only non-theistic moral theory that Craig has discussed in any detail, and therefore it is worthy of further consideration. Craig responds to Harris' account as follows[285]:

> "He (Harris) says, 'questions about values... are really questions about the well-being of conscious creatures.' Therefore, he concludes, 'It makes no sense... to ask whether maximizing well-being is 'good'.' Why not? Because he's redefined the word 'good' to mean the well-being of conscious creatures. So to ask, 'why is maximizing creatures' well-being good?' is on his definition the same as asking, 'why does maximizing creatures' well-being maximize creatures' well-being?' It is simply a tautology - talking in a circle. Thus, Harris has 'solved' his problem simply by redefining his terms. It is mere word play. At the end of the day Harris is not really talking about moral values. He is just talking about what's conducive to the flourishing of sentient life on this planet."

Here Craig is right to say that claiming two phrases are identical in meaning is to make a very strong claim, as it follows that any instance of one can be replaced with an instance of the other. So, for example, if Harris is right that 'morally good' means the same thing as 'conducive to the well-being of conscious creatures', then as Harris says it is not meaningful to ask 'is it morally good to maximise well-being?' since this would be equivalent to asking 'is it morally good to be morally good?' Yet whether morality is about well-being is a question that philosophers have long debated, and certainly seems to be a reasonable question to ask. As such, it seems wrong to say that this claim is actually true by definition, and thus no more meaningful than asking 'are bachelors unmarried?' The latter is a question that no competent user of the English language can ask in good faith, while the former question seems at the very least to be a perfectly reasonable question that a competent, honest speaker of English could ask. As such, Craig is right to argue that Harris' semantic identification of moral value with what is conducive to well-being cannot be correct.

This objection to Harris' account, however, is really only an objection to the particular way in which Harris formulated his argument. The problem was in asserting a semantic equivalence between what is moral and what is conducive to well-being, a strong claim that is hard to defend philosophically. The real concern here, however, is not to provide an account of the meaning of moral terms (which Craig denies he is doing anyway), but rather to provide an account of how moral facts can be grounded without appeal to God. Such an account is easily obtained by modifying Harris' account to say that 'morally good' and 'conducive to the well-being of conscious creatures', while having different meanings, nevertheless refer to the same thing. Thus, saying that 'morality is about maximising well-being' is a similar sort of claim to that expressed by 'water is H20'. The words 'water' and 'H20' do not have the same meaning, for one could sensibly ask for the chemical formula of water but not for the chemical formula of 'H20'. These two words do, however, refer to the same real-world substance, and so in philosophical jargon they can be said to share the same referent. In this way, it is possible to provide an account of the foundation for objective moral values in terms of something more fundamental and (arguably) less mysterious, namely the promotion of the well-being of conscious creatures. Indeed, this is precisely the approach Craig adopts in outlining what he agrees amounts to an 'informative reduction' of moral values to divine commands. Thus, the naturalist can provide a grounding of objective moral values at least as good as that provided by Craig. Both consist of an informative identification of moral values in terms of objective facts, in the former case with what is conducive to well-being, and in the latter case with what God commands.

A more carefully formulated version of reductive moral naturalism could articulate the relationship between morality and natural, non-moral facts by appealing to the philosophical concept of supervenience. One set of properties is said to supervene on another if any difference in the first set of properties must be associated with a difference in the second set of properties – for example, the property of temperature supervenes on the more fundamental property of average kinetic energy. In the case of moral naturalism, the idea would be that moral facts supervene on natural non-moral facts, such as facts about human flourishing or promoting the well-being of conscious creatures. Craig does not think such a position is feasible, arguing[286]:

> "The claim that moral properties necessarily supervene on certain physical states of affairs at best gives us reason to think that if moral properties do supervene on certain natural states, then they do so necessarily. But that gives us no reason at all to think that, given a naturalistic worldview, there are any moral properties or that they do supervene on natural states. Why think that on an atheistic view of the world the curious, non-physical property of moral goodness would supervene on a human female's nursing her infant?"

This objection is exceptionally weak, however, since the answer to Craig's question is simple and straightforward. According to reductive moral naturalism, the reason for thinking that moral states of affairs supervene (whether necessarily or not) on certain non-moral states of affairs is simply because we have good reason to think that objective moral facts exist, and that the idea of supervenience provides a cogent explanation of how they could exist in a naturalistic world. In particular, if moral properties are to be informatively identified with non-moral natural properties, then there is no puzzle at all in seeing how the moral properties supervene on the natural properties (since they actually both refer to the same thing). Craig cannot object to the notion of informative identification since he appeals to exactly the same notion when explaining how God's perfectly good nature grounds objective moral values. Thus, Craig's real objection isn't with the notion of supervenience at all, but rather with the idea that objective moral values can plausibly be informatively identified with facts about the wellbeing of conscious creatures. While there are many possible ways of arguing for the plausibility of such an identification, the most straightforward in this case is simply to adopt the very same argument Craig uses in his formulation of the moral argument:

- Premise one: If reductive moral naturalism is false, then objective moral values do not exist.
- Premise two: Objective moral values do exist.
- Conclusion: Reductive moral naturalism is true.

What is most striking about this argument is that Craig seems to think that an atheist should endorse both premises. Since Craig argues that moral values cannot exist without a foundation, and rejects non-reductive alternatives, it seems that Craig would say that atheists should affirm the first premise. More importantly, Craig also clearly endorses premise two, and goes so far as to say that[287]:

"There is no more reason to deny the objective reality of moral values than the objective reality of the physical world."

If it is true that the existence of objective moral values can be known with such a high degree of confidence, then any argument implying the non-existence of objective morality should be rejected. An atheist who believes there is good reason to doubt the existence of God would therefore be perfectly justified in rejecting Craig's premise that "if God does not exist, objective moral values would not exist" and instead affirming the first premise of the above argument. This would hold even if the atheist found themselves unable to provide any particular account of how such moral values could exist, since the fact that they *do* exist can be so firmly established, it follows that there must be *some explanation* for their existence, even if we currently cannot determine what this explanation is. This is a fatal flaw in Craig's argument: he argues that we can be extremely confident in the existence of objective moral values even without knowledge of God, but then somehow thinks we should also doubt the existence of objective moral values unless we can provide a secure grounding for them. If we can be as sure that objective moral values exist as Craig says we can, then the mere inability to provide an account of the grounding of such values should not be enough to convince us of their non-existence. We should instead simply conclude either that no such account is needed (i.e. moral facts are fundamental), that such an account simply has yet to be developed, or that we have made some unidentified mistake in our reasoning. As such, Craig's objection that the core premise of reductive moral natural is insufficiently motivated is thoroughly unpersuasive.

Craig's objection to reductive moral naturalism faces a second major difficulty. This is the fact that his objection represents an epistemological objection to an ontological argument, and thus by Craig's own standards is irrelevant and beside the point. To see why this is so, suppose for the sake of argument that we grant that Craig is right, and that there is no particular reason to think that moral values exist under naturalism. It clearly does not follow, however, that objective moral values *do not exist* under naturalism, since they may exist even if we had no particular reason to believe in them. This might seem like an odd sort of rebuttal, until one recalls that the key assertion of Craig's moral argument is that without God, there *cannot be* any objective moral values, as there is nothing in which they could be grounded. Craig is very clear to emphasise he is not making an epistemological claim about what we can *know* about morality; rather he is making an ontological claim about what can *exist*. He clearly says for instance[288]:

"I have been astonished at the confusion of moral ontology with moral epistemology on the part of prominent moral philosophers responding to premise (1). Moral ontology deals with the reality of moral values and properties; moral epistemology deals with our knowledge of moral truths."

Yet in his objection Craig is falling into exactly this trap of confusing epistemology with ontology. Indeed, on the very same page of the same book, Craig immediately contradicts himself by making a purely epistemological objection to an ontological argument[289]:

"If there is no God, then it's hard to see any reason for thinking that the herd morality evolved by homo sapiens is objectively true or that the property of moral goodness supervenes on certain natural states of such creatures."

As Craig says, it simply doesn't matter if it is hard to see any reason for thinking that moral goodness supervenes on natural states of affairs, since this is an epistemological objection. All that matters is whether Craig can show that moral goodness cannot supervene on natural states of affairs. That is, in order to substantiate an ontological conclusion, Craig must provide *ontological* reasons that relate to what does or does not exist. The problem is that in the responses quoted above, Craig is only making an *epistemological* objection, asserting that we have no reason to regard the proffered naturalistic foundation for moral values as a true account. Such a response is insufficient, however, since as long as there remains a possible ontological foundation that *could* furnish truth-makers for moral values without reference to God, Craig has failed to justify his conclusion that no such grounding exists. It is unnecessary for the naturalist to demonstrate that any particular thing does serve this function. To carry his point, Craig needs to show that the proposal *cannot* serve the foundational role attributed to it, not merely that no reason has been given to think that it does.

Most egregious of all is the manner in which Craig's response to ethical naturalism represents such a clear double standard. In responding to the criticism that Craig never provides a reason for believing that his preferred version of divine command theory is true (he responds to objections against the theory but never offers positive arguments in its favour), Craig says[290]:

> *"My goal in defending the first contention is to sketch a moral theory according to which objective moral values and duties exist; the intention, at least at this point, is not to prove that that theory is true."*

Craig fails to give any actual reason for thinking that his preferred version of divine command theory is true. Concerning Craig's assertion that God's nature is the objective moral yardstick, Stephen Law has responded[291]:

> *"This is just a claim, isn't it? Why suppose the yardstick is a god? What's the argument both that there's such a yardstick and it can only be the Judeo-Christian, Craig-type God? It's a huge leap from 'There's an objective moral yardstick' to 'The Judeo-Christian God exists'. Even if the case for the yardstick could be made."*

If all that Craig need do is establish that his theory would account for objective moral values if it were true, without actually having to establish that it actually is true, then it seems ethical moral naturalism should have the same standard applied to it. That is, we should consider 'if ethical moral naturalism were true, would there be an objective grounding for moral values?' Craig himself seems to agree that there would be, as is clear from the passage above. His problem was not that the theory does not account for objective moral values, but simply that we have no reason to regard the theory as true. But, of course, if all that one needs to establish is the conditional claim 'if reductive moral naturalism is true than objective moral values are secure', then Craig's concern about why we should believe reductive moral naturalism is true becomes irrelevant. Thus, it seems evident that Craig is engaging in blatant special pleading: he requires that theories he disagrees with provide positive arguments to establish their truth, but for his preferred theory he only requires that *if* it were true then it would account for the phenomena in question. Moreover, while he states that his aim is to "show the explanatory inadequacy of competing theories (of morality)," he does not in fact give any reason as to why reductive ethical naturalist theories are explanatorily lacking – all he says is that we have no reason to believe that it is true. As such, I regard Craig's criticisms of reductive moral naturalism as unpersuasive and contradictory with other remarks he makes about morality.

EXPLANATORY STOPPING POINTS

Having set aside Craig's argument that there is no reason to believe in a reductive naturalistic account of moral values, one final objection remains to be considered concerning the issue of explanatory stopping points. For any philosophical argument, one can always continue to press the question 'but why should we believe that to be true?' In order to avoid an infinite regress, at some point in our explanation we must reach an endpoint, or what Craig calls an 'explanatory stopping point' where the explanation ends. An explanatory stopping point has no further explanation – it simply is. Craig himself acknowledges this, saying in the context of a discussion about grounding moral values[292]:

> "*The difference between the theist and (atheist philosopher) Sinnott-Armstrong is not that one has an explanatory ultimate and the other does not. It is rather that the theist has a different explanatory ultimate.*"

According to Craig, the problem with atheistic theories of morality is not that they have an explanatory stopping point, but rather that all attempts to ground objective moral values in an explanatory ultimate other than God are implausible and arbitrary[293]:

> *"The atheistic humanist must simply insist... that whatever contributes to human flourishing is morally good and whatever detracts from human flourishing is bad and take that as his explanatory stopping point. But the problem is that such an explanatory stopping point seems premature because of its arbitrariness and implausibility."*

This assertion that human flourishing is an arbitrary foundation for moral values, however, strikes me as exceptionally implausible, since human well-being is obviously so fundamental to morality. Indeed, Craig's response is especially bizarre given that he specifically identifies promotion of human flourishing as a key component of what makes a judgement moral[294]:

> *"A judgment is moral only if it makes reference to proper human flourishing, human dignity, the welfare of others, the prevention of harm and the provision of benefit. Inasmuch as this criterion makes exclusive reference to human beings, it is clearly inadequate as a necessary condition for morality. Animals and the environment are, arguably, appropriate objects of moral concern in their own right and not merely because such concern is of benefit to human flourishing. But if this caveat is kept in mind, (the) criterion is a good one. It focuses attention on the fact that much of the point of morality is to preserve the dignity, welfare and richness of human life."*

Craig seems to have an almost schizophrenic attitude towards morality. On the one hand he says[295]:

> *"Actions like rape, torture, child abuse, and brutality aren't just socially unacceptable behavior – they're moral abominations. By the same token, love, generosity, equality, and self-sacrifice are really good. People who fail to see this are just morally handicapped, and there is no reason to allow their impaired vision to call into question what we see clearly."*

Here he does not say that these moral claims hold only relative to God's commands, but are true absolutely, with reference only to the goodness and badness of the acts in question themselves. Yet on the other hand Craig also asks[296]:

"Why think that on atheism we have a moral obligation to maximize the well-being of conscious creatures? Why, given atheism, think that inflicting harm on other people would have any moral dimension at all? Why would it be wrong to hurt another member of our species?."

It seems that Craig believes that while there may well be facts about what is conducive to the well-being of conscious creatures, he can see no reason outside of God's commands as to why these facts constitute *moral* facts, or why in virtue of these facts humans would have any moral obligations. To me this seems to be a disturbing position, to assert that one can see no reason why sentient creatures capable of experiencing hope, desire, pleasure, pain, wonder, and all the rest, have no moral value. Rather than the naturalist needing to provide an account of what makes it wrong to cause suffering to human beings, it seems far more plausible that Craig needs to provide an account as to why such acts can *only* be wrong if God decrees that they are so.

In support of his contention that human flourishing is an arbitrary explanatory stopping point, Craig argues that we can conceive of aliens for whom rape would not be immoral, and we can conceive of possible worlds in which moral values do not supervene on states conducive to human flourishing. However, the mere fact that something is conceivable does not render it possible for such a thing to exist. For example, we can conceive of a perfectly round circle or of an infinitely large hotel, or of a universe that existed without God, even though Craig would deny that any of these things is possible. The idea of a world in which moral truths do not supervene on states conducive to human flourishing also contradicts the generally accepted principle that a non-moral copy of the world would also be a moral copy of the world.

Finally, Craig argues that even if some moral facts supervene necessarily upon natural facts, this is a "curious" and mysterious state of affairs that needs "some sort of explanation"[297]. Essentially here Craig is saying that if particular natural facts always necessarily give rise to certain moral facts, this is an unusual state of affairs that needs some explanation if we are to think it is so. One problem with this objection is that it is question-begging, as atheism asserts precisely that no such explanation is necessary. More importantly, as Erik Wielenberg has pointed out, if naturalists require an explanation for why moral facts necessarily supervene upon certain natural facts, then so too does Craig require an explanation for why moral facts or duties are necessarily entailed by God's nature. That is, if necessary moral truths require an explanation, then we must also have an explanation of God's distinctive set of necessary properties, or why it is necessarily true that God's nature gives rise to objective moral values. Wielenberg gives the following example[298]:

> "Because God is loving, He necessarily commands that we love one another. This claim has a certain ring of plausibility to it, but notice that it posits a logically necessary connection between being loving and issuing the command that we love one another. P2 (logically necessary moral connections require explanation) implies that unless Craig provides an explanation for this necessary connection, his meta-ethical approach is unacceptable. To my knowledge, Craig nowhere provides such an explanation."

The only argument Craig provides as to why God is a more plausible stopping point is the following[299]:

> "The question might be pressed as to why God's nature should be taken to be definition of goodness. But unless we are nihilists, we have to recognize some ultimate standard of value, and God seems to be the least arbitrary stopping point. Moreover, God's nature is singularly appropriate to serve as such a standard. For by definition, God is a being worthy of worship. And only a being that is the locus and source of all value is worthy of worship."

Craig's bold assertion that 'God seems to be the least arbitrary stopping point' is unlikely to convince anyone not already a theist. The only argument he provides in favour of this assertion is that God is by definition worthy of worship, and only a being that is the 'locus and source of all value' is worthy of worship. To simply assert, however, that God is 'by definition' worthy of worship in no way establishes that the existence of a being so defined is in any way plausible or likely. Furthermore, it fails to explain why God is worthy of worship. If God is only worthy of worship because he embodies properties like goodness, justice, kindness, etc., then it seems that these properties are the real explanatory stopping point for morality. On the other hand, if God is worthy of worship independently of his possession of these properties, then it does indeed seem that God is pretty arbitrary as a stopping point for morality. Even if God possesses all his properties necessarily, it is nevertheless still possible to inquire which properties are most fundamental, and which properties are dependent upon these most fundamental properties. Either way, however, it seems that Craig faces a dilemma which renders God quite implausible as an explanatory 'stopping point'.

In the end, therefore, Craig's preferred account of objective moral values offers no greater insights than alternatives that make no reference to God. As Wes Morriston aptly summarises the issue[300]:

> "It may be said that God's moral attributes just are the ultimate standard of goodness. But how is this any more satisfying than saying that love (for example) just is good-making? As far as I can see, building God and God's attributes into the account of moral values merely complicates things and replaces one set of puzzles with another."

SUMMARY OF THE ARGUMENT

In his moral argument, Craig attempts to show that the existence of objective moral values is powerful evidence for the existence of God. His argument proceeds by first arguing that objective moral facts exist, second by showing how God can provide a foundation for these facts, and finally by arguing that without God there could not be any foundation for moral facts. The moral argument is, in my view, by far the weakest of Craig's four main arguments for the existence of God. It seems that Craig has little interest in defending the argument robustly in philosophical journals, for he has published almost nothing scholarly about the argument, nor has he attempted to respond to any of the many non-theistic theories of morality that have been developed. Craig's defence of his key premise, that without God objective moral values would not exist, is not rigorously developed or carefully structured in the way most of his other arguments are, indicating its relatively underdeveloped status.

As a result of these factors, Craig's moral argument is positively riddled with flaws and unjustified assumptions. At the outset, Craig fails to provide sufficient justification for his underlying premise that moral values require some sort of grounding, as opposed to simply being brute facts. In defending the existence of objective moral values, he says relatively little about non-cognitivist theories of morality, and the few arguments he does provide in defence of cognitivism are unconvincing. Craig's formulation divine command theory, while avoiding the classic Euthyphro dilemma, is still subject to the arbitrariness critique, and fails to adequately explain what precisely it is about God's 'nature' which underpins moral values. The weakest part of Craig's argument is his defence of the premise that no non-theistic foundation for objective moral values is possible. His arguments on the basis of the smallness of humanity, comparisons of humans to animals, and the lack of libertarian free will, are confused and lack any real relevance to the issue. Craig's criticism of reductive moral naturalism is based upon applying a double standard, requiring the naturalistic theory of morality to provide answers to questions that he exempts his theistic account from. As a result of these numerous failings, Craig's moral argument for the existence of God is unsound and unconvincing.

James Fodor

Chapter Five
The Christological Argument

Overview of the Argument

The Structure of Craig's Argument

The Christological argument attempts to move beyond generic theism to establish the truth of Christianity. The basic idea is to show that God raised Jesus from the dead, thereby vindicating the central claims of Christianity. Craig's argument for the historicity of the bodily resurrection of Jesus proceeds as follows. First, he outlines four historical facts which he argues have been established by the majority of biblical scholars. Second, he provides a series of criteria according to which the quality of an explanation is to be judged. Third, he argues that the resurrection hypothesis – that God miraculously raised Jesus from the dead – meets these explanatory criteria far better than do any other proposed explanations for the four historical facts. Finally, he concludes on the basis of inference to the best explanation that the resurrection hypothesis is probably true. We can summarise his argument as follows:

- Premise one: Four historical facts regarding the death of Jesus have been established by the consensus of biblical scholars.

- Premise two: A set of criteria describes the quality of a proposed explanation in accounting for a given body of facts.

- Premise three: The resurrection hypothesis meets these criteria for explaining the four facts far better than any rival hypothesis.

- Premise four: If one explanation is far superior to all others, it should be accepted as probably true.

- Conclusion: The resurrection hypothesis should be accepted as probably true.

Most of the responses to Craig's argument reject premise one by disputing one or more of the four historical facts that Craig attempts to establish. Another common strategy is to implicitly challenge premise two by arguing, in effect, that miraculous interventions are an illegitimate explanatory option, thereby essentially adding an additional criterion for a good explanation, namely that it not be miraculous or supernatural. Most of Craig's responses to his critics, therefore, have focused on defending his first two premises. He also devotes some time to defending premise three by criticising some alternate explanations for the historical facts that have been put forward, particularly that of Gerd Lüdemann.

In this chapter, I wish to pursue quite a different strategy, one that I believe has been largely (though not completely) neglected in the discourse thus far. Specifically, subject to only a few relatively minor qualifications, I will accept both of the first two premises of Craig's argument. I believe Craig has provided adequate evidence to attest to the four historical facts, even if I believe he does overstate his case at times. I also largely accept the criteria that he presents for judging explanations, though I do differ somewhat in my interpretation of some of them. Instead, I want to focus my attention on Craig's third premise, that the resurrection hypothesis is the best explanation for the four historical facts. I will present an alternate explanation for Craig's historical facts, defend it against various objections, and then argue that this alternate explanation better fulfils the criteria for a good explanation than does Craig's resurrection hypothesis. As such, I argue that Craig fails to show that the resurrection of Jesus is the best explanation for the historical facts, and therefore his argument for the truth of Christianity fails. Note that it doesn't follow from this that Christianity is *false*; only that Craig's argument for establishing its truth is not successful.

CRITERIA FOR JUDGING AN EXPLANATION

An explanation consists of a set of propositions which, taken together, entail the facts to be explained. The facts don't have to follow with deductive certainty, but they should follow with reasonable probability. In the words of philosopher Charles Pierce, given an explanation, the facts to be explained should follow as "a matter of course."[301] Without an explanation, a given set of facts may initially seem unusual, strange, or mysterious, but given an appropriate explanation, these facts should seem to make perfect sense and not be strange at all. Explanations should account for strange features and render the otherwise inexplicable readily understandable.

Explanations are judged in accordance with three main criteria:

1. Explanatory scope: the larger the range of facts that an explanation can account for, the better is that explanation.

2. Explanatory power: the more likely the facts are rendered by the explanation, the more clearly they are accounted for by it, the better is the explanation.

3. Plausibility: the more likely are the propositions posited by the explanation given existing background knowledge (outside of the facts to be explained), the better is the explanation.

To illustrate how these criteria work, let me provide a simple example. Suppose we return home from a day out to discover the following two facts:

1. A flower vase is smashed next to a small table.
2. The cat is found nearby with wet fur.

These facts are somewhat unusual – we don't normally find the vase smashed or the cat wet, so we naturally seek an explanation for them. One explanation for these facts would be that the vase had been left too close to the edge, and fell as the result of a slight breeze or shifting of air. This explanation has good *explanatory power*, since if the vase was just on the edge of falling it seems very likely (not merely somewhat likely) that it would end up smashed on the floor. However, this explanation does not have very good *explanatory scope*, for it would not explain why the cat is wet, unless it also just happened to be passing by when the vase fell, which is unlikely. Since the explanation doesn't account for all of the facts, we say it is limited in explanatory scope. In addition, the explanation is also not very *plausible*, since it is unlikely that the vase could have been balanced so exactly precariously as not to fall in our presence, but only after we had left. An alternative explanation, that the cat walked into the table and knocked off the vase, has greater explanatory scope, since it explains both the smashed vase and the wet cat without any implausible assumptions (cats are indeed liable to walk into table legs). If we were to subsequently learn, however, that the vase was made of especially sturdy material which usually does not break when dropped from this height, then the explanatory power of this explanation would be reduced, because even if the cat did knock the vase off the table, it doesn't follow that it would necessarily have broken. In this circumstance, we would have to search for a new explanation, which in turn would need to be weighed against these criteria.

These three criteria are very similar, but not identical to, the set of seven criteria (originally formulated by C. Behan McCullagh) that Craig outlines as being the method by which historians judge the quality of explanations[302]:

> "1. The hypothesis, together with other true statements, must imply further statements describing present, observable data.
> 2. The hypothesis must have greater explanatory scope (that is, imply a greater variety of observable data) than rival hypotheses.
> 3. The hypothesis must have greater explanatory power (that is, make the observable data more probable) than rival hypotheses.
> 4. The hypothesis must be more plausible (that is, be implied by a greater variety of accepted truths, and its negation implied by fewer accepted truths) than rival hypotheses.
> 5. The hypothesis must be less ad hoc (that is, include fewer new suppositions about the past not already implied by existing knowledge) than rival hypotheses.
> 6. The hypothesis must be disconfirmed by fewer accepted beliefs (that is, when conjoined with accepted truths, imply fewer false statements) than rival hypotheses.
> 7. The hypothesis must so exceed its rivals in fulfilling conditions (2) through (6) that there is little chance of a rival

hypothesis, after further investigation, exceeding it in meeting these conditions."

I prefer the set of three over Craig's seven because three criteria are far more manageable than six, and furthermore Craig's six criteria are redundant. For example, Craig has separate criteria for plausibility, accordance with accepted beliefs, and degree of ad hocness, even though it is very unclear how these are distinct from one another. Criterion five is particularly dubious because every explanation is in some sense contrived to explain a set of data; what matters is how *plausible* the explanation is given our background knowledge. Furthermore, it is somewhat odd that Craig appeals to these specifically *historical* criteria given that elsewhere he agrees that strictly speaking historical explanations do not countenance the supernatural, and thus he is really arguing that his explanation is the best explanation *overall*, not the best purely *historical* explanation. I have no problem with this approach, but it clearly belies appealing to specifically historical criteria for judging the quality of an explanation, and indicates that it may be more appropriate to use broader, philosophical criteria. Nevertheless, my argument could fairly easily be reformulated in terms of Craig's six criteria, losing nothing essential other than some clarity and conciseness.

Regarding the criterion of plausibility, I believe it is necessary to provide some additional clarification since I believe Craig utilises a deficient conception of plausibility. Craig adopts McCullagh's conception of plausibility, according to which a hypothesis is more plausible if it is "implied by a greater variety of accepted truths." Applying this understanding of plausibility, Craig has argued that[303]:

> *"With respect to our background knowledge alone, the supernaturalist agrees with the naturalist that the resurrection hypothesis has virtually zero plausibility in McCullagh's sense, for nothing in our background information implies that Jesus' resurrection took place. But by the same token, the hypotheses that the disciples stole the body or that Jesus was not really dead also have zero plausibility with respect to the background information, for nothing in that information implies that any of these events took place either."*

Such a conception of plausibility, however, is mistaken because it is very rare for our background beliefs to *imply* any particular explanatory hypothesis. Indeed, if a hypothesis was entailed by existing accepted beliefs then it would not be a hypothesis, but it would be a *corollary* of existing beliefs. Rather, I argue that the correct conception is that an explanation is more plausible to the degree that its postulates are rendered *more probable* by existing background beliefs. This distinction is important because while background beliefs seldom *imply* (that is with deductive certainty) an explanatory hypothesis, they very often affect the *probabilities* of various postulates or assumptions necessary for that hypothesis. As such, explanations with assumptions that are rendered more probably true given our background evidence are accorded higher plausibility than explanations whose assumptions are not rendered as probable by such background evidence. By this conception of plausibility, I think Craig is incorrect in stating that both naturalistic and resurrection hypotheses have zero plausibility, since our background evidence does have implications for the plausibility of the postulates of these respective hypotheses. I will discuss this in greater detail later in this chapter.

The Four Historical Facts

Craig's four historical facts are as follows[304]:

> 1. After his crucifixion Jesus was buried by Joseph of Arimathea in the tomb.
> 2. On the Sunday following the crucifixion, Jesus' tomb was found empty by a group of his women followers.
> 3. On multiple occasions and under various circumstances, different individuals and groups of people experienced appearances of Jesus alive from the dead.
> 4. The original disciples came to believe that Jesus had risen from the dead despite considerable predisposition to the contrary.

I will not review the considerable evidence that Craig presents in defence of these facts. For more information on this I invite readers to consult his published works[305]. For the purposes of this chapter, I will accept as historical each of Craig's four facts. My response to Craig's arguments, therefore, will be based entirely on critiquing his proposed explanation of these facts, and not on denying any of the facts themselves. I should note, however, that accepting these four facts does not amount to accepting the historicity of *every detail* recorded in the New Testament, or in the gospels specifically. In particular, I do not necessarily grant the historicity of all the details surrounding Jesus' death, burial, and appearances, nor that each appearance recorded in one of the gospels is necessarily historical. I grant that experiences of the risen Jesus occurred, and that they took place on multiple occasions, in different circumstances, with individuals and groups of people. This does not, however, entail that all details of such accounts in the gospels are completely accurate, or can be uncritically appealed to. Craig's argument, however, does not appeal to the accuracy of all such details, and Craig himself has specifically denied that his historical argument for the resurrection of Jesus is dependent upon the general reliability of the gospels[306].

THE RHBS HYPOTHESIS

OVERVIEW OF THE HYPOTHESIS

The model in brief

The naturalistic explanation of Craig's four historical facts that I will defend incorporates a number of ideas originally developed by Gerd Lüdemann[307], Bart Ehrman[308], and Richard Carrier[309]. However, many of the details in this model, as well as its precise formulation, are my own. I have termed this explanatory hypothesis the RHBS model, which stands for Reburial, Hallucination, Biases, and Socialisation, corresponding to the key elements of the model. A summary of the model follows (see figure 13 for a diagrammatic presentation):

- Reburial: Between Jesus' burial on Friday afternoon and the discovery of the empty tomb on Sunday morning, Jesus' body was removed from the tomb and subsequently reburied. Exactly why is a secondary matter, but in my view the most likely explanation is that Joseph of Arimathea himself wished to remove Jesus' corpse from his family tomb.

- Individual Hallucinations: Following the discovery of the empty tomb, and exacerbated by grief, emotional excitement, one or more of Jesus' followers experienced individual hallucinations of the risen Jesus (the most likely candidates are Mary and Peter, though that is not essential to the argument).

- Group Religious Experiences: These followers then discussed their experiences with the disciples, generating an expectation that they might experience something similar. Partly as a result of this expectancy, and also mediated by social reinforcement, strong emotions, sensory distortions, and environmental influences, the early disciples had several collective religious experiences of the risen Jesus. These experiences were social in nature and so not purely psychological hallucinations, but were delusory in the sense that they did not involve the disciples actually seeing a physically resurrected Jesus. These sorts of group experiences of strange phenomena have been documented many times, for instance Marian apparitions, certain UFO sightings, miracles in other religious traditions, and instances of mass hysteria. I will give more specific examples later on in this chapter.

- Memory and Cognitive Biases: In the process of discussing these experiences among themselves afterwards, the disciples' memories of what they experienced were reshaped through processes of reconstructive recall and social memory contagion in the direction of increased coherence between individual accounts, and also greater impressiveness of the experiences. In the process, a 'standard version' of these experiences began to develop. Cognitive dissonance, confirmation bias, selective perception, and other similar biases combined to reduce any inconsistencies or discrepancies in the accounts or memories. All of these phenomena have been well documented by psychologists and sociologists, and some of the evidence for them I will discuss in more detail later.

- Socialisation and Marginalisation of Doubt: Public expressions of doubt, disagreement, and scepticism were further muted because few disbelievers cared enough about Christianity to engage much with early Christians or disprove their claims, and most of those exposed to these claims had neither the inclination nor the ability to check them for themselves.

Unreasonable Faith

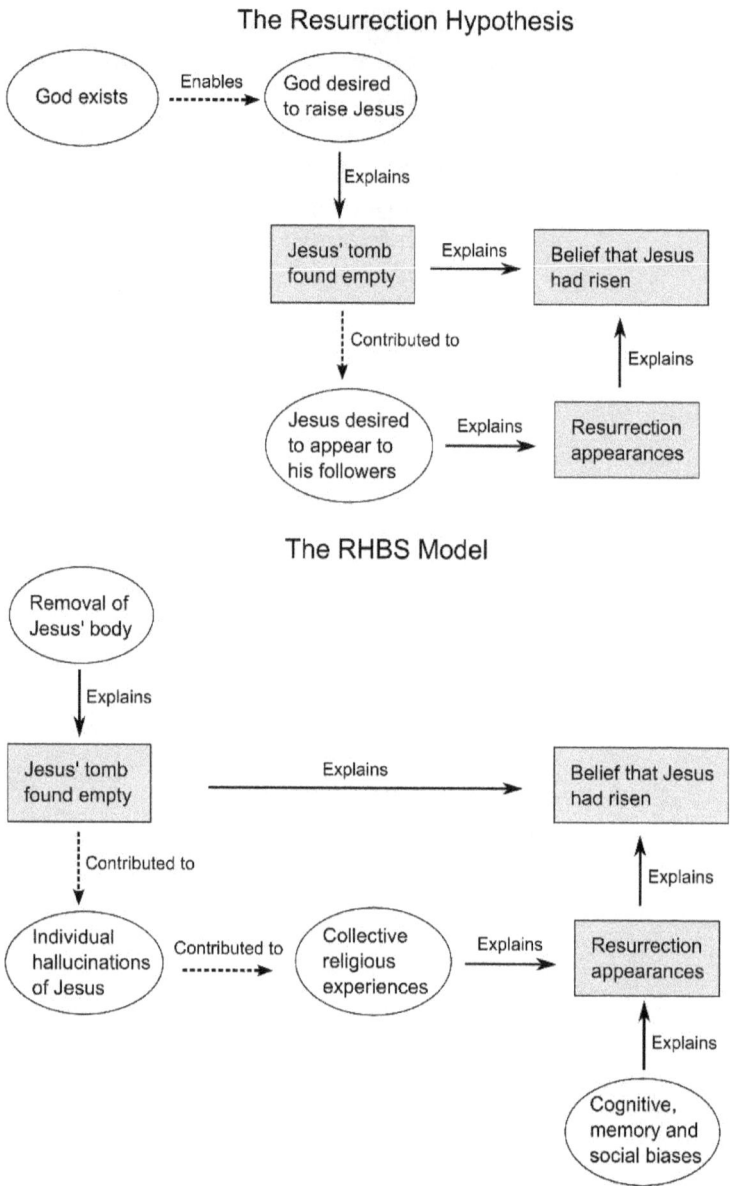

Figure 13. An overview of the explanatory relationships for the resurrection hypothesis (top) and the RHBS model (bottom). Shaded boxes indicate historical

facts to be explained (the burial is omitted as it is the same in both models), while unshaded circles indicate postulates necessary to explain the historical facts. Full arrows indicate explanatory relationships that account for the historical facts. Dashed arrows indicate other contributory or enabling relationships in the model which do not directly account for any of the historical facts.

Simplicity and Occam's Razor

Without question my RHBS model is much more complicated to state than Craig's simple formulation 'God rose Jesus from the dead'. This, however, does not imply that by Occam's Razor we should prefer the resurrection hypothesis for its apparent simplicity. This is because, contrary to how it is often stated, Occam's Razor does *not* say that 'simpler explanations are more likely to be true'. Rather, it states that explanations which require fewer new (that is previously unestablished) assumptions, are to be preferred over those which require more such assumptions. Thus, it is essentially equivalent to the criterion of plausibility – given our background information, how likely is the proposed explanation? I will discuss the relative plausibility of the RHBS and resurrection hypotheses in subsequent sections. My purpose here is simply to highlight the fact that the length of time it takes to explain a hypothesis, or the number of internal parts that it has, is not relevant when judging simplicity or plausibility. Rather, what is important is the number of *new assumptions* the explanation needs to make, and how *plausible* these assumptions are given generally-accepted background evidence.

Key assumptions of RHBS model

My proposed explanation requires four assumptions that are not already established on the basis of known facts or general background evidence:

1. Jesus' body was removed from the tomb before its discovery by Jesus' women followers.

2. Some of Jesus' followers experienced individual hallucinations of Jesus appearing to them.

3. Reports of the empty tomb and these first appearances triggered a series of collective experiences of the risen Jesus among the disciples.

4. The memories and understanding of these experiences were reshaped over time by psychological and sociological forces towards being more consistent and impressive.

In order to establish the plausibility of the RHBS model, it is necessary to establish the plausibility of each of these postulates, given generally accepted background evidence. I will therefore consider each of these postulates in turn, arguing that while none of them can be demonstrated to be true with certainty, all of them are *plausible* given our background knowledge.

POSTULATE ONE: REMOVAL OF THE BODY

The RHBS model postulates that between Jesus' burial on Friday afternoon and the discovery of the empty tomb on Sunday morning, Jesus' body was removed from the tomb and subsequently reburied. Exactly why this occurred is a secondary question, but in my view the most likely explanation is that Joseph of Arimathea himself wished to remove Jesus' corpse from his family tomb.

There are four main possible routes by which Jesus' body could have come to be removed from its original resting place:

1. Joseph of Arimathea moved the body for reburial.

2. Tomb robbers stole the body.

3. One, or a small subset, of the disciples removed the body without informing the others.

4. An unknown third party (but not robbers) removed the body for unknown reasons.

I consider options three and four to be relatively unlikely, however I still include them here for completeness. Note that option three corresponds to a form of the 'conspiracy theory', the classical form of which holds that the disciples themselves stole Jesus' body. Craig argues that this is absurdly implausible because such a conspiracy would have come to light, and furthermore the disciples would not have suffered persecution and death for Jesus' resurrection if they had known it was a lie. These responses, however, assume quite an extensive conspiracy involving most or all of the disciples. A more limited conspiracy, involving only a small number of disciples and possibly none of the actual twelve, would be much easier to keep secret, and would explain why the other disciples, not involved in the conspiracy, would be willing to die for what they still believed to be true. Nevertheless, I think that options one and two are by far the most likely possibilities for how Jesus' body came to be removed from Joseph's tomb.

Reburial by Joseph

I propose that it is likely Joseph of Arimathea had always planned Jesus' original burial to be temporary, intending to rebury the body at another location after the Sabbath was over. Jewish law required bodies to be taken down before evening, as per Deuteronomy 21:22, "if a man has committed a sin worthy of death... and you hang him from a tree, his corpse shall not hang all night on the tree, but you shall surely bury him on the same day." John 19:31 also mentions that Jesus' body was taken down "so that the bodies would not remain on the cross on the Sabbath." Joseph's tomb may have been selected for the temporary burial as it was very close to the site of execution, and time was short before the onset of the Sabbath. This hypothesis is supported by the gospels, which indicate the burial was rushed. In Mark 15:42, for instance, we read that Joseph asked for Jesus' body "when evening had already come, because it was the preparation day, that is, the day before the Sabbath." Likewise, John 19:42 states that "therefore because of the Jewish day of preparation, since the tomb was nearby, they laid Jesus there." The fact that the women came on Sunday morning to anoint Jesus shows that the burial had not been completed on Friday night, yielding further evidence of significant time constraints on the original burial. Thus, a temporary burial at a nearby tomb seems consistent with the requirements of Jewish burial practise and the specific facts of the case. Yet another reason for selecting Joseph's garden tomb as a temporary burial site is that the Jewish and Roman authorities were concerned about keeping public order following the great uproar surrounding Jesus' arrest and execution, and so wanted Jesus' burial to be as private as possible to minimise the risk of any trouble or further riots. As such, the authorities wanted a quiet, private site to place Jesus' body for a couple of days until the commotion surrounding his crucifixion had died down. A temporary burial in Joseph's tomb is consistent with the time constraints under which the original burial took place, and the desire of the authorities to keep the matter as private as possible.

Another possibility is that Joseph may have originally *intended* to leave Jesus' body in his family tomb, perhaps because he was a sympathiser or even secret supporter of Jesus. However, after spending time with family and/or friends over the Sabbath and telling them what he had done, he had second thoughts and was prevailed upon to move the body of a convicted criminal from his expensive rock-hewn family tomb. In Jewish burial custom criminals were buried in a separate location to ordinary Jews, and having Jesus buried in one's tomb (or even nearby to one's tomb) would have been considered to be an insult. Furthermore, tombs in Jewish tradition were owned and utilised by the family, and having Jesus placed in the family tomb, even if Joseph himself had wanted to do this, might well have elicited sufficient opposition from his family to prevail upon him to change his mind. Indeed, one can just imagine Joseph going home and his wife yelling incredulously 'you did *what* with our family tomb!?' As the Encyclopaedia Judaica notes[310]:

> "Bodies would be laid on rock shelves provided on three sides of the chamber, or on the floor, and as generations of the same family used the tomb, skeletons and grave goods might be heaped up along the sides or put into a side chamber to make room for new burials. This practice of family burial, though not universal if only because not all could afford it... was common enough to give rise to the Hebrew expressions 'to sleep with one's fathers' and 'to be gathered to one's kin' as synonyms for 'to die'."

Craig has objected that the burial site for common criminals was very close to site of the crucifixion, and thus there is no reason why Joseph should have placed Jesus' body temporarily in his own tomb.

Even if successful, this response would not rule out the possibility that Joseph originally intended to bury Jesus in his family tomb but subsequently changed his mind. There are, however, two problems with this response. First, we do not know the relative distances of Joseph's tomb and the common burial ground from the site of execution, as there is simply insufficient evidence of the detailed layout of Jerusalem at the time. What specific evidence we do have, namely the quotes from the gospels indicating specifically that Joseph's tomb was selected because it was nearby, seems to indicate that whatever the exact geography was, Joseph's tomb was close enough to the site of execution for it to be a very convenient burial site in a circumstance when time was of the essence. Second, even if the common criminal grave was closer than Joseph's tomb, as I noted above the latter may have been selected because it was a quiet, private location away from the potential disruption of a crowd. The Romans would have wanted to avoid the potential for more public upheaval, while the Jews would have wanted to ensure their Sabbath laws were obeyed, and so would have wanted to prevent any additional delays in getting the body buried.

Some have argued that if Joseph had reburied Jesus, he would have told people: either to counter claims that the body had been stolen by the disciples, or to counter claims that Jesus had actually been resurrected (depending upon where his ultimate sympathies lay). I do not agree with this assertion since we know almost nothing about Joseph of Arimathea. In Mark 15:43 it says that he was "a prominent member of the Council, who himself was waiting for the kingdom of God." Mathew 27:57 says simply that he "had also become a disciple of Jesus." John 19:38 describes him as "a disciple of Jesus, but a secret one for fear of the Jews." Luke 23:50-51 provides the most detail, calling him "a good and righteous man... who, though a member of the council, had not agreed to their plan and action. He came from the Jewish town of Arimathea." This is very little information on which to speculate about Joseph's motives and personality. It is easily possible that he later regretted his involvement with Jesus, or wanted to distance himself from such a controversial and radical movement as the early Christians. Perhaps he had a change of heart and lost his faith following Jesus' death. Perhaps pressure was placed on him by his family, friends, the council, or others, to keep quiet about the whole matter afterwards. Perhaps he did speak openly about it, telling people that he had moved the body, but for whatever reason he was ignored, or his message was not widely heard (see my discussion below about irrational belief persistence). Perhaps he died very shortly afterwards, moved away, or otherwise lost contact with the early Christian movement – after all, how well did any of the disciples actually know Joseph? All in all, there seem to be far too many unknowns, and far too many plausible alternatives, to justify jumping to the conclusion that Joseph of Arimathea would *necessarily* have made his actions widely known had he moved Jesus' body. As such, I consider this to be a fairly weak argument against the plausibility of reburial.

Another occasional objection to the reburial hypothesis is that reburial was illegal under Jewish law. While this is true in general, as the Encyclopaedia Judaica notes, there were some exceptional circumstances under which this prohibition was lifted. One of these exceptions stated that "where a grave is in danger of water seepage or if it is not safe against robbers, etc, transfer is permitted." [311] As such, Joseph may have justified the reburial on the grounds that his tomb was publically known and therefore not safe from tomb robbers. Even if this was not his *actual* reason for reburying Jesus, he could still have used this as a plausible justification. Furthermore, Mary Magdelene herself didn't seem to think that a reburial was implausible, as in John 20:2 she says, "they have taken away the Lord out of the tomb, and we do not know where they have laid Him."

Craig has argued that a reburial is unlikely since the earliest Jewish polemic assumes not that the body was moved by Joseph, but that the body was stolen by the disciples[312]:

> "Behind the story (of the guards at the tomb) evidently lies a developing pattern of assertion and counter-assertion:
>
> Christian: 'The Lord is risen!'
>
> Jew: 'No, his disciples stole away his body.'
>
> Christian: 'The guard at the tomb would have prevented any such theft.'
>
> Jew: 'No, the guard fell asleep.'

James Fodor

Christian: 'The chief priests bribed the guard to say this.'"

Craig asserts that this pattern "probably goes right back to controversies in Jerusalem following the disciples' proclamation of the resurrection,"[313] however he has no evidence to substantiate this. His only argument is that "the time span involving such a developing pattern of response and counter-response pushes the dispute back prior to the destruction of Jerusalem." This is quite evidently an absurd argument, however, as all these responses are quite natural and could easily have been developed within the course of a single conversation, not requiring the lengthy period of time Craig seems to suppose. Furthermore, we have no record of these controversies anywhere outside of Matthew's gospel (in particular they are not found in the earlier Gospel of Mark), and thus there is no particular reason to think they must have originated in the immediate aftermath of the death of Jesus, as opposed to being developed many years or decades later. Even if this exchange *does* date back to within a short time after the crucifixion, all that would establish is that a guard at the tomb was *one* argument or narrative utilised by Jewish polemic, not that it was the *only* one. Since we have no examples of anti-Christian polemic from the first century, we are not in any position to say what the Jewish authorities were saying in response to the resurrection claims in this early period. As such, Craig's appeal to the 'earliest anti-Christian polemic' fails to establish that Jesus' body could not have been reburied.

Tomb robbery

Craig argues that tomb robbery is implausible because nothing valuable was buried with Jesus' body, and furthermore in the event of robbery the body itself would not have been taken, only any goods it was buried with[314]. That nothing valuable was buried with the body seems questionable given that several of the gospels state that Jesus was buried with significant quantities of valuable spices, which robbers may have been interested in obtaining. This would also explain why the body was carried off, since the robes in which the body was wrapped were covered in oils which they would wish to drain off. Presumably it would have been easier to simply carry off the body and untangle all the linen later, rather than take the time to do that in the tomb while they risked being discovered. Another quite different possibility is that whoever robbed the tomb was some sort of political or religious enemy of Jesus who wanted to desecrate his body, in which case the absence of any valuables in the tomb would have been irrelevant. Yet another possibility is that tomb robbers may have hoped to obtain valuable relics from such a renowned holy man.

Craig also argues that no one other than "Joseph and his companions and the women even knew where Jesus was buried."[315] To this already not insubstantial list must be added anyone whom Joseph or his companions or the women told the location of the tomb. Since we have no idea how many 'companions' Joseph had, or how many people they, or Joseph himself may have told over the course of the Sabbath, it seems very premature of Craig to assume that 'no one knew.' Even if we assume that all these people kept quiet about their role in such a noteworthy event, it is perfectly possible that others could have surreptitiously followed at a distance (as the gospels indicate the disciples did at times), and thereby found out where the body was buried. Lack of knowledge of the location of Jesus' body is thus a weak objection to the possibility of tomb robbery.

Another objection presented by Craig is that the theft of Jesus' body is inconsistent with the discovery of grave clothes at the tomb, which one would expect to have been carried off with the body had the latter been stolen[316]. Regarding the existence of grave clothes, Luke 24:12 simply says that John saw "the strips of linen (variously translated as 'linen cloths' or 'linen wrappings') lying by themselves," while John 20:6-7 says that Peter saw "the linen wrappings (or 'cloths' or 'strips of linen') lying there, and the face-cloth which had been on His head, not lying with the linen wrappings, but rolled up in a place by itself." This latter passage about the face-cloth being "rolled up" is particularly controversial. Other translations state that it was "folded up," "wrapped together," or simply "still lying in its place."[317] First and foremost, it should be noted that there is no particular reason to regard these minor details as historical. Craig himself acknowledges that the authors of the gospels added details in order to make their accounts feel more believable and realistic, as in the context of Mark he has stated[318]:

> "I think it's worth adding too that these 'progressions', as Gundry calls them (additions), are not in general taken to be indicative of legendary development, but of the Evangelists' editorial changes in the tradition they received."

He has also argued that[319]:

> "We need not therefore worry about inconsistencies in the circumstantial details of the Gospel resurrection. The case for the historicity of Jesus' resurrection doesn't depend on such details."

Second, even if we do regard these specific details as historical, these passages only refer to *some* remaining strips of cloth, out of the many that would have been used to dress the body originally, being left behind by whoever moved the body. I see no reason to interpret the passage from John 20:7 as indicating anything other than that some linen used to cover the face was found lying separately from the other linen. I do not see this as being inconsistent with the fact that *most* of the linen, including most of the valuable linen containing the spices, had been removed with the body, leaving just some residual strips.

Yet another objection Craig raises against tomb robbery is that such a robbery would represent a 'conspiracy', which would most likely have come to light in the course of events[320]. To describe such tomb robbery as a 'conspiracy', however, seems to be significantly overstating the importance of this event. Removal of the body would only have required a few people and would not have needed much in the way of complex organisation, and as such I find it odd that Craig chooses such a grandiose word as 'conspiracy'. Grave robbery happened all the time in the ancient world, and even so, we have very few records of particular conspiracies to commit it. While Craig argues that we have no trace of such a conspiracy "even in Jewish propaganda," he neglects to mention that we in fact do not have *any* propaganda from the Jewish authorities dating to this period. All we have to go on are some later Christian reports of what the authorities were saying and doing contained in Acts. As such, I regard this as a particularly weak argument against the possibility of tomb robbery.

In some of his earlier publications, Craig defended the view that the tomb guards would have prevented any tampering with the body[321]. Most biblical scholars, however, would regard this as a later apologetic insertion, and I see no compelling reason to believe that there were ever any tomb guards. Of the four gospels, only Matthew mentions there being any guards. In the same passage in which they are mentioned (Matthew 27:63-65), Matthew also provides details of a private conversation between the chief priests and Pilate, conspiring to ensure that the Christians could not steal Jesus' body and then claim a resurrection by placing a guard at the tomb. Given that neither Matthew nor any of the other disciples could possibly have been present at such a meeting, it is not clear to me why any part of this particular tale should be taken seriously. Many scholars have also argued that the tale of the guard was a later apologetic assertion. Even if we take the story at face value, the guard was only set on the Sabbath after Friday night was over, as reported in Matthew 27:62-64, "Now on the next day, the day after the preparation, the chief priests and the Pharisees gathered together with Pilate, and said... give orders for the grave to be made secure until the third day, otherwise His disciples may come and steal Him away and say to the people." This event implausibly involves the Pharisees breaking the Sabbath, but even so it still leaves the Friday night open for a theft to have taken place. Thus, even in the unlikely event that a guard was present, theft is still a possibility.

The 'no evidence' objection

Craig has argued that we have no evidence that the body was removed, and that such a proposal is mere speculation[322]. In saying this, however, Craig exhibits an inconsistency compared to how he treats his own resurrection hypothesis, and misconstrues the nature of the argument being made. The entire premise of Craig's Christological argument is that it is an inference to the best explanation. All such arguments begin by establishing the facts to be explained, and then making certain postulates which, taken together, would explain the facts in question. If the postulates have sufficient explanatory force, power, and plausibility, then we take their ability to explain the facts as evidence that the postulates are true. This is why Craig is not question-begging in assuming that God exists in his resurrection argument, since this is not a premise which must be substantiated in order to establish the conclusion. Rather, it is a postulate which, taken with the other postulates, aims to explain the set of facts at hand. If successful, the explanatory power is taken as evidence of truth of the postulates.

Once we properly understand what the argument is doing, therefore, we see that this objection is irrelevant, since it is unnecessary to have specific evidence for the postulates made when presenting inferences to the best explanation. The whole point of such explanations is that the explanatory power they generate with respect to the facts to be explained constitutes evidence for the truth of the postulates. This is exactly the same standard that Craig uses when analysing his own proposed explanation, since he has no specific, direct evidence that God resurrected Jesus. Rather, he is *postulating* the resurrection on the basis of its explanatory power. This is precisely what I am doing in appealing to a reburial or removal of the body. As such, we are *both* postulating a previously unestablished fact in order to appeal to the explanatory power generated by this postulate. The relevant question is not whether there is specific evidence for the postulate, but whether the postulate is *plausible* given generally accepted background knowledge. In this section, I have argued that reburial and tomb robbery are both plausible given our background evidence about Jewish burial practices and the circumstances surrounding Jesus' death. That is to say, even absent any specific positive evidence for removal of the body, the postulate that Jesus' body was removed from the tomb is quite plausible.

The production of Jesus' body

Sometimes it is claimed that if Jesus had not risen from the dead, the Jewish authorities could have produced his body and this would have stopped the growth of Christianity in its tracks[323]. I think this claim is almost certainly false, because it rests upon several premises I regard as highly dubious.

First, it assumes that the Jewish authorities were interested in debating or disproving specific factual claims made by the early Christians. I see no reason to believe that this was the case. What the Jewish authorities objected to was the early Christians making claims they regarded as blasphemous, stirring up trouble among the people, and building up a rival religious power structure. The activities of the Jewish authorities as recorded in Acts are consistent with these focuses: they persecute, they arrest, they bring to trial, they criticise and forbid from teaching. They make no attempt, however, to persuade or present counter-evidence to the Christian claims, as they had no interest in engaging in reasoned discourse with the Christian movement. Such an attitude is perfectly understandable – after all, how many Christians or atheists today have any interest in engaging in reasoned arguments with fringe groups like Scientologists or Raelians? Even if the Jewish authorities *had* shown an interest in refuting Christian claims, it is likely that any significant acts that they might have taken, in particular exhuming Jesus' corpse and displaying it publicly, would have required the approval of the Roman authorities. Craig himself, however, discusses how disinterested the Roman authorities were in the early Christian movement[324]:

> "As for the Gentile reaction to Christianity, it generally followed the pattern of contempt prior to investigation. Christianity shared at first in the low esteem given to Judaism. The relative silence of Tacitus and Pliny concerning what was then widespread Christianity can only be accounted for as the result of ignorance and apathy."

Given the disinterest of the Roman authorities, and their desire to maintain public order and not incite further upheavals, it is unlikely the Roman authorities would have permitted the Jewish authorities to do anything as drastic as publicly display an exhumed body (which, as noted previously, is something Jewish law typically did not allow and thus would have caused great controversy), even had the Jewish authorities wanted to do so. In response to this rebuttal Craig has argued that at least the Jewish authorities took an active interest in the early Christians[325]:

> "It won't do to suggest that the Jewish authorities didn't take the Christian movement seriously and so they didn't bother dealing with it. They were, after all, the same men who were

responsible for Jesus' condemnation and delivery to the Romans for execution. As their engaging the Pharisee named Saul of Tarsus to persecute Jewish Christians amply illustrates, the Jewish authorities in Jerusalem were bent on squelching the budding Jesus movement."

The trouble with this response is that it fails to appreciate the importance of the exact timing of events. Obviously, the Jewish authorities took the Jesus movement seriously while Jesus was still alive; the question is whether they *continued* to do so in the immediate period after his death. The fact that they were so intent on arresting and executing Jesus while seemingly having no interest at all in his disciples seems to indicate that they believed that killing Jesus would successfully end the movement, or at least consign it to political irrelevance. From this we would therefore expect that the Jewish authorities would lose interest in the Jesus movement following the death of its leader. As to the engagement of Saul to persecute the early Christian movement, this did not occur until several *years* after Jesus' crucifixion, whereas the Jewish authorities would have had to have acted within weeks, if not days, in order to provide persuasive evidence that Jesus had indeed remained dead (see below about the problem of decay). There is simply no evidence that the Jewish authorities continued to take an interest in the early Christian movement in the period immediately following Jesus' death. None of his other disciples or followers was arrested, nor is there any indication of efforts to purge the synagogues of those sympathetic to his teachings. All the evidence points to the fact that immediately following the crucifixion, the Jewish authorities did not take any interest in the residual Christian movement until it was *already too late* for them to do anything to disprove the resurrection.

Second, Craig's argument regarding the production of the body assumes that the Jewish authorities knew where Jesus' body was. If the body of Jesus was reburied in a mass grave, disfigured or dismembered by enemies, stolen by some third party, or simply misplaced in some other way, there is no reason why the Jewish authorities would have known where it was. It is not at all clear why they would initially have cared what happened to the body or have made any effort to keep tabs

Unreasonable Faith

on it. After all, as Craig himself often points out, no one was expecting Jesus to rise from the dead!

Third, the argument assumes that if the Jewish authorities had presented the body of Jesus publicly in some way, we would have a record of this fact. However, we have *no records at all* about the early Christian movement from the first century Jewish authorities whom the Christians were dealing with. The only accounts we have are those found in Acts and in other early Christian sources; nothing from the Jewish authorities themselves. If the authorities had presented the body of Jesus, it seems very plausible that this is something Christians would not have recorded, since they would have regarded it as a Jewish plot and not taken it seriously. Since we don't have records from anybody else, there is no reason to suppose that we would have any written records of this occurrence at all. In other words, all we know is that we don't have any record of the body being produced, which given the lack of data from this early period is really not very strong evidence that it did not occur. Craig himself, in discussing the lack of corroboration of the period of darkness described in the gospels, says that[326]:

> "Given the paucity of surviving literature from the first century, as well as the possibly merely local impact of the events, an argument from silence is by nature tenuous."

I would make precisely the same argument with respect to the lack of evidence that there was any identification of Jesus' corpse.

Fourth, Craig's argument assumes that if the Jewish authorities had presented the body of Jesus publicly, the corpse would have been recognised by the disciples. Corpses decay quite quickly, especially in the Mediterranean conditions of Palestine. There is no clear cut-off as to exactly how long it takes a corpse to become unrecognisable, but the time span would be on the order of days, or at most a couple of weeks. Thus, the Jewish authorities had a very short window in which a corpse could be presented with any chance that the disciples would accept it as Jesus. It seems eminently reasonable that, even had they wanted to produce the body and known where it could be found, by the time it could be done it was too late to bother, or too late to make any difference, as the corpse had decaying beyond clear and incontrovertible recognition. Craig responds to this argument by saying[327]:

> "*Even if the remains of the corpse were no longer recognizable due to putrefaction, the burden of proof would have still been upon anyone who said that these were not Jesus' remains. But no such dispute over the identification of Jesus' corpse ever seems to have taken place.*"

Craig's response is quite strange since the burden of proof always lies with the person making the claim ("this is the body of Jesus"), not on those who are dubious about the claim ("how can you be sure, it looks very decayed to me..."). More to the point, it is irrelevant who *we* regard the burden of proof to have lain with – what matters is what would have been persuasive to *first century Palestinian Jews*. Given what is known about cognitive biases and irrational belief persistence (see the sections on these below), especially in the context of new religious movements, it is highly improbable that anyone who believed that the Messiah had appeared to them after being raised from the dead would be persuaded otherwise by an unidentifiable, decayed corpse which their religious and political enemies claimed was their dead leader. As to Craig's second response, that we have no record of a dispute over the identification of a corpse, I see no reason to believe we would have any record of such dispute, since as I just noted we have no record *at all* about what the Jewish authorities were saying other than the few anecdotes preserved in Acts. Furthermore, it is unlikely that any dispute ever took place, since even if the authorities knew where Jesus' corpse was, they would likely not have bothered to display it since they would have been fully aware that it would be decayed beyond recognition and thus would persuade no one. They would not have gone to all that trouble and risked the wrath of the Roman authorities (for stirring up more trouble) for something that would so obviously fail to persuade its intended targets. Fifth, Craig's argument assumes that if the disciples had recognised the corpse as that of Jesus, they would have given up their claims, or at least been unable to persuade anyone else that he had risen from the dead. However, I believe that there is more than sufficient psychological and historical evidence to demonstrate that people are perfectly capable of believing things in spite of overwhelming evidence to the contrary (see my subsequent section on 'irrational belief persistence'). As such, even if the followers of Jesus believed that the corpse they saw was that of Jesus, it is quite plausible, and indeed probable given their deep religious convictions, that they would have found some way to rationalise this away. Being regarded as a devious Jewish plot, the incident was either not recorded or records of it were lost, and thus it was eventually dropped from the Christian narrative and lost to history. Craig himself provides an example for this sort of reaction, since he has said that he regards his private, subjective experience of the risen Jesus to constitute an 'intrinsic defeater-defeater' sufficient to overcome any possible counterevidence to Christianity. While I doubt the early disciples had the same sophisticated model of justified basic beliefs as Craig, the same basic way of thinking would quite likely have applied had the Jewish authorities attempted to present Jesus' body. As I have said previously, however, I do not regard this as the most likely outcome. What I regard as most likely is that the Jewish authorities never bothered to find or present the body until it was already too late for it to be located or recognised. As a result, Craig's argument that the possibility of the Jewish leaders producing the body rules out a reburial is unconvincing.

POSTULATE TWO: PRIVATE HALLUCINATORY EXPERIENCES

The second postulate of the RHBS model is that following the discovery of the empty tomb, and exacerbated by grief and emotional excitement, one or more of Jesus' followers experienced individual hallucinations of the risen Jesus. In this section I argue that this postulate is plausible given evidence from psychology, and respond to several pertinent objections that Craig has provided against the possibility of individual hallucinations.

The plausibility of individual hallucinations

Private hallucinations are quite common, and contrary to what Craig has claimed, they are not mostly confined to the mentally ill or those using particular drugs. Here I cite some evidence in favour of the proposition that hallucinations are not unusual or a necessary sign of pathology, but are quite common in the general population. Craig states[328]:

"Hallucinations require a very special psychobiological preparation and are usually associated with mental illness or substance abuse."

Such a claim stands in stark contrast to the psychological literature on hallucinations, for it has been established for some time that hallucinations are not at all restricted to the mentally ill. I include several illustrative quotes from recent reviews to illustrate the point that according to the best available evidence from psychology, hallucinations do not require 'very special preparation,' nor are they necessarily 'associated with mental illness or substance abuse.'

- 'Surveys of hallucinatory experiences suggest that 10-25% of the general population have had such experiences (auditory hallucinations) at least once...Morrison concluded that these findings suggest that hallucinations may be normal responses to certain events or triggers.' [329]

- 'Hallucinations are perceptual phenomena involved in many fields of pathology. Although clinically widely explored, studies in the general population of these phenomena are scant. This issue was investigated using representative samples of the non-institutionalized general population of the United Kingdom, Germany and Italy aged 15 years or over (N=13 057)... Overall, 38.7% of the sample reported hallucinatory experiences (19.6% less than once in a month; 6.4% monthly; 2.7% once a week; and 2.4% more than once a week). These hallucinations occurred, (1) At sleep onset (hypnagogic hallucinations 24.8%) and/or upon awakening (hypnopompic hallucinations 6.6%), without relationship to a specific pathology in more than half of the cases... (2) During the daytime and reported by 27% of the sample: visual (prevalence of 3.2%) and auditory (0.6%) hallucinations were strongly related to a psychotic pathology... Haptic hallucinations were reported by 3.1% with current use of drugs as the highest risk factor.' [330]

- 'Although there is no comprehensive model that explains the occurrence of auditory hallucinations, current accounts emphasize the importance of cognitive factors, in particular, the misattribution of internal cognitive events to external sources... With respect to the latter explanation, it appears that the predisposition to hallucinate is not an all or nothing affair but one based on a continuum of probability. This mirrors research on psychoticism, which shows that psychosis is not separate from normality but is merely an extreme along a continuum of normality-abnormality. According to Claridge, psychotic characteristics are not the prerogative of the classically psychotic patient, rather there is a continuity of behaviour blending into a spectrum of illness. Not surprisingly, therefore, studies of normal populations have found that between 10 and 37% of people report having experienced auditory hallucinations.' [331]

- 'While auditory hallucinations (AH) are prototypic psychotic symptoms whose clinical presence is often equated with a psychotic disorder, they are commonly found among those without mental illness as well as those with nonpsychotic disorders not typically associated with hallucinations in DSM-IV... Auditory hallucinations found among "normal" people suggest that either AH are not as pathologic as they are typically taken to be, or that less-than-hallucinatory experiences are routinely mischaracterized as AH. Such hallucinations in the context of conversion disorder, trauma, sensory deprivation, and certain cultural settings strengthen an association between AH and psychopathology but suggest limited diagnostic specificity and relevance. It may be useful to think of AH like coughs — common experiences that are often, but not always, symptoms of pathology associated with a larger illness.' [332]

- 'Charles Bonnet Syndrome (CBS) is characterized by vivid, elaborate and recurrent visual hallucinations in psychologically normal people. It most often occurs in older, visually impaired persons. The prevalence of the syndrome has been reported at 1-40% in Asia, Europe and North America... The hallucinations that are experienced by patients suffering from CBS are described as 'complex', and can contain both familiar and unfamiliar images of people, animals, buildings, plants, trees and kaleidoscope-type patterns.' [333]

Bereavement hallucinations are a particularly common form of hallucination. Although the disciples' experiences were obviously atypical in a number of respects (most people's deceased relatives after all did not claim to be the Messiah!), nevertheless I believe that the frequency of such hallucinations renders it quite likely that the disciples could have experienced individual hallucinations of the risen Jesus partly prompted by grief.

- 'The heterogeneous concept of grief hallucinations is described and discussed, focusing particularly on the difficulties of reaching a differentiation between hallucination and pseudohallucination. Basic theses of the article are: (1) Contrary to a widely held view, grief hallucinations can display all the characteristics of 'true' hallucinations. (2) The concept of grief hallucinations probably comprises a heterogeneous group of disturbances of perception and of thought processes. They can be experienced as comforting but can also cause considerable distress.' [334]

- 'Ratings of grief reactions, post-bereavement hallucinations and illusions and quality of life were made during the first year after the death of a spouse among 14 men and 36 women in their early seventies. In both sexes, the reactions were generally moderate or mild and characterized by loneliness, low mood, fatigue, anxiety and cognitive dysfunctioning. Feeling lonely was the most persistent problem during the year. Post-bereavement hallucinations or illusions were very frequent and considered helpful. Half of the subjects felt the presence of the deceased (illusions); about one third reported seeing, hearing and talking to the deceased (hallucinations).' [335]

There is also substantial evidence that some people are considerably more likely to experience hallucinations than others. Such people have been described as exhibiting a 'fantasy-prone personality', and are more likely to be involved in paranormal or new religious movements, both of which facilitate opportunities for unusual experiences. Many of Jesus' followers would have fitted into this category, and therefore would have been particularly susceptible to hallucinations. Here I document some of the evidence concerning 'fantasy-prone personalities', participants in new religious movements, and predisposition to experience hallucinations.

- 'Members of New Religious Movements (NRMs)... scored higher on the Unusual Experiences factor, which measures positive symptomatology, and the Schizotypal Personality questionnaire, than the two control groups (non-religious and mainstream Christians)... The NRMs did not score significantly differently to the two religious controls on the factors of Cognitive Disorganisation, Impulsive Nonconformity, Extraversion and the anxiety measure. The NRMs were more depressed than the Christian, but not the non-religious group, and their mean score was well within the normal range.' [336]

- 'As predicted, individuals from the New Religious Movements scored significantly higher than the control groups on all the delusional measures apart from levels of distress. They did not show as much florid symptomatology as the psychotic patients, but could not be differentiated from the deluded group on the number of delusional items endorsed on the Peters et al. delusions Inventory, or on levels of conviction. However, they were significantly less distressed and preoccupied by their experiences. No differences were found between the two control groups on any of the delusional measures, suggesting that religious beliefs per se do not account for the NRMs members' scores.' [337]

- '(This study) evaluated the fantasy-prone (FP) personality by selecting subjects who ranged along the continuum of fantasy proneness and administering measures designed to assess hypnotic susceptibility, absorption, vividness of mental imagery, responses to waking suggestion, creativity, and social desirability... Results show strong support for J. R. Hilgard's (1970, 1979) construct of imaginative involvement and S. C. Wilson and T. X. Barber's (1983) contention that FP persons can be distinguished from others in terms of fantasy and related cognitive processes. FP subjects outscored subjects in both comparison groups on all of the measures of fantasy, imagination, and creativity, with social desirability used as a covariate.' [338]

- 'Psychopathological interpretations of individuals who claim contacts with extraterrestrials typify the few psychiatric evaluations of such behavior. Biographical analyses of 152 subjects who reported temporary abductions or persistent contacts with UFO occupants show that these subjects are remarkably devoid of a history of mental illness. However, in 132 cases, one or more major characteristics were found of... the fantasy-prone personality (FPP). Although they appear to function as normal, healthy adults, FPPs experience rich fantasy lives and score dramatically higher (relative to control groups) on such characteristics as hypnotic susceptibility, psychic ability, healing, out-of-body experiences, automatic writing, religious visions, and apparitional experiences. In the present study, UFO "abductees" and "contactees" exhibit a pattern of symptomatology similar to that of FPPs. Thus, clinicians should consider testing UFO abductees or contactees for fantasy proneness in cases in which a particular psychopathological diagnosis is not obvious.' [339]

- 'This study defines spiritual experiences in terms of "psychism," or psychic intrusions in the stream of consciousness that are perceived by the actor as not originating within the "self." Intrusions interpreted as psychism are regarded by the actor as having the same facticity as empirical experience and are regarded as "proof" of an esoteric belief system. Psychism originated beliefs are therefore resistant to refutation or change, and support spiritual autonomy.' [340]

These considerations should lead us to reject Craig's claim that[341]:

> "The disciples had no anticipation of seeing Jesus alive again; all they could do was wait to be reunited with him in the Kingdom of God. There were no grounds leading them to hallucinate him alive from the dead."

Instead, the evidence that I have cited demonstrates two key points. First, hallucinations are not especially uncommon, and no particularly astounding cause is needed to explain their occurrence. Second, since the disciples were in a mindset of great turmoil and emotional upheaval following the unexpected death of their master, the evidence from bereavement hallucinations, new religious movements, and emotional excitement all point toward their particular susceptibility to experiencing individual hallucinations. It should also be recalled that some of Jesus' women followers found his tomb empty and reported this to the male disciples, thereby providing further impetus for a post-mortem sighting. Finally, there is the simple point that the disciples would dearly have wished their lives following Jesus not to have been in vain, and therefore would have been highly predisposed to have some sort of experience to vindicate their leader. Overall, therefore, it is quite plausible to hypothesise that one or more of his disciples had an individual hallucination of the risen Jesus.

Would hallucinations have led to belief in a resurrection?

Craig argues that hallucinatory hypotheses fail to explain the origin of the disciples' belief in the resurrection. In particular, he argues that even if the disciples had hallucinated appearances of Jesus, this would merely have led them to believe that he had been taken up into heaven with God, not that he had been bodily resurrected from the dead[342]:

> *"The Hallucination Hypothesis has weak explanatory power with respect to the origin of the disciples' belief in Jesus' resurrection. Subjective visions, or hallucinations, have no extramental correlate but are projections of the percipient's own brain. So if... Paul or Peter were to have projected visions of Jesus alive, they would have envisioned him in Paradise, where the righteous dead awaited the eschatological resurrection. But such exalted visions of Christ leave unexplained their belief in his resurrection. The inference 'He is risen from the dead,' so natural to our ears, would have been wholly unnatural to a first century Jew. In Jewish thinking there was already a category perfectly suited to describe Peter's postulated (hallucinatory) experience: Jesus had been assumed into heaven. An assumption is a wholly different category from a resurrection. To infer from heavenly visions of Jesus that he had been resurrected ran counter to Jewish thinking in two fundamental respects... whereas Jesus' assumption into heaven would have been the natural conclusion."*

Craig typically raises this objection against hypotheses which deny the empty tomb and argue that the belief in Jesus' resurrection originated as a result of hallucinations alone. Craig's key point is that such appearances alone would not have led to the inference 'he is risen from the dead', because appearances by themselves would fit more naturally (given the Jewish context) into the category of a vision of Jesus having been assumed into heaven. While this objection might be applicable to accounts which deny the empty tomb, the RHBS model is predicated upon the historicity of the empty tomb. It is important to emphasise that I do not argue that the disciples experienced hallucinations of a resurrected Jesus per se. Rather, the RHBS model holds that they experienced collective experiences of Jesus appearing and speaking with them. They later came to *interpret* these experiences as resurrection appearances, as they found this to be the best fit with their theological beliefs, as well as with the fact of the empty tomb. As such, the RHBS model holds that the disciples came to believe that Jesus had been resurrected by *exactly the same process* that Craig thinks led them to this belief. Namely, they came to believe that Jesus had been resurrected because they found his tomb empty and subsequently had experiences of Jesus appearing to them. If this combination of 'empty tomb plus appearances' is sufficient to elicit belief in the resurrection under Craig's argument, then it should likewise be sufficient in the case of the RHBS model, since in both cases the same requisite factors are present. The RHBS model differs only in what *caused* the empty tomb and the appearances, but since it affirms the reality of both, the effects or consequences of these events should be exactly the same as in Craig's account.

Craig also argues that the Christian understanding of the resurrection was different from the Jewish conception of resurrection, in that the latter always occurred for all righteous persons at the end of the world, and did not apply to the Messiah alone during the middle of history[343]:

> "But the Jewish conception of resurrection differed in two important, fundamental respects from Jesus' resurrection. In Jewish thought the resurrection always (1) occurred after the end

of the world, not within history, and (2) concerned all the people, not just an isolated individual."

Craig believes that it would take a substantial transformative experience to cause the disciples to abandon or alter their beliefs about the resurrection, something that mere hallucinations cannot account for. He does not, however, provide any evidence for this claim. What reason do we have to believe that the disciples' theological understanding of the nature of resurrection was so important to them that they would only be willing to modify it following a substantive transformative experience? Christians, Jews, and Muslims to this day regularly change their minds about minor theological points that are of little great concern to them, without needing any particularly transformative event to explain the change. Furthermore, Craig overlooks the fact that the disciples most probably believed that they *were* living at the end of history, and that Jesus' resurrection *was* part of a broader resurrection of the saints. As numerous scholars have argued, the early Christian movement was at least in part an apocalyptic movement[344], with Jesus making numerous statements about the imminent destruction of Jerusalem and the coming of God's kingdom. Thus, when his early followers believed that he had been resurrected, they would not have viewed this as an event in the 'middle' of history as we do today, but rather as a further sign of the beginning of the end times.

Further evidence for this perspective is found in the report of the 'opening of the tombs' recorded in Matthew 27:52-53, where the bodies of 'many saints' are said to come to life and 'appear to many.' At the very least, the author of Matthew seems to have thought that Jesus' resurrection was part of a more general resurrection of the saints. Paul describes Jesus as 'the firstfruits of them that slept' (1 Cor 15:20), indicating that Jesus was believed to be but the first of a general resurrection that was to come very soon, when the final end would come. Craig himself even supplies support for this view when he refers to "the New Testament expectation that in light of Jesus' resurrection the general resurrection of the dead was imminent"[345]. In sum, all this evidence supports the view that the disciples did not (at least not at first) give up their belief that the resurrection was something that would happen at the end of history. Rather, the belief was only somewhat modified such that Jesus was regarded as the 'firstfruits' of this general resurrection, with the remainder to follow very shortly at the (imminent) end of the world. Craig's argument that hallucinations are implausible because they cannot account for the change in the concept of resurrection is thus mistaken.

Craig also argues that the Jewish Messiah was not supposed to be killed, and therefore his death would have been a crushing blow to his disciples[346]:

> "*Jews had no conception whatsoever of a Messiah who, instead of triumphing over Israel's enemies, would be shamefully executed by them as a criminal. Messiah was supposed to be a triumphant figure who would command the respect of Jew and Gentile alike, and who would establish the throne of David in Jerusalem. Yet Jesus' disciples held deeply a conviction that he was the promised Messiah – a Messiah who failed to deliver and to reign; was defeated, humiliated, and slain by his enemies; and was a contradiction in terms. Nowhere do ancient Jewish texts speak of this sort of 'Messiah.'*"

That the Jews did not expect their Messiah to be executed is beyond question. The question, rather, is what the disciples would likely have done in the event that the figure they thought to be the Messiah was executed. Craig thinks that it is implausible that the disciples would have had hallucinations of the risen Jesus and started to proclaim his resurrection, as they would have been too disillusioned by his failure to fulfil Jewish expectations, their hopes and dreams completely dashed. Instead, Craig believes that their only possible responses to such a catastrophe were to find a new Messiah or return home[347]:

> "*Failed messianic movements were nothing new in Judaism, and they left their followers with basically two alternatives: either go home or else find a new Messiah. These were no doubt hard choices... but they were nevertheless the choices they had. After surveying such failed messianic movements before and after Jesus, N. T. Wright remarks: 'So far as we know, all the followers of these first-century messianic movements were*

fanatically committed to the cause. They, if anybody, might be expected to suffer from this blessed twentieth century disease called 'cognitive dissonance' when their expectations failed to materialize. But in no case, right across the century before Jesus and the century after him, do we hear of any Jewish group saying that their executed leader had been raised from the dead and he really was the Messiah after all.' Wright raises the interesting question: if the disciples did not want simply to go home, then why didn't they pick someone else, like James, to be the Messiah?... Based on the typical experience of failed messianic movements, it is to be expected that the disciples should have either gone home or fastened upon someone else – but we know that they did not, which needs explaining."

Despite their strong assertions, neither Craig nor N.T. Wright present any comparative analysis or evidence of the many failed messianic movements they cite, concerning what the followers of these messiahs did after their leader was killed. Nearly all the extant accounts of such movements conclude at the death of their leaders, never saying anything about what happened to their followers afterwards. Given this dearth of evidence, how does Craig know that the only two choices were to 'go home or find a new Messiah'? Most of these Messiah figures are only mentioned in passing by authors, such as Josephus, who were interested primarily in civil disorders or military revolts, and had little interest in documenting what happened to peaceful remnants of such movements afterwards. Even if these movements did eventually fail, this does not prove that the death of their Messiah is what caused them to fail. In fact, the experience of more recent new religious movements about which we have better documentation indicates that the norm for such movements is *not* to 'go home or find a new Messiah (or prophet)'.

For example, Menachem Mendel Schneerson was a rabbi hailed as the Messiah by many of his followers before his unexpected death in 1994[348]. Nevertheless, some of his followers continued to believe that he was still alive, reporting seeing him intermittently in various settings. He retains a following to this day, many of whom believe that in due course he will be resurrected in glory. More such examples are documented in the subsequent section on irrational belief persistence. On the basis of these considerations, I conclude that an analysis of the historical evidence does not support Craig's contention that disciples of failed messiahs could only opt to go home or find another messiah. Rather, there is good reason to believe that the disciples responded to the shock of Jesus' death much as the adherents to other new religious movements do when faced with such shocks: by reinterpreting existing beliefs to come up with a new framework consistent with the course of events. They pondered, soul-searched, discussed with each other, and thanks in part to the empty tomb, they developed a hope that Jesus might still be alive in some sense. This hope led to the initial hallucinatory experiences, which then in turn led to the collective experiences, as I have outlined. Subsequent further pondering and searching of the scriptures led them to understand their experiences in terms of the Jewish concept of the resurrection.

Indeed, given all the alleged barriers to belief in the resurrection that Craig presents, it is unclear how, even under Craig's account, the disciples came to believe in the resurrection at all. Craig speaks as if the fact that Jesus rose from the dead and appeared to the disciples explains why the disciples came to believe in his resurrection, but this obviously is not the case; after all, something being true doesn't by itself explain why people believe in that thing. There must be some *connection* between the event in question and the beliefs of those who come to accept it. In the case of the disciples, we are driven to ask how they were able to overcome their predilections against belief in a resurrection. The answer to this question, clearly, cannot be simply to state that Jesus was resurrected, because he could have been resurrected without the disciples believing he had. As such, it seems that an answer must appeal to the *beliefs* and *mindset* of the disciples. Specifically, that they came to believe in the resurrection because of their belief in the empty tomb, plus the appearances, plus their concerted efforts to make sense of what they have been involved in without having to reject belief in their Messiah. This explanation, of course, is equally consistent with either the RHBS model or with Craig's resurrection hypothesis.

A further point to be made is that the arguments Craig makes concerning the difficulty in explaining changes in the Jewish conceptions of the Messiah and resurrection can be taken to an extreme which would preclude the possibility of any sort of religious innovation. As New Testament scholar Larry Hurtado writes[349]:

> "It is simplistic to regard religious experiences as only derivative from prior beliefs and to fail to see that religious experiences can modify beliefs and/or generate new ones, in some cases resulting in significant innovations... Several decades ago Rodney Stark made similar observations about the capacity of certain "revelational" experiences to generate religious innovations, even 'to contradict and challenge prevailing theological 'truths',' noting that such innovations can produce 'new theologies, eschatological prophecies, or commissions to launch social reforms'."

Religious innovation, including development of new ideas and re-conceptualising and rethinking old ones, is common throughout history, and indeed I would argue forms a crucial part of the birth of most new religions. For example, Joseph Smith claimed to have seen a vision of God and Jesus as distinct persons even though he grew up in a Trinitarian environment, Muhammad claimed to receive revelation from the one true God in a polytheistic environment (and though there was some degree of Jewish and Christian presence, neither of these faiths had 'room' for a new prophet of God), while the Buddha broke substantially with most of the orthodox tradition of Indian religious thought by rejecting the authority of the Vedas. To say that the disciples of Jesus could not alter or innovate within their existing religious framework in order to make sense of their experiences is to fly in the face of religious history. As such, there is no reason to think that hallucinatory experiences of Jesus could not have subsequently given rise to a belief that Jesus had been resurrected.

One final argument that Craig makes is that the New Testament makes a distinction between visions of Jesus and resurrection appearances, which only makes sense if there was a difference between the two types of experiences. Craig says[350]:

> "Now visions of the exalted Christ such as Stephen's (Acts 7:55-56), Paul's (Acts 22:17-21) or John's (Rev 1:10-18) were

not regarded as hallucinatory; but neither did they count as resurrection appearances of Christ. Why not? Because appearances of Jesus, in contrast to veridical visions of Jesus, involved an extramental reality that anyone present could experience. Even Paul's experience on the Damascus road, which was semi-visionary in nature, could count as a real appearance because the light and the voice were experienced by Paul's travelling companions (though they were not experienced by them as a revelation of Christ). As I say, this seems to be the consistent answer throughout the New Testament to the question of what the difference was between a vision and an appearance of Jesus... Now if this is correct, it is devastating for the claim that the postmortem appearances of Christ were visionary experiences. For then the distinction running throughout the New Testament between a vision of Christ and a resurrection appearance of Christ becomes inexplicable. Years ago I challenged skeptical scholars to provide any plausible explication of this distinction other than the difference between intra and extramental reality. That challenge, to my knowledge, has never been taken up."

It is hard to see why an answer to Craig's challenge has been so long in coming, since it is fairly straightforward and well-known in the study of religious movements. Rodney Stark has developed a set of criteria for determining whether new religious movements will be successful, based on the study of groups such as the Mormons. He argues that "as they become successful, religious movements founded on revelations will attempt to curtail revelations or to at least prevent novel (heretical) revelations" [351]. Religions that do not do this tend to become unstable owing to a profusion of competing claims to revelation disrupting organisational authority and unity. In the case of the early Christian movement, the break was determined to have occurred after Pentecost. Experiences of Jesus which occurred after this were judged to be visions rather than full-blown resurrection appearances, and were thereby accorded different spiritual status. As Craig himself admits in the above passage, the case of Paul's experience is somewhat of an anomaly, falling somewhere between an appearance and a vision. This is perfectly consistent with Stark's theory, however, since Paul had to campaign long and hard to have his experience accepted as genuine by the other disciples, something that no other figure was able to achieve for experiences occurring after Pentecost. The distinction between resurrection appearances and visions, therefore, is perfectly explicable in terms of Stark's theory of an emerging religious movement enforcing greater structure and orthodoxy by restricting the forms new revelations could take.

The appearance to James the brother of Jesus

Craig appeals to the conversion of James as evidence against any hallucination account of the appearances, arguing that[352]:

> "The Hallucination Hypothesis has weak explanatory power with respect to (the appearance to James), since James, as an unbeliever and no part of the Christian community, was unlikely to experience a 'secondary vision' of the Risen Jesus."

This argument commits the fallacy of arguing that because one event follows another in time that therefore the second event must have been caused by the first event. Such reasoning is fallacious because two temporally ordered events may not necessarily have any causal connection at all. With regard to the conversion of James, there is no biblical record that he was converted *as a result of* a resurrection appearance. All the New Testament indicates is that James was not a believer during part of Jesus' ministry, and then later it records that he was a believer who had an experience of Jesus appearing to him. Absent further information, we are not justified in simply inferring that the appearance was the *cause* of James' conversion. I propose that it is more probable that James, if he did experience an appearance of Jesus, had been converted prior to this, and thus was affected by the same psychological and sociological processes as the other followers of Jesus. This hypothesis is plausible given our background evidence, and equally as consistent with the textual evidence as Craig's hypothesis that James was converted as a result of a resurrection appearance. If Craig wishes to use the conversion of James as an argument against a hallucination account of the resurrection appearances, he first must provide sufficient evidence to demonstrate that James was likely converted as a direct result of such an experience.

James Fodor

The appearance to Thomas

Craig also appeals to Thomas as a sceptic who witnessed an appearance of Jesus, saying[353]:

> *"It was not merely true believers that saw appearances of Jesus but also people like Thomas, James the brother of Jesus and the Pharisee Saul of Tarsus."*

The account Craig is referring to is found in John 20:26-31:

> *"Jesus came, the doors having been shut, and stood in their midst and said, 'Peace be with you.' Then He said to Thomas, 'Reach here with your finger, and see my hands; and reach here your hand and put it into my side; and do not be unbelieving, but believing.' Thomas answered and said to Him, 'My Lord and my God!' Jesus said to him, 'Because you have seen me, have you believed? Blessed are they who did not see, and yet believed.' Therefore many other signs Jesus also performed in the presence of the disciples, which are not written in this book; but these have been written so that you may believe that Jesus is the Christ, the Son of God; and that believing you may have life in His name."*

Many scholars have noted that clear apologetic intent of this passage, which combined with the fact that it is reported only in John, the latest of the gospels, has led many scholars to doubt its historicity[354]. Furthermore, claims to prior scepticism as seen in the case of Thomas and elsewhere in the gospels are a well-known narrative device used in reporting miraculous or paranormal events. As psychologist Anna Stone explains[355]:

> *"The avowal of prior scepticism is a narrative device designed to enhance the credibility of the narrator and the likelihood of attribution of the event to a paranormal cause. The technique works like this: a typical narrative account starts with the avowal of prior scepticism ('at first I was sceptical'), followed by a description of an anomalous occurrence ('but a psychic told me things she could not have known'), which in turn is followed by a conversion ('I realised that something out of the ordinary*

was occurring'). This technique highlights the strength of evidence that caused a change in the narrator's attitude from initial scepticism to belief. By highlighting the narrator's reliance on evidence the account also positions the narrator as a rational thinker."

The accounts of 'doubting Thomas' are therefore best explained as later apologetic accretions to the core appearances narrative, made (likely unconsciously) in accordance with the common motif of the avowal of prior scepticism concerning miraculous claims. Craig has not provided evidence to show that Thomas truly was as sceptical as John claims he was, or that the events in this passage occurred exactly as John claims they did. As such, Craig's appeal to the appearance to Thomas adds no compelling evidence to his case for the resurrection.

The appearance to the five hundred

In 1 Corinthians 15:6 Paul says that Jesus "appeared to more than five hundred brothers at one time, most of whom are still alive, though some have fallen asleep." Craig argues that this large number of surviving witnesses could have been consulted by sceptical hearers of Paul's message, and any discrepancies or inventions uncovered in this way. As such, the fact of so many surviving eyewitnesses provides strong evidence for the real bodily appearance of Jesus, as inaccuracies would not have been able to propagate with so many surviving witnesses. There are two major defects with this argument. First, it is not clear that this event can be characterised as among the core historical bedrock that Craig appeals to in making his argument. Our only evidence for it is Paul's word that it happened, without any details or specifics. It is not mentioned in any of the gospels, which seems strange for such a remarkable event. This does not mean that it did not occur, but it is not one of the key facts that Craig originally outlined, and therefore if he wishes to appeal to it as evidence then he will first need to establish that it is likely to have been a real historical event. Second, supposing the appearance to the five hundred did occur, it is unclear how Paul knows that all the witnesses actually saw Jesus. It seems highly improbable that he interviewed any significant number of them

James Fodor

individually to find out exactly what they saw. We do not know with any confidence how many people were really present, or how many of them even saw anything at all. We do not know whether those who did see something saw the same thing, or whether each person saw something quite different. What we have, therefore, is not five hundred independent accounts of seeing Jesus, but a single account of a large group of people who had a collective experience of seeing Jesus. This sort of account is relatively common, and is similar to the many reports of Marian apparitions, Buddha statues that drink, collective UFO sightings, and other group miracle reports that I document in the next section. It is perfectly consistent with the RHBS model that large crowds of people falsely came to believe (through the mechanisms I outline) that they saw Jesus in some form. It does not follow that such sightings would in any way have prevented the spread of inaccuracies, especially those based on unreliable memories.

Craig advances another distinct argument concerning the appearance to the five hundred. Quoting C.H. Dodd, he argues that[356]:

"There can hardly be any purpose in mentioning the fact that the most of the 500 are still alive, unless Paul is saying, in effect, 'The witnesses are there to be questioned'. Paul would not have said this if the event had not occurred. He wouldn't have challenged people to talk to the eyewitnesses if the event had never taken place and there were no eyewitnesses."

This remark is strange because there is a very obvious reason why Paul would have made such a statement – because he was trying to convince people to believe in the risen Jesus! Paul was an accomplished orator and would use whatever tools he had at his disposal to present his case in a manner compelling to his audience. I don't mean to imply that Paul thought he was lying, just that we need not interpret this remark as a literal challenge to go and investigate. Rather it should be interpreted as a rhetorical flourish to emphasise that the facts are true and one could verify them if one wished, even though Paul would have been fully aware that very few people would have had both the means and the inclination to actually do so. He was not, therefore, literally challenging people to check his claims. Additionally, it must be

Unreasonable Faith

remembered that travel in the Roman world was considerably more difficult and expensive than it is in our time. By my calculations using the Stanford geospatial network model of the Roman world[357], the quickest trip (by sea) from Corinth to Jerusalem would take 10 days (in summer), and cost about 300 denarii, which is something like ten months wages for an average labourer[358]. Such a journey would only be feasible for the rich, or those supported by the church. Thus, while not impossible, going to investigate Paul's claims would not have been something that anyone who was curious about them could simply have done over the weekend in the sort of cavalier way Craig seems to imagine. There were also further complications, such as the potential difficulty in finding the persons Paul refers to some twenty years after the fact, and the likelihood that the Greeks Paul was addressing would not have spoken the same language as the predominantly Aramaic-speaking Jews who would have witnessed the event. The actual ability to check any such claim seems extremely tenuous, with the exception of those in close temporal and spatial proximity to the original event.

POSTULATE THREE: COLLECTIVE RELIGIOUS EXPERIENCES

The third postulate of the RHBS model is that reports of Jesus' empty tomb and the initial individual hallucinations of the risen Jesus triggered a serious of collective experiences of the risen Jesus among the disciples through expectation and socialisation effects. In this section I first outline the psychological evidence for the perceptual, expectation, and social influence mechanisms that this postulate appeals to, and then provide a number of historical cases of groups of people reporting miraculous or highly unusual phenomena, thereby demonstrating the plausibility of my claim that such collective experiences could also have occurred in the case the resurrection appearances.

Expectation and perceptual biases

Below I cite a few studies which illustrate how expectations and preconceptions can lead us to find meaning in ambiguous stimuli, to observe things that we otherwise would not, and to interpret what we observe through the framework of what we are expecting to see. These processes would have been important in generating the collective religious experiences of the risen Jesus, given that the original private hallucinations generated an expectation in the rest of the disciples that they might experience something similar.

- 'This study assessed the degree to which the contents of religious experiences agree with the expectations and rated desirability of various experiential contents... In sum, the data suggest that those who have religious experiences get what they anticipate, and their expectations emphasize highly desirable components in such experience.' [359]

- 'Recent work on visual integration and change direction reveals that we are surprisingly unaware of the details of our environment from one view to the next: we often do not detect large changes to objects and scenes ('change blindness'). Furthermore, without attention, we may not even perceive objects ('inattentional blindness'). Taken together, these findings suggest that we perceive and remember only those objects and details that receive focused attention.' [360]

- 'The data also demonstrated a significant difference between the high versus low expectancy subjects for both patient and (faith) healer groups, as well as a significant relationship between high expectancy in patients and healer and the effectiveness of the spiritual healing encounter. The results of the study therefore suggest that high healer and patient expectancy may be important elements which can serve as both predictors as well as facilitators of the healing process. The degree of bonding or communication between the healer and patient was postulated as an important factor in this regard.' [361]

- 'Near-death experiences (NDEs) include a set of subjective experiences encountered by people who were close to death or were faced with life-threatening situations. Reports have suggested that the phenomenology of NDE might differ across cultures... This article concludes that although there are common themes, there are also reported differences in NDEs. The variability across cultures is most likely to be due to our interpretation and verbalizing of such esoteric events through the filters of language, cultural experiences, religion, education and their influence on our belief systems either shedding influence as an individual variable or more often perhaps by their rich interplay between these factors.[1] [362]

The social construction of miracles

The idea that hallucinatory or delusory experiences can occur in group settings is unfamiliar to many people, and some regard it as a very strange and implausible idea. Nevertheless, this is a known phenomenon in the psychological literature that has been the subject of some considerable study. Describing how such collective experiences take place, psychologist Donovan H. Rawcliffe writes[363]:

> *"The same factors which operate for a single individual in the induction of hallucinations... may become even more effective in an excited or expectant crowd, and on occasion may result in mass hallucinations. This is not to say that any two people are capable of having precisely the same hallucination identical in every respect. But similar preconceptions and expectations can undoubtedly result in hallucinatory visions so alike that subsequent comparisons would not disclose any major discrepancy... dissimilar hallucinatory experiences often attain a spurious similarity by a process of harmonisation in subsequent recollection and conversation."*

It is important to emphasise that, as Rawcliffe explains, during these experiences it is not necessary for each person present to experience *exactly the same thing*. Rather, they all have experiences that are *similar enough*, with details later rectified through processes of memory conformity and other cognitive biases that I discuss in the next section. While Rawcliffe gives a broad overview of the psychological and sociological processes thought to be responsible for such experiences, a more detailed understanding of precisely how groups of people come to report unusual collective experiences is still under active study. Below I provide a number of further examples from the literature to illustrate both what types of collective experiences have been documented, and some of the mechanisms thought to be responsible for them.

James Fodor

- 'Pentecostal miracles and healings have often been described and interpreted, but rarely explained in their sociological workings. As former research implies, actual biomedical effects of Pentecostal healings are possible (the so-called placebo effect), but quite limited. In Pentecostal healing services, however, very impressive miracles and healings are routinely produced: paralytics arise from wheelchairs, cancerous ulcers disappear, legs grow, cavities are mysteriously filled, and the deaf suddenly hear. Drawing on a case study and qualitative interviews, this paper offers a sociological, mechanism-based, explanatory scheme for the observed phenomena. It is argued that a number of "social techniques" (e.g., suggestion, rhythm, music), context factors (e.g., audience size and beliefs), and causal mechanisms (e.g., probability, latency, selection, and editing effects) are combined in an ingenious way in order to produce miracles and healings.' [364]

- 'The communal creation of religious meaning is here examined in the context of an Irish Catholic Charismatic prayer meeting. Through a micro-analysis of the "spontaneous" ritual language of one such meeting, various discursive strategies are revealed which function to create for the participants an experience of divine/human communication. These include an explicit effort on the part of speakers to construct a thematically consistent and coherent ritual event out of a sequence of apparently spontaneous individual speech acts, as well as a marked use of evidentials to attribute spiritual authorship and authority to personal speech acts.' [365]

- 'This paper is based on interviews with 160 persons who were participants in spiritual healing groups in Baltimore between 1981 and 1983. Survey data are used to describe how participants in spiritual healing groups presented their health problems, and how and if these problems were resolved or 'healed' over a six-month period. The majority of respondents claimed some degree of healing, associated mainly with symptom alleviation rather than cure. A process of health problem redefinition occurred among some respondents, that provided better 'fit' with outcome descriptions of healing than original problem formulations. Redefined health problems were often less serious, less medical, more chronic, and more 'emergent' than those initially defined, and respondents who redefined problems were significantly more likely to claim a healing experience. 'Psychologisation' of problems suggest that healing experiences can be conceived as socially constructed events.' [366]

- 'Hauntings and poltergeist-like episodes are argued to be products of contagious reactions to ambiguous environmental or cognitive events. In particular, evidence suggests that the subjective and objective effects reported by percipients are the function of independent, non-paranormal etiologies whose constitutions have been previously established and described. According to this multivariate model, the labelling of ambiguous events as "abnormal" or "paranormal" initiates the reactive process which is subsequently sustained by perceptual contagion, i.e., flurries of paranormal observations due self-reinforcing attentional processes.' [367]

- 'Participants were required to spend 50 min in a specially constructed chamber, within which they were exposed to infrasound, complex EMFs, both or neither... A considerable proportion of the participants reported a number of anomalous sensations in response to a fairly mild suggestion that in our white, round, featureless room they might feel some unusual sensations. Such an explanation is in line with the observations of Houran and Lange. They asked two volunteers to keep a diary for 30 days of unusual events of the type that are traditionally associated with hauntings and poltergeists in a residence with no prior history of such activity. As expected, the instructions themselves were sufficient for the volunteers to note, with increasing frequency, anomalous or unusual events presumably simply because the volunteers were now primed to notice... The most parsimonious explanation for our findings is in terms of suggestibility.' [368]

Findings such as these enable us to develop a schematic picture of how the disciples may have come to have collective experiences of the risen Jesus. The literature indicates that both expectation and an appropriate environmental setting are necessary for such events to occur.

James Fodor

According to the RHBS model, the expectation existed as a result of the disciples having heard of reports both of the empty tomb, and also of the initial appearances of Jesus to individual followers (perhaps Peter or Mary). The appropriate emotionally-charged setting imbued with religious significance would likely have been generated by a meeting of the disciples, perhaps sharing a meal or discussing what they should do following the death of their leader. Some ritual action, perhaps a prayer, singing a hymn, or collective silent reflection, further consolidated the context and mindsets of those present to focus on the person of Jesus. The appearance may then have begun with a private hallucination that was transmitted by means of suggestion, or as an initial ambiguous stimulus, was interpreted as the voice or image of Jesus (this may be hinted at by the non-recognition motifs found in some of the appearance narratives, though this may also have other origins). Given the effects of expectation and appropriate social setting, the experience then developed and took its course through an iterative process of social feedback, primed attentional processes, emotional excitement and suggestion. These processes would have been augmented by the harmonising effects of the disciples fitting a comprehensible narrative account to their experiences consistent with their worldview and expectations, a process which would have begun during the experience itself, but also continued long afterwards. While the details of precisely what occurred can never be known, and the RHBS model does not pretend to explain *exactly* how these collective experiences occurred (there is too little data to do so), nevertheless I believe that the account I provide here is quite plausible given the psychological and sociological evidence that I cite in this section.

The diversity of the appearances

Craig has argued that, even if some of the disciples had experienced individual hallucinations of Jesus, this cannot explain the origin of the reports of collective experiences. He states[369]:

> *"The* diversity of the appearances *is not well explained by means of such visions (hallucinations). The appearances were experienced many different times, by different individuals, by*

> *groups, at various locales and under various circumstances, and by not only believers, but also by unbelievers like James the brother of Jesus and the Pharisee Saul of Tarsus. This diversity is very difficult to explain by recourse to hallucinations. For hallucinations require a special psychological state on the part of the percipient."*

Craig does not give any evidence to substantiate his claim that hallucinations require a 'special psychological state'. Of course, in one sense this is trivially true, since every single perception or experience requires its own particular psychological state. If what Craig is trying to say, however, is that some special psychological characteristics are required in order to experience a hallucination, then this is incorrect, as indicated by the literature I cited previously. Furthermore, while the geographical location and exact participants involved were variable, these are not of primary importance in explaining the appearances. What is important is that all of the appearances of Jesus occurred to various of his followers (I discussed the case of James in a previous section), who were members of a new religious movement who were grieving following the loss of their charismatic leader, and who had various levels of expectancy to experience an encounter as a result of the empty tomb and prior reports of individual hallucinations by some of the disciples. I believe that I have provided sufficient evidence that members of new religious movements, people experiencing grief, and those with prior expectations, are all particularly predisposed to experience relevant forms of hallucinations. The only exception to this description would be the appearance to Paul, however this really ought to be discussed separately since this was not a resurrection appearance, but a visionary experience occurring years later to someone who never knew Jesus while alive. As such, I do not believe Craig's 'diversity' objection provides sufficient grounds to discredit hallucinations as an explanation of the appearances.

Craig further argues that[370]:

> *"Even if one could compile from the casebooks an amalgam consisting of stories of hallucinations over a period of time (like the visions in Medjugorje), mass hallucinations (as at Lourdes),*

hallucinations to various individuals, and so forth, the fact remains that there is no single instance in the casebooks exhibiting the diversity involved in the postmortem appearances of Jesus. It is only by compiling unrelated cases that anything analogous might be constructed."

This statement is problematic for two main reasons. First, one of the very examples he cites disproves Craig's own argument, since the visions in Medjugorje occurred over a period of many years, to a group of several individuals. Second, Craig is just wrong to assert that there are no other such examples, for I document many other cases that demonstrate similar diversity of appearances as the resurrection accounts in the subsequent three sections, including hallucinations to various individuals, group and individual hallucinations, and hallucinations over a period of time. Craig's claim is thus simply not supported by the evidence.

Historical examples of public miracles

If the psychological and sociological processes that I discuss above are capable of generating collective experiences of miraculous or paranormal phenomena, then we would expect to see many examples of this occurring throughout history and continuing to the present day. In particular, we would expect that collective reports of miracles witnessed by groups of people would be found in other religious traditions, meaning that the resurrection appearances are not unique in this respect. I believe that this is, in fact, exactly what we do observe, and that the evidence of collective miracle experiences I outline in this section constitutes powerful evidence in favour of the RHBS model.

On the question of competing collective miraculous experiences, Craig has made conflicting statements. He has stated[371]:

"It still remains an empirical question whether a miracle supporting a counter-Christian claim is equally or better attested than Jesus' miracles and resurrection. There is no way to settle the issue apart from an investigation."

Elsewhere, however, he asserts that[372]:

> *"The fact remains that there is no single instance in the casebooks exhibiting the diversity involved in the postmortem appearances of Jesus."*

This indicates that rather than still being open, he regards the question settled in the negative. It seems to me, however, that Craig's confident assertion in the latter quote is an empty declaration made without any supporting evidence. Craig has devoted very little space in any of his writings to addressing the question of competing miracle claims, and so even though he recognises in principle the need for comparative empirical investigation, in practise the only miracle claim that he has devoted any significant effort into investigating is that of Christianity. This, of course, does not prove the resurrection of Jesus did not occur. It should, however, raise significant suspicions about Craig's bold claims to the superiority of the resurrection over any other miracle claim, and highlight the importance of actually making a sincere effort to carry out the comparative empirical analysis that Craig mentions.

As I have stated above, and contrary to Craig's baseless assertions, I believe that there are many claims of publicly performed miracles throughout history that are comparably well documented as the New Testament appearances of Jesus. In this section, I briefly outline several dozen of the most promising cases that I have been able to uncover; doubtless there are also many more I am not aware of, and there are also many more that I have found but not included here. I have attempted only to include miracles that are claimed to have occurred in some public setting with multiple witnesses, thereby excluding figures like Mohammed who claimed only to have received private revelations. I also have attempted to include only those miracles of which we have written accounts dating to within several decades of the event, a comparable timespan to the gospels. In many of the modern examples, the documentary evidence dates effectively to the year or even the day of the event itself. Conversely, in some examples from the ancient world the timeline is somewhat expanded, with a few of the examples having been recorded a bit over a century after the events in question. This is a longer time span than the gospels (up to seventy years for the Gospel of John), however not dramatically longer. I have, however, omitted miracles that are only reported many centuries after the fact, which is why for instance none of the many miracles of the Buddha are included. I do not claim that each example provided below is equally well evidenced as the resurrection appearances – for some I believe the evidence is somewhat better, and for others it is somewhat worse. Nevertheless, I have attempted to provide an illustrative sample of cases to give the reader an idea of the range of examples to be found when one actually attempts to conduct a review of what Craig calls 'the casebooks.'

In these examples I have also tried to focus on miracles being reported outside of either early Christianity or post-reformation protestant traditions, since apologists like Craig may be inclined to accept such accounts as genuine supernatural occurrences. I have focused instead on miracles occurring in traditions at odds with protestant Christianity, including Catholicism, Judaism, paganism, Buddhism, Hinduism, and new religious movements. The reader should also bear in mind that in the majority of cases, original documents are not available in English and have not received a great deal of scholarly attention, so it can be difficult to say exactly how well attested the claims are.

Catholic Miracles

- Our Lady of Fátima: The Virgin Mary was reported to have appeared to crowds of up to 70,000 people at Fatima, Portugal in 1917. Initially the sightings were reported by a group of children, but subsequently were witnessed by groups of many thousands as pilgrims were drawn from throughout the country. The most famous of these appearances is called the Miracle of the Sun, where an expectant crowd reported seeing the sun move about erratically across the sky and produce strange colours and other sights. A quote from an eyewitness[373]:

"The sun's disc did not remain immobile. This was not the sparkling of a heavenly body, for it spun round on itself in a mad whirl, when suddenly a clamor was heard from all the people. The sun, whirling, seemed to loosen itself from the firmament and advance threateningly

upon the earth as if to crush us with its huge fiery weight. The sensation during those moments was terrible."

- Our Lady of Assiut: Thousands experienced apparitions of the Virgin Mary in Egypt in 2000, with both Muslims and Christians witnessing the event. The apparitions continued for a period of about five months. Representative quotes from witnesses as reported in contemporary newspapers[374]:

"I saw the Virgin Mary, flashing lights and big white doves."
"Light was emanating from her hands, then doves start flying, they were as big as ducks."

- Our Lady of Zeitoun: A series of Marian apparitions reported in Cairo for several years in the late 1960s. Tens of thousands of people reported seeing the apparitions, including many Muslims and non-Christians. One representative quote[375]:

"The whole scene was bathed with a luminous halo surrounded with a blue circular frame all ablaze. Little by little the vision became more distinct until the figure of Mary became more evident to the vast multitudes who filled the space surrounding the church of Zeitun. The luminous circle seemed to symbolize to me the perfection of eternity in contradistinction to the fragmentary limitations of our seemingly dreary mechanical measure of time."

- Our Lady of Medjugorje: A group of six people in former Yugoslavia have been reporting visions of Mary since 1981. There have been many investigations into this phenomenon which provide much more information. A brief description follows[376]:

"On June 24, 1981, at about 6pm, six young parishioners from Medjugorje: Ivanka Ivankovic, Mirjana Dragicevic, Vicka Ivankovic, Ivan Dragicevic, Ivan Ivankovic and Milka Pavlovic, saw on the hill Crnica (on the place called Podbrdo) an apparition, a white form with a child in her arms. Surprised and scared, they did not approach. The next day at the same time, June 25, 1981, four of them, Ivanka Ivankovic, Mirjana Dragicevic, Vicka Ivankovic and Ivan Dragicevic, felt strongly drawn towards the place where, the day before, they saw the One who they had recognised as Our Lady. Marija

Pavlovic and Jakov Colo joined them. The group of Medjugorje visionaries was formed. They prayed with Our Lady and talked to her. From that day onward, they had daily apparitions, together or separately. Milka Pavlovic and Ivan Ivankovic have never seen Our Lady any more."

- William of Newburgh: A twelfth century English historian who recorded a number of miracles and wondrous occurrences, including the bizarre tale of the green children of Woolpit. He also reports a number of cases of people rising from the dead and terrorising the local village. One account, which he received from a monk said to be an eyewitness, is given below concerning the death of a young outlaw[377]:

"A Christian burial, indeed, he received, though unworthy of it; but it did not much benefit him: for issuing, by the handiwork of Satan, from his grave at night-time, and pursued by a pack of dogs with horrible barkings, he wandered through the courts and around the houses while all men made fast their doors, and did not dare to go abroad on any errand whatever from the beginning of the night until the sunrise, for fear of meeting and being beaten black and blue by this vagrant monster. But those precautions were of no avail; for the atmosphere, poisoned by the vagaries of this foul carcass, filled every house with disease and death by its pestiferous breath."

- Convulsionnaires of Saint-Médard: An interesting case from eighteenth century France in which hundreds of people reported witnessing healings, convulsions, and other strange events when visiting the grave of a recently deceased heretical Deacon called François de Pâris. We have many accounts from the time, though most of the relevant source material is only available in French[378].

New Christian Movements

- Simon Kimbangu: A twentieth century African religious leader who claimed to be a special envoy of Christ, and to whom is attributed many miracles, including healings and raising the dead[379]. He was imprisoned by the colonial authorities as a result of his drawing such large crowds. Although there is much early documentation of his ministry and purported miracles, most of the literature is in French[380].

- Oral Roberts: Renowned twentieth century faith healer and televangelist who also claims to have raised the dead[381]. He wrote a book where he outlines some of his greatest miracles[382], many of which are also listed on his website and on various online videos.

- Three Witnesses to the Book of Mormon: Three companions of Mormon founder Joseph Smith, who declared that an angel appeared to them and showed them the Gold Plates that Smith had translated. Their signed declaration was printed in the first edition of the Book of Mormon within about a year of the event[383], and reads:

"We declare with words of soberness, that an angel of God came down from heaven, and he brought and laid before our eyes, that we beheld and saw the plates, and the engravings thereon; and we know that it is by the grace of God the Father, and our Lord Jesus Christ, that we beheld and bear record that these things are true. And it is marvelous in our eyes. Nevertheless, the voice of the Lord commanded us that we should bear record of it; wherefore, to be obedient unto the commandments of God, we bear testimony of these things."

Jewish Miracle Workers

- Theudas: A first century AD Jewish rebel whom both Josephus and the author of Acts record as having convinced a large number of people that he was able to perform miracles. The following is reported by Josephus[384]:

"While Cuspius Fadus was procurator of Judea, that a certain charlatan, whose name was Theudas, persuaded a great part of the people to take their effects with them, and follow him to the Jordan river; for he told them he was a prophet, and that he would, by his own command, divide the river, and afford them an easy passage over it. Many were deluded by his words."

- Eliezer ben Hurcanus: A rabbi of the first and second centuries AD said to have performed a number of miracles in support of a particular doctrinal claim he was advocating. These are recorded in the Mishnah, and so were written within decades of his life. One example [385]:

> "On that day R. Eliezer brought forward every imaginable argument, but they did not accept them. Said he to them: 'If the Halacha (Jewish law) agrees with me, let this carobtree prove it!' Thereupon the carob tree was torn a hundred cubits out of its place; others affirm, four hundred cubits. 'No proof can be brought from a carob-tree,' they retorted. Again he said to them: 'If the Halacha agrees with me, let the stream of water prove it!' Whereupon the stream of water flowed backwards. 'No proof can be brought from a stream of water,' they rejoined... Again he said to them: 'If the Halacha agrees with me, let it be proved from Heaven!' Whereupon a Heavenly Voice cried out: 'Why do ye dispute with Rabbi Eliezer, seeing that in all matters the Halacha agrees with him!'."

- Sabbatai Zevi: A seventeenth century Turkish rabbi and Messiah claimant said to have performed many miracles, including predicting the future. He is also notable because he attracted many followers throughout the Jewish world, and even retained a core following after his forced conversion to Islam at the hands of the Ottomans. He still has followers to this day. An extract from a modern biography reads[386]:

> "Sabbati Sevi, or the new Shadday, had transformed their world into one huge miracle where everything was possible... Reports send to Amsterdam stated as early as December 1665 that Sabbatai Sevi had confirmed his mission by miracles. He had predicted the sudden death of certain people, as well as a day of darkness and the fall of 'great Hail-stones, Fire and Brimstone'... Sabbatai also 'commanded a fire to be made in a public place, in the presence of many beholders; as well as of Christians, as of Turks, and Jews; and entered into the fire twice or thrice, without any hurt to his Garments, or to an hair of his head'."

- Baal Shem Tov: An eighteenth century Polish mystical Rabbi credited with a large number of miracles. Many of these are recorded in the book *In Praise of the Ba'al Shem Tov*[387], which contains many stories passed down orally by his followers and published around fifty years after his death.

- Menachem Mendel Schneerson: A twentieth century Jewish Rabbi accredited with many healings, and who many of his followers report having seen appear to them since his death. A documentary has also been made about him called *A Glimpse Through the Veil: Eight First-Person Accounts of the Rebbe's Miracles*. A study of postmortem apparitions reports[388]:

> "Most Hasidim have acquiesced to his death while still hoping for his resurrection as the Messiah. But a significant minority of radical Hasidim called meshichistim ('messianists') flatly denies the Rabbi's demise claiming that he continues to live, invisible but intact, in '770', his abode and the movement's epicentre... Visual encounters with the Rabbi increase over the years. Of the 76 apparitions reported throughout 1994–2010, yielding an annual average of 4–5 cases, 75 percent occurred in the second half of that period... Most seers reported a single apparition, but in some cases the Rabbi is seen twice or more on different occasions by one individual. A few simultaneous apparitions, usually involving a dyad, were reported."

Ancient Roman Miracle Workers

- Emperor Vespasian: Suetonius, writing about fifty years after the death of this Roman emperor, reports an interesting anecdote[389]:

> "A man of the people who was blind, and another who was lame, came to him together as he sat on the tribunal, begging for the help for their disorders which Serapis had promised in a dream; for the god declared that Vespasian would restore the eyes, if he would spit upon them, and give strength to the leg, if he would deign to touch it with his heel. Though he had hardly any faith that this could possibly succeed, and therefore shrank even from making the attempt, he was at last prevailed upon by his friends and tried both things in public before a large crowd; and with success."

- Apollonius of Tyana: A first century AD Greek philosopher and popular orator credited with many miracles. Our main source of information is Apollonius' biographer Philostratus who wrote his Life of Apollonius of Tyana between 217 and 238, about 100-150 years after the event. Around AD 180 Lucian wrote a pamphlet where he attacked Alexander of Abonoteichus, a student of one of Apollonius' students, as a charlatan, suggesting that the whole school was based on fraud. From this we can infer that Apollonius really had students and that his school survived at least until Lucian's time.

- Alexander of Abonoteichus: Leader of a second century AD Roman cult. The main account we have of his alleged miracles comes from the hostile source Lucian, who wrote *Alexander the False Prophet* some ten years after the death of Alexander in AD 170. In this book he outlines a number of Alexander's alleged miracles and how he duped people into believing that he had magical powers. What is most interesting is how many people believed him despite apparently quite compelling counter-evidence. Consider for instance this report from Lucian[390]:

"He (Alexander) published an oracle at the height of the war in Germany, when the late Emperor Marcus himself had at last come to grips with the Marcomanni and Quadi. The oracle recommended that two lions be cast into the Danube alive, together with a quantity of perfumes and magnificent offerings... But when all this had been done as he had directed... that tremendous disaster befell our side, in which a matter of twenty thousand were wiped out at a blow... To meet this issue, Alexander was flat enough to adduce the Delphian defence in the matter of the oracle given to Croesus, that the God had indeed foretold victory, but had not indicated whether it would go to the Romans or to the enemy."

- Simon Magus: A first century religious figure mentioned in the gospels and by Josephus, his miracles are described in several apocryphal works written a century or more after his life, including Acts of Peter, Pseudo-Clementines, and the Epistle of the Apostles[391]. We have quite a number of independent sources for his deeds and some of his miracles, most of them dating to the late second century. Acts 8:9-11 reports that he was a sorcerer:

Unreasonable Faith

> *"Now there was a man named Simon, who formerly was practicing magic in the city and astonishing the people of Samaria, claiming to be someone great; and they all, from smallest to greatest, were giving attention to him, saying, 'This man is what is called the Great Power of God.' And they were giving him attention because he had for a long time astonished them with his magic arts."*

Indian Miracles

- Mirza Ghulam Ahmad: A Muslim religious leader from the nineteenth century and founder of the founder of the Ahmadiyya Movement. He made many prophecies, which believers consider to be evidence of his prophethood, along with various other miracles and divine signs[392]. Anandamayi Ma: A twentieth century Indian saint credited with many healings and other miracles. As an example from an eyewitness[393]:

"At Kalibari, I used to hear many interesting conversations among the devotees about Ma's supernatural powers and miracles. Some devotees would describe Ma as Antarjamini (knower of everything that passes in other's heart), others remarked that at a single glance at one's face, Ma could at once know the uppermost thought in the devotee's mind, while some others said that Ma had appeared to different persons at different places in different forms, such as, Ma Durga, Ma Kali etc. But I was not impressed by such anecdotes which sounded to me as nothing but fairy-tales...

I knew that Ma was a great lover of songs and during each darshan time Ma used to ask somebody from among the assembled devotees to sing... I therefore devised a plan for testing Ma. I decided to go henceforth for Ma's darshan with a strong desire in my mind to sing before her only if Ma asked me to sing. I did not divulge this decision either to my parents or anybody else. I then started to practice a particular song thoroughly at home... On the third afternoon, I volunteered to go for Ma's darshan and my mother accompanied me to Kalibari. When we reached there, we found Ma sitting on a cot in the big hall and radiating a transcendental Light all around...

After some time, Ma answered to some questions put to her by two devotees. Ma then asked one girl to sing and when she finished, she asked another... An hour ticked by and during this period, Ma did not even cast a single glance towards me...After a while... my own mother told me that it was time for us also to leave. I agreed. I went near Ma, did my pranam and as I raised my head to get up Ma said 'Are you leaving now? Won't you let me hear your song? Just sing at least one song for me'. I was stunned and dumbfounded to hear Ma's words...I therefore sat down and as I was getting ready, Ma said with a smile: 'Sing that very song which you have practised so hard'. At this, my astonishment knew no bounds and I wondered how Ma knew all about my plan. After I finished singing, I looked up and found Ma looking straight towards me with a bewitching smile on Her face. The smile seemed to communicate the message that I have lost the contest and Ma has won. My heart filled with joy. I felt a wonderful delight which was hitherto unknown to me. I also realised that this was one of thousands of mysterious incidents that very often take place around Ma."

- Raghavendra Swami: A seventeenth century Indian saint credited with many miracles during and after his life. There is even an interesting story of a nineteenth century British officer called Sir Thomas Munroe who allegedly had a vision of the guru while visiting his tomb[394]. At least some of the miracle claims from during his lifetime come from a biography written by his nephew titled *Raghavendra Vijaya*. His devotees continue to report miracles to this day, many of which can be found online[395].

- Shirdi Sai Baba: A nineteenth century Indian saint said to have performed many miracles, including healings, exorcisms, levitation, and bilocations. We have a number of contemporary or near-contemporary sources, including Ganesh Srikrishna Khaparde. One example[396]:

"Sai Baba was to them (his followers) as real as their homes and their fields and their cattle and the distant hills. Das Ganu once had an unforgettable experience. On a festive occasion, he sought Baba's permission to go to a place called Singba on the banks of the Godavari to have a bath in the holy waters. 'No', Baba replied resolutely, 'where is the need to go all the way when the Godavari is here right at my feet?' Das Ganu was vexed. He was willing to concede that Ganga the holy river (Baba frequently referred to Godavari as Ganga) rose from the feet of Sri Narayana *(one among the Hindu trinity of Gods) himself, but his faith was not deep enough to believe that the waters of the Godavari could spring form the feet of his master, Sri Sai Baba who was reading Das Ganu's mind decided that this was the time to strengthen Das Ganu's faith. He told his devotee: 'come closer to me and hold the hollow of your palms at my feet!' As soon as he did so water flowed freely out of the toes of the master's feet and filled the hollow of Das Ganu's palms in no time. His joy knew no limits. He sprinkled the water on his head and his body and distributed some more among the assembled devotees as tirtha (holy water)."*

- Sathya Sai Baba: A twentieth century Indian guru credited with a very large number of miracles by his followers, including levitation, bilocation, healing, and resurrection of the dead. As an example[397]:

"On the morning of the third day the body was more than ever like a corpse - dark, cold, quite stiff and beginning to smell. Other people who came to see and sympathise told Mrs. Radhakrishna that she should have the corpse removed from the ashram. But she replied, 'Not unless Swami orders it'... The minutes dragged by - an hour passed – but Swami Baba did not come. Then, when they were beginning to despair entirely, the door opened and there stood Baba in His red robe, copious hair, and shining smile. It was then about half past two in the afternoon of the third day... Gently, Baba asked the tearful women and sorrowful Mr. Hemchand to leave the room. As they left, He closed the door behind them. They do not know – no man knows – what happened in that room where there were only Swami and the 'dead' man. But after a few minutes Baba opened the door and beckoned the waiting ones in. There, on the bed, Radhakrishna was looking up at them and smiling!"

- Chaitanya Mahaprabhu: A fifteenth century Indian saint with many miracles attributed to them. There are multiple biographies of him written within a few decades of his death[398].

As an example of a miracle claim[399]:

"At Puri a miracle happened. During the car festival, the car of Jagannath did not move. All the pilgrims tried their combined strength. It proved futile. The gigantic elephants of the Raja of Puri also failed to move the car. All were in a stage of suspense and dilemma. Gauranga came just then. He pushed the car by his head and the car moved at once."

Chinese and Japanese Miracles

The following are not individual miracle workers but rather compendia of miracles prepared by various Japanese and Chinese authors. Very little scholarly work has been published in English on these compilations, and so it is impossible for me to identify specific cases. Nevertheless, I include them to illustrate that many other miracle claims exist, and Craig cannot simply assert that there are no parallel cases without having examined the claims made by these sorts of texts.

- Nihon Ryoiki: An early ninth century compilation of folktales and miraculous events from Japan[400]. At least some of these events are supposed to have occurred within a few decades of this book being written.

- Du Guangting: A recorder of miracles in support of Daoism in his text *Daojiao lingyan ji*. The text was written around AD 900, and many of the miracles it relates date from the preceding two centuries[401].

- Dauxuan: A sixth century Chinese Buddhist author who wrote a work entitled *Continued Biographies of Eminent Monks*, which outlines many miracles said to have been formed by Buddhist monks[402]. At least some of these tales seem to have been based on biographical accounts written by the disciples of the monk in question, though the exact origin of many stories is unclear.

- Fu Liang: Another Chinese recorder of miracles, from the late fourth century. He wrote a work called *Guangshiyin yingyanji* detailing many Buddhist miracles, some of which seem to have been very recent events[403].

I have provided this lengthy list of examples of publicly-attested miracle claims in order to demonstrate that the post-mortem appearances of Jesus are not as unparalleled as Craig suggests. Of course, no single case is completely analogous to the resurrection appearances of Jesus, but this is to be expected since all historical events of this sort are unique. What these examples demonstrate is that we do have ample documentary evidence from throughout history and across the world that in certain situations, groups of people can report having seen apparently miraculous events. This, I argue, is precisely what would be expected given the various biases and social construction processes that I have discussed above, and belies Craig's claims that the resurrection appearances of Jesus are historically unique in this regard.

Mass hysteria and psychogenic illness

In this section I outline some interesting cases of what appear to be mass delusions or psychogenic illnesses. While these are not miracle claims as such, I believe that these examples lend further credence to my claim that through social reinforcement, cognitive biases, expectation, and other such effects, large groups of people can come to confidently believe very bizarre things in spite of the absence of any genuine phenomenon.

- Seattle Windshield Pitting Epidemic[404]: widespread observation of previously unnoticed windshield holes, pits and dings on cars.

- Angels of Mons[405]: an apocryphal tale of angels seen at the trenches in World War One, very widely reported and believed but with no apparent basis in any original report.

- N-rays[406]: a form of radiation whose existence was independently confirmed by many scientists in the early 20th century, but which was later found to be totally non-existent, the findings purely due to experimenter artefacts.

- Mad Gasser of Mattoon[407]: an alleged series of gas attacks in Illinois in the 1940s which may have been a case of mass hysteria.

- German air raids on Canada[408]: widespread reports of and belief in German aircraft being seen over Canada during the First World War, despite the fact that the Germans never conducted any such raids, nor had aircraft with sufficient range.

- Genital-Shrinking Epidemic[409]: a widespread belief among males that their genitals are shrinking due to some kind of disease, which has been recorded on numerous occasions throughout history.

Of course, mass hysterias of this magnitude are rare, but as I have shown they are documented to have occurred in modern times when sufficient written documents and other evidence is available to establish their non-veridical nature. It is therefore probable that such events have also occurred in the past, at times when the means were not available to establish them as cases of mass hysteria, and may instead have been reported as miraculous or supernatural in origin. I should clarify that I am not necessarily claiming that the resurrection appearances constituted an instance of mass hysteria. Rather, my point is simply that we do know that groups of people can quite quickly come to believe exceptionally implausible things even given obvious evidence to the contrary, purely as a result of psychological and sociological processes. As a part of the explanation for the resurrection appearances, therefore, such processes cannot simply be ignored or blithely dismissed as absurd.

Apparitions of the dead

Mainstream academics are seldom interested in collecting cases of people reporting having witnessed the dead being raised, or of seeing or speaking to someone who has died. There are however, a number of specialised literature sources where one can find such reports. One such source is the clinical psychology literature relating to what is termed 'complicated bereavement', which includes study of bereavement hallucinations and cases of delusory belief that dead loved ones are still alive. Another source is an amorphous subfield of anthropology variously described as anomalous anthropology, anthropology of consciousness, or shamanistic anthropology. In this literature a number of cases have been documented of raising or seeing the dead by field anthropologists working with tribal peoples. The third major source of such cases is the late nineteenth and early twentieth century spiritualist literature, as well as its modern continuation in the field of parapsychology. Drawing upon these literatures, here I document a number of cases of people reporting to have seen the dead being raised, or to have witnessed an apparition of someone who has recently died. In many of these cases, the event in question is said to have taken place in public, and/or been observed by multiple persons. Many of the cases also concern people witnessing the appearance of persons they knew while alive. Here I only include cases documented within a short span (years to decades at most) of the events in question, thereby excluding vague legendary accounts. I also exclude 'pop phenomena' sightings of dead celebrities, such as Elvis sightings.

Though no single case is analogous to the resurrection appearances in all respects, I believe that the selection of cases presented here establishes conclusively that individuals and groups of people do, with reasonable frequency, report experiences of seeing and interacting with those who have recently died. This, of course, does not prove that the RHBS model is correct, or that Jesus could not have been resurrected. However, I do think that these cases are consistent with the prediction of the RHBS model that the sociological and psychological processes I postulate as responsible for the resurrection appearances would also be operative in other times and places in history. These cases therefore constitute evidence for my contention that the resurrection appearances represent but one of the more impressive of a large and diverse class of similar sorts of sightings of the dead, thereby increasing the plausibility of my claim that such experiences are the result of sociological and psychological processes. If the resurrection was the result of a divine miracle, there is no reason to expect these other cases would exist. The fact that they do exist therefore lends support to my claim that collective hallucinatory experiences of the dead occur, and that they are explicable through naturalistic processes.

Complicated Bereavement

- Case report of an elderly woman who continued to believe that her son was alive for 35 years after his death. She was not otherwise diagnosed with a mental illness. They report[410]:

"On mental status examination, her higher mental functions were intact. When asked about her son she said she could not talk about him, but requested us to arrange for his return."

- Case report of a twenty-six-year-old businessman who believed that his mother, who had died six months previously, was visiting and talking to him for extended periods of time every day.

No mental illness or organic pathology was identified. They report[411]:

> "The patient described seeing his mother regularly, almost every evening at different times. According to him, his mother would appear in different dresses that she used to wear when alive and would not allow him to touch her. The patient firmly believes that his mother appears to him in the real world; he does accept that dead people do not return to earth but attributes this exception to his strong bond with his mother."

- Thai newspapers report a number of 'mass hallucination' sightings of dead tourists following the 2004 tsunami[412]:

> "There were reports of ghost sightings involving foreign tourists in the six worst-hit southern provinces in Thailand following the tsunami tragedy. This phenomenon of 'mass hallucinations' is understandable from the cultural perspective: the Thais believe that spirits can only be put to rest by relatives at the scene of the disaster."

- *Mu Ghayeb* is an Omani culturally-sanctioned bereavement process in which relatives ardently deny that the deceased is really dead, and hold expectations of their imminent return[413]:

> "Grieving the deceased by the family, friends and acquaintances seems to indicate their acceptance of the reality of the loss. However, they continue to believe that the individuals are still alive. They are, therefore, expected to rise from the grave, and move around to lead a shadowy existence, sleeping naked in a cave during the day, and rising at night to wander the countryside, feeding on leaves, and performing the orders of the magician, the master or the controller. During this period, the dead may be seen as a wraith-like figure at night by their family and friends. Alternatively, such individuals may be reported as being seen normally clothed (during daylight) in rapidly passing cars, or in other situations, not easily amenable to verification."

Anthropological Reports

- Sir George Grey was a British explorer who, in his journey to an aboriginal tribe living North of Perth in 1838, reported an experience whereby he was believed to be the son of one of the aboriginal families reborn as a white man. This belief has been documented by other white explorers who were believed by natives to be dead relatives reborn. Here I quote a passage from Grey's diary[414]:

"After we had tethered the horses and made ourselves tolerably comfortable we heard loud voices from the hills above us... Our guides shouted in return and gradually the approaching cries came nearer and nearer. I was however wholly unprepared for the scene that was about to take place. A sort of procession came up headed by two women down whose cheeks tears were streaming. The eldest of these came up to me and looking for a moment at me said – 'Gwa gwa bundo bal' – 'Yes yes in truth it is him'; and then throwing her arms round me cried bitterly her head resting on my breast... the other younger one knelt at my feet also crying. At last the old lady emboldened by my submission deliberately kissed me on each cheek just in the manner a Frenchwoman would have done; she then cried a little more and at length relieving me assured me that I was the ghost of her son who had some time before been killed by a spear-wound in his breast. The younger female was my sister...

My new mother expressed almost as much delight at my return to my family as my real mother would have done had I been unexpectedly restored to her. As soon as she left me my brothers and father (the old man who had previously been so frightened) came up and embraced me after their manner – that is they threw their arms round my waist placed their right knee against my right knee and their breast against my breast holding me in this way for several minutes... This belief that white people are the souls of departed blacks is by no means an uncommon superstition amongst them; they themselves never having an idea of quitting their own land cannot imagine others doing it; – and thus when they see white people suddenly appear in their country and settling themselves down in particular spots they imagine that they must have formed an attachment for this land in some other state of existence; and hence conclude the settlers were at one period black men and their own relations. Likenesses whether real or imagined complete the delusion; and from the manner of the old woman I have just alluded to from her many tears and from her warm caresses I feel firmly convinced that she really believed I was her son whose first thought upon his return to earth had been to re-visit his old mother and bring her a present."

- Bruce T. Grindal is a respected academic anthropologist who wrote a scholarly account of his experience 'seeing' a person raised from the dead in an African ritual. Note that he doesn't believe the event really happened this way, but that is what he claims to have seen.[415]

- Clairvius Narcisse is a Haitian man believed to have died in 1962 and subsequently turned into a 'zombie' by pharmacological means. Eventually his captor died and he regained his sanity and returned to his family.[416]

- Anthropologist Jean-Guy A. Goulet reports the following experience[417]:

"In the summer of 1982, I was in Ottawa after a six-month period of fieldwork, the third in three consecutive years. I had left the field following the tragic death of a young girl. Her family and I had seen her leave happily with friends in the morning to go to a nearby river, where she was accidentally shot in the head by a young hunter carrying a hunting rifle as he was stepping out of a canoe... These events were to have a major impact on my involvement in the Dene community, beginning with a vision of the young girl while I was back in Ottawa. Imagine the setting: a large university auditorium, in which over 150 participants were listening to sociologists, historians, theologians, and a Metis shaman discuss the topic of secularization.' As I listened to the shaman tell of experiences of spirits among aboriginal people in the Canadian north, my eye was caught suddenly by an apparition to my right, in midair. I couldn't believe my eyes. I saw the young Dene Tha girl who had died the violent death described above. The young girl looked at me, smiled, and extended open hands towards me. The life-sized figure was radiant with light and smiled as it moved a little closer to me from a distance of approximately fifty feet. I looked at the figure, then turned my eyes towards the podium. Yes, the speaker was still there. I looked at my hand and at the paper on which I had been taking notes. Yes, I was wide-awake. I looked back up to my right. Yes, the figure was still there. A few moments later the vision subsided, the figure disappeared, and everything returned to normal. In January 1983 when I was back among the Dene Tha, I visited the mother and grandparents of the deceased child to tell them of my vision. They listened attentively and thanked me for reporting it to them. A few days

later, a relative of the child came to visit me... (They reported). 'I saw [her]. One night last summer, I was dreaming and woke up. I looked outside and [she] was sitting on a pile of wood, smiling to me. Very peaceful. I told her grandma I saw [her], and to keep praying, that she would see [her] too'."

Spiritualist and Parapsychology Accounts

With respect to the cases reported in parapsychology, Craig has argued that[418]:

> "A second possible explanation for the resurrection appearances comes from the casebooks of parapsychology: the appearances were veridical visions of the departed Jesus. This theory... is masterfully expounded by Michael Perry... (but) as Perry admits, in order to find parallels to the appearance stories one must ransack the literature of parapsychology and build up a composite picture of striking aspects from many different cases. The fact is, no single parapsychological case is fully analogous to a resurrection appearance."

This is a totally unreasonable requirement, for no single miraculous or paranormal report is ever 'fully analogous' to any other such case. The precise circumstances in which such events occur are very rarely replicated exactly, and even similar events seldom reoccur in exactly the same way. Thus, there is no reason we should expect to see any case that is fully analogous to the resurrection appearances. All that we can reasonably expect are cases that are sufficiently similar in relevant respects, including groups reporting sightings of people known to be deceased, especially in cases where the deceased was known to these witnesses. I believe that there are such sufficiently similar cases, exactly as would be expected on the basis of the operation of the psychological and sociological processes outlined in the RHBS model.

- Reported in the Proceedings of the Society for Psychical Research[419]:

"s 25. In March 1846, the wife and two adult daughters of Dr R., in their home in West Philadelphia, Pa., all saw at the same time an apparition

which they instantly and independently recognised as Dr R.'s mother, who had died ten years before. The apparition conformed with a promise made by the old lady before her death, and coincided with the purchase of a house by her son along lines which she had advised. That same evening the ladies related their experience to the Rev. Y. He later told the story to Robert Dale Owen. Mr Owen then secured an account of the story direct from the elder daughter, and afterwards secured confirmation from the mother. The direct accounts from the percipients tallied exactly with the story as it had been told by Mr Y. Both the mother and the daughter recollected the precise dress of the apparition and their accounts agreed entirely that the apparition had crossed the room, approached a portrait of Dr R., fingered to look at it, recrossed to the door, and inexplicably vanished."

- Reported in the Proceedings of the Society for Psychical Research[420]:

"s 29. Julia Murray died in Yonkers, N.Y., on 23 March 1901. At about 3 a.m. the next morning, seven relatives and friends (all Catholics) each saw and recognised an apparition of the deceased which came into view near a picture of the Virgin Mary, on the wall of a room next to the one where the body lay. Katie Cain, Rose Kearne and Mrs Corbalis, when interviewed separately, all agreed on the following facts: a wreath or crown (of 'flowers', 'leaves and flowers', or 'evergreens') was on the head; rosary beads hung from the hands, which were crossed on the breast or in a position of prayer, or both successively; the figure wore a robe which ended at the bottom in clouds. Points mentioned by two, but not all three of the percipients interviewed were as follows : The apparition was seen in profile ; the hair was hanging down the back ; the robe was white ; the figure appeared to be solid (or was seen as plainly as in life) ; it faded toward the ceiling, or disappeared slowly through the ceiling. The newspapers made a great sensation about these events. James H. Hyslop heard about it and interviewed Mrs Corbalis on 30 March, and Katie Cain and Rosie Kearns on 5 April 1901, but did not secure signed statements from them."

- Reported in the Proceedings of the Society for Psychical Research[421]:

"s 32. On Easter Monday, 1920, a State Tax Commissioner in a New England State committed suicide. He had been greatly devoted to a church of which he was senior warden. On the next Sunday morning, when the offering was brought to the chancel steps by the new warden and his associate, the rector and two parishioners, in widely separated parts of the church, saw an apparition of the suicide at his usual place near the other two wardens. He was as life-like and realistic to each of the three percipients as on any Sunday of the thirty years during which he had officiated there. One of the Parishioner percipients wrote out an account, some seven or eight years later, and this account was assented to as correct by the rector."

- Reported in the Proceedings of the Society for Psychical Research[422]:

"p 34. In June 1931, a chimney-sweep named Samuel Bull died of cancer in Ramsbury, Wilts., England, leaving an aged invalid wife and a grandson, James Bull, twenty-one years of age, living in the cottage where he died. In August 1931, a married daughter, Mrs Edwards, came with her five children and her husband to live with them. Sometime in or after February 1932, Mrs Edwards saw the deceased man ascend stairs and pass through a door, which was shut, into the room in which he died, and in which his widow had been lying for some time, but which was then shut up and unused. Almost immediately after Mrs Edwards saw the apparition, James Bull also saw it. Later all the members of the family together saw the apparition. Even the smallest girl (aged 5?) recognised it as 'grandpa Bull'. The appearances continued at frequent intervals from that time until about 9 April. Whenever the apparition was seen, all the persons present were able to see it. The apparition seemed solid, and twice laid his hand on the brow of Mrs Bull. Once she heard him call her 'Jane'. On one occasion the figure was visible continuously for a period thought to have been a half-hour. It always appeared to be quite lifelike. The features were clearly recognised. Mrs Edwards spoke of noting the appearance of the hands, with the knuckles seeming to be protruding through the skin...

The case was originally reported by the local vicar, the Rev. G. H. Hackett. Through him Lord Selborne and Admiral Hyde Parker heard of the case as early as 3 April 1932. Sometime between 7 and 11 April the vicar, at Admiral Parker's request, visited the family and put to Mrs Edwards *a series of questions covering the reported phenomena, which she answered perfectly consistently with earlier statements made by the family. On 14 April, Admiral Parker, Mr Hackett, Lord Balfour and Mr Piddington called at the cottage and interviewed Mrs Edwards and Mrs Bull, who confirmed the information previously supplied. On 31 May 1932, the vicar visited the family and secured the signatures of Mr and Mrs Edwards to the statement of facts which he had previously secured from them."*

- A parapsychology study was able to elicit various forms of 'contact experiences' with dead relatives of a significant fraction of participants through suggestion and mirror gazing. One such report was[423]:

"I believe a group of 'guardians' were there in the beginning (aunts, grand-mothers, friends – folks I randomly sense from time to time) – knowing my uncle, he probably invited them all. There was an intense warmth (physically/spatially) around me. My uncle's presence was felt but it was slight and somewhat guarded. He repeated 'Don't worry' and 'Do what's best for you,' which I somehow can't hear enough of."

- Alfred Russel Wallace reports the following account in his book *On Miracles and Modern Spiritualism*[424]:

"Sir John Sherbroke and General George Wynyard were Captain and Lieutenant in the 33rd Regiment, stationed in the year 1785 at Sydney, in the island of Cape Breton, Nova Scotia. On the 15th of October of that year, about nine in the morning, as they were sitting together at coffee in Wynyard's parlour, Sherbroke, happening to look up, saw the figure of a pale youth standing at a door leading into the passage. He called the attention of his companion to the stranger, who passed slowly through the room into the adjoining bed-chamber. Wynyard, on seeing the figure, turned as pale as death, grasped his friend's arm, and, as soon as it had disappeared, exclaimed, 'Great God! My brother!' Sherbroke thinking there was some trick, had a search immediately made, but could find no one either in the bed-room or about the premises. A brother officer, Lieutenant Gore, coming in at the time assisted in the search, and at his suggestion Sherbroke made a memorandum of the date, and all waited with anxiety for letters from England, where Wynyard's brother was. The expected letter came to Captain Sherbrooke, asking him to break to his

friend the news of his brother John's death, which had occurred on the day and hour when he had been seen by the two officers. In 1823 Lieutenant-Colonel Gore gave this account in writing to Sir John Harvey, Adjutant- General of the Forces in Canada. He also stated that some years afterwards Sir Sherbroke, who had never seen John Wynyard alive, recognised in England a brother of the deceased, who was remarkably like him, by the resemblance to the figure he had seen in Canada. Mr. Owen has obtained additional proof of the correctness of these details from Captain Henry Scott, R.N., who was told by General Paul Anderson, C.B., that Sir John Sherbroke had, shortly before his death, related the story to him in almost exactly the same words as Mr. Owen has given it and which was communicated in manuscript to Captain Scott."

- The famous case of the Ghost of Versailles, which resulted in the ladies in question being subject to a great deal of ridicule for their story. A short summary[425]:

"In that year (1911) two eminent English women academics, Charlotte Anne Moberly and Eleanor Jourdain, the principal and vice-principal, respectively, of St. Hugh's College, Oxford, published under the pseudonyms 'Miss Morison' and 'Miss Lamont' a book entitled An Adventure in which they asserted that while on a sightseeing tour of the gardens of the Petit Trianon near Versailles on 10 August 1901, they had encountered the apparitions of Marie Antoinette and several members of her court precisely as they had existed in the year 1789. After jointly researching the matter for nearly ten years in the French national archives, Moberly and Jourdain wrote, they had been forced to conclude that they had travelled backwards in time-perhaps by entering telepathically into 'an act of memory' performed by Marie Antoinette herself during her incarceration following the sacking of the Tuileries. In the central chapters of An Adventure (which quickly became a best-seller) they laid out this bizarre theory in detail, along with a mass of so-called historical and topographical evidence supposedly confirming it."

Summary of collective religious experiences

I believe that the evidence cited in this section is sufficient to establish as plausible the postulate that, after they heard reports of individual sightings of the risen Jesus, the disciples had collective religious experiences of the risen Jesus as a product of expectation and perceptual biases and social influences. I have documented how perception is influenced by expectation, how collective experiences of miraculous phenomena are generated through subtle social and environmental interactions, and provided evidence of numerous religious and non-religious historical cases in which such processes led to groups of people experiencing collective experiences of highly unusual phenomena, including some cases of apparitions of the dead. I do not argue that the foregoing proves that Jesus' disciples experienced a similar such experience, because the psychological and sociological evidence is incomplete, and no single historical case is totally comparable in all respects. What I do argue, however, is that the third postulate of the RHBS model concerning collective religious experiences of the risen Jesus is plausible given existing background knowledge from science and history.

POSTULATE FOUR: COGNITIVE, MEMORY, AND SOCIAL BIASES

The final postulate of the RHBS model is that the stories of Jesus' appearances that came to be told by Jesus' followers do not correspond exactly to what the disciples originally experienced in their collective religious experiences of the risen Jesus, even though the disciples really did *believe* they were truthfully reporting their experiences. This is the result of the disciple's memories of what they experienced being altered over time, leading to a general increase in impressiveness of the accounts, incorporating new elements from the recollections of other disciples, and also to enhance the overall coherence of the accounts of different disciples. This would not primarily have been a conscious process, but largely was the natural product of the repeated retelling and reflecting upon the same few emotionally charged events in a close-knit communal setting.

Memory biases and eyewitness testimony

There is ample evidence from the psychological literature to substantiate the notion that false memories are quite common and relatively easy to form, and in particular it is common for eyewitnesses to incorporate details from the testimony of others and recall them as their own. Some illustrative findings are outlined below.

- 'One hundred participants completed a News Coverage Questionnaire concerning personal memories of where they were, what they were doing and who they were with when footage of dramatic news events was first shown on television, as well as asking them to recall details of the footage itself. These news items included four events that are known to have been captured on film and one item concerning non-existent footage of the bombing of a nightclub in Bali. Overall, 36% of respondents reported false memories of the alleged footage of the Bali bombing.' [426]

- 'This research investigated whether generating misinformation impairs memory for actual information. After watching a videotaped robbery, some witnesses were interviewed about it, but others did not rehearse the event details. One week later, the witnesses tried to remember the robber's appearance... In both experiments, deceptive witnesses sometimes reported invented details on the memory test, suggesting that they may have come to believe some fabrications.' [427]

- 'Three studies investigated change-of-meaning processes following decisions to conform or dissent. Study 1 demonstrated that conformity decisions relative to a group standard, but not agreement decisions relative to a purely informational standard, caused changes in subject's construal of a stimulus story. Studies 2 and 3 extended these findings to a real-world stimulus story (an actual newspaper account of a police shooting incident) and showed that postconformity change-of-meaning effects were maintained over a 1-week test period and in fact increased over time for female subjects.' [428]

- 'Students described two important autobiographical events twice. In between the two recall sessions, participants from the experimental group viewed two films. The first was a short, televised account of the two events; the second was a corresponding videotaped description of the personal experiences of a young woman. In addition, participants were asked to imagine what she had been talking about. Most of the participants from the experimental group incorporated elements of the woman's description into their own subsequent accounts. In spite of this, they rated the vividness and the accuracy of their post-test memories as very high.' [429]

- 'In their study, student participants tune their retelling of a witnessed incident to their audience's evaluation of the suspects in the incident. It is found that participants' own memories and judgments regarding the incident are more biased toward their audience when they are more (vs. less) motivated to create a shared view with a particular audience (a student with a similar vs. dissimilar academic background).' [430]

After the disciples had their initial collective experiences of the risen Jesus, they undoubtedly would have discussed this experience extensively among themselves, comparing accounts, debating details, discussing their emotional and spiritual reactions, and trying to understand the meaning of what they had experienced. This sort of detailed and ongoing recollection, reprocessing, and communal discussion of a memory is precisely the set of circumstances most conducive to the formation of false memories and alteration of existing memories, as the studies cited below clearly indicate. It is important to note that I am not asserting that the disciples concocted their experience completely from nothing; rather my argument is that an *initial* collective experience, which each disciple would have experienced differently, was through this process of collective reconstruction of memory shaped into a single, unified, consistent account, in which the details became agreed upon, and likely was more impressive and 'spiritualised' than had been their initial experience. This was not a conscious process of deception, but rather the result of the natural operation of psychological and sociological processes.

- 'Loftus and Bernstein (2005) claim that rich false memories are usually created by increasing processing requirements (e.g., participants are asked to imagine an event, to elaborate on some new information, etc). Elaborating the new information (e.g., imagining it) increases the perceived level of familiarity of the event; in turn this increased familiarity is erroneously attributed to childhood experience, rather than to the recent elaboration. In a similar vein, a "familiarity plus corroboration" model proposes that false memories are due to a surreptitiously enhanced feeling of familiarity of a specific item, which triggers the search for corroborating (and false) memories. Although initially proposed in a different context, this model can easily explain how rich false autobiographical memories are created.' [431]

- 'In contrast to laboratory free recall (which emphasizes detailed and accurate remembering), conversational retellings depend upon the speaker's goals, the audience, and the social context more generally. Because memories are frequently retrieved in social contexts, retellings of events are often incomplete or distorted, with consequences for later memory. Selective rehearsal contributes to the memory effects, as does the schema activated during retelling. Retellings can be linked to memory errors observed in domains such as eyewitness testimony and flashbulb memories; in all of these situations, people retell events rather than engage in verbatim remembering.' [432]

The fact that the disciples were highly confident in their beliefs, even potentially willing to die for what they believed they witnessed, is not in conflict with the psychological evidence. Numerous studies have shown that, even when warned about the possibility of their memories being contaminated by co-witnesses or incorporating inaccurate information, people typically remain highly confident in their reports. I cite two illustrative examples below.

- 'Participants were shown a crime video and then asked to discuss the video in groups, with some receiving misinformation about the event from their discussion partners. After a one week delay some participants were warned about possible misinformation before all participants provided their own account of the event. Co-witness information was incorporated into participants testimonies, and this effect was not reduced by warnings or source monitoring instructions, suggesting memory change may have occurred.' [433]

- 'In two studies, participants read a story and then completed a multiple-choice recognition test assessing recall for facts from the story. After answering some of the recognition test items, participants were shown a (bogus) tally of other participants' responses to the same items... Later, participants' memory for story facts was again assessed, this time using a cued recall test. The data indicate that participants' memory responses on the story cued recall test sometimes changed from the memory responses given on the initial story recognition test... these response alterations were observed even when participants were explicitly told that the responses of others were bogus. We conclude that attending to the bogus responses of others sometimes influenced participants' recall for story facts.' [434]

The processes of memory conformity and creation of false memories are not isolated to trivial details, but have been documented to occur for highly emotionally salient and unusual events, as would have been the appearance of Jesus to his disciples. The following three examples from the literature illustrate the formation of false memories even in highly emotionally salient contexts.

- 'On September 12, 2001, 54 Duke students recorded their memory of first hearing about the terrorist attacks of September 11 and of a recent everyday event. They were tested again either 1, 6, or 32 weeks later. Consistency for the flashbulb and everyday memories did not differ, in both cases declining over time. However, ratings of vividness, recollection, and belief in the accuracy of memory declined only for everyday memories. Initial visceral emotion ratings correlated with later belief in accuracy, but not consistency, for flashbulb memories... Flashbulb memories are not special in their accuracy, as previously claimed, but only in their perceived accuracy.' [435]

- 'Numerous studies have shown that eyewitness testimony for pseudo-psychic demonstrations, such as fake séances and fork bending, may be inaccurate and vulnerable to memory distortion. Wiseman and Morris (1995), for example, have presented evidence suggesting that believers in the paranormal had poorer memories for pseudo-psychic demonstrations (i.e., conjuring tricks) than non-believers. Furthermore, the memory differences between believers and non-believers were particularly marked for information that was crucial to explaining how a particular effect had been achieved. For example, the fact that a key disappeared from view during a metal-bending demonstration was critical because it was at this point that a straight key was switched for a bent key.' [436]

- 'Granhag, Stromwall, and Billings (2003) found that 76% of participants came to remember seeing non-existent film footage of the sinking of the passenger liner the Estonia, when they heard the confederate say she had seen the footage of the film, compared to 36% of those who did not hear the confederate report seeing the footage... Hence, memory conformity effects can occur for significant and emotional autobiographical events.' [437]

Contrary to what is sometimes claimed, inaccuracy of eyewitness testimony is not found only in disinterested bystanders to an event who only see a fleeting glimpse of the events or person they are later asked to identify. Some of the most dramatic examples of the inaccuracy of eyewitness testimony can be found in rape cases. I present two such example cases below.

- 'Donald Thomson, an Australian psychologist, was bewildered when the police informed him that he was a suspect in a rape case, his description matching almost exactly that provided by the victim. Fortunately for Thomson, he had a watertight alibi. At the time of the rape, he was taking part in a live TV interview – ironically, on the fallibility of eyewitness testimony. It turned out that the victim had been watching Thomson on TV just before the rape occurred and had confused her memory of him with that of the rapist.' [438]

- 'She picked out his eyebrows, his nose, his pencil-thin moustache. She picked out his photo. A week later, she sat across a table from six men holding numbered cards. She picked No. 5. "That's my rapist," she told Gauldin. In court, she put her right hand on the Bible and swore to tell the truth... She had never been so sure of anything. His name was Ronald Cotton and he was the same age as she. Local man, headed down the wrong road, had already been in trouble with the law. Served 18 months in prison for attempted sexual assault. She was white. He was black. Police knew he liked white women. When Thompson picked him out of the line-up, everyone was sure they had the right man. Everyone, that is, except Ronald Cotton...

The knife at her throat was cold, the voice menacing. "Shut up or I'll cut you." Even as she screamed, even as her attacker shoved her down on the bed, pinning her hands behind her, even as her head exploded with revulsion and fear, the 22-year-old college student knew exactly what to do. She would outsmart her rapist. She would remember everything about this night: his voice, his hair, his leering eyes. She would trick him into turning on a light. She would study his features for scars, tattoos, anything that would help identify him later... She'd send him to prison for the rest of his life... On Jan. 17, 1985, the day Cotton was sentenced to life in prison, Thompson toasted her victory with champagne. "It was the happiest day of my life," she said...

One day, about a year after Cotton was convicted, another man joined him working in the prison kitchen. His name was Bobby Poole. He was serving consecutive life sentences for a series of brutal rapes. And he was bragging to other inmates that Cotton was doing some of his time. Cotton hated Poole... And when he learned he had won a second trial, his heart filled with hope. Another woman had been raped just an hour after Thompson: same Burlington neighborhood, same kind of attack... At the new trial, the witnesses would get a look at Poole, who was subpoenaed by Cotton's lawyer. Finally, Cotton thought, he would be set free. He had forgotten the power of Jennifer Thompson. Back on the stand, she was as confident as ever. She looked directly at Poole and she looked directly at Cotton. Fifteen feet away, he could feel the hatred in her heart. Cotton is the man who raped me, she told the jury. Are you sure? Yes, I'm sure. The second victim was less convincing, but she pointed to him, too. Cotton hung his head...

The knock on the door of her Winston Salem home came out of the blue. The detective hadn't just dropped by casually to say hello. It had been 11 years. Standing in Thompson's kitchen, Gauldin struggled to break the news. "Jennifer," he said. "You were wrong. Ronald Cotton didn't rape you. It was Bobby Poole..." There was new evidence, Gauldin was saying. DNA tests. New scientific proof that hadn't been available before. Eleven years of nightmares, of Cotton's face taunting her in the dark. Eleven years of struggling to move on, of building a life with her husband and children. Eleven years of being wrong. There must be some mistake. She could still hear his voice: "Shut up or I'll cut you." She could still see his face in her head... How could she have been wrong?'[439]

Irrational belief persistence

Craig has argued that if the location of Jesus' body was known, or if counterevidence to the resurrection had been available and presented by the Roman or Jewish authorities, there is no possibility that the belief in the resurrection would have been able to survive in Jerusalem in the period following the death of Jesus[440]. This argument overlooks that fact that many people, especially in the context of new religious movements, engage in what has been called 'irrational belief persistence', firmly adhering to beliefs in spite of overwhelming evidence to the contrary. A review of religious groups which made falsified prophecies found that twelve of the thirteen groups they analysed survived the failure of specific prophecies[441]. Jehovah's Witness' multiple failed end of world predictions are a well-known example of this. Another famous example was the 1844 so-called "Great Disappointment" following the failed prediction of the Millerites that Jesus would return in that year. There were many attempted justifications, and some fell away, but the movement continued and gave rise to the contemporary Seventh Day Adventist church. One form such of rationalisation has been described by religious scholar J. Gordon Melton as 'spiritualisation'[442]:

> *"The prophesied event is reinterpreted in such a way that what was supposed to have been a visible, verifiable occurrence is seen*

to have been in reality an invisible, spiritual occurrence. The event occurred as predicted, only on a spiritual level."

Further insight into the operation of irrational belief persistence in the context of new religious movements is found in Joseph Zygmunt's account of the general pattern followed by the Watch Tower Society in response to the various prophetic failures they experienced[443]:

- The initial reaction by both rank and file and the movement's leaders was usually a combination of disappointment and puzzlement.

- Proselytism declined, but members maintained an attitude of watchful waiting for the predictions to materialize. The doctrinal bases for the prophecies were re-examined and conjectures offered as to why the expected events might have been "delayed."

- The group asserted that the prophecies had, in fact, been partially fulfilled, or that some event of prophetic significance — usually supernatural and hence not open to disconfirmation — had actually transpired on the nominated dates. Belief was sustained that God's plan was continuing to unfold.

- Unfulfilled portions of the failed prophecies were projected into the future by issuing redated predictions, in association with retrospective reinterpretation of earlier failures.

- The group engaged in a selective interpretation of newly developing historical events as confirmation of the signs of the approaching end. A pessimistic worldview sensitized the group to perceive almost every social disturbance and natural disaster as an indicator of the impending end of the world.

These or similar techniques are likely to have been employed (consciously or unconsciously) by the disciples to discount counterevidence or other potential discrepancies with respect to the evidence for the resurrection. Experimental studies also provide further support for and insight into the phenomenon of irrational belief persistence, some examples of which I present below.

- 'An accomplice presented three common magician's tricks, which resembled "psychic" performances, to six introductory psychology classes. In the two classes comprising the Psychic condition, the instructors skeptically introduced the accomplice as an alleged psychic; in the Weak Magic condition, as an amateur magician; in the Strong Magic condition, as an amateur magician who would perform stunts which resembled psychic phenomena, but were really not. Belief was assessed through free-form written response, in the form of feedback to the performer. These instructional sets succeeded in manipulating proportion of occult belief. However, proportion of occult belief was above 50% and far exceeding magic beliefs in each experimental condition, even though, as indicated by a manipulation check, subjects in the Magic conditions heard and understood the instructors' assertions that the accomplice was a magician who would be faking a psychic performance.' [444]

- 'A study is reported in which 50 adolescent female high school students were given a chance to commit themselves publicly to a religious belief and were then faced with information which seemed to disconfirm that belief. Consistent with dissonance interpretations of earlier field studies, subjects who both expressed belief and accepted the veracity of the disconfirming information subsequently expressed a significant increase in intensity of belief. This reaction was not found among subjects who either had not expressed initial belief or had not accepted the veracity of the disconfirming information.' [445]

- 'When people are motivated to cling to a belief, they do not feel comfortable with blithely ignoring adverse evidence or simply shutting their ears to anyone who opposes their views. Instead, they engage in more subtle forms of ad hoc reasoning, rationalization, and special pleading to arrive at their desired conclusions and to justify their beliefs to others, e.g., reinterpreting the facts, weighing them against background knowledge, finding some reason to discredit the source, etc. This practice allows them to uphold an 'illusion of objectivity' concerning the manner in which... inferences were derived.' [446]

The operation of irrational belief persistence is not limited to experimental or religious settings, but is evident in numerous historical case studies in all sorts of other contexts. These cases demonstrate that beliefs can gain a following despite overwhelming evidence of their falsity, that charismatic individuals can retain adherents even after they have been clearly and decisively shown to be fraudulent or hypocritical, and that grossly implausible claims can be readily accepted by many despite little or no evidence ever being presented. A small selection of notable examples is given below. I believe such cases show conclusively that people can hold to very unusual beliefs even in the presence of overwhelming counterevidence. Furthermore, in many of these cases believers are clearly willing to suffer for their beliefs, thereby demonstrating their genuine sincerity and true commitment to their beliefs.

- Andrew Wakefield[447]: a doctor who published a now thoroughly discredited study which cast doubt on the safety of the MMR vaccine. Despite the huge quantity of evidence that he deliberately engaged in fraud for his own gain, and the overwhelming evidence for the efficacy of the MMR vaccines, Wakefield continues to be defended as a hero by many in the anti-vaccination movement. Those who refuse vaccinations place the lives of their own children at risk, and have in several documented cases led to outbreaks of preventable infectious diseases.

- Breatharianism[448]: the belief that one can survive without food or water, a phenomenon which has been documented to result in the death of some of its adherents.

- Holocaust denial[449]: disbelief that millions of Jews were murdered by Nazi Germany during the Holocaust, despite the huge amount of physical, photographic, documentary, and testimonial evidence that such events took place. Some proponents have been jailed for their advocacy of such views.

- Anti-fluoridation[450]: continued opposition to the fluoridation of municipal water supplies despite overwhelming evidence of efficacy and no plausible evidence of harm.

- Touchless knockouts[451]: certain martial arts practitioners believe that they are able to knock out or otherwise defeat their opponents without even touching them, by harnessing the power of chi. Despite some very notable public failures involving considerable physical and reputational damage, such techniques are still believed in by some practitioners.

Socialisation effects

Social reinforcement has been shown to play a very important role in consolidating belief in unusual events, as well as membership in new religious movements. This is important because under the RHBS model, the effects of identity consolidation and socialisation are posited to have acted to mute any potential lingering doubts or scepticism that any disciples may have had concerning their experiences. Craig totally neglects these forces in his discussion of the disciples, speaking as if they would have behaved strictly as rational agents, individually following the evidence as an impartial observer. The psychological literature, however, shows clearly that this is not how most religious adherents behave, especially those involved in charismatic new religious movements. For its adherents, their identity, source of meaning, and purpose in life were all bound up in the Jesus movement. Not only would this result in a very powerful motivation to find a way to continue the movement following the death of Jesus, but also it would generate very strong internal and external pressures not to cast doubt on the experiences that were so central to the disciples' renewed faith. If disciples had doubts, would likely attribute them their own lack of worthiness, and not to the insufficiency of the evidence. Their entire identities became bound up in the Jesus movement in such a manner that they were not in a position to dispassionately evaluate the evidence objectively. This does not of course mean they were necessarily mistaken, but it does considerably reduce the evidential value of their firm confidence in their beliefs and lack of apparent doubts. Below I provide some illustrative quotes from the literature studying such effects, which I believe demonstrate how powerful and formative they can be, particularly in religious contexts. Readers desiring more detailed discussion of these effects are encouraged to consult the original papers.

- 'The authors characterize religions as social groups and religiosity as the extent to which a person identifies with a religion, subscribes to its ideology or worldview, and conforms to its normative practices. They argue that religions have attributes that make them well suited to reduce feelings of self-uncertainty. According to uncertainty-identity theory, people are motivated to reduce feelings of uncertainty about or reflecting on self; and identification with groups, particularly highly entitative groups, is a very effective way to reduce uncertainty. All groups provide belief systems and normative prescriptions related to everyday life... (Religions) provide a moral compass and rules for living that pervade a person's life, making them particularly attractive in times of uncertainty. The authors document data supporting their analysis and discuss conditions that transform religiosity into religious zealotry and extremism.' [452]

- '*When Prophets Die* contends that few nonconventional religious groups die as a result of their founder's death. Actually, these new religions usually die because the public has failed to respond to the founder's ideas or the founder has not organized his or her followers into a strong group. If new religions are going to die, they will die in the first decade. In various degrees, the next eleven essays defend such arguments. The movements selected as case studies are as follows: the Shakers, the Amana Society, American Indian prophetic groups, the Latter-day Saints, the Hutterites, the Theosophical Society, Christian Science, the Spirit Fruit Society, Rastafarianism of Jamaica, Krishna Consciousness, Siddha Yoga, and the Unification Church.' [453]

- 'As a social identity anchored in a system of guiding beliefs and symbols, religion ought to serve a uniquely powerful function in shaping psychological and social processes. Religious identification offers a distinctive "sacred" worldview and "eternal" group membership, unmatched by identification with other social groups. Thus, religiosity might be explained, at least partially, by the marked cognitive and emotional value that religious group membership provides. The uniqueness of a positive social group, grounded in a belief system that offers epistemological and ontological certainty, lends religious identity a twofold advantage for the promotion of well-being.'[454]

- 'According to social identity theory, identity competition plays a central role in the inception and escalation of intergroup conflict, even when economic and political factors also are at play... Religions often serve these psychological needs more comprehensively and potently than other repositories of cultural meaning that contribute to the construction and maintenance of individual and group identities. Religions frequently supply cosmologies, moral frameworks, institutions, rituals, traditions, and other identity-supporting content that answers to individuals' needs for psychological stability in the form of a predictable world, a sense of belonging, self-esteem, and even self-actualization.'[455]

Overall, I believe that the evidence I have cited in the previous sections demonstrates that the processes appealed to in postulate four of the RHBS model, including false memory formation, social memory contagion, socialisation effects, and persistence of these beliefs in spite of contrary evidence, are plausible in the light of the extant psychological and sociological literature.

The role of legendary development

Craig has argued that the control that the disciples had over the developing Christian tradition, and their continued presence in the early Christian community for decades following the events of the crucifixion, would have acted as a check to prevent the sort of legendary embellishments based on hallucinations which I propose[456]. This response assumes that the embellishments in question were later developments not directly tied to or constrained by the disciples' own stories. This, however, is not my argument. Rather, according to the RHBS model it was the disciples themselves who came to believe that they had experienced appearances of the bodily risen Jesus. The embellishments that occurred to the story, therefore, were not primarily gradual legendary accretions (though I do not rule out this occurring to some degree and possibly leading to some of the discrepancies in secondary details found in the gospels), but largely were the result of the psychological and sociological processes I have just outlined, shaping and reshaping the disciples' memories and understandings of what *they themselves* had experienced. As such, the RHBS model that I am here defending is in no way dependent upon gradual legendary accretion or on the gospels not having access to original eyewitness testimony. Although I regard it unlikely that any of the gospels were directly written by eyewitnesses, nevertheless my account is consistent with this possibility, since the RHBS model seeks to explain how the eyewitnesses themselves came to believe that the risen Jesus appeared to them in the flesh. It does not posit some runaway legendary process that occurred outside the control of the disciples and contrary to their wishes.

EXPLANATORY SCOPE AND POWER OF THE POSTULATES

Having considered the individual plausibility of all the key postulates of the RHBS model, we must now consider the explanatory scope and power of the model in accounting for the key historical facts. As outlined previously, the four facts the RBHS model attempts to account for are as follows:

1. After his crucifixion Jesus was buried by Joseph of Arimathea in the tomb.

2. On the Sunday following the crucifixion, Jesus' tomb was found empty by a group of his women followers.

3. On multiple occasions and under various circumstances, different individuals and groups of people experienced appearances of Jesus alive from the dead.

4. The original disciples came to believe that Jesus had risen from the dead despite considerable predisposition to the contrary.

The postulates whose plausibility I defended in the previous sections are as follows:

1. Jesus' body was removed from the tomb before its discovery by Jesus' women followers.

2. Some of Jesus' followers experienced individual hallucinations of Jesus appearing to them.

3. Reports of the empty tomb and these first appearances triggered a serious of collective experiences of the risen Jesus among the disciples.

4. The memories and understanding of these experiences were reshaped over time by psychological and sociological forces towards being more consistent and impressive.

First, I will examine explanatory scope: can the explanation account for the facts in question? The first postulate, that Jesus' body was removed from the tomb, accounts for facts one and two, that Jesus was buried and the tomb was found empty. This is only natural, since if Jesus' body was removed from the tomb by a third party, it is only to be expected that the tomb would be found empty. The second and third postulates, concerning the individual and group hallucinations of Jesus' appearances, account for fact three, that there were various reported experiences of Jesus appearing to his disciples alive. If there were individual hallucinations followed by collective experiences, these would be reported as encounters with the risen Jesus. The fourth postulate, relating to memory, social, and other biases, accounts for fact four, that the disciples came to confidently believe that Jesus had risen from the dead. As such, I believe that the RHBS model has sufficient explanatory scope to account for all of Craig's four historical facts.

The question of the explanatory power of the RHBS model is more difficult to assess, for it is often very unclear as to how to judge *how well* a given set of postulates explain a set of facts, or how likely the facts are rendered by the explanation. Overall, however, I would argue that the RHBS model has strong explanatory power with respect to facts one, two, and four, and moderate explanatory power with respect to fact three. If we accept the postulate that Jesus' body was removed before Sunday morning, most likely either by Joseph himself or by tomb robbers, then it seems very likely that this would have led to Jesus' devoted women followers finding the tomb empty when they first were able to return to it on the Sunday morning. It is very unlikely that any party in the position to move the body would have informed the women, and equally improbable (given what is reported of their devotion) that the women would not bother going to the tomb. As such, I think postulate one renders the fact of the discovery of the empty tomb highly probable, while being completely consistent with Jesus' prior death and burial.

By contrast, I believe that postulates two and three, concerning individual hallucinations leading to group appearances, renders the third fact only reasonably probable. This is because, even given all of the literature I cite about memory and social biases and comparable miracle claims, nevertheless human psychology and memory are both fickle and unpredictable, and it is entirely possible that had certain particular people not been involved or responded differently, events could have taken a very different course such that either we would have no miracle claims or only much smaller, less impressive ones. Thus, while I believe that postulates two and three can account for the fact of group appearances, they only do so with moderate explanatory power, since it is still plausible that these postulates could have pertained without the appearance reports as we know them from developing. The final postulate relating to the operation of memory and social biases has perhaps the strongest explanatory power, since the firmness of belief and deep conviction of the disciples stated by fact four is precisely what we would expect based on the fourth postulate.

Overall, therefore, I conclude that each of the four key postulates of the RHBS model is plausible, and that taken together they have adequate explanatory scope and moderately high explanatory power in accounting for Craig's four historical facts. As such, I think the RHBS model provides a reasonably good explanation for the historical facts. It is certainly not a perfect explanation – it does not account for every detail, nor does it do so with maximal degrees of plausibility or explanatory power. Nevertheless, I think it accounts for the facts in question in as good as manner as can reasonably be expected given the paucity of the evidence for such an ancient event. In the subsequent section I will examine Craig's resurrection hypothesis to see how it fairs with respect to the same criteria, arguing that it provides a substantially inferior explanation for the historical facts when compared to the RHBS model.

THE RESURRECTION HYPOTHESIS

OVERVIEW OF THE HYPOTHESIS

Craig's proposed explanation (which I call the resurrection hypothesis) for the four historical is as follows:

> Resurrection hypothesis: God bodily raised Jesus from the dead by means of a divine miracle.

Craig says that this hypothesis[457]:

> "Explains why the tomb was found empty, why the disciples saw postmortem appearances of Jesus, and why the Christian faith came into being."

Quite evidently, however, this is simply not the case, for there is nothing in this hypothesis which entails or provides any means to account for why the risen Jesus, after vacating his tomb, would appear to anyone at all. It is perfectly possible, after all, that God could have raised Jesus from the dead only for Jesus to ascend directly to heaven, without making any appearances. Craig's resurrection hypothesis as it stands, therefore, has nothing to say on the matter, and no tools for explaining why anyone should have seen Jesus after he was raised. The bodily resurrection of Jesus implies that he *could* have appeared to people, but does not imply that he *would* so appear, or really say anything about whether he would be *likely* to appear or not. Thus, it has insufficient explanatory scope to account for the resurrection appearances.

Craig may argue that Christians have access to knowledge of God's intentions and desires through revealed theology, which therefore enables them to infer that appearing to his followers is something Jesus would be likely to do following his resurrection. Even if we grant this, however, it is nevertheless still necessary to *specify* that such knowledge is being assumed as part of the explanation. That is, Craig's explanation for the four historical facts needs to state explicitly the basis on which appearances are rendered probable. Otherwise, his explanation simply fails to account for the phenomena that Craig says it does. It is relatively easy to rectify this problem, but it requires modifying the original hypothesis to form what I shall call the augmented resurrection hypothesis:

> Augmented resurrection hypothesis: God bodily raised Jesus from the dead by means of a divine miracle, after which the risen Jesus physically appeared his followers.

Thus modified, Craig's proposed explanation requires the following assumptions not already established on the basis of known facts or general background evidence (see figure 13 for a diagrammatic presentation):

1. God exists.
2. God desired to (or had reason to) raise Jesus from the dead.
3. Subsequent to being raised, Jesus desired to (or had reason to) appear to his followers.

Craig generally fails to acknowledge the dependence of his proposed explanation on postulates two and three, often speaking as if given the mere existence of God, it follows that God would wish to raise Jesus from the dead and that Jesus would then appear to his followers. The fact these things do not follow from God's mere existence, however, is trivially evident when considering the fact that many intelligent, educated people believe in God but do not accept that God would want to raise Jesus from the dead, or deny that this is something God would have any reason or desire to do. Deists, for example, believe that a creator God exists but does not intervene in human affairs, so they would accept postulate one but deny two and three. Muslims would also accept postulate one, and presumably would also agree that God intervenes in human affairs and so *could* have raised Jesus from the dead if he had so desired, but deny that God had any such desire; they do not regard this as something that God would actually do. It also possible to accept both postulates one and two while denying postulate three, which for instance one might do if one had only read the original ending of Mark's gospel, which describes the empty tomb but not the post-mortem appearances. It is even possible to accept postulates one and three while denying postulate two, as for example certain early Gnostics who denied the bodily resurrection but believed that Jesus nevertheless did appear to his followers. In order for Craig's explanation to account for the four historical facts, therefore, it is necessary that he establish *all three* of these postulates as individually plausible given accepted background knowledge. I will therefore examine the plausibility of each of these postulates in turn.

POSTULATE ONE: GOD EXISTS

Clearly the plausibility of this postulate depends upon how successful we judge Craig's other arguments for the existence of a personal God. Since the rest of this book is devoted to analysing these arguments, I will say nothing more here other than to note that clearly, given its dependence on this postulate, the resurrection argument is unlikely to be successful on its own as an argument for the existence of God, but will need to be developed in tandem with further arguments in a 'cumulative case'.

POSTULATE TWO: GOD DESIRED TO RAISE JESUS

Craig claims that the resurrection hypothesis is plausible because[458]:

> "The hypothesis: 'God raised Jesus from the dead' does not in any way conflict with the accepted belief that people don't rise naturally *from the dead. The Christian accepts* that belief as wholeheartedly as he accepts the hypothesis that God raised Jesus from the dead."

This claim is incorrect, since even if we grant that God exists or that supernatural resurrections are possible, an analysis of history clearly shows that such events are extremely rare. That is, it is not merely the case that everyone who has died has not *naturally* resurrected from the dead, but neither has anyone, except possibly for Jesus and maybe a handful of other claimed cases, been *supernaturally* resurrected from the dead. Supernatural resurrection therefore might occur, but if it does it is clearly an extremely *rare* event. As such, in any given case it is extraordinarily unlikely that a supernatural resurrection did occur, even if we believe that a God capable of performing such resurrections exists.

Craig might argue that the case of Jesus is unique because of his unusual claims about himself, his unique life and teachings, etc. This would be consistent with his statement that[459]:

> "Given the historical context of Jesus' own unparalleled life and claims, the resurrection serves as divine confirmation of those radical claims."

While it is reasonable to say that such considerations place Jesus into a special reference class (i.e., it is more likely Jesus would be raised from the dead than some person chosen at random), I do not accept that this isolates Jesus as *uniquely* likely to have been resurrected compared to *all other humans* who have ever lived. Rather, I believe it places him in a reference class alongside a sizeable number of similar such individuals, who throughout history have made claims to be God, or the son of God, or God's special and unique messenger, or the Jewish Messiah, or something similar. There are a great many such people who have made extravagant claims about themselves, acquired followings, taught particular ethical and theological precepts, and are claimed to have done miracles. For an interesting comparative historical analysis of fifteen such figures, readers are invited to consult the paper *Charisma and Religious Leadership: An Historical Analysis*[460]. Given the existence of a sizeable number of such charismatic religious claimants, unless we assume from the outset that Jesus was the son of God, there seems no justifiable basis to assert that God would be any more likely to resurrect Jesus than any of these others. What we can infer from this is that, *even if* God does occasionally raise particularly special or unique prophets or spiritual figures from the dead, even among this special reference class of such claimed prophets and religious leaders, such an occurrence is highly unusual. In other words, even most Messiah claimants, or most charismatic prophets, and most people who claim to be God, are not resurrected by a divine miracle. Craig thus goes too far in saying that Jesus' life and ministry establish it is as likely that God would have reason to raise him from the dead, since even among such figures resurrection is a very rare occurrence. This does not mean that God couldn't have raised Jesus from the dead, only that

Unreasonable Faith

God has shown throughout history that this isn't something he is in the business of doing very often, so on face value it is not very plausible as a postulate. Perhaps there are additional reasons to think Jesus was the one special case, as in fact Christians believe, but I do not think that Craig has given any such reasons which will be compelling to those who do not already accept the divinity of Jesus.

Craig exhibits his neglect of this crucial assumption when he makes remarks such as the following[461]:

> "In all honesty, we have to say that the only basis for denying the physical, bodily nature of the post-mortem appearances of Jesus is not historical, but philosophical; namely, such appearances would be stupendous miracles, and many critics simply cannot swallow that claim. But if that's the problem, then we need to go back to square one and think about the question of God's existence; if God exists, there's no good reason to be skeptical about miracles."

There is, however, quite obviously ample reason to be sceptical about miracles even if God does exist. There are many examples of people who accept the existence of God but deny the existence of miracles, such as the eighteenth Deists who denied Jesus' bodily resurrection despite belief in God. Other groups believe in the possibility of miracles but deny the particular on in question (e.g. Jews, Muslims). Craig totally ignores the many other philosophical issues relevant to assessing these miracles claims, including whether resurrecting Jesus is something that God would want to or have an interest in doing, and whether such a resurrection is consistent with Old Testament prophecies about the Messiah. Regarding the relationship between the resurrection and out background evidence, Craig has stated[462]:

> "I cannot think of any accepted beliefs that disconfirm the resurrection hypothesis – unless one thinks that 'dead men do not rise' is disconfirmatory. But then we are just back to the problem of miracles again. This belief would disconfirm a naturalistic revivification hypothesis, but it does nothing to disconfirm the hypothesis that God raised Jesus from the dead."

It seems, however, that Craig is exhibiting severe lack of

imagination on this point, for depending upon one's accepted background beliefs there are a potentially large range of things that would render the resurrection hypothesis unlikely, wholly apart from the question of whether or not miracles are possible. As noted above, if one were a Muslim then one would accept the possibility of miracles, but would regard the resurrection of Jesus as improbable given background beliefs about what sort of miracles God would be inclined to perform. Though I suspect relatively few of my readers will come from a theological tradition which affirms miracles but denies the resurrection of Jesus, nevertheless my point holds that Craig's characterisation of the issue as a question of openness to miracles is simply inaccurate. Rather, in order for the resurrection to be judged as the most plausible explanation, one must begin with the belief not simply that God can do miracles, but that God would have particular reason to perform the *specific miracle* of raising Jesus from the dead. Even many people who accept the possibility of miracles, however, would not accept this as being plausible, and therefore would perfectly justifiably not regard Craig's explanation of the historical facts as the most plausible.

There are also additional reasons relating to Jewish theology, in virtue of which it is less likely that God would have reason to raise Jesus from the dead. Craig himself argues that according to Jewish theology as understood at the time, Jesus of Nazareth simply failed to uphold what was expected of a Messiah. I have already quoted Craig as arguing that the Jews had no notion that their Messiah would be killed rather than triumphing over Israel's enemies, or that that the Messiah would be resurrected individually during the middle of history. Jesus also failed to fulfil many Messianic prophesies, such as gathering Jews back to Israel and rebuilding the temple[463]. These facts therefore count against the plausibility of the hypothesis that Jesus was actually the Jewish messiah, since he doesn't seem to match the description of this Messiah given in the Jewish scriptures. Such considerations are, indeed, one of the major reasons why most Jews refused to accept Jesus at the time, and why they continue to regard him as a false Messiah to this day[464]. Typically, Christians respond to such criticisms by reinterpreting the meaning of some of these prophecies and adjusting their conception of the Messiah in light of Jesus' experiences. While this may be perfectly valid theologically if one begins with Christian presuppositions, this approach is completely ad hoc with respect to explaining Craig's core historical facts, as the only reason for adjusting any of these beliefs about the Messiah is because one *already* believes in the divinity of Jesus. After all, as Craig goes to some lengths to point out, prior to the death of Jesus there simply weren't any Jews who interpreted the Old Testament's claims about the Messiah in the way that Christians currently do. An orthodox Jew facing the evidence for Jesus' resurrection is thus faced with two choices: either reject the traditional interpretation of what the Old Testament says about the Messiah and accept the divinity of Jesus, or hold to the traditional interpretation and reject Jesus as a false Messiah. My point is not to argue that it is impossible that the evidence for the resurrection of Jesus could ever be good enough to lead an orthodox Jew to the first option. Rather, my point is that the contradictions between Jesus' life and the traditional Jewish understanding of the Messiah render the postulate 'God desired to raise Jesus from the dead' relatively less probable than it would otherwise be. Craig neglects to consider this, and thereby inflates his assessment of the plausibility of his resurrection hypothesis.

I conclude, therefore, that it is relatively unlikely that Craig's second postulate is true. To accept it as probably true would require that independent evidence be provided in its favour: i.e. evidence that is separate from the resurrection appearances in question here. The only way that Craig can argue for the plausibility of postulate two, however, is by appealing to particular theological beliefs that are not widely accepted and so are not among our shared background beliefs. An explanation that is dependent upon postulate two, therefore, is not a very plausible explanation unless one already accepts certain theological claims about Jesus. To those unconvinced of such claims (even if they believe in a God who does miracles), the postulate remains implausible.

POSTULATE THREE: JESUS DESIRED TO APPEAR TO HIS FOLLOWERS

In addition to the postulate that God had reason to raise Jesus from the dead, Craig also fails to acknowledge that his proposed explanation depends upon the assumption that Jesus himself had some reason or desire to appear to his followers after being raised. As noted above, this assumption presumes some particular theological views which are not part of our widely shared background beliefs. One may argue, for instance, that Jesus' purpose in appearing to his followers was to consolidate their faith by providing evidence of his conquest over death, and also to task the disciples with the job of spreading this good news throughout the world. Such beliefs, however, are theological positions which, while very familiar to Christians, are not at all entailed by the assumption that God exists or even that Jesus rose from the dead, and thus must be adopted as an additional assumption.

To see this, one need only consider the situation from the perspective of alternate theologies, and observe how such viewpoints lead to different conclusions about what is probable. Under Mormon theology, Jesus had reason to visit the Americas following his crucifixion to preach to the isolated group of Israelites living there. This motivation or reason is totally absent from orthodox Christian theology, and therefore a visitation of Christ to the people of the Americas, while not impossible, is generally regarded as implausible and without motivating reason. This arises, however, only as a result of adopting *particular theological views* at the expense of others. Conversely, some Gnostics believed that while Jesus was not bodily resurrected, he did appear spiritually (in some sense) to the disciples. The idea of Jesus rising from the dead without appearing to any of his followers is even preserved in the canonical gospels in the form of the original ending of Mark, which lacks any post-mortem appearances. Mark may or may not have been familiar with the appearance traditions through the writings of Paul, but my point is simply that Mark's original ending illustrates how as a matter of logic, narrative, and theology, the appearances are not entailed by the resurrection itself, but must be motivated separately.

Craig is quick to demand evidence of the assumptions necessary for the various naturalistic proposals to explain the resurrection appearances[465]; however, he provides no evidence at all in favour of the postulate that Jesus had some reason or motive to appear to his followers. The mere fact that he *might* have had such reasons does not constitute evidence that he actually *did*. What is Craig's evidence or basis, referring to generally accepted facts and not merely Christian theology, for postulating that Jesus had a reason for appearing to his disciples after his death? I do not believe he provides any, and therefore I do not believe he provides sufficient plausibility for this crucial aspect of his explanation.

Most fundamentally, this problem (as well as that of postulate two) arises because Craig is attempting to explain the resurrection appearances by appealing to the actions of an agent. As Craig has said[466]:

> "There are two kinds of explanations. There are scientific explanations which are given in terms of laws of nature and initial conditions. On the other hand, there are personal explanations which are given in terms of an agent and his volitions, what he wills to do."

Craig's proposed explanation for his minimal facts is obviously of the second type, a personal explanation appealing to an agent and their volitions. In order for such an explanation to carry force, however, it is necessary to have prior knowledge of, or to make assumptions about, that agent's beliefs, desires, and goals, in order to be able to say anything about their likely actions. Kevin Scharp has dubbed this the 'problem of divine psychology[467].' It refers to the fact that absent such assumptions, explanations which appeal to personal agency are completely unable to constrain the possible range of actions, and hence have no explanatory power. Only when outcomes can be constrained by postulating particular motivations, objectives, or reasons is it possible for personal explanations to provide explanatory insight. In this case, however, some reason needs to be given for why those motivations, objectives, or reasons are more plausible than other possibilities. As I have argued, Craig has failed to do this with respect to the crucial postulates that God would want to raise Jesus from the dead, or that Jesus would have reason to appear to his followers following his resurrection.

EXPLANATORY SCOPE AND POWER OF THE POSTULATES

The augmented resurrection hypothesis has sufficient explanatory scope and strong explanatory power with respect to both the empty tomb and the post-mortem appearances (facts one through three), however I do not believe it has much explanatory power with respect to the fourth fact, namely that the original disciples came to believe that Jesus had risen from the dead. This is because witnessing miracles is insufficient to guarantee conversion, as is clear from the case of Judas for instance, and also the fact that only a very small fraction of early Jews came to believe that Jesus was the Messiah. Craig's hypothesis is thus unable to explain why the disciples responded to the events Craig believes they witnessed in the way that they did, while others responded very differently. As I noted previously, even if Jesus *was* resurrected and *did* appear to his disciples in the manner that Craig believes, this event itself is insufficient to explain why the disciples would necessarily come to *believe* that Jesus had risen from the dead. Craig himself acknowledges this possibility when he says[468]:

> "For a Jew, although he might recognize the reality of miracles, there was still a good way to go before he could persuade himself to recognize Jesus as the Messiah. The gospels themselves are filled with examples of Jews who admitted Jesus' miracles, but refused to bow the knee to him."

Further confirmation of this possibility is found in the equivocal reactions of the disciples to many of the miracles found in the gospels, and their sceptical attitude to the women's reports of the empty tomb. Fundamentally, this difficulty arises because Craig's hypothesis makes no reference at all to the psychological state or beliefs of the disciples, while at the same time attempting to explain facts directly relevant to those attitudes and beliefs. Craig needs to explain why the disciples were thinking and feeling what they were, but he attempts to do so without making any explicit reference to these facts, as his proposed hypothesis only concerns the actions and intentions of God, not the disciples. By contrast, I believe that my RHBS model, which makes explicit reference to the psychological state of the disciples and the effects of their social interactions on the basis of the best available scientific literature, has far greater explanatory power with respect to accounting for why they came to believe that Jesus rose from the dead.

SUMMARY OF THE ARGUMENT

The historical argument for the resurrection of Jesus attempts to show that God's divine intervention is the best explanation for a set of key historical facts surrounding the death of Jesus of Nazareth. While most responses to this argument attempt to cast doubt on one or more of Craig's alleged historical facts, I have instead followed the approach of granting all of Craig's facts, and then attempting to provide an alternative explanation of them that does not appeal to divine intervention. The alternate explanation that I propose is called the Reburial, Hallucinations, Biases, and Socialisation (RHBS) model, named after the key mechanisms which the model appeals to. My claim is not that the RHBS model provides a perfect explanation of all the data, nor do I attempt to show that it is a true description of what actually happened. Rather, my argument is only that the RHBS model provides a *better explanation* for Craig's historical facts, as judged by essentially the same criteria that Craig uses in his own argument.

The RBHS model attempts to explain the historical facts of Jesus' empty tomb, the reports of his post-mortem appearances, and the origin of his disciples' sincere belief that he had risen from the dead. According to the model, the empty tomb is explained by the fact that Jesus' body was removed and reburied, probably on the orders of Joseph of Arimathea. Jesus' followers were not informed of this removal and so went to the original tomb, hence accounting for why it was found empty. The reports of Jesus' post-mortem appearances are explained by the disciples having experienced collective religious experiences of Jesus appearing to them, initially triggered by previous private hallucinations leading to an expectancy of further sightings. Individual accounts of these collective experiences were subsequently rendered more impressive and coherent through processes of cognitive, memory, and social biases. The origin of the disciples' belief in the resurrection is explained as the result of their subsequent attempts to make sense of the empty tomb and subsequent experiences, which was also consistent with their theological worldviews and firm conviction that Jesus was the Messiah.

Craig's resurrection hypothesis, that God raised Jesus from the dead, is very obviously insufficient to account for all of the facts, as this hypothesis says nothing about any subsequent appearances or beliefs that the disciples may form. In order to account for all of the facts, Craig's hypothesis must be augmented to state that God raised Jesus from the dead, and Jesus desired to appear to his disciples after his resurrection. This augmented hypothesis is then able to explain the empty tomb and the post-mortem appearances.

Since both explanations have been designed to account for the same set of facts (see figure 13), they have approximately equivalent explanatory scope and depth — though as I argued above I think the RHBS model still has some advantages here. Nevertheless, in adjudicating between the two explanations the primary criterion to consider is how plausible are the assumptions that each theory needs to make. I have thus presented extensive empirical evidence in defence of the key postulates of the RHBS model, including comparative cases of group reports of miraculous events, and evidence of a wide range of cognitive, memory, and social biases that are known to lead to the formation and strengthening of false memories. I have argued that various details of history and Jewish custom render it quite plausible to suppose that either Joseph of Arimathea or some other third party removed Jesus' body from the tomb without the knowledge of the disciples, and without them coming to know of the final resting place of the body. Finally, I have also presented evidence to show that new religious movements do not engage in the sort of critical evaluation of the evidence that Craig imagines the disciples did, but instead are much more liable to engage in all sorts of illogical thinking and biased interpretation of evidence in order to maintain their belief system. Overall, therefore, I have shown that the key postulates of the RBHS model are plausible in the light of shared, widely accepted background evidence.

By contrast, I have argued that the assumptions Craig requires for his augmented resurrection hypothesis are both more numerous and less plausible than he asserts. First, I showed that Craig must assume not only that God exists, but also the two additional assumptions that God would want to raise Jesus from the dead, and also that Jesus would have reason to appear to his disciples. I demonstrated that both of these are distinct issues, separable from and largely independent of the postulate that God exists, and so their plausibility must be considered separately. Considering then all of Craig's three key assumptions, I showed that they are all subject to significant dispute depending upon our prior theological assumptions, and none are among our widely accepted set of background beliefs. These beliefs, of course, will be very plausible if one is already disposed to believe that Jesus was divine (as does Craig), however they are not among the generally accepted background beliefs that can be appealed to in judging the plausibility of Craig's explanation. The fundamental problem is that the second two of these assumptions rely on knowledge of God's intentions, which is something that we do not have access to without making prior theological assumptions. By contrast, the RHBS model relies only on assumptions which can be shown to be plausible given shared background knowledge from history, psychology, and sociology. As such, the RBHS model is a superior explanation of the historical facts surrounding the death of Jesus of Nazareth. One may still believe that God did raise Jesus from the dead if one has independent reasons (theological or experiential) for this belief, however I argue that it is not a belief that can be justified solely by appeal to the best explanation of Craig's historical facts. Craig's historical argument for the resurrection of Jesus is thus ultimately unsuccessful. The historical evidence for the resurrection of Jesus provides some evidence for the truth of Christianity, but not nearly as much as Craig claims that it does.

Chapter Six
Other Arguments

The Leibnizian Cosmological Argument

The Leibnizian cosmological argument is similar to the kalam cosmological argument in that both attempt to demonstrate the existence of God by appealing to the origin of the universe. They differ in the manner by which they attempt to do this. While the kalam cosmological argument argues that the universe must have had a cause of its *beginning* (which is identified with God), the Leibnizian cosmological argument contends that the universe must have a reason for *existing at all* (which reason is again identified with God). The key difference, therefore, is that the Leibnizian argument does not depend on establishing that the universe began to exist, nor is it dependent on a particular philosophy of time. Craig summarises the Leibnizian cosmological argument as follows (premises renumbered)[469]:

> "Premise 1. Anything that exists has an explanation of its existence, either in the necessity of its own nature or in an external cause.
>
> Premise 2. If the universe has an explanation of its existence, that explanation is God.
>
> Premise 3. The universe exists.
>
> Conclusion 1. Therefore, the universe has an explanation of its existence.
>
> Conclusion 2. Therefore, the explanation of the existence of the universe is God."

Obviously, the soundness of this argument rests on the

plausibility of the first two premises, so I will discuss each of these in turn. Craig's first premise is a more moderate version of what is called the principle of sufficient reason, which in its more general form states that everything must have a reason or explanation for being the way it is. Craig believes that some entities, called necessary beings, exist by virtue of their own nature and so have no external cause of their existence. God is a supposed example of such a being, while mathematical objects are another possible example. The second type of entity, contingent beings, exists as a result of some external cause. To motivate the plausibility of his first premise, Craig provides the following analogy[470]:

> *"Suppose you were hiking through the forest and came upon a ball lying on the ground. You would naturally wonder how it came to be there. If your hiking buddy said to you, "Forget about it! It just exists!" you would think he was either joking or just wanted you to keep moving. No one would take seriously the idea that the ball just exists without any explanation. Now notice that merely increasing the size of the ball until it becomes coextensive with the universe does nothing to either provide, or remove the need for, an explanation of its existence."*

The main problem with this principle is that Craig does not define what he means by an 'explanation'. The notion of explanation is quite complex and disputed by philosophers. This may not matter a great deal for many applications (including scientific) of the concept of explanation, but when we are considering the question of the explanation of the entire universe, it is necessary to be more precise about exactly what would count as such an explanation. One of the most popular positions is that to give an explanation for something is to cite the causes in virtue of which that thing exists or occurred. According to this view, to provide an explanation for the universe would be to cite the cause or causes in virtue of which the universe exists. Under this understanding, however, Craig's version of the Leibnizian cosmological argument becomes very similar to the kalam cosmological argument, in that both are ultimately concerned with establishing the cause of the beginning of the universe. As I discussed in Chapter two, Craig has not adequately established that the universe must have a cause. For example, if the universe began as an infinitesimally small region of spacetime which expanded as a result of some sort of quantum fluctuation, it is not at all clear that the existence of such a tiny initial region of spacetime need have any cause of its existence. Plausibly, nothing caused it to come into being; it simply exists.

Craig's analogy of finding a sphere in the forest is inapt because it refers to an object *within* the universe, and objects within the universe nearly always have an explanation (in terms of causes) as to why they exist. As I have argued, however, Craig has not established that this principle can be extrapolated to the very existence of the initial tiny region of spacetime that gave rise to the universe as a whole. The two situations are drastically different, and I do not believe we should have any confidence in simply extrapolating our intuitions formed on the basis of the sorts of examples that Craig sites to vastly different situations which we have no familiarity with (e.g. the cause of the universe itself). Furthermore, it is fallacious to argue that because everything in the universe has an explanation, that therefore the universe as a whole (which is simply the totality of everything that exists) therefore also has an explanation. This would be like arguing that because every student at a university is enrolled in a course, the student body as a whole is therefore enrolled in a course. As a result of these considerations, I do not believe Craig has established his first premise as being particularly likely to be true.

Craig defends his second premise by arguing that most atheists, in responding to the Leibnizian argument, implicitly endorse the view that if the universe did have an explanation then that explanation would be God. He argues as follows[471]:

> "*Atheists typically assert that, since there is no God, it is false that everything has an explanation of its existence, for the universe, in this case, just exists inexplicably. So in affirming that*
> A. *If atheism is true, then the universe has no explanation of its existence,*
> *atheists are also affirming the logically equivalent claim that*
> A´. *If the universe has an explanation of its existence, then atheism is not true,*

> *that is to say, that God exists. Hence, most atheists are implicitly committed to (premise 2)."*

I think it is fairly clear, however, that this is a gross misstatement of the position of most atheists. For atheism entails no commitment about whether or not the universe has a cause, and as such atheists need not adopt any particular view on this matter. Atheists would generally say that if God exists then the universe would have an explanation of its existence, but if God does not exist then the universe need not have such an explanation. As such, Craig's proposition A would be more accurately stated as 'if theism is true then the universe has an explanation of its existence, but otherwise it does not necessarily have an explanation of its existence'. The entire force of Craig's argument, therefore, derives from his unfair presentation of the atheist position.

Craig also provides a second argument in defence of this second premise, in which he asserts that a personal God is the only possible explanation for the universe[472]:

> *"The universe, by definition, includes all of physical reality. So the cause of the universe must (at least causally prior to the universe's existence) transcend space and time and therefore cannot be physical or material. But there are only two kinds of things that could fall under such a description: either an abstract object (like a number) or else a mind (a soul, a self). But abstract objects don't stand in causal relations... So if the universe has an explanation of its existence, that explanation must be a transcendent, unembodied Mind which created the universe – which is what most people have traditionally meant by the word 'God.'"*

The problem with this argument is that, as with the kalam cosmological argument, Craig simply ignores all other proposals for non-physical entities that could potentially provide an explanation for the universe. I discuss some of these possibilities in section four of Chapter two. Since Craig is making the argument that God is the explanation of the universe, he bears the burden of proof to show that no other possible non-physical explanation could account for the existence of the universe. Since he makes no effort to do this, and simply assumes that a personal agent is the only alternative, I regard Craig's argument for his second premise as unconvincing.

Another possible rebuttal to Craig's second premise is to argue that the universe does not have any explanation external to it, but that existence is an inherent necessary property of the universe. One argument Craig gives against this possibility is that we can imagine that every object in the universe did not exist, and thus it seems possible that there was no universe at all. Craig thinks that if we can trust our intuitions about the fact that we can imagine the non-existence of Earth, then we should also trust them in the fact that we can imagine the non-existence of everything else in the universe. This does not strike me as a very persuasive argument. The fact that I can imagine something does little to indicate that such a thing is really possible. For instance, I can imagine that God does not exist, even though Craig thinks that God's existence is necessary and thus it would be impossible for God not to exist. It seems that for Craig's argument to work, he must hold the position that no one can ever even imagine that God does not exist. This seems deeply implausible, and as a result I think this argument should be rejected. As such, just because we can imagine the non-existence of the universe, it does not follow that such non-existence is actually possible. Of course, it may be that the universe could have failed to exist, but I don't think Craig has given sufficient reason to rule out this possibility.

A second argument that Craig gives against the possibility of a necessarily existing universe is that we know that the fundamental particles that make up the universe could have been replaced by a different set of fundamental particles. He explains[473]:

> "A universe consisting of a totally different collection of quarks, say, seems quite possible. But if that's the case, then the universe does not exist by a necessity of its own nature. For a universe composed of a wholly different collection of quarks is not the same universe as ours."

The problem with this argument is that it assumes that the contingent or necessary existence of the universe is ultimately dependent upon the contingency or necessity of the fundamental particles that currently make up macroscopic objects within the universe. Modern cosmology, however, shows that all fundamental particles only came into existence sometime *after* the very beginning of the universe, following the time when the four fundamental forces of matter decouple from one another. If the universe exists by the necessity of its own nature, therefore, it is clearly not the particles themselves that exist necessarily, but something more fundamental from which the particles were formed. What this 'something' is exactly is not currently known, because we do not have the quantum theory of gravity that would be necessary in order to properly describe the universe at this very early time. However, we might suppose that a quantum mechanical field, an infinitesimally small region of spacetime, or something similar is the original entity which exists necessarily by its own nature. This field or spacetime manifold might then have given rise to any number of subsequent contingent entities and events (including the fundamental particles Craig mentions), even though it itself exists necessarily by its own nature.

Overall, therefore, I think that Craig fails to provide sufficient justification for either of the two key premises of the Leibnizian cosmological argument. Though both premises are somewhat plausible and the argument is at least more persuasive than the kalam, I do not regard it as a particularly compelling argument for the existence of God.

THE ONTOLOGICAL ARGUMENT

The ontological argument is perhaps the single most unusual argument for the existence of God. The argument attempts to show that the mere *possibility* of God's existence entails that God must *actually* exist. There are different versions of the ontological argument, with the version propounded by Craig having been originally developed by philosopher Alvin Plantinga. This formulation relies on the concept of 'possible worlds'. A possible world refers to a total configuration of the way things could be in reality. Some states of affairs, for example a married bachelor, are impossible and so do not exist in any possible world. By contrast, many other states of affairs do not pertain in the actual world, but could potentially exist, and so exist in some possible world. Thus, we can say that in some possible world Craig became an electrician rather than a philosopher, while in another possible world Germany won the First World War.

Plantinga defines God to be a being who is 'maximally great', which he in turn defines as being 'maximally excellent' (omniscient, omnipotent, morally perfect, etc) in every possible world. With this definition, so long as such a being possibly exists (i.e. so long as God exists in at least one possible world) then God must also exist in every possible world. This is because God is *by definition* said to be a being who is maximally excellent in every possible world, so either such a being is simply impossible (and so exists in no possible world), or is necessary and so exists in every possible world. If God exists in every possible world, then of course he must exist in the actual world. So long as it is possible for a maximally great being to exist, therefore, such a being must exist.

Although Plantinga formulated his argument in the language of modal logic and the conclusion he establishes might appear to be grandiose, his argument asserts little more than the historically widely-held view that if God exists, he exists necessarily. That is, God could not be the sort of being that might or might not have existed, like a planet or animal or country. If things had gone differently in the early universe, for instance, the Milky Way galaxy might never have formed, and thus Earth might never have existed. God, however, simply isn't the sort of being whose existence could be contingent in this way – either he must necessarily exist, or he could not possibly exist at all. Plantinga's argument is simply a modern reformulation of this idea. Essentially, it shows that either it is impossible for God to exist, or else God must necessarily exist.

Correctly understood, therefore, Plantinga's formulation isn't really an argument for the existence of God so much as an argument for the fact that God's existence is either impossible or necessary. Craig, however, has presented Plantinga's ontological argument as if it can establish that the mere possibility that God exists implies that he must exist. He says[474]:

Unreasonable Faith

> *"As we've seen, there are other arguments for God's existence which at least suggest that it's possible that God exists. So I'll just leave it with you. Do you think, as I do, that it's at least possible that God exists? If so, then it follows logically that He does exist."*

The problem with this remark is that Craig is conflating metaphysical possibility with epistemic possibility. Craig himself explains the importance of keeping the two distinct[475]:

> *"In dealing with this issue, it's crucial that we distinguish clearly between metaphysical and merely epistemic possibility. The first concerns what is really possible; the second concerns what is consistent with what we know. One is tempted to say, 'It's possible that God exists, and it's possible that he doesn't exist!' But this assertion is true only with respect to epistemic possibility: for all we know, God may exist or he may not exist. On the other hand, if God is conceived as a maximally great being, then his existence is either necessary or impossible, regardless of our epistemic uncertainty."*

When Craig asks 'do you think, as I do, it's at least possible God exists?', it is not completely clear what sort of possibility Craig is referring to, but I think given the way it is phrased and the context in which it is uttered, most people not versed in the subtleties of modal logic would interpret this to be referring to *epistemic* possibility. Craig is therefore implying that Plantinga's ontological argument demonstrates that unless one closed-mindedly denies even the possibility of God's existence, then one must affirm his actual existence. As Craig explains, however, the argument concerns not epistemic but *metaphysical* possibility, and therefore in denying the possibility of God's existence the atheist is not saying that he is absolutely certain that God exists, but merely that he does not think the existence of God is metaphysically possible. Thus, some of his ambiguous remarks on the subject notwithstanding, Craig has not shown that anyone who thinks that God might exist should believe that he actually does exist.

Another problem with Craig's phrasing of Plantinga's ontological argument is that he falsely conflates logical and metaphysical possibility. Once again, this is despite Craig's own injunctions against so doing[476]:

> "When philosophers speak of metaphysical necessity/possibility, they are thinking in terms of a modality that lies somewhere in between the strict logical modality that characterizes the laws of logic and the broader physical modality that characterizes what is permitted by nature's laws and boundary conditions... Metaphysical necessity has to do with what must be the case, even though its denial does not involve a contradiction. For example, I think it is metaphysically necessary that everything that begins to exist has a cause, even though there is no logical inconsistency in saying that a certain thing came into being without a cause... There is no strict logical contradiction in the statement 'God does not exist,' just as there is not a strict logical contradiction in saying 'Jones is a married bachelor', but both are unactualizable states of affairs. Thus, it is metaphysically necessary that God exists."

Craig thus agrees that Plantinga's argument establishes only that God is metaphysically necessary, not that he is logically necessary. Given this, Craig is mistaken when he says elsewhere that[477]:

> "In order for the ontological argument to fail, the concept of a maximally great being must be incoherent, like the concept of a married bachelor."

The ontological argument does not say anything about God being logically necessary, only metaphysically necessary. An atheist therefore does not have to assert that the concept of a maximally great being is logically incoherent, only that it is not metaphysically possible.

Craig's formulation of the ontological argument relies on Craig's misleading conflation of different types of possibility. It is therefore not only unpersuasive to anyone who does not already believe in God, but also potentially disingenuous for Craig to make the argument in the way that he does.

THE ARGUMENT FROM INTENTIONALITY

Craig argues that the mental phenomenon of intentionality fits much better in a theistic than a naturalistic worldview[478]:

> "Intentionality is the property of being about something or of something. It signifies the object-directedness of our thoughts. For example, I can think about my summer vacation, or I can think of my wife. No physical object has intentionality in this sense. A chair or a stone or a glob of tissue like the brain is not about or of something else. Only mental states or states of consciousness are about other things... By contrast, for theists, because God is a mind, it's hardly surprising that there should be other, finite minds, with intentional states. Thus intentional states fit comfortably into a theistic worldview."

The biggest problem with this argument is simply that it is not an argument for theism, but simply an argument against naturalism (a view which denies the existence of immaterial minds). This can be seen most easily be examining Craig's summary form of the argument (premises renumbered)[479]:

> "Premise 1. If God did not exist, intentional states of consciousness would not exist.
> Premise 2. But intentional states of consciousness do exist.
> Conclusion. Therefore, God exists."

Nothing Craig has said, however, grants him warrant to posit the first premise that intentional states of consciousness would not exist without God. Even if we accept his argument that physical objects cannot exhibit intentionality, all that follows is something beyond the physical (such as immaterial minds) must exist which do exhibit such intentionality. This could be used as an argument for substance dualism or against naturalism, but by itself it is not an argument for the existence of God because it says nothing about God at all, only material minds in the abstract.

There are also further problems with this argument. First, there are strong arguments against the plausibility of substance dualism which I discuss in section four of Chapter two. Second, Craig makes no effort to engage with the many naturalistic theories of intentionality that philosophers have developed. Information-theoretic accounts of intentionality, for instance, explain intentionality as deriving from the informational content of particular states of affairs[480]. Since Craig blithely ignores all such theories without any engagement or discussion of their merits, he has no justification for simply asserting that naturalism cannot be reconciled with the existence of intentionality. Third, Craig's argument that 'a chair or a stone or a glob of tissue like the brain is not about or of something else' commits a category mistake. Intentionality is a property, not an object that exists, and so it is a mistake to say that an object like a brain is not the same thing as the property of intentionality. The question is rather whether it is possible for a physical object like a brain to manifest the property of intentionality through its patterns of electrochemical activity. Phrased in this way the idea that a brain can exhibit intentionality as a result of complex interactions between billions of neurons is much less absurd than Craig's misleading characterisation that a brain cannot be about something. Fourth, Craig's proposed explanation for the origin of intentionality is completely explanatorily vacuous. He simply asserts that non-material minds just do exhibit intentionality, without explaining how or why this should be the case. After all, if a material entity like a brain cannot exhibit intentionality, why should an immaterial entity be able to do so? What difference does the fact that the entity is immaterial make in its ability to be about something else? Since Craig does not provide any justification for this, there is really no reason to prefer his immaterial explanation over a naturalistic explanation.

THE UNREASONABLE EFFECTIVENESS OF MATHEMATICS

Craig has argued that the amazing effectiveness of mathematics in describing the physical world is a phenomenon best explained by theism. He introduces the matter by asking[481]:

> "*How is it, for example, that a mathematical theorist like Peter Higgs can sit down at his desk and, by pouring over*

mathematical equations, predict the existence of a fundamental particle which 30 years later, after investing millions of dollars and thousands of man hours, experimentalists are finally able to detect? Mathematics is the language of nature. But how is this to be explained?"

Craig argues that the naturalist has no ability to explain why nature has a complex underlying mathematical structure. The theist, by contrast, can explain the mathematical structure of the universe by appealing to the fact that God created the universe and the laws of physics on the basis of a mental 'blueprint' that he had in mind. Craig therefore summarises this argument as follows (premises renumbered)[482]:

"Premise 1. If God did not exist, the applicability of mathematics would be just a happy coincidence.
Premise 2. The applicability of mathematics is not just a happy coincidence.
Conclusion. Therefore, God exists."

What is strange about this argument is that Craig never explains how it is that theism is supposed to explain the effectiveness of mathematics in understanding nature. He says that God created the physical world on the basis of a blueprint he had in mind, but then also says that[483]:

"There are any number of blueprints he might have chosen."

So why, then, did God choose a mathematical blueprint, instead of any of the non-mathematical ones he could have chosen? Craig's proposed 'explanation' is thus completely explanatorily vacuous, as it is equally consistent with literally any possible way the universe could have been. Physicist Sean Carroll eloquently expressed this critique in a slightly different context during a debate with Craig[484]:

"In a similar context, he (Craig) said, 'Suppose God is more like the cosmic artist who wants to splash his canvas with the extravagance of design and who enjoys creating this fabulous cosmos designed with fantastic detail for observers'. My point is that this is not some sort of sophisticated apologetic strategy. This is an admission of defeat. This is saying we should never

expect theism to explain why the universe is one way, rather than some other way. You know God – God is an artist. You know artists; they're kind of quirky and unpredictable. We can't expect to know what they're going to do ahead of time. Anything you might possibly observe about the universe, according to this view, I can explain as saying, 'That is what God would have done.'"

If a physicist were able to design the laws of nature from scratch, they would surely choose something far more tractable than the laws which describe our actual universe. The two most successful of current physical theories, general relativity and quantum mechanics, are both mathematically intractable for all but the simplest of systems. Nearly all real-world applications of these theories can only be made using numerical methods involving many approximations. It would be far more elegant if these fundamental theories admitted of much simpler analytic solutions which could then comparatively easily be computed in a variety of real world cases. Of course, it could be that a designer God has different priorities than terrestrial physicists, or a different sense as to what counts as 'simple' or 'elegant'. This, however, is precisely the problem that Carroll points out with appeals of this sort – since the designer can do anything and there are no established principles for restricting his behaviour, design is equally consistent with all possible outcomes, and therefore is not able to explain why any particular outcome comes to be. In the case of the mathemetisability of the laws of nature, therefore, design is a completely impotent explanatory hypothesis, and we are left without any reason to accept Craig's first premise.

In addition to the failure of theism to offer any plausible explanation for the effectiveness of mathematics, it is by no means clear that said effectiveness is in any way 'unreasonable' in the first place. Mathematics is a disciple which studies the abstract structures and rules associated with concepts such as space, number, symmetry, and probability. These concepts are so abstract and general that they can be applied to nearly any field, and so it is not surprising that they also find application in describing the laws of physics. The field of geometry, for example, is capable of describing the structure of almost any imaginable space, and so would find application in describing the structure of the world we live in even if the number of dimensions were different. Craig also overlooks the fact that many important mathematical techniques and concepts were developed in large part precisely in order to serve the purpose of describing laws of nature. For example, differential calculus was developed by Newton specifically in order to describe the motion of objects under the influence of forces. It is no surprise that mathematical concepts are so useful in describing the world when they are developed with that exact purpose in mind. There are of course many other cases where mathematical concepts were first developed with no particular intended application, and then later found application in an unexpected physical domain. In yet other cases, many mathematical concepts have been developed from their own merit and find essentially no application in describing the laws of nature. Overall, the applicability of mathematics to nature seems to be a 'mixed bag', partly the result of design and partly the result of luck, and not something that is in any way 'unreasonable'.

Craig also ignores the many examples of systems which are describable using the language of mathematics that seem clearly not to have been something designed by God based on a mental blueprint. Many mathematical tools are used extensively in the fields of finance and economics, yet few theists would want to infer from this that stock markets or international trade flows were designed by God. Likewise, the behaviour of cars in traffic jams[485], people waiting in a line, and warehouse inventories[486] are all very profitably modelled as stochastic processes using queuing theory[487]. Should we infer from this that God designed the concept of 'queues' in accordance with some mental blueprint? The implausibility of this suggests that we cannot simply infer that because something is describable using mathematics, that therefore that thing must have been designed by God using a mathematical blueprint.

In light of all these considerations, it is most reasonable to regard mathematics as a set of abstract tools and concepts developed for many different purposes. Given its broad scope and abstract nature, it is not surprising that many physical phenomena can be usefully described in mathematical terms, just as can many phenomena unrelated to natural physical laws. As such, there is no reason to regard the applicability of mathematics as particularly 'unreasonable', nor has Craig given any reason to think that God provides any explanatory power with respect to the applicability of mathematics to the natural world.

CHAPTER SEVEN
CONCLUSIONS

AN OVERALL EVALUATION OF CRAIG'S ARGUMENTS

In this final section, I present some brief concluding remarks concerning Craig's arguments, with a focus on evaluating the arguments in accordance with the criteria set out in the introduction, namely how persuasively they demonstrate that Christianity is true. Considering Craig's cumulative case for Christianity as a whole, I think it is helpful to divide his arguments into two classes. In the first class are those arguments which I believe are not at all persuasive, and thus do not provide any significant reason to accept their conclusions. In this class I would place the kalam cosmological argument, the moral argument, the argument from intentionality, and the unreasonable effectiveness of mathematics, and the ontological argument. In the second class are the arguments which are somewhat persuasive, and thus do provide at least some reason to accept their conclusions, even if it is less than Craig claims. This class I would place the Leibnizian cosmological argument, the fine-tuning argument, and the argument for the resurrection of Jesus.

The kalam cosmological argument is a failure first and foremost because it is internally inconsistent. Its inconsistency lies in the fact that Craig cannot provide a philosophy of time that allows him to simultaneously affirm that the universe began to exist, and that the cause of the universe must have been an immaterial agent. As I argued, the presentist philosophy of time that Craig adopts, according to which only the present exists, undercuts both of his arguments for the finitude of the past, since under presentism the past does not represent an actual infinite as the past does not exist. Furthermore, the only plausible answer to the problem of the extent of the present is that the present exists as an infinitesimal instant. This means that if past events are real then there must be infinitely many of them even if there *was* an absolute beginning of the universe, thereby again undercutting Craig's arguments for the finitude of the past. Craig's presentist philosophy of time is also inconsistent with general relativity, and renders it impossible for him to appeal to the Borde-Guth-Vilenkin theorem to establish the beginning of the universe. Finally, Craig fails to show that agent causation is either the only possible nonphysical cause of the universe, or that agent causation has any advantages over any other possible causative mechanism. In particular, Craig's assertion that an agent exercising their causative powers does not require a cause contradicts his premise that everything that begins to exist requires a cause. His ad hoc attempts to avoid this contradiction by asserting that this premise only applies to substances that begin to exist undercuts its application to the universe, for the universe as a whole is likewise not a substance that began to exist, but rather the totality of all physical existence. The underlying inconsistency in the kalam lies, I believe, in the fact that Craig developed this argument before he developed the philosophy of time needed to underpin the kalam. Taken individually, I think each project faces considerable problems, but when combined I think they are simply impossible to reconcile. As such, I do not think the kalam cosmological argument provides any good reasons for believing in the existence of God.

The moral argument is unsuccessful largely because Craig gives so little reason to accept its key fourth premise that without God there could be no grounding for objective moral values. In particular, he does not engage at all with any of the philosophical literature concerning the basis of moral values, and so simply ignores the numerous accounts that have been developed to explain the nature of moral values. The main technique Craig uses when presented with any atheistic account of moral values is to question what reason we have for believing this account, which conflicts both with his own statement that he does not need to give any reasons for believing his theistic account of the basis of moral values, and also conflicts with his assertion that his argument is about the ontological foundation of moral values and not about moral epistemology. For the moral argument to work, therefore, Craig needs to show not that we have no reason to believe that any particular atheistic account of moral values is true, but rather that no atheistic account of moral values could be true, which he simply makes no effort to do. Furthermore, there is an intrinsic tension between the second and fourth premises of Craig's argument, since somebody convinced of the truth of the fourth premise (that objective moral values cannot exist without God), is likely to simply reject the truth of the second premise (that objective moral values exist), and conclude that moral values are not objective in the way Craig asserts. That is, the nonexistence of objective moral values would for such persons constitute evidence against the existence of God. Conversely, those who accept the truth of premise two that objective moral values exist are likely to reject the fourth premise that objective morality is dependent upon God. That is, they will take the nonexistence of God and the existence of objective moral values as reason to believe there must be some account of moral values which can succeed without appealing to God, even if they currently cannot provide one. This is analogous to the Christian who takes the coexistence of God and evil as reason to believe that God must have some reason for allowing evil, even if they don't know what that reason is. The moral argument is thus ultimately unconvincing because Craig is unable to simultaneously provide sufficient reasons for accepting all of its premises.

The arguments from intentionality and the unreasonable effectiveness of mathematics are both relatively new arguments that Craig has only recently begun to defend. Perhaps as a result, Craig has simply given relatively little reason to accept the premises of either of these arguments. In particular, he fails to establish that there is anything particularly mysterious to explain about intentionality or the effectiveness of mathematics. The argument from intentionality is also not even an argument for the existence of God, but merely an argument for some form of mind-body dualism. The argument from the unreasonable effectiveness of mathematics fails to give any reason as to why the existence of God would explain the application of mathematics to the physical world, since there is no particular reason why we should expect God to prefer a mathematical over any other type of universe. As a result of these considerations, I do not think either of these arguments provides any reason for believing in the existence of God.

The Leibnizian cosmological argument is more successful than the kalam cosmological argument because it does not depend upon any particular philosophy of time in order to be effective. The main problem with this argument is that both of its premises are highly controversial and very difficult to establish with any confidence. 'Explanation' is a notoriously difficult concept which Craig does not adequately define when arguing that 'everything that exists must have an explanation for its existence'. If explanation is understood as providing a cause, then this premise becomes very similar to the argument that everything that begins to exist has a cause, which renders it extremely similar to the kalam cosmological argument. As to the second premise of this argument, Craig must establish that the universe does not exist necessarily. His only arguments for this are that we could imagine the universe not existing, and that we know that the particles that make up the universe are contingent. Neither is very compelling, however, since we can also imagine God not existing, yet Craig thinks he is metaphysically necessary, and it is not clear that because fundamental particles are contingent that therefore the whole universe must be. Craig's justification of his two key premises, therefore, falls short of firmly establishing his desired conclusion. Nevertheless, it does seem that both premises are at least plausible, with the degree of plausibility largely dependent upon how much credence we accord to appeals to various metaphysical intuitions. The Leibnizian argument therefore provides some modest support for the contention that God exists, though much less than Craig claims.

The fine-tuning argument is similarly more successful than the kalam because it is not susceptible to the same sorts of internal contradictions. The core intuitive thrust of the fine-tuning argument is that the existence of God would render the suitability of the universe for life much more plausible, while in the absence of God there seems no particular explanation as to why this should be the case. This key insight I think is sound, and provides some modest reason for believing in the existence of a creator God, though this is undermined to some degree by the inability to provide a non-question-begging reason for why God should prefer to create life through the operation of natural laws. Most importantly, however, Craig fails to establish that the probability that the universe would be life-permitting without explicit design is especially low. Craig's appeals to the findings of physicists that the constants of nature are 'fine-tuned' for life to extremely high precision are misplaced because the sort of life referred to in such studies is always biochemically-based life living on rocky planets orbiting long-lived stars – that is, the sort of life we are familiar with. Craig, however, gives no reason why God would be likely to create a universe conducive to this specific form of life. Instead, all his argument establishes is that God would have a reason to create a universe conducive to the existence of some form of embodied life. Since we do not know what conditions are necessary for such life to exist, we simply do not know what combinations of constants would be able to support such life. This problem is especially pronounced given the large number of constants in question (what I called the 'dimensionality problem'), and the immense difficulty of inferring what proportion of the total phase-space of possible constant values is life-permitting based on knowledge of only small parts of that space (what I termed the 'representativeness problem'). As a result of these difficulties, I do not believe that Craig has established that the universe is fine-tuned for life in the way that he claims, and as such most of the persuasive force of the fine-tuning argument is undermined.

Perhaps surprisingly to many non-theists, I regard the argument for the resurrection of Jesus as the strongest of Craig's arguments. I think there is little doubt that the case of Jesus is a highly unusual one, and the historical evidence for his rising from the dead is far better than most atheists are willing to admit. Nevertheless, I think that while this evidence does provide some reason for thinking that Jesus rose from the dead, I do not think it is nearly as compelling as Craig claims. In particular, Craig's claim that there is no plausible naturalistic explanation for the core historical facts is undermined by my presentation of the RHBS model, which is able to explain these facts with reference only to findings from history, psychology, and sociology that are generally accepted by Christians and non-Christians alike. Craig's explanation, by contrast, appeals to key assumptions about the intentions and plans of God which are contested, and which are not part of our shared background knowledge. Craig also overstates the uniqueness of the resurrection claims, overlooking the wide range of miracle and paranormal occurrences which clearly demonstrate that groups of people can come to report having experienced very unusual phenomena. Through careful documentation of the numerous memory and cognitive biases that shape human recollection, I have shown how it is possible to explain the emergence of the resurrection appearance narratives without any deliberate deception or extensive legendary embellishment. As such, I believe that the RHBS model provides a superior explanation for Craig's key historical facts than does the resurrection hypothesis, thereby significantly (though not completely) undermining the persuasiveness of Craig's argument.

WHAT SHOULD WE BELIEVE?

In this book, I have confined myself to an analysis of a certain set of arguments attempting to show the truth of Christianity. While I have contended that these arguments are not very persuasive and are subject to problems of various sorts, I have not attempted to show that the conclusion of these arguments is false. That is, I have only argued that Craig's apologetic case for Christianity is not particularly compelling, not that Christianity is false or that one ought not to be a Christian. In order to address this question, I would first need to establish a framework for determining what it is reasonable to believe in, and how we should adjust our beliefs in response to evidence. This would require a detailed discussion of many issues in epistemology, psychology, Christian theology, and the relationship between faith and reason, all of which fall well outside the scope of this book. Since I have not considered most of the relevant issues, it would be invalid to draw any firm conclusions about what we should believe with respect to the truth claims of Christianity. As such, at no point in this book have I attempted to argue that God did *not* create the universe, or that Jesus did *not* rise from the dead. All I have contended is that the arguments Craig gives for believing these things are not very good. Whether one should believe them anyway for some other reason (or even for no reason at all), is quite another question. One exception is the moral argument, where I did argue that God is not the ultimate ground of objective morality in the way that Craig claims. Of course, it does not follow from this that God does not exist, for many prominent theists agree with me on this point.

Ultimately, of course, what most people are truly interested in is the question of what they should believe, and not merely whether a given argument is a sound or not. As such, it seems appropriate at the conclusion of this book to offer a few brief thoughts on this issue. My position is that all of the arguments both for and against the existence of the Christian God are inconclusive, such that on the basis of reason and evidence alone, belief in the core claims of Christianity is neither rationally prohibited nor rationally required. In other words, there is insufficient evidence to adjudicate the question with any high confidence one way or the other. Note that I *do* think that particular claims made by some Christians, such as young Earth creationism or the literal truth of Noah's flood, *can* be decisively refuted by appeal to argument and evidence. I do not, however, think this is true of the core theological and philosophical claims of Christianity as such. By my current best assessment of the arguments and evidences, I would accord the Christian God around a five to ten percent probability of existing, while acknowledging that these epistemic probability estimates are necessarily vague and hard to justify rigorously. I do, nevertheless, think that on balance the world we observe is best explained by atheism rather than Christian theism.

This itself, however, is not enough to answer the question as to what we should believe, for in the case of Christianity belief is not merely an intellectual assent to some abstract proposition. Instead, true adoption of the Christian worldview entails a thoroughgoing alteration of one's attitude to and priorities in life. It is, Christians say, to enter into a personal relationship with God himself, to allow him to change oneself from the inside out, and to follow his teachings and example for the rest of one's life. Faith, then, is not a passive endorsement of some belief, but an active engagement with a new way of living. If this is the case, then whether or not Christianity provides the best explanation for the totality of phenomena in the world may not be the most important consideration. Christians claim that all mankind are 'drowning' and Jesus is the only 'life raft' that we can cling to. If one really were drowning and were thrown a life raft, one would hardly refuse to grab hold on the basis that the most likely explanation given all the available evidence is that the life raft is unseaworthy. In these circumstances, one would still be inclined to place one's trust in the life raft, and make a choice to cling to it in hope that it just might be able to save us. One might similarly make a decision to choose to become a Christian, even in the face of significant doubts, if one thought that such a life was the best way to live.

For myself at the present time, I do not regard becoming a Christian as the best way for me to live my life, which is why I remain an atheist. Nevertheless, I do not suppose to make this judgement on behalf of anyone else, and thus do not claim that anyone else ought not to be a Christian. I think there are a great many particular things that people calling themselves Christians believe, say, and do which I do not believe they ought to; however adherence to the key doctrines of Christianity itself is not one of those things. All I have attempted to show in this book is that one should not be a Christian solely or primarily on the basis of the arguments presented by Craig. Beyond that, everyone must consult their own reason and conscience, and do what is right by their best judgement, always remaining open to new evidence, arguments, and ways of looking at things. It is my hope that this book has been of use to those seeking what to believe, how to think critically, and the best place to put their trust.

BIBLIOGRAPHY

Abbott, Benjamin P, Richard Abbott, TD Abbott, MR Abernathy, Fausto Acernese, Kendall Ackley, Carl Adams, Thomas Adams, Paolo Addesso, and RX Adhikari. "Observation of Gravitational Waves from a Binary Black Hole Merger." *Physical review letters* 116, no. 6 (2016): 061102.

"About Reasonable Faith." http://www.reasonablefaith.org/about-reasonable-faith.

Adams, Glenn, and Vivian Afi Dzokoto. "Genital-Shrinking Panic in Ghana: A Cultural Psychological Analysis." *Culture & Psychology* 13, no. 1 (2007): 83-104.

Aguirre, Anthony, Brendan Foster, and Zeeya Merali. *It from Bit or Bit from It?: On Physics and Information*: Springer, 2015.

Al-Adawi, Samir, Rustam Burjorjee, and Ihsan Al-Issa. "Mu-Ghayeb: A Culture-Specific Response to Bereavement in Oman." *International Journal of Social Psychiatry* 43, no. 2 (1997): 144-51.

"All They Need Is the Air." *BBC News*, 1999, http://news.bbc.co.uk/2/hi/uk_news/454313.stm.

"Animated spaceships.gif", 2009, https://commons.wikimedia.org/wiki/File:Animated_spaceships.gif.

Asmodelle, Estelle. "Tests of General Relativity: A Review." *arXiv preprint arXiv:1705.04397* (2017).

Association, Ahmadiyya Muslim. "Truthfulness of the Promised Messiah: Vi – Miracles." http://whyahmadi.org/claims-of-promised-messiah/truthfulness-of-the-promised-messiah-vi-miracles.html.

Baethge, Christopher. "Grief Hallucinations: True or Pseudo? Serious or Not?" *Psychopathology* 35, no. 5 (2002): 296-302.

Barnes, Douglas F. "Charisma and Religious Leadership: An Historical Analysis." *Journal for the Scientific Study of Religion* (1978): 1-18.

Bartholomew, Robert. "Phantom German Air Raids on Canada: War Hysteria in Québec and Ontario During the First World War." *Canadian Military History* 7, no. 4 (2012): 3.

Bartholomew, Robert E, Keith Basterfield, and George S Howard.

"UFO Abductees and Contactees: Psychopathology or Fantasy Proneness?" *Professional Psychology: Research and Practice* 22, no. 3 (1991): 215.

Bartholomew, Robert E, and Jeffrey S Victor. "A Social-Psychological Theory of Collective Anxiety Attacks: The "Mad Gasser" Reexamined." *The Sociological Quarterly* 45, no. 2 (2004): 229-48.

Batson, C Daniel. "Rational Processing or Rationalization? The Effect of Disconfirming Information on a Stated Religious Belief." *Journal of Personality and Social Psychology* 32, no. 1 (1975): 176.

Beamon, Benita M., and Stephen A. Kotleba. "Inventory Modelling for Complex Emergencies in Humanitarian Relief Operations." *International Journal of Logistics Research and Applications* 9, no. 1 (2006): 1-18.

Beer, Randall D. "Autopoiesis and Cognition in the Game of Life." *Artificial Life* 10, no. 3 (2004): 309-26.

Belanti, John, Mahendra Perera, and Karuppiah Jagadheesan. "Phenomenology of near-Death Experiences: A Cross-Cultural Perspective." *Transcultural psychiatry* 45, no. 1 (2008): 121-33.

Benassi, Victor A, Barry Singer, and Craig B Reynolds. "Occult Belief: Seeing Is Believing." *Journal for the Scientific Study of Religion* (1980): 337-49.

Betz, Andrew L, John J Skowronski, and Thomas M Ostrom. "Shared Realities: Social Influence and Stimulus Memory." *Social Cognition* 14, no. 2 (1996): 113.

BibleHub. "John 20:7 Parallel Verses." http://biblehub.com/john/20-7.htm.

Bilu, Yoram. ""We Want to See Our King": Apparitions in Messianic Habad." *Ethos* 41, no. 1 (2013): 98-126.

Blacker, Carmen, Michael Loewe, and J Martin Plumley. *Ancient Cosmologies*: F Allen & Unwin, 1975.

Borde, Arvind, Alan H Guth, and Alexander Vilenkin. "Inflationary Spacetimes Are Not Past-Complete." *arXiv preprint gr-qc/0110012* (2001).

Boudry, Maarten, and Johan Braeckman. "How Convenient! The Epistemic Rationale of Self-Validating Belief Systems." *Philosophical Psychology* 25, no. 3 (2012): 341-64.

Bourget, David, and David J Chalmers. "What Do Philosophers Believe?" *Philosophical Studies* 170, no. 3 (2014): 465-500.

Buehler, Roger, and Dale Griffin. "Change-of-Meaning Effects in Conformity and Dissent: Observing Construal Processes over Time." *Journal of Personality and Social Psychology* 67, no. 6 (1994): 984.

Carroll, Sean. "Does the Universe Need God." *The Blackwell companion to science and christianity* (2012): 185-97.
Castle, Terry. "Contagious Folly: 'An Adventure' and Its Skeptics." *Critical Inquiry* 17, no. 4 (1991): 741-72.
Chaudhuri, Haridas. "The Concept of Brahman in Hindu Philosophy." *Philosophy East and West* 4, no. 1 (1954): 47-66.
Chaudhuri, Narayan. *That Compassionate Touch of Ma Anandamayee*. Delhi: Motilal Banarsidass, 1980.
Clarke, David. "Rumours of Angels: A Legend of the First World War." *Folklore* 113, no. 2 (2002): 151-73.
Collins, Robin. "The Teleological Argument: An Exploration of the Fine-Tuning of the Universe." In *The Blackwell Companion to Natural Theology*, 202-81, 2009.
Copan, Paul, and William Lane Craig. *The Kalam Cosmological Argument, Volume 1: Philosophical Arguments for the Finitude of the Past.* Vol. 1: Bloomsbury Publishing USA, 2017.
Coren, Michael. "William Lane Craig Vs Michael Payton: Does God Exist?", 2009.
Craig, William Lane. "Apologetics Training - Advice to Christian Apologists." *Reasonable Faith*.
— — —. *Assessing the New Testament Evidence for the Historicity of the Resurrection of Jesus*. Lewiston, N.Y., USA: E. Mellen Press, 1989.
— — —. "The Caused Beginning of the Universe: A Response to Quentin Smith." *British Journal for the Philosophy of Science* (1993): 623-39.
— — —. "Contemporary Scholarship and the Historical Evidence for the Resurrection of Jesus Christ." *Truth* 1 (1985): 89-95.
— — —. "Curriculum Vitae."
— — —. "Debate with Dr. Kevin Scharp Part 3." (2016).
— — —. "Debate on the Kalam Argument." http://www.reasonablefaith.org/debate-on-the-kalam-argument.
— — —. *Did Jesus Rise from the Dead?*: Impact 360 Institute, 2014.
— — —. *Did Jesus Rise from the Dead?* Pine Mountain, Georgia: Impact 360 Institute, 2001.
— — —. "Does God Exist?" http://www.reasonablefaith.org/does-god-exist-1#ixzz4LstLFjFs.
— — —. "Does God Exist?" *Philosophy Now* (2013).
— — —. "God and the 'Unreasonable Effectiveness of Mathematics'." *Christian Research Journal* 36, no. 6 (2013).
— — —. "Graham Oppy on the Kalām Cosmological Argument." *Sophia* 32, no. 1 (1993): 1-11.
— — —. "Has the Multiverse Replaced God?"

— — —. "The Historical Argument for the Resurrection of Jesus During the Deist Controversy." (1988).

— — —. "'Honesty, Transparency, Full Disclosure" and the Borde-Guth-Vilenkin Theorem." *Reasonable Faith* (2013).

— — —. "The Indispensability of Theological Meta-Ethical Foundations for Morality." *Foundations* 5 (1997): 9-12.

— — —. *The Kalam Cosmological Argument*: Wipf and Stock Publishers, 2000.

— — —. "The Kalam Cosmological Argument." (2015).

— — —. "Must the Beginning of the Universe Have a Personal Cause?" *Faith and Philosophy* 19, no. 1 (2002): 94-105.

— — —. "Navigating Sam Harris' the Moral Landscape." *Reasonable Faith* (2012).

— — —. "Oaklander on Mctaggart and Intrinsic Change." *Analysis* 59, no. 264 (1999): 319-20.

— — —. "The Plausibility of Grounding Moral Values in God." *Reasonable Faith* (2012).

— — —. "The Problem of Miracles: A Historical and Philosophical Perspective." *Gospel Perspectives, The Miracles of Jesus.(ed.)*. Wenham D. and C. Blomberg (1986): 9-48.

— — —. "Q&A 68: The Witness of the Holy Spirit." *Reasonable Faith* (2008).

— — —. "Q&A 78: Personal Testimony of Faith." *Reasonable Faith* (2008).

— — —. "Q&A 83: Double Doctorates." *Reasonable Faith* (2008).

— — —. "Q&A 118: God's Necessity." *Reasonable Faith* (2009).

— — —. "Q&A 127: Is a Beginningless Past Actually Infinite?" *Reasonable Faith* (2009).

— — —. "Q&A 155: Debating." *Reasonable Faith* (2010).

— — —. "Q&A 370: Still More Reflections on the Sean Carroll Debate." *Reasonable Faith* (2014).

— — —. "Q&A 437: Nominalism and Natural Law." *Reasonable Faith* (2015).

— — —. "Q&A 462: Gravitational Waves Detected!" *Reasonable Faith Q&A* (2016).

— — —. "Q&A 476: Divine Psychology." *Reasonable Faith* (2016).

— — —. *Reasonable Faith: Christian Truth and Apologetics*: Crossway, 2008.

— — —. "Reflections on "Uncaused Beginnings"." *Faith and Philosophy* 27, no. 1 (2010): 72-78.

— — —. "Replies to Evan Fales: On the Empty Tomb of Jesus." (2001).

— — —. "Reply to Evan Fales: On the Empty Tomb of Jesus."

Philosophia Christi 3 (2001): 67-76.
———. *The Son Rises: Historical Evidence for the Resurrection of Jesus*: Wipf and Stock Publishers, 2000.
———. "The Scientific Kalam Cosmological Argument."
———. "Taking Tense Seriously in Differentiating Past and Future." *Faith and Philosophy* 27, no. 4 (2010): 451-56.
———. *The Tensed Theory of Time: A Critical Examination*. Vol. 293: Springer Science & Business Media, 2000.
———. *The Tenseless Theory of Time: A Critical Examination*. Vol. 294: Springer Science & Business Media, 2000.
———. "Theistic Critiques of Atheism." In *The Cambridge Companion to Atheism*, edited by Michael Martin, 69-85: Cambridge University Press, 2007.
———. *Time and Eternity: Exploring God's Relationship to Time*. Wheaton, Ill.: Crossway Books, 2001.
———. *Time and the Metaphysics of Relativity*: Springer Science & Business Media, 2001.
———. "Transcript: Existence of God (Part 13)." *Excursus On Natural Theology* (2011).
———. "Transcript: Existence of God (Part 16)." *Excursus On Natural Theology* (2011).
———. "Visions of Jesus: A Critical Assessment of Gerd Lüdemann's Hallucination Hypothesis." *Edwin Mellen Press.* (2000).
Craig, William Lane, and Sean Carroll. *God and Cosmology: William Lane Craig and Sean Carroll in Dialogue*: Fortress Press, 2016.
Craig, William Lane, Gerd Lüdemann, Paul Copan, and Ronald K Tacelli. *Jesus' Resurrection: Fact or Figment?: A Debate between William Lane Craig & Gerd Ludemann*: InterVarsity Press, 2000.
Craig, William Lane, and Massimo Pigliucci. "Does God Exist?: William Lane Craig Vs. Massimo Pigliucci Debate Transcript." http://www.reasonablefaith.org/does-god-exist-the-craig-pigliucci-debate.
Craig, William Lane, and Kevin Scharp. ""Is There Evidence for God?": William Lane Craig Vs. Kevin Scharp Debate Transcript." (2016), http://www.reasonablefaith.org/debate-is-there-evidence-for-god.
Craig, William Lane, and James D Sinclair. "The Kalam Cosmological Argument." In *The Blackwell Companion to Natural Theology*, 101-201: Wiley-Blackwell Oxford, 2009.
Craig, William Lane, and Walter Sinnott-Armstrong. *God?: A Debate between a Christian and an Atheist*: Oxford University Press, 2003.
Craig, William Lane, and Quentin Smith. *Einstein, Relativity and*

Absolute Simultaneity: Routledge, 2007.Datta, Amaresh, and Akademi Sahitya. *Encyclopaedia of Indian Literature: A-Devo*. New Delhi: Sahitya Akademi, 1987.

Davies, Martin F, Murray Griffin, and Sue Vice. "Affective Reactions to Auditory Hallucinations in Psychotic, Evangelical and Control Groups." *British Journal of Clinical Psychology* 40, no. 4 (2001): 361-70.

Davies, Paul, and Niels Henrik Gregersen. *Information and the Nature of Reality: From Physics to Metaphysics*: Cambridge University Press, 2014.

Dawson, Lorne L. "When Prophecy Fails and Faith Persists: A Theoretical Overview." *Nova Religio: The Journal of Alternative and Emergent Religions* 3, no. 1 (1999): 60-82.

Day, Samantha, and Emmanuelle Peters. "The Incidence of Schizotypy in New Religious Movements." *Personality and Individual Differences* 27, no. 1 (1999): 55-67.

Dorato, Mauro. "Review of William Lane Craig." *Time and Metaphysics of Relativity. Republished (2003) in Studies in History and Philosophy of Modern Physics* 34, no. 1 (2001): 154-58.

Douven, Igor. "Peirce on Abduction." *Stanford Encyclopedia of Philosophy* (2011).

Dov Baer ben, Samuel, Dan Ben-Amos, and Jerome R. Mintz. *In Praise of the Baal Shem Tov [Shivhei Ha-Besht] : The Earliest Collection of Legends About the Founder of Hasidism*. Bloomington: Indiana University Press, 1970.

Easwaran, Arcot. "Manthralayam for That Healing Touch " *The Hindu*, 2002, http://www.thehindu.com/thehindu/fr/2002/10/18/stories/2002101801350500.htm.

Echterhoff, Gerald, and William Hirst. "Social Influence on Memory." *Social psychology* 40, no. 3 (2009): 106-10.

Eells, Ellery. "Quentin Smith on Infinity and the Past." *Philosophy of science* (1988): 453-55.

Ehrman, Bart D. *How Jesus Became God: The Exaltation of a Jewish Preacher from Galilee*, 2014.

Fagg, Lawrence W. *The Becoming of Time: Integrating Physical and Religious Time*: Scholars Press, 1995.

Faucher, Kane X. *Metastasis and Metastability: A Deleuzian Approach to Information*: Springer Science & Business Media, 2013.

Ferreiro, Alberto. *Simon Magus in Patristic, Medieval and Early Modern Traditions*. Vol. 125: Brill, 2005.

Flavius, Josephus. "The Antiquities of the Jews, 20.97-98,"

http://lexundria.com/j_aj/20.97-20.117/wst.
Frazer, James George. "Lecture 6: The Belief in Immortality among the Other Aborigines of Australia." In *The Belief in Immortality and the Worship of the Dead. Vol. 1.* London: Macmillan, 1913.
French, Chris. "False Memories of Sexual Abuse Lead to Terrible Miscarriages of Justice." *The Guardian*, 2010.
French, Christopher C, Usman Haque, Rosie Bunton-Stasyshyn, and Rob Davis. "The "Haunt" Project: An Attempt to Build a "Haunted" Room by Manipulating Complex Electromagnetic Fields and Infrasound." *Cortex* 45, no. 5 (2009): 619-29.
Gadit, Amin A Muhammad. "Insightful Hallucination: Psychopathology or Paranormal Phenomenon?" *BMJ case reports* 2011 (2011): bcr1020103456.
Garcia, Robert K, and Nathan L King. *Is Goodness without God Good Enough?: A Debate on Faith, Secularism, and Ethics*: Rowman & Littlefield, 2009.
Glik, Deborah C. "The Redefinition of the Situation: The Social Construction of Spiritual Healing Experiences." *Sociology of Health & Illness* 12, no. 2 (1990): 151-68.
Goulet, Jean-Guy. "Ways of Knowing: Experience, Knowledge, and Power among the Dene Tha." University of Nebraska Press.
Grimby, Agneta. "Bereavement among Elderly People: Grief Reactions, Post-Bereavement Hallucinations and Quality of Life." *Acta Psychiatrica Scandinavica* 87, no. 1 (1993): 72-80.
Grindal, Bruce T. "Into the Heart of Sisala Experience: Witnessing Death Divination." *Journal of Anthropological Research* (1983): 60-80.
Hahn, Patrick D. "Dead Man Walking: Wade Davis and the Secret of the Zombie Poison." (2007), http://www.biology-online.org/articles/dead_man_walking.html.
Harris, Celia B, Helen M Paterson, and Richard I Kemp. "Collaborative Recall and Collective Memory: What Happens When We Remember Together?" *Memory* 16, no. 3 (2008): 213-30.
Harvey, Peter. *An Introduction to Buddhist Ethics: Foundations, Values and Issues*: Cambridge University Press, 2000.
Hastings, Arthur, Michael Hutton, William Braud, Constance Bennett, Ida Berk, Tracy Boynton, Carolyn Dawn, Elizabeth Ferguson, Adina Goldman, and Elyse Greene. "Psychomanteum Research: Experiences and Effects on Bereavement." *OMEGA-Journal of Death and Dying* 45, no. 3 (2002): 211-28.
Hedrick, Landon. "Heartbreak at Hilbert's Hotel." *Religious studies* 50, no. 01 (2014): 27-46.
Helm, Paul. "Time and Time Again: Two Volumes by William Lane

Craig." *Religious studies* 38, no. 04 (2002): 489-98.

Hogg, Michael A, Janice R Adelman, and Robert D Blagg. "Religion in the Face of Uncertainty: An Uncertainty-Identity Theory Account of Religiousness." *Personality and Social Psychology Review* 14, no. 1 (2010): 72-83.

Hoogendoorn, Serge P, and Piet HL Bovy. "State-of-the-Art of Vehicular Traffic Flow Modelling." *Proceedings of the Institution of Mechanical Engineers, Part I: Journal of Systems and Control Engineering* 215, no. 4 (2001): 283-303.

Houran, James, and Rense Lange. "Hauntings and Poltergeist-Like Episodes as a Confluence of Conventional Phenomena: A General Hypothesis." *Perceptual and motor skills* 83, no. 3 suppl (1996): 1307-16.

Hurtado, Larry W. "Revelatory Experiences and Religious Innovation in Earliest Christianity." *The Expository Times* 125, no. 10 (2014): 469-82.

Hyman, Frieda Clark. *The Pharisees: The Preservers of Judaism*. Jerusalem; Hewlett, NY: Gefen, 2001.

Jackson, Frank, and Philip Pettit. "Moral Functionalism, Supervenience and Reductionism." *The Philosophical Quarterly* 46, no. 182 (1996): 82-86.

Jacob, Pierre. "Intentionality." In *The Stanford Encyclopedia of Philosophy*, edited by Edward N. Zalta, 2014.

Johnson, W. J. "Guṇa." In *A Dictionary of Hinduism*: Oxford Reference, 2009.

Johnston, Francis. *Fatima: The Great Sign*: Tan Books, 1980.

Judaica, Encyclopaedia. "Death & Bereavement in Judaism: Ancient Burial Practices." (2008), https://www.jewishvirtuallibrary.org/jsource/Judaism/ancientburial.html.

— — —. "Disinterment." (2008), https://www.jewishvirtuallibrary.org/jsource/judaica/ejud_0002_0005_0_05253.html.

Kivilu, Sabakinu. "Kimbangu, Simon." In *The Encyclopaedia Africana Dictionary of African Biography, Volume Two: Sierra Leone-Zaire*, edited by L. H. Ofosu-Appiah: Reference Publications Inc., 1979.

Klinghoffer, David. *Why the Jews Rejected Jesus: The Turning Point in Western History*. New York: Doubleday, 2005.

Kyle, Richard. "When Prophets Die: The Postcharismatic Fate of New Religious Movements. Edited by Timothy Miller. Suny Series in Religious Studies. Albany, Ny: State University of New York Press, 1991." *Church History* 64, no. 03 (1995): 536-38.

Laubach, Marty. "The Social Effects of Psychism: Spiritual Experience and the Construction of Privatized Religion." *Sociology of Religion* 65, no. 3 (2004): 239-63.

Law, Stephen. "Craig's Website Response Re Our Debate " (2011), http://stephenlaw.blogspot.com.au/2011/11/craigs-website-response-re-our-debate.html.

Lowry, R. J. "Fluoridation: What the Papers Say: How Does the United Kingdom Press Treat Water Fluoridation and Does It Matter?" *Br Dent J* 189, no. 1 (2000): 14-18.

Lucian of Samosata. *Alexander the False Prophet*, http://www.tertullian.org/rpearse/lucian/lucian_alexander.htm.

Lüdemann, Gerd, and Alf Özen. *What Really Happened to Jesus: A Historical Approach to the Resurrection*. Louisville, Ky.: Westminster John Knox Press, 1995.

Lynn, Steven J, and Judith W Rhue. "The Fantasy-Prone Person: Hypnosis, Imagination, and Creativity." *Journal of Personality and Social Psychology* 51, no. 2 (1986): 404.

Maire, Catherine. "Les Convulsionnaires De Saint-Médard. Miracles, Convulsions Et Prophéties À Paris Au Xviiie Siècle." (1985).

Marsh, Elizabeth J. "Retelling Is Not the Same as Recalling Implications for Memory." *Current Directions in Psychological Science* 16, no. 1 (2007): 16-20.

Mazzoni, Giuliana, and Manila Vannucci. "Hindsight Bias, the Misinformation Effect, and False Autobiographical Memories." *Social Cognition* 25, no. 1 (2007): 203.

McAllister, Blake. "The Universe Began to Exist? Craig's Philosophical Argument for a Finite Past." Stance, 2011.

Medalia, Nahum Z, and Otto N Larsen. "Diffusion and Belief in a Collective Delusion: The Seattle Windshield Pitting Epidemic." *American Sociological Review* (1958): 180-86.

Miller, Alexander. "Naturalism 1: Cornell Realism." In *An Introduction to Contemporary Metaethics*, 138-77. Cambridge, UK; Malden, MA: Polity Press ; Distributed in the USA by Blackwell Publishers, 2003.

Milo, Ronald. "Contractarian Constructivism." *The Journal of Philosophy* 92, no. 4 (1995): 181-204.

"Miracles of Raghavendra." http://www.gururaghavendra.in/miracles1.htm.

Moreland, James Porter, and William Lane Craig. *Philosophical Foundations for a Christian Worldview*: InterVarsity Press, 2003.

Moreland, JP. "Libertarian Agency and the Craig/Grünbaum Debate About Theistic Explanation of the Initial Singularity." *American*

Catholic Philosophical Quarterly 71, no. 4 (1997): 539-54.
Morrison, Anthony P. "The Interpretation of Intrusions in Psychosis: An Integrative Cognitive Approach to Hallucinations and Delusions." *Behavioural and Cognitive Psychotherapy* 29, no. 03 (2001): 257-76.
Morriston, Wes. "Beginningless Past, Endless Future, and the Actual Infinite." *Faith and Philosophy* 27, no. 4 (2010): 439-50.
— — —. "A Critical Examination of the Kalam Cosmological Argument." (2009).
— — —. "God and the Ontological Foundation of Morality." *Religious studies* 48, no. 1 (2012): 15-34.
— — —. "Is Goodness without God Good Enough? A Debate on Faith, Secularism, and Ethics." *International Journal for Philosophy of Religion* 70, no. 1 (2011): 85-89.
Mulligan, James. *Medjugorje: A Portfolio of Images from the Early Years of the Apparitions*: CreateSpace Independent Publishing Platform, 2014.
Murphet, Howard. *Sai Baba: Man of Miracles*. London: Muller, 1971.
Nakamura, Kyoko Motomuchi. *Miraculous Stories from the Japanese Buddhist Tradition: The Nihon Ryoiki of the Monk Kyokai*: Routledge, 2013.
Narlikar, Jayant V. *An Introduction to Relativity*: Cambridge University Press, 2010.
Newburgh, William of. *The History of English Affairs*: Lulu Press, Inc, 2015.
Newell, C. *Applications of Queueing Theory*. Vol. 4: Springer Science & Business Media, 2013.
Ng, By. "Grief Revisited." *Annals-Academy of Medicine Singapore* 34, no. 5 (2005): 352.
Niedźwieńska, Agnieszka. "Distortion of Autobiographical Memories." *Applied Cognitive Psychology* 17, no. 1 (2003): 81-91.
Nye, Mary Jo. "N-Rays: An Episode in the History and Psychology of Science." *Historical studies in the physical sciences* 11, no. 1 (1980): 125-56.
O'Neill, Helen. "The Perfect Witness." *The Washington Post*, 2001, https://www.washingtonpost.com/archive/lifestyle/2001/03/04/the-perfect-witness/a7fa0461-c15c-4237-86db-52ab5069fbea.
Oaklander, L Nathan. "Craig on Mctaggart's Paradox and the Problem of Temporary Intrinsics." *Analysis* 59, no. 264 (1999): 314-18.
— — —. "Two Versions of the New B-Theory of Language." *Time, Tense, and Reference* (2003): 271.
— — —. *The Ontology of Time*. Amherst, N.Y.: Prometheus Books, 2004.

Ohayon, Maurice M. "Prevalence of Hallucinations and Their Pathological Associations in the General Population." *Psychiatry research* 97, no. 2 (2000): 153-64.

Oppy, Graham. *Arguing About Gods*. New York: Cambridge University Press, 2006.

— — —. "From the Tristram Shandy Paradox to the Christmas Shandy Paradox: Reply to Oderberg." *Ars Disputandi* 3, no. 1 (2003): 172-95.

"Oral Roberts Tells Conference He Has Raised People from the Dead." *The New York Times*, 1987, http://www.nytimes.com/1987/06/27/us/oral-roberts-tells-conference-he-has-raised-people-from-the-dead.html.

Palmquist, Chris. "No Touch Martial Arts Master Meets Reality." http://www.mixedmartialarts.com/news/No-touch-martial-arts-master-meets-reality.

Paterson, Helen M, Richard Kemp, and Sarah McIntyre. "Can a Witness Report Hearsay Evidence Unintentionally? The Effects of Discussion on Eyewitness Memory." *Psychology, Crime & Law* 18, no. 6 (2012): 505-27.

Peters, Emmanuelle, Samantha Day, Jacqueline McKenna, and Gilli Orbach. "Delusional Ideation in Religious and Psychotic Populations." *British Journal of Clinical Psychology* 38, no. 1 (1999): 83-96.

Pickel, Kerri. "When a Lie Becomes the Truth: The Effects of Self-Generated Misinformation on Eyewitness Memory." *Memory* 12, no. 1 (2004): 14-26.

Pierre, Joseph M. "Hallucinations in Nonpsychotic Disorders: Toward a Differential Diagnosis of "Hearing Voices"." *Harvard review of psychiatry* 18, no. 1 (2010): 22-35.

Price, Robert M, and Jeffery Jay Lowder. *The Empty Tomb: Jesus Beyond the Grave*: Prometheus Books, 2005.

Pruss, Alexander. "The Grim Reaper Paradox." http://alexanderpruss.blogspot.com.au/2008/01/grim-reaper-paradox.html.

Railton, Peter. "Moral Realism." *The Philosophical Review* 95, no. 2 (1986): 163-207.

Rao, T. S. Sathyanarayana, and Chittaranjan Andrade. "The Mmr Vaccine and Autism: Sensation, Refutation, Retraction, and Fraud." *Indian Journal of Psychiatry* 53, no. 2 (2011): 95-96.

Rawcliffe, Donovan Hilton. *Illusions and Delusions of the Supernatural and the Occult*: Kessinger Publishing, 2006.

Rees, Martin J. *Just Six Numbers: The Deep Forces That Shape the Universe*: Basic Books, 2000.

Rehg, William. *Insight and Solidarity: The Discourse Ethics of Jürgen Habermas*. Vol. 1: Univ of California Press, 1994.
Reyes, Reinabelle, Rachel Mandelbaum, Uros Seljak, Tobias Baldauf, James E Gunn, Lucas Lombriser, and Robert E Smith. "Confirmation of General Relativity on Large Scales from Weak Lensing and Galaxy Velocities." *Nature* 464, no. 7286 (2010): 256.
Roberts, Oral. *Twelve Greatest Miracles of My Ministry*: Pinoak Publications, 1974.
Romero, Gustavo E. "Present Time." *Foundations of Science* 20, no. 2 (2015): 135-45.
Scheidel, Walter, and Elijah Meeks. "Orbis: Stanford Geospatial Network Model of the Roman World." 2017.
Scholem, Gershom. *Sabbatai Sevi; the Mystical Messiah, 1626-1676*. Princeton, N.J: Princeton University Press, 1973.
Seul, Jeffrey R. "Ours Is the Way of God': Religion, Identity, and Intergroup Conflict." *Journal of peace research* 36, no. 5 (1999): 553-69.
Shermer, Michael, and Alex Grobman. *Denying History: Who Says the Holocaust Never Happened and Why Do They Say It?*: Univ of California Press, 2009.
Shirdi Sai Global Foundation. "Miracles of Sai Baba." http://www.saibabaofshirdi.net/.
Simmons, Shraga. "Why Jews Don't Believe in Jesus." 2004, http://www.aish.com/jw/s/48892792.html.
"Simon Kimbangu." In *Encyclopaedia Britannica*, 2013, https://www.britannica.com/biography/Simon-Kimbangu.
Simons, Daniel J, and Christopher F Chabris. "Gorillas in Our Midst: Sustained Inattentional Blindness for Dynamic Events." *Perception* 28, no. 9 (1999): 1059-74.
Sivananda, Swami. "Lord Gauranga (Sri Krishna Chaitanya Mahaprabhu)." In *Lives of Saints*. Distt. Tehri-Garhwal, U.P., Himalayas, India: Divine Life Society, 1999.
Small, Robin. "Tristram Shandy's Last Page." *The British Journal for the Philosophy of Science* 37, no. 2 (1986): 213-16.
Society for Psychical Research. *Proceedings of the Society for Psychical Research*. London: Trubner, 1883.
Solomon, Susan, and Swapnil Gupta. "The Denial of Death: A Three-Decade Long Case of Absent Grief." *Indian journal of psychological medicine* 36, no. 1 (2014): 82.
Spilka, Bernard, Kevin L Ladd, Daniel N McIntosh, Sara Milmoe, and Carl O Bickel. "The Content of Religious Experience: The Roles of Expectancy and Desirability." *The international journal for the*

psychology of religion 6, no. 2 (1996): 95-105.
Stafforini, Pablo. "William Lane Craig: A Complete List of Debates." http://www.stafforini.com/blog/william-lane-craig-a-complete-list-of-debates/.
Stark, Rodney, and Reid L Neilson. *The Rise of Mormonism*: Columbia University Press, 2012.
Stillings, Neil A, Steven W Weisler, Christopher H Chase, Mark H Feinstein, Jay L Garfield, and Edwina L Rissland. *Cognitive Science: An Introduction*: MIT press, 1995.
Stolz, Jörg. ""All Things Are Possible": Towards a Sociological Explanation of Pentecostal Miracles and Healings." *Sociology of Religion* 72, no. 4 (2011): 456-82.
Stone, Anna. "An Avowal of Prior Scepticism Enhances the Credibility of an Account of a Paranormal Event." *Journal of Language and Social Psychology* (2013): 0261927X13512115.
Stratton-Lake, Philip. "Intuitionism in Ethics." In *The Stanford Encyclopedia of Philosophy* edited by Edward N. Zalta, 2016.
Swingrover, Louis J. "Difficulties with William Lane Craig's Arguments for Finitism," 2014, http://www.academia.edu/7068171/Difficulties_With_William_Lane_Craigs_Arguments_for_Finitism
Szuchewycz, Bohdan. "Evidentiality in Ritual Discourse: The Social Construction of Religious Meaning." *Language in Society* 23, no. 03 (1994): 389-410.
Talarico, Jennifer M, and David C Rubin. "Confidence, Not Consistency, Characterizes Flashbulb Memories." *Psychological Science* 14, no. 5 (2003): 455-61.
Temin, Peter. "The Economy of the Early Roman Empire." *The Journal of economic perspectives* 20, no. 1 (2006): 133-51.
Tranquillus, C. Suetonius. "The Life of Vespasian, 7:2-3." In *The Lives of the Caesars*.
Ullmann, F. "The Testimony of Three Witnesses." *Times and Seasons* 3, no. 21 (1841): 895-910.
Verellen, Franciscus. ""Evidential Miracles in Support of Taoism": The Inversion of a Buddhist Apologetic Tradition in Late Tang China." *T'oung Pao* (1992): 217-63.
Vukicevic, Meri, and Kerry Fitzmaurice. "Butterflies and Black Lacy Patterns: The Prevalence and Characteristics of Charles Bonnet Hallucinations in an Australian Population." *Clinical & experimental ophthalmology* 36, no. 7 (2008): 659-65.
Wagner, Robin Beth. *Buddhism, Biography and Power: A Study of Daoxuan's Continued Lives of Eminent Monks*. Vol. 1995: Harvard

University, 1995.
Wallace, Alfred Russel. *Miracles and Modern Spiritualism* London: G. Redway, 1896.
Wielenberg, Erik J. "An Inconsistency in Craig's Defence of the Moral Argument."
Wilkins, Michael J., and James Porter Moreland. "Did Jesus Rise from the Dead?" In *Jesus under Fire: Modern Scholarship Reinvents the Historical Jesus*. Grand Rapids, Mich.: Zondervan, 1995.
Wilson, Krissy, and Christopher C French. "Memory Conformity and Paranormal Belief." Paper presented at the The Parapsychological Association Convention 2004: Proceedings of Presented Papers, 2004.
— — —. "The Relationship between Susceptibility to False Memories, Dissociativity, and Paranormal Belief and Experience." *Personality and Individual Differences* 41, no. 8 (2006): 1493-502.
Wirth, Daniel P. "The Significance of Belief and Expectancy within the Spiritual Healing Encounter." *Social Science & Medicine* 41, no. 2 (1995): 249-60.
Ysseldyk, Renate, Kimberly Matheson, and Hymie Anisman. "Religiosity as Identity: Toward an Understanding of Religion from a Social Identity Perspective." *Personality and Social Psychology Review* 14, no. 1 (2010): 60-71.
Yu, Chun-fang. "Eye on Religion: Miracles in the Chinese Buddhist Tradition." *Southern medical journal* 100, no. 12 (2007): 1243-45.
Zaki, Pearl. *Our Lord's Mother Visits Egypt in 1968 and 1969*: St. Mary Coptic Orthodox Church, 1982.
Zeitun-eg. "Our Lady Appears in Assiut, Upper Egypt." http://www.zeitun-eg.org/assiut.htm.
Zkchong, Lorenz Attractor (2010), https://titanlab.org/2010/04/08/lorenz-attractor/.
Zygmunt, Joseph F. "Prophetic Failure and Chiliastic Identity: The Case of Jehovah's Witnesses." *American Journal of Sociology* (1970): 926-48.

ENDNOTES

[1] William Lane Craig, "Q&A 78: Personal Testimony of Faith," *Reasonable Faith* (2008).
[2] ———, "Curriculum Vitae."
[3] ———, "Q&A 83: Double Doctorates," *Reasonable Faith* (2008).
[4] Pablo Stafforini, "William Lane Craig: A Complete List of Debates," http://www.stafforini.com/blog/william-lane-craig-a-complete-list-of-debates/.
[5] William Lane Craig, "Q&A 155: Debating," *Reasonable Faith* (2010).
[6] "About Reasonable Faith," http://www.reasonablefaith.org/about-reasonable-faith.
[7] ———, *Reasonable Faith: Christian Truth and Apologetics* (Crossway, 2008), 43-6.
[8] Ibid., 48.
[9] ———, "Q&A 68: The Witness of the Holy Spirit," *Reasonable Faith* (2008).
[10] Craig, *Reasonable Faith: Christian Truth and Apologetics*, 58.
[11] Ibid., 56.
[12] William Lane Craig, *The Kalam Cosmological Argument* (Wipf and Stock Publishers, 2000).
[13] Ibid., 63-4.
[14] William Lane Craig and James D Sinclair, "The Kalam Cosmological Argument," in *The Blackwell Companion to Natural Theology* (Wiley-Blackwell Oxford, 2009), 183-4.
[15] William Lane Craig, "Graham Oppy on the Kalām Cosmological Argument," *Sophia* 32, no. 1 (1993).
[16] ———, *The Tensed Theory of Time: A Critical Examination*, vol. 293 (Springer Science & Business Media, 2000), 22.
[17] Ibid., 68.
[18] L. Nathan Oaklander, "Two Versions of the New B-Theory of Language," *Time, Tense, and Reference* (2003).
[19] L. Nathan Oaklander, *The Ontology of Time* (Amherst, N.Y.: Prometheus Books, 2004), 287-8.
[20] Note that I have changed Oaklander's use of 'A-sentence' and 'B-

sentence' to 'tensed' and 'tenseless' sentence respectively, to minimise use of unnecessary jargon.

[21] Craig, *The Tensed Theory of Time: A Critical Examination*, 78.
[22] Ibid., 80.
[23] Ibid., 95.
[24] William Lane Craig, *The Tenseless Theory of Time: A Critical Examination*, vol. 294 (Springer Science & Business Media, 2000), 8.
[25] David Bourget and David J Chalmers, "What Do Philosophers Believe?," *Philosophical Studies* 170, no. 3 (2014): 38.
[26] Craig, *The Tensed Theory of Time: A Critical Examination*, 62-3.
[27] Ibid., 60.
[28] Ibid., 58.
[29] Ibid., 58-9.
[30] Ibid., 22.
[31] Ibid., 220.
[32] William Lane Craig, *Time and the Metaphysics of Relativity* (Springer Science & Business Media, 2001), 186.
[33] ———, "Q&A 437: Nominalism and Natural Law," *Reasonable Faith* (2015).
[34] Craig, *The Tensed Theory of Time: A Critical Examination*, 131.
[35] Ibid., 138.
[36] Ibid., 164.
[37] Paul Helm, "Time and Time Again: Two Volumes by William Lane Craig," *Religious studies* 38, no. 04 (2002): 496.
[38] Craig, *The Tensed Theory of Time: A Critical Examination*, 139-40.
[39] Ibid., 148.
[40] Ibid., 152.
[41] Ibid., 159.
[42] Ibid., 160.
[43] Oaklander, *The Ontology of Time*, 236.
[44] Craig, *The Tensed Theory of Time: A Critical Examination*, 161.
[45] Ibid., 162.
[46] Ibid., 163.
[47] Jayant V Narlikar, *An Introduction to Relativity* (Cambridge University Press, 2010), 17-8.
[48] Craig, *The Tenseless Theory of Time: A Critical Examination*, 74.
[49] Ibid., 83.
[50] Narlikar, *An Introduction to Relativity*, 34-41.

[51] Craig, *The Tenseless Theory of Time: A Critical Examination*, 126.
[52] Gustavo E. Romero, "Present Time," *Foundations of Science* 20, no. 2 (2015): 4.
[53] Estelle Asmodelle, "Tests of General Relativity: A Review," *arXiv preprint arXiv:1705.04397* (2017).
[54] Narlikar, *An Introduction to Relativity*, 146-9.
[55] Reinabelle Reyes et al., "Confirmation of General Relativity on Large Scales from Weak Lensing and Galaxy Velocities," *Nature* 464, no. 7286 (2010).
[56] Benjamin P Abbott et al., "Observation of Gravitational Waves from a Binary Black Hole Merger," *Physical review letters* 116, no. 6 (2016).
[57] Narlikar, *An Introduction to Relativity*, 158-9.
[58] William Lane Craig, "Q&A 462: Gravitational Waves Detected!," *Reasonable Faith Q&A* (2016).
[59] Craig, *Time and the Metaphysics of Relativity*, 189.
[60] ———, *The Tenseless Theory of Time: A Critical Examination*, 142; William Lane Craig, "Apologetics Training - Advice to Christian Apologists," *Reasonable Faith*.
[61] Craig, *Time and the Metaphysics of Relativity*, 189.
[62] Ibid., 190.
[63] Ibid., 191.
[64] Ibid., 192.
[65] William Lane Craig and Quentin Smith, *Einstein, Relativity and Absolute Simultaneity* (Routledge, 2007), 125.
[66] Craig and Sinclair, "The Kalam Cosmological Argument," 192.
[67] Romero, "Present Time," 5.
[68] Craig, *The Tenseless Theory of Time: A Critical Examination*, 203.
[69] Ibid., 202.
[70] Ibid., 204.
[71] Ibid., 206.
[72] Ibid., 211.
[73] Ibid., 208.
[74] Ibid., 150.
[75] Ibid., 159.
[76] Helm, "Time and Time Again: Two Volumes by William Lane Craig," 493.
[77] Craig, *The Tenseless Theory of Time: A Critical Examination*, 161.
[78] Ibid., 151.

[79] ———, *The Tensed Theory of Time: A Critical Examination*, 155.
[80] Oaklander, *The Ontology of Time*, 104-12.
[81] Craig, *The Tensed Theory of Time: A Critical Examination*, 213.
[82] L. Nathan Oaklander, "Craig on McTaggart's Paradox and the Problem of Temporary Intrinsics," *Analysis* 59, no. 264 (1999): 318.
[83] William Lane Craig, "Oaklander on McTaggart and Intrinsic Change," *Analysis* 59, no. 264 (1999): 320.
[84] Craig, *The Tensed Theory of Time: A Critical Examination*, 213-4.
[85] Ibid., 214.
[86] Ibid., 238-9.
[87] Ibid., 243.
[88] Ibid., 245.
[89] Ibid., 247.
[90] Ibid., 247-8.
[91] Ibid., 194.
[92] Ibid., 246.
[93] Helm, "Time and Time Again: Two Volumes by William Lane Craig," 496.
[94] Craig and Sinclair, "The Kalam Cosmological Argument," 108.
[95] Ibid., 109.
[96] Landon Hedrick, "Heartbreak at Hilbert's Hotel," *Religious studies* 50, no. 01 (2014): 32.
[97] Craig and Sinclair, "The Kalam Cosmological Argument," 110.
[98] Wes Morriston, "Beginningless Past, Endless Future, and the Actual Infinite," *Faith and Philosophy* 27, no. 4 (2010): 441.
[99] Willian Lane Craig, "Debate on the Kalam Argument," http://www.reasonablefaith.org/debate-on-the-kalam-argument.
[100] Blake McAllister, "The Universe Began to Exist? Craig's Philosophical Argument for a Finite Past," (Stance, 2011), 111.
[101] Craig, "Graham Oppy on the Kalām Cosmological Argument."
[102] McAllister, "The Universe Began to Exist? Craig's Philosophical Argument for a Finite Past," 113.
[103] Louis J Swingrover, "Difficulties with William Lane Craig's Arguments for Finitism," (2014), 12-3.
[104] Craig and Sinclair, "The Kalam Cosmological Argument," 112.
[105] Ibid., 112-3.
[106] Ibid., 113.
[107] Alexander Pruss, "The Grim Reaper Paradox,"

http://alexanderpruss.blogspot.com.au/2008/01/grim-reaper-paradox.html.
[108] Craig and Sinclair, "The Kalam Cosmological Argument," 115-6.
[109] Morriston, "Beginningless Past, Endless Future, and the Actual Infinite," 446, 49.
[110] Craig, "Debate on the Kalam Argument."
[111] Paul Copan and William Lane Craig, *The Kalam Cosmological Argument, Volume 1: Philosophical Arguments for the Finitude of the Past*, vol. 1 (Bloomsbury Publishing USA, 2017), 306.
[112] Craig, "Graham Oppy on the Kalām Cosmological Argument."
[113] ———, *The Tensed Theory of Time: A Critical Examination*, 228.
[114] William Lane Craig, "Q&A 127: Is a Beginningless Past Actually Infinite?," *Reasonable Faith* (2009).
[115] ———, "Taking Tense Seriously in Differentiating Past and Future," *Faith and Philosophy* 27, no. 4 (2010).
[116] Ibid.
[117] Ibid.
[118] Craig, *The Tensed Theory of Time: A Critical Examination*, 179.
[119] Hedrick, "Heartbreak at Hilbert's Hotel," 42.
[120] Craig and Sinclair, "The Kalam Cosmological Argument," 117.
[121] Ibid., 117-9.
[122] Ibid., 119.
[123] Ibid., 117.
[124] Ibid., 118.
[125] Ibid.
[126] Ibid.
[127] Ibid.
[128] Ibid., 119.
[129] Ibid.
[130] Ibid., 120.
[131] Ibid., 121.
[132] Craig, "Graham Oppy on the Kalām Cosmological Argument."
[133] Ibid.
[134] Robin Small, "Tristram Shandy's Last Page," *The British Journal for the Philosophy of Science* 37, no. 2 (1986).
[135] Craig and Sinclair, "The Kalam Cosmological Argument," 121.
[136] Ellery Eells, "Quentin Smith on Infinity and the Past," *Philosophy of science* (1988).

[137] Graham Oppy, "From the Tristram Shandy Paradox to the Christmas Shandy Paradox: Reply to Oderberg," *Ars Disputandi* 3, no. 1 (2003): 8-9.
[138] Craig and Sinclair, "The Kalam Cosmological Argument," 121-2.
[139] Ibid., 117.
[140] Craig, "Graham Oppy on the Kalām Cosmological Argument."
[141] Arvind Borde, Alan H Guth, and Alexander Vilenkin, "Inflationary Spacetimes Are Not Past-Complete," *arXiv preprint gr-qc/0110012* (2001): 3.
[142] William Lane Craig, "The Kalam Cosmological Argument," (2015).
[143] Craig, *Time and the Metaphysics of Relativity*, 150.
[144] Craig and Sinclair, "The Kalam Cosmological Argument," 114.
[145] Craig, *Time and the Metaphysics of Relativity*, 150.
[146] Ibid., 187.
[147] Ibid., 154.
[148] Ibid., 160.
[149] Ibid., 193.
[150] Mauro Dorato, "Review of William Lane Craig," *Time and Metaphysics of Relativity*. Republished (2003) in Studies in History and Philosophy of Modern Physics 34, no. 1 (2001): 4.
[151] Graham Oppy, *Arguing About Gods* (New York: Cambridge University Press, 2006), 146.
[152] Craig, "Graham Oppy on the Kalām Cosmological Argument."
[153] Craig and Sinclair, "The Kalam Cosmological Argument," 133.
[154] Ibid., 134.
[155] William Lane Craig, "The Scientific Kalam Cosmological Argument."
[156] Craig and Sinclair, "The Kalam Cosmological Argument," 191.
[157] William Lane Craig and Sean Carroll, *God and Cosmology: William Lane Craig and Sean Carroll in Dialogue* (Fortress Press, 2016), 42.
[158] Craig and Sinclair, "The Kalam Cosmological Argument," 179.
[159] William Lane Craig, ""Honesty, Transparency, Full Disclosure" and the Borde-Guth-Vilenkin Theorem," *Reasonable Faith* (2013).
[160] Craig and Carroll, *God and Cosmology: William Lane Craig and Sean Carroll in Dialogue*, 29.
[161] See for example Craig, *Time and the Metaphysics of Relativity*, 191.
[162] Craig and Sinclair, "The Kalam Cosmological Argument," 182.
[163] William Lane Craig, "Must the Beginning of the Universe Have a Personal Cause?," *Faith and Philosophy* 19, no. 1 (2002).
[164] William Lane Craig, "The Caused Beginning of the Universe: A

Response to Quentin Smith," *British Journal for the Philosophy of Science* (1993).
[165] Ibid.
[166] Craig, "Must the Beginning of the Universe Have a Personal Cause?."
[167] ———, "The Caused Beginning of the Universe: A Response to Quentin Smith."
[168] ———, "Must the Beginning of the Universe Have a Personal Cause?," 3.
[169] Craig and Sinclair, "The Kalam Cosmological Argument," 186.
[170] Wes Morriston, "A Critical Examination of the Kalam Cosmological Argument," (2009): 102.
[171] Craig, "Graham Oppy on the Kalām Cosmological Argument," 7.
[172] William Lane Craig, "Reflections on "Uncaused Beginnings"," *Faith and Philosophy* 27, no. 1 (2010).
[173] Ibid.
[174] Craig and Sinclair, "The Kalam Cosmological Argument," 192.
[175] Craig and Carroll, *God and Cosmology: William Lane Craig and Sean Carroll in Dialogue*, 26-7.
[176] Craig, "The Caused Beginning of the Universe: A Response to Quentin Smith," 1993.
[177] Craig and Sinclair, "The Kalam Cosmological Argument," 192.
[178] Ibid., 193.
[179] Lawrence W Fagg, *The Becoming of Time: Integrating Physical and Religious Time* (Scholars Press, 1995), 85.
[180] Ibid., 81.
[181] Haridas Chaudhuri, "The Concept of Brahman in Hindu Philosophy," *Philosophy East and West* 4, no. 1 (1954): 47-8.
[182] Anthony Aguirre, Brendan Foster, and Zeeya Merali, *It from Bit or Bit from It?: On Physics and Information* (Springer, 2015), 129.
[183] Paul Davies and Niels Henrik Gregersen, *Information and the Nature of Reality: From Physics to Metaphysics* (Cambridge University Press, 2014), 49.
[184] Kane X Faucher, *Metastasis and Metastability: A Deleuzian Approach to Information* (Springer Science & Business Media, 2013), 8.
[185] Carmen Blacker, Michael Loewe, and J Martin Plumley, *Ancient Cosmologies* (F Allen & Unwin, 1975), 122.
[186] W. J. Johnson, "Guṇa," in *A Dictionary of Hinduism* (Oxford Reference, 2009).

[187] Craig and Carroll, *God and Cosmology: William Lane Craig and Sean Carroll in Dialogue*, 37.
[188] Craig and Sinclair, "The Kalam Cosmological Argument," 193.
[189] Craig, *The Tensed Theory of Time: A Critical Examination*, 246.
[190] Craig and Sinclair, "The Kalam Cosmological Argument," 194.
[191] Craig, "Must the Beginning of the Universe Have a Personal Cause?."
[192] JP Moreland, "Libertarian Agency and the Craig/Grünbaum Debate About Theistic Explanation of the Initial Singularity," *American Catholic Philosophical Quarterly* 71, no. 4 (1997): 548.
[193] Craig and Sinclair, "The Kalam Cosmological Argument," 194.
[194] Ibid.
[195] William Lane Craig, *Time and Eternity: Exploring God's Relationship to Time* (Wheaton, Ill.: Crossway Books, 2001), 156.
[196] Moreland, "Libertarian Agency and the Craig/Grünbaum Debate About Theistic Explanation of the Initial Singularity," 548-9.
[197] James Porter Moreland and William Lane Craig, *Philosophical Foundations for a Christian Worldview* (InterVarsity Press, 2003), 283-9.
[198] Bourget and Chalmers, "What Do Philosophers Believe?."
[199] Moreland and Craig, *Philosophical Foundations for a Christian Worldview*, 239.
[200] Ibid.
[201] Ibid., 242.
[202] Ibid., 261.
[203] Ibid.
[204] See for example Neil A Stillings et al., *Cognitive Science: An Introduction* (MIT press, 1995).
[205] Craig has said "When I wrote *The Kalam Cosmological Argument* I was vaguely aware of theories of tenseless time but did not really take them seriously. Since then I have come to appreciate that tenseless time theorists like Oppy himself need to be taken very seriously." Craig, "Graham Oppy on the Kalām Cosmological Argument."
[206] ———, *The Tensed Theory of Time: A Critical Examination*, 165.
[207] Craig and Sinclair, "The Kalam Cosmological Argument," 186.
[208] William Lane Craig, "Has the Multiverse Replaced God?."
[209] Craig and Carroll, *God and Cosmology: William Lane Craig and Sean Carroll in Dialogue*, 32.
[210] Craig, *Reasonable Faith: Christian Truth and Apologetics*, 158.
[211] WIllIam Lane Craig, "Q&A 476: Divine Psychology," *Reasonable Faith*

(2016).
[212] Robin Collins, "The Teleological Argument: An Exploration of the Fine-Tuning of the Universe," in *The Blackwell Companion to Natural Theology* (2009), 252.
[213] Craig, *Reasonable Faith: Christian Truth and Apologetics*, 160.
[214] Ibid., 159.
[215] William Lane Craig, "Transcript: Existence of God (Part 16)," *Excursus On Natural Theology* (2011).
[216] Willian Lane Craig, "Q&A 370: Still More Reflections on the Sean Carroll Debate," *Reasonable Faith* (2014).
[217] Craig, "Q&A 476: Divine Psychology."
[218] Sean Carroll, "Does the Universe Need God," *The Blackwell companion to science and christianity* (2012): 15-6.
[219] Martin J Rees, *Just Six Numbers: The Deep Forces That Shape the Universe* (Basic Books, 2000), 30-1.
[220] Ibid., 48-51.
[221] Ibid., 86-9.
[222] Ibid., 125-6.
[223] Ibid., 115.
[224] Ibid., 135-6.
[225] Randall D Beer, "Autopoiesis and Cognition in the Game of Life," *Artificial Life* 10, no. 3 (2004).
[226] *Animated spaceships.gif*, (2009).
[227] Collins, "The Teleological Argument: An Exploration of the Fine-Tuning of the Universe," 248.
[228] Ibid., 253.
[229] Craig, *Reasonable Faith: Christian Truth and Apologetics*, 164.
[230] Collins, "The Teleological Argument: An Exploration of the Fine-Tuning of the Universe," 245.
[231] Zkchong, Lorenz Attractor (2010), https://titan-lab.org/2010/04/08/lorenz-attractor/.
[232] ———, "The Teleological Argument: An Exploration of the Fine-Tuning of the Universe," 262.
[233] Craig, *Reasonable Faith: Christian Truth and Apologetics*, 166.
[234] Ibid., 171.
[235] William Lane Craig, "Does God Exist?," http://www.reasonablefaith.org/does-god-exist-1#ixzz4LstLFjFs.
[236] Moreland and Craig, *Philosophical Foundations for a Christian*

Worldview, 530-1.

[237] Robert K Garcia and Nathan L King, *Is Goodness without God Good Enough?: A Debate on Faith, Secularism, and Ethics* (Rowman & Littlefield, 2009), 121.

[238] Wes Morriston, "God and the Ontological Foundation of Morality," *Religious studies* 48, no. 1 (2012): 29.

[239] Craig, *Reasonable Faith: Christian Truth and Apologetics*, 178.

[240] Morriston, "God and the Ontological Foundation of Morality," 30.

[241] William Lane Craig and Massimo Pigliucci, "Does God Exist?: William Lane Craig Vs. Massimo Pigliucci Debate Transcript," http://www.reasonablefaith.org/does-god-exist-the-craig-pigliucci-debate.

[242] Moreland and Craig, *Philosophical Foundations for a Christian Worldview*, 398.

[243] Ibid.

[244] William Lane Craig, "Theistic Critiques of Atheism," in *The Cambridge Companion to Atheism*, ed. Michael Martin (Cambridge University Press, 2007), 75.

[245] Stephen Law, "Craig's Website Response Re Our Debate "(2011), http://stephenlaw.blogspot.com.au/2011/11/craigs-website-response-re-our-debate.html.

[246] Garcia and King, *Is Goodness without God Good Enough?: A Debate on Faith, Secularism, and Ethics*, 30.

[247] Moreland and Craig, *Philosophical Foundations for a Christian Worldview*, 491.

[248] Morriston, "God and the Ontological Foundation of Morality," 21.

[249] Moreland and Craig, *Philosophical Foundations for a Christian Worldview*, 395.

[250] Garcia and King, *Is Goodness without God Good Enough?: A Debate on Faith, Secularism, and Ethics*, 173.

[251] Ibid., 169.

[252] Wes Morriston, "Is Goodness without God Good Enough? A Debate on Faith, Secularism, and Ethics," *International Journal for Philosophy of Religion* 70, no. 1 (2011): 86.

[253] Morriston, "God and the Ontological Foundation of Morality," 22.

[254] Garcia and King, *Is Goodness without God Good Enough?: A Debate on Faith, Secularism, and Ethics*, 172.

[255] Ibid., 171.

[256] Morriston, "God and the Ontological Foundation of Morality," 32.
[257] Moreland and Craig, *Philosophical Foundations for a Christian Worldview*, 491.
[258] Ibid; Garcia and King, *Is Goodness without God Good Enough?: A Debate on Faith, Secularism, and Ethics*, 31.
[259] Michael Coren, "William Lane Craig Vs Michael Payton: Does God Exist?," (2009), see video at 19:42 mark.
[260] Craig, *Reasonable Faith: Christian Truth and Apologetics*, 173-4.
[261] William Lane Craig and Walter Sinnott-Armstrong, *God?: A Debate between a Christian and an Atheist* (Oxford University Press, 2003), 33.
[262] Peter Railton, "Moral Realism," *The Philosophical Review* 95, no. 2 (1986).
[263] Frank Jackson and Philip Pettit, "Moral Functionalism, Supervenience and Reductionism," *The Philosophical Quarterly* 46, no. 182 (1996).
[264] Alexander Miller, "Naturalism 1: Cornell Realism," in *An Introduction to Contemporary Metaethics* (Cambridge, UK; Malden, MA: Polity Press ; Distributed in the USA by Blackwell Publishers, 2003).
[265] William Rehg, *Insight and Solidarity: The Discourse Ethics of Jürgen Habermas*, vol. 1 (Univ of California Press, 1994).
[266] Ronald Milo, "Contractarian Constructivism," *The Journal of Philosophy* 92, no. 4 (1995).
[267] Philip Stratton-Lake, "Intuitionism in Ethics," in *The Stanford Encyclopedia of Philosophy* ed. Edward N. Zalta (2016).
[268] Peter Harvey, *An Introduction to Buddhist Ethics: Foundations, Values and Issues* (Cambridge University Press, 2000).
[269] William Lane Craig and Kevin Scharp, ""Is There Evidence for God?": William Lane Craig Vs. Kevin Scharp Debate Transcript,"(2016), http://www.reasonablefaith.org/debate-is-there-evidence-for-god.
[270] William Lane Craig, "Debate with Dr. Kevin Scharp Part 3," (2016).
[271] Craig, *Reasonable Faith: Christian Truth and Apologetics*, 177.
[272] William Lane Craig, "The Plausibility of Grounding Moral Values in God," *Reasonable Faith* (2012).
[273] Bourget and Chalmers, "What Do Philosophers Believe?."
[274] Garcia and King, *Is Goodness without God Good Enough?: A Debate on Faith, Secularism, and Ethics*.
[275] Ibid., 31.
[276] Morriston, "God and the Ontological Foundation of Morality," 24.
[277] William Lane Craig, "Navigating Sam Harris' the Moral Landscape,"

Reasonable Faith (2012).
[278] ———, "The Indispensability of Theological Meta-Ethical Foundations for Morality," *Foundations* 5(1997).
[279] Morriston, "God and the Ontological Foundation of Morality," 24.
[280] Ibid.: 25.
[281] Craig, "Navigating Sam Harris' the Moral Landscape."
[282] ———, "The Indispensability of Theological Meta-Ethical Foundations for Morality."
[283] Bourget and Chalmers, "What Do Philosophers Believe?."
[284] Garcia and King, *Is Goodness without God Good Enough?: A Debate on Faith, Secularism, and Ethics*, 135.
[285] Craig, "Navigating Sam Harris' the Moral Landscape."
[286] ———, *Reasonable Faith: Christian Truth and Apologetics*, 177.
[287] ———, "The Indispensability of Theological Meta-Ethical Foundations for Morality."
[288] ———, *Reasonable Faith: Christian Truth and Apologetics*, 176.
[289] Ibid.
[290] Garcia and King, *Is Goodness without God Good Enough?: A Debate on Faith, Secularism, and Ethics*, 127.
[291] Law, "Craig's Website Response Re Our Debate."
[292] Garcia and King, *Is Goodness without God Good Enough?: A Debate on Faith, Secularism, and Ethics*, 173.
[293] Craig, *Reasonable Faith: Christian Truth and Apologetics*, 177.
[294] Moreland and Craig, *Philosophical Foundations for a Christian Worldview*, 395.
[295] Craig, *Reasonable Faith: Christian Truth and Apologetics*, 181.
[296] ———, "Navigating Sam Harris' the Moral Landscape."
[297] Garcia and King, *Is Goodness without God Good Enough?: A Debate on Faith, Secularism, and Ethics*, 135.
[298] Erik J Wielenberg, "An Inconsistency in Craig's Defence of the Moral Argument," 70.
[299] Moreland and Craig, *Philosophical Foundations for a Christian Worldview*, 532.
[300] Morriston, "God and the Ontological Foundation of Morality," 31.
[301] Igor Douven, "Peirce on Abduction," *Stanford Encyclopedia of Philosophy* (2011).
[302] Michael J. Wilkins and James Porter Moreland, "Did Jesus Rise from the Dead?," in *Jesus under Fire: Modern Scholarship Reinvents the*

Historical Jesus (Grand Rapids, Mich.: Zondervan, 1995).
[303] Ibid.
[304] William Lane Craig et al., *Jesus' Resurrection: Fact or Figment?: A Debate between William Lane Craig & Gerd Ludemann* (InterVarsity Press, 2000), 32-4.
[305] Ibid; William Lane Craig, *Assessing the New Testament Evidence for the Historicity of the Resurrection of Jesus* (Lewiston, N.Y., USA: E. Mellen Press, 1989); ———, *Did Jesus Rise from the Dead?* (Impact 360 Institute, 2014).
[306] Craig, *Reasonable Faith: Christian Truth and Apologetics*, 298.
[307] Gerd Lüdemann and Alf Özen, *What Really Happened to Jesus: A Historical Approach to the Resurrection* (Louisville, Ky.: Westminster John Knox Press, 1995).
[308] Bart D. Ehrman, *How Jesus Became God: The Exaltation of a Jewish Preacher from Galilee* (2014).
[309] Robert M Price and Jeffery Jay Lowder, *The Empty Tomb: Jesus Beyond the Grave* (Prometheus Books, 2005).
[310] Encyclopaedia Judaica, "Death & Bereavement in Judaism: Ancient Burial Practices,"(2008), https://www.jewishvirtuallibrary.org/jsource/Judaism/ancientburial.html.
[311] ———, "Disinterment,"(2008), https://www.jewishvirtuallibrary.org/jsource/judaica/ejud_0002_0005_0_05253.html.
[312] Craig et al., *Jesus' Resurrection: Fact or Figment?: A Debate between William Lane Craig & Gerd Ludemann*, 178.
[313] Ibid.
[314] William L Craig, *The Son Rises: Historical Evidence for the Resurrection of Jesus* (Wipf and Stock Publishers, 2000), 86.
[315] Ibid.
[316] Ibid., 86.
[317] BibleHub, "John 20:7 Parallel Verses," http://biblehub.com/john/20-7.htm.
[318] Craig et al., *Jesus' Resurrection: Fact or Figment?: A Debate between William Lane Craig & Gerd Ludemann*, 170.
[319] Craig, *Did Jesus Rise from the Dead?*, 55.
[320] ———, *Assessing the New Testament Evidence for the Historicity of the Resurrection of Jesus*, 376-7.

[321] Ibid.
[322] ———, *The Son Rises: Historical Evidence for the Resurrection of Jesus*, 86.
[323] Wilkins and Moreland, "Did Jesus Rise from the Dead?."
[324] William Lane Craig, "The Historical Argument for the Resurrection of Jesus During the Deist Controversy," (1988): 349.
[325] Craig, *Did Jesus Rise from the Dead?*, 16.
[326] William Lane Craig, "Replies to Evan Fales: On the Empty Tomb of Jesus," (2001): 6.
[327] Craig, *Did Jesus Rise from the Dead?*, 15-6.
[328] Craig et al., *Jesus' Resurrection: Fact or Figment?: A Debate between William Lane Craig & Gerd Ludemann*, 190.
[329] Anthony P Morrison, "The Interpretation of Intrusions in Psychosis: An Integrative Cognitive Approach to Hallucinations and Delusions," *Behavioural and Cognitive Psychotherapy* 29, no. 03 (2001).
[330] Maurice M Ohayon, "Prevalence of Hallucinations and Their Pathological Associations in the General Population," *Psychiatry research* 97, no. 2 (2000).
[331] Martin F Davies, Murray Griffin, and Sue Vice, "Affective Reactions to Auditory Hallucinations in Psychotic, Evangelical and Control Groups," *British Journal of Clinical Psychology* 40, no. 4 (2001).
[332] Joseph M. Pierre, "Hallucinations in Nonpsychotic Disorders: Toward a Differential Diagnosis of "Hearing Voices"," *Harvard review of psychiatry* 18, no. 1 (2010).
[333] Meri Vukicevic and Kerry Fitzmaurice, "Butterflies and Black Lacy Patterns: The Prevalence and Characteristics of Charles Bonnet Hallucinations in an Australian Population," *Clinical & experimental ophthalmology* 36, no. 7 (2008).
[334] Christopher Baethge, "Grief Hallucinations: True or Pseudo? Serious or Not?," *Psychopathology* 35, no. 5 (2002).
[335] Agneta Grimby, "Bereavement among Elderly People: Grief Reactions, Post-Bereavement Hallucinations and Quality of Life," *Acta Psychiatrica Scandinavica* 87, no. 1 (1993).
[336] Samantha Day and Emmanuelle Peters, "The Incidence of Schizotypy in New Religious Movements," *Personality and Individual Differences* 27, no. 1 (1999).
[337] Emmanuelle Peters et al., "Delusional Ideation in Religious and Psychotic Populations," *British Journal of Clinical Psychology* 38, no. 1

(1999).

[338] Steven J Lynn and Judith W Rhue, "The Fantasy-Prone Person: Hypnosis, Imagination, and Creativity," *Journal of Personality and Social Psychology* 51, no. 2 (1986).

[339] Robert E Bartholomew, Keith Basterfield, and George S Howard, "UFO Abductees and Contactees: Psychopathology or Fantasy Proneness?," *Professional Psychology: Research and Practice* 22, no. 3 (1991).

[340] Marty Laubach, "The Social Effects of Psychism: Spiritual Experience and the Construction of Privatized Religion," *Sociology of Religion* 65, no. 3 (2004).

[341] William Lane Craig, "Contemporary Scholarship and the Historical Evidence for the Resurrection of Jesus Christ," *Truth* 1(1985).

[342] ———, "Visions of Jesus: A Critical Assessment of Gerd Lüdemann's Hallucination Hypothesis," *Edwin Mellen Press.* (2000).

[343] Craig, "Contemporary Scholarship and the Historical Evidence for the Resurrection of Jesus Christ."

[344] See for example Ehrman, *How Jesus Became God: The Exaltation of a Jewish Preacher from Galilee.*

[345] William Lane Craig, "Reply to Evan Fales: On the Empty Tomb of Jesus," *Philosophia Christi* 3(2001): 3.

[346] Craig, *Did Jesus Rise from the Dead?*, 51.

[347] Craig et al., *Jesus' Resurrection: Fact or Figment?: A Debate between William Lane Craig & Gerd Ludemann*, 182-3.

[348] Yoram Bilu, ""We Want to See Our King": Apparitions in Messianic Habad," *Ethos* 41, no. 1 (2013).

[349] Larry W Hurtado, "Revelatory Experiences and Religious Innovation in Earliest Christianity," *The Expository Times* 125, no. 10 (2014).

[350] Craig et al., *Jesus' Resurrection: Fact or Figment?: A Debate between William Lane Craig & Gerd Ludemann*, 196-7.

[351] Rodney Stark and Reid L Neilson, *The Rise of Mormonism* (Columbia University Press, 2012), 55.

[352] Craig, "Visions of Jesus: A Critical Assessment of Gerd Lüdemann's Hallucination Hypothesis."

[353] Craig et al., *Jesus' Resurrection: Fact or Figment?: A Debate between William Lane Craig & Gerd Ludemann*, 189.

[354] For example Gerd Lüdemann makes this point in his debate with Craig, see Ibid., 55.

[355] Anna Stone, "An Avowal of Prior Scepticism Enhances the Credibility of an Account of a Paranormal Event," *Journal of Language and Social Psychology* (2013): 5.
[356] Craig, *Did Jesus Rise from the Dead?*, 36.
[357] Walter Scheidel and Elijah Meeks, "Orbis: Stanford Geospatial Network Model of the Roman World," (2017).
[358] Peter Temin, "The Economy of the Early Roman Empire," *The Journal of economic perspectives* 20, no. 1 (2006): 138.
[359] Bernard Spilka et al., "The Content of Religious Experience: The Roles of Expectancy and Desirability," *The international journal for the psychology of religion* 6, no. 2 (1996).
[360] Daniel J Simons and Christopher F Chabris, "Gorillas in Our Midst: Sustained Inattentional Blindness for Dynamic Events," *Perception* 28, no. 9 (1999).
[361] Daniel P Wirth, "The Significance of Belief and Expectancy within the Spiritual Healing Encounter," *Social Science & Medicine* 41, no. 2 (1995).
[362] John Belanti, Mahendra Perera, and Karuppiah Jagadheesan, "Phenomenology of near-Death Experiences: A Cross-Cultural Perspective," *Transcultural psychiatry* 45, no. 1 (2008).
[363] Donovan Hilton Rawcliffe, *Illusions and Delusions of the Supernatural and the Occult* (Kessinger Publishing, 2006), 113.
[364] Jörg Stolz, ""All Things Are Possible": Towards a Sociological Explanation of Pentecostal Miracles and Healings," *Sociology of Religion* 72, no. 4 (2011).
[365] Bohdan Szuchewycz, "Evidentiality in Ritual Discourse: The Social Construction of Religious Meaning," *Language in Society* 23, no. 03 (1994).
[366] Deborah C Glik, "The Redefinition of the Situation: The Social Construction of Spiritual Healing Experiences," *Sociology of Health & Illness* 12, no. 2 (1990).
[367] James Houran and Rense Lange, "Hauntings and Poltergeist-Like Episodes as a Confluence of Conventional Phenomena: A General Hypothesis," *Perceptual and motor skills* 83, no. 3 suppl (1996).
[368] Christopher C French et al., "The "Haunt" Project: An Attempt to Build a "Haunted" Room by Manipulating Complex Electromagnetic Fields and Infrasound," *Cortex* 45, no. 5 (2009).
[369] Craig, "Visions of Jesus: A Critical Assessment of Gerd Lüdemann's Hallucination Hypothesis."

[370] Ibid.
[371] William Lane Craig, "The Problem of Miracles: A Historical and Philosophical Perspective," *Gospel Perspectives, The Miracles of Jesus.(ed.). Wenham D. and C. Blomberg* (1986): 19.
[372] Craig, "Visions of Jesus: A Critical Assessment of Gerd Lüdemann's Hallucination Hypothesis."
[373] Francis Johnston, *Fatima: The Great Sign* (Tan Books, 1980), 62.
[374] Zeitun-eg, "Our Lady Appears in Assiut, Upper Egypt," http://www.zeitun-eg.org/assiut.htm.
[375] Pearl Zaki, *Our Lord's Mother Visits Egypt in 1968 and 1969* (St. Mary Coptic Orthodox Church, 1982), 9.
[376] James Mulligan, *Medjugorje: A Portfolio of Images from the Early Years of the Apparitions* (CreateSpace Independent Publishing Platform, 2014), 3.
[377] William of Newburgh, *The History of English Affairs* (Lulu Press, Inc, 2015), 361.
[378] See for example Catherine Maire, "Les Convulsionnaires De Saint-Médard. Miracles, Convulsions Et Prophéties À Paris Au Xviiie Siècle," (1985).
[379] "Simon Kimbangu," in *Encyclopaedia Britannica* (2013).
[380] Sabakinu Kivilu, "Kimbangu, Simon," in *The Encyclopaedia Africana Dictionary of African Biography, Volume Two: Sierra Leone-Zaire*, ed. L. H. Ofosu-Appiah (Reference Publications Inc., 1979).
[381] "Oral Roberts Tells Conference He Has Raised People from the Dead," *The New York Times* 1987.
[382] Oral Roberts, *Twelve Greatest Miracles of My Ministry* (Pinoak Publications, 1974).
[383] F. Ullmann, "The Testimony of Three Witnesses," *Times and Seasons* 3, no. 21 (1841): 898.
[384] Josephus Flavius, "The Antiquities of the Jews, 20.97-98."
[385] Frieda Clark Hyman, *The Pharisees: The Preservers of Judaism* (Jerusalem; Hewlett, NY: Gefen, 2001), 377.
[386] Gershom Scholem, *Sabbatai Sevi; the Mystical Messiah, 1626-1676* (Princeton, N.J: Princeton University Press, 1973), 390.
[387] Samuel Dov Baer ben, Dan Ben-Amos, and Jerome R. Mintz, *In Praise of the Baal Shem Tov [Shivhei Ha-Besht] : The Earliest Collection of Legends About the Founder of Hasidism* (Bloomington: Indiana University Press, 1970).

[388] Bilu, ""We Want to See Our King": Apparitions in Messianic Habad," 98-101.
[389] Gaius Suetonius Tranquillus, "The Life of Vespasian, 7:2-3," in *The Lives of the Caesars.*
[390] Lucian of Samosata, *Alexander the False Prophet*, 48.
[391] See for example discussion in Alberto Ferreiro, *Simon Magus in Patristic, Medieval and Early Modern Traditions*, vol. 125 (Brill, 2005).
[392] See for example discussion in Ahmadiyya Muslim Association, "Truthfulness of the Promised Messiah: Vi – Miracles," http://whyahmadi.org/claims-of-promised-messiah/truthfulness-of-the-promised-messiah-vi-miracles.html.
[393] Narayan Chaudhuri, *That Compassionate Touch of Ma Anandamayee* (Delhi: Motilal Banarsidass, 1980), 159-63.
[394] Arcot Easwaran, "Manthralayam for That Healing Touch " *The Hindu* 2002.
[395] "Miracles of Raghavendra," http://www.gururaghavendra.in/miracles1.htm.
[396] Shirdi Sai Global Foundation, "Miracles of Sai Baba," http://www.saibabaofshirdi.net/.
[397] Howard Murphet, *Sai Baba: Man of Miracles* (London: Muller, 1971), 132-3.
[398] Amaresh Datta and Akademi Sahitya, *Encyclopaedia of Indian Literature: A-Devo* (New Delhi: Sahitya Akademi, 1987), 607-9.
[399] Swami Sivananda, "Lord Gauranga (Sri Krishna Chaitanya Mahaprabhu)," in *Lives of Saints* (Distt. Tehri-Garhwal, U.P., Himalayas, India: Divine Life Society, 1999).
[400] Kyoko Motomuchi Nakamura, *Miraculous Stories from the Japanese Buddhist Tradition: The Nihon Ryoiki of the Monk Kyokai* (Routledge, 2013).
[401] Franciscus Verellen, ""Evidential Miracles in Support of Taoism": The Inversion of a Buddhist Apologetic Tradition in Late Tang China," *T'oung Pao* (1992).
[402] Robin Beth Wagner, *Buddhism, Biography and Power: A Study of Daoxuan's Continued Lives of Eminent Monks*, vol. 1995 (Harvard University, 1995).
[403] Chun-fang Yu, "Eye on Religion: Miracles in the Chinese Buddhist Tradition," *Southern medical journal* 100, no. 12 (2007): 1243.
[404] Nahum Z Medalia and Otto N Larsen, "Diffusion and Belief in a

Collective Delusion: The Seattle Windshield Pitting Epidemic," *American Sociological Review* (1958).

[405] David Clarke, "Rumours of Angels: A Legend of the First World War," *Folklore* 113, no. 2 (2002).

[406] Mary Jo Nye, "N-Rays: An Episode in the History and Psychology of Science," *Historical studies in the physical sciences* 11, no. 1 (1980).

[407] Robert E Bartholomew and Jeffrey S Victor, "A Social-Psychological Theory of Collective Anxiety Attacks: The "Mad Gasser" Reexamined," *The Sociological Quarterly* 45, no. 2 (2004).

[408] Robert Bartholomew, "Phantom German Air Raids on Canada: War Hysteria in Québec and Ontario During the First World War," *Canadian Military History* 7, no. 4 (2012).

[409] Glenn Adams and Vivian Afi Dzokoto, "Genital-Shrinking Panic in Ghana: A Cultural Psychological Analysis," *Culture & Psychology* 13, no. 1 (2007).

[410] Susan Solomon and Swapnil Gupta, "The Denial of Death: A Three-Decade Long Case of Absent Grief," *Indian journal of psychological medicine* 36, no. 1 (2014).

[411] Amin A Muhammad Gadit, "Insightful Hallucination: Psychopathology or Paranormal Phenomenon?," *BMJ case reports* 2011(2011).

[412] By Ng, "Grief Revisited," *Annals-Academy Of Medicine Singapore* 34, no. 5 (2005).

[413] Samir Al-Adawi, Rustam Burjorjee, and Ihsan Al-Issa, "Mu-Ghayeb: A Culture-Specific Response to Bereavement in Oman," *International Journal of Social Psychiatry* 43, no. 2 (1997).

[414] James George Frazer, "Lecture 6: The Belief in Immortality among the Other Aborigines of Australia," in *The Belief in Immortality and the Worship of the Dead. Vol. 1* (London: Macmillan, 1913).

[415] Bruce T Grindal, "Into the Heart of Sisala Experience: Witnessing Death Divination," *Journal of Anthropological Research* (1983).

[416] Patrick D. Hahn, "Dead Man Walking: Wade Davis and the Secret of the Zombie Poison," (2007).

[417] Jean-Guy Goulet, "Ways of Knowing: Experience, Knowledge, and Power among the Dene Tha," University of Nebraska Press.

[418] Craig, *Assessing the New Testament Evidence for the Historicity of the Resurrection of Jesus*, 400-02.

[419] Society for Psychical Research, *Proceedings of the Society for Psychical Research* (London: Trubner, 1883), s25.

[420] Ibid., s29.
[421] Ibid., s32.
[422] Ibid., s34.
[423] Arthur Hastings et al., "Psychomanteum Research: Experiences and Effects on Bereavement," *OMEGA-Journal of Death and Dying* 45, no. 3 (2002).
[424] Alfred Russel Wallace, *Miracles and Modern Spiritualism* (London: G. Redway, 1896), 70-1.
[425] Terry Castle, "Contagious Folly: "An Adventure" and Its Skeptics," *Critical Inquiry* 17, no. 4 (1991): 743.
[426] Krissy Wilson and Christopher C French, "The Relationship between Susceptibility to False Memories, Dissociativity, and Paranormal Belief and Experience," *Personality and Individual Differences* 41, no. 8 (2006).
[427] Kerri Pickel, "When a Lie Becomes the Truth: The Effects of Self-Generated Misinformation on Eyewitness Memory," *Memory* 12, no. 1 (2004).
[428] Roger Buehler and Dale Griffin, "Change-of-Meaning Effects in Conformity and Dissent: Observing Construal Processes over Time," *Journal of Personality and Social Psychology* 67, no. 6 (1994).
[429] Agnieszka Niedźwieńska, "Distortion of Autobiographical Memories," *Applied Cognitive Psychology* 17, no. 1 (2003).
[430] Gerald Echterhoff and William Hirst, "Social Influence on Memory," *Social psychology* 40, no. 3 (2009).
[431] Giuliana Mazzoni and Manila Vannucci, "Hindsight Bias, the Misinformation Effect, and False Autobiographical Memories," *Social Cognition* 25, no. 1 (2007).
[432] Elizabeth J Marsh, "Retelling Is Not the Same as Recalling Implications for Memory," *Current Directions in Psychological Science* 16, no. 1 (2007).
[433] Helen M Paterson, Richard Kemp, and Sarah McIntyre, "Can a Witness Report Hearsay Evidence Unintentionally? The Effects of Discussion on Eyewitness Memory," *Psychology, Crime & Law* 18, no. 6 (2012).
[434] Andrew L Betz, John J Skowronski, and Thomas M Ostrom, "Shared Realities: Social Influence and Stimulus Memory," *Social Cognition* 14, no. 2 (1996).
[435] Jennifer M Talarico and David C Rubin, "Confidence, Not Consistency, Characterizes Flashbulb Memories," *Psychological Science* 14, no. 5

(2003).
[436] Krissy Wilson and Christopher C French, "Memory Conformity and Paranormal Belief" (paper presented at the The Parapsychological Association Convention 2004: Proceedings of Presented Papers, 2004).
[437] Celia B Harris, Helen M Paterson, and Richard I Kemp, "Collaborative Recall and Collective Memory: What Happens When We Remember Together?," *Memory* 16, no. 3 (2008).
[438] Chris French, "False Memories of Sexual Abuse Lead to Terrible Miscarriages of Justice," *The Guardian* 2010.
[439] Helen O'Neill, "The Perfect Witness," *The Washington Post* 2001.
[440] Craig, *Reasonable Faith: Christian Truth and Apologetics*, 338.
[441] Lorne L Dawson, "When Prophecy Fails and Faith Persists: A Theoretical Overview," *Nova Religio: The Journal of Alternative and Emergent Religions* 3, no. 1 (1999).
[442] Ibid.: 65.
[443] Joseph F Zygmunt, "Prophetic Failure and Chiliastic Identity: The Case of Jehovah's Witnesses," *American Journal of Sociology* (1970).
[444] Victor A Benassi, Barry Singer, and Craig B Reynolds, "Occult Belief: Seeing Is Believing," *Journal for the Scientific Study of Religion* (1980).
[445] C Daniel Batson, "Rational Processing or Rationalization? The Effect of Disconfirming Information on a Stated Religious Belief," *Journal of Personality and Social Psychology* 32, no. 1 (1975).
[446] Maarten Boudry and Johan Braeckman, "How Convenient! The Epistemic Rationale of Self-Validating Belief Systems," *Philosophical Psychology* 25, no. 3 (2012).
[447] T. S. Sathyanarayana Rao and Chittaranjan Andrade, "The Mmr Vaccine and Autism: Sensation, Refutation, Retraction, and Fraud," *Indian Journal of Psychiatry* 53, no. 2 (2011).
[448] "All They Need Is the Air," *BBC News* 1999.
[449] Michael Shermer and Alex Grobman, *Denying History: Who Says the Holocaust Never Happened and Why Do They Say It?* (Univ of California Press, 2009).
[450] R. J. Lowry, "Fluoridation: What the Papers Say: How Does the United Kingdom Press Treat Water Fluoridation and Does It Matter?," *Br Dent J* 189, no. 1 (2000).
[451] Chris Palmquist, "No Touch Martial Arts Master Meets Reality," http://www.mixedmartialarts.com/news/No-touch-martial-arts-master-meets-reality.

[452] Michael A Hogg, Janice R Adelman, and Robert D Blagg, "Religion in the Face of Uncertainty: An Uncertainty-Identity Theory Account of Religiousness," *Personality and Social Psychology Review* 14, no. 1 (2010).

[453] Richard Kyle, "When Prophets Die: The Postcharismatic Fate of New Religious Movements. Edited by Timothy Miller. Suny Series in Religious Studies. Albany, Ny: State University of New York Press, 1991.," *Church History* 64, no. 03 (1995).

[454] Renate Ysseldyk, Kimberly Matheson, and Hymie Anisman, "Religiosity as Identity: Toward an Understanding of Religion from a Social Identity Perspective," *Personality and Social Psychology Review* 14, no. 1 (2010).

[455] Jeffrey R Seul, "Ours Is the Way of God': Religion, Identity, and Intergroup Conflict," *Journal of peace research* 36, no. 5 (1999).

[456] Craig, *The Son Rises: Historical Evidence for the Resurrection of Jesus*, 119-20.

[457] Craig et al., *Jesus' Resurrection: Fact or Figment?: A Debate between William Lane Craig & Gerd Ludemann*, 37.

[458] Ibid.

[459] Ibid.

[460] Douglas F Barnes, "Charisma and Religious Leadership: An Historical Analysis," *Journal for the Scientific Study of Religion* (1978).

[461] William Lane Craig, *Did Jesus Rise from the Dead?* (Pine Mountain, Georgia: Impact 360 Institute, 2001).

[462] Wilkins and Moreland, "Did Jesus Rise from the Dead?," 165.

[463] Shraga Simmons, "Why Jews Don't Believe in Jesus," http://www.aish.com/jw/s/48892792.html.

[464] See for instance David Klinghoffer, *Why the Jews Rejected Jesus: The Turning Point in Western History* (New York: Doubleday, 2005).

[465] Craig, *Did Jesus Rise from the Dead?* , 52.

[466] William Lane Craig, "Transcript: Existence of God (Part 13)," *Excursus On Natural Theology* (2011).

[467] Craig and Scharp, ""Is There Evidence for God?": William Lane Craig Vs. Kevin Scharp Debate Transcript."

[468] Craig, "The Historical Argument for the Resurrection of Jesus During the Deist Controversy," 349.

[469] ———, *Reasonable Faith: Christian Truth and Apologetics*, 106.

[470] WIlliam Lane Craig, "Does God Exist?," *Philosophy Now* (2013).

[471] Craig, *Reasonable Faith: Christian Truth and Apologetics*, 108.
[472] Ibid.
[473] Ibid., 109.
[474] ———, "Does God Exist?," 6.
[475] ———, *Reasonable Faith: Christian Truth and Apologetics*, 185.
[476] William Lane Craig, "Q&A 118: God's Necessity," *Reasonable Faith* (2009).
[477] Craig, *Reasonable Faith: Christian Truth and Apologetics*, 185.
[478] ———, "Does God Exist?," 4.
[479] Ibid.
[480] Pierre Jacob, "Intentionality," in *The Stanford Encyclopedia of Philosophy*, ed. Edward N. Zalta (2014).
[481] William Lane Craig, "God and the 'Unreasonable Effectiveness of Mathematics'," *Christian Research Journal* 36, no. 6 (2013).
[482] Craig, "Does God Exist?," 3.
[483] ———, "God and the 'Unreasonable Effectiveness of Mathematics'."
[484] Craig and Carroll, *God and Cosmology: William Lane Craig and Sean Carroll in Dialogue*, 73.
[485] Serge P Hoogendoorn and Piet HL Bovy, "State-of-the-Art of Vehicular Traffic Flow Modelling," *Proceedings of the Institution of Mechanical Engineers, Part I: Journal of Systems and Control Engineering* 215, no. 4 (2001).
[486] Benita M. Beamon and Stephen A. Kotleba, "Inventory Modelling for Complex Emergencies in Humanitarian Relief Operations," *International Journal of Logistics Research and Applications* 9, no. 1 (2006).
[487] C Newell, *Applications of Queueing Theory*, vol. 4 (Springer Science & Business Media, 2013).

www.ingramcontent.com/pod-product-compliance
Lightning Source LLC
Chambersburg PA
CBHW020147090426
42734CB00008B/725